Political Economy of the Swiss National Bank

Contributions to Economics

Christoph M. Schneider
Research and Development Management: From the Soviet Union to Russia
1994. ISBN 3-7908-0757-5

Bernhard Böhm/Lionello F. Punzo (Eds.)
Economic Performance
1994. ISBN 3-7908-0811-3

Lars Olof Persson/Ulf Wiberg
Microregional Fragmentation
1995. ISBN 3-7908-0855-5

Ernesto Felli/Furio C. Rosati/Giovanni Tria (Eds.)
The Service Sector: Productivity and Growth
1995. ISBN 3-7908-0875-X

Giuseppe Munda
Multicriteria Evaluation in Fuzzy Environment
1995. ISBN 3-7908-0892-X

Giovanni Galizzi/Luciano Venturini (Eds.)
Economics of Innovation: The Case of Food Industry
1996. ISBN 3-7908-0911-X

David T. Johnson
Poverty, Inequality and Social Welfare in Australia
1996. ISBN 3-7908-0942-X

Rongxing Guo
Border-Regional Economics
1996. ISBN 3-7908-0943-8

Oliver Fratzscher
The Political Economy of Trade Integration
1996. ISBN 3-7908-0945-4

Ulrich Landwehr
Industrial Mobility and Public Policy
1996. ISBN 3-7908-0949-7

Arnold Picot/Ekkehard Schlicht (Eds.)
Firms, Markets, and Contracts
1996. Corr. 2nd printing 1997.
ISBN 3-7908-0947-0

Thorsten Wichmann
Agricultural Technical Progress and the Development of a Dual Economy
1997. ISBN 3-7908-0960-8

Ulrich Woitek
Business Cycles
1997. ISBN 3-7908-0997-7

Michael Carlberg
International Economic Growth
1997. ISBN 3-7908-0995-0

Massimo Filippini
Elements of the Swiss Market for Electricity
1997. ISBN 3-7908-0996-9

Giuseppe Gaburro (Ed.)
Ethics and Economics
1997. ISBN 3-7908-0986-1

Frank Hoster/Heinz Welsch/Christoph Böhringer
CO_2 Abatement and Economic Structural Change in the European Internal Market
1997. ISBN 3-7908-1020-7

Christian M. Hafner
Nonlinear Time Series Analysis with Applications to Foreign Exchange Rate Volatility
1997. ISBN 3-7908-1041-X

Sardar M. N. Islam
Mathematical Economics of Multi-Level Optimisation
1998. ISBN 3-7908-1050-9

Sven-Morten Mentzel
Real Exchange Rate Movements
1998. ISBN 3-7908-1081-9

Lei Delsen/Eelke de Jong (Eds.)
The German and Dutch Economies
1998. ISBN 3-7908-1064-9

Mark Weder
Business Cycle Models with Indeterminacy
1998. ISBN 3-7908-1078-9

Tor Rødseth (Ed.)
Models for Multispecies Management
1998. ISBN 3-7908-1001-0

Michael Carlberg
Intertemporal Macroeconomics
1998. ISBN 3-7908-1096-7

Sabine Spangenberg
The Institutionalised Transformation of the East German Economy
1998. ISBN 3-7908-1103-3

continued on page 271

Bruno Jeitziner

Political Economy of the Swiss National Bank

With 29 Figures
and 57 Tables

Physica-Verlag
A Springer-Verlag Company

Series Editors
Werner A. Müller
Martina Bihn

Author
PD Dr. Bruno Jeitziner
University of Freiburg
Miséricorde
CH-1700 Freiburg, Switzerland

Cataloging-in-Publication Data applied for
Die Deutsche Bibliothek – CIP-Einheitsaufnahme
Jeitziner, Bruno: Political economy of the Swiss National Bank; with 57 tables / Bruno Jeitziner. – Heidelberg: Physica-Verl., 1999
(Contributions to economics)

ISBN-13: 978-3-7908-1209-1 e-ISBN-13: 978-3-642-99811-9
DOI: 10.1007/978-3-642-99811-9

Softcover Design: Erich Kirchner, Heidelberg

SPIN 10726404 88/2202-5 4 3 2 1 0 – Printed on acid-free paper *for Christa, Anja, Andrea Sara and Marc*

„Eine Notenbank ist ständigen Pressionen ausgesetzt. Das Dilemma ist, dass man immer in einem Zwiespalt ist zwischen der Langfristigkeit der Geldpolitik und den kurzfristigen Wünschen von Wirtschaft und Politik."
Markus Lusser

(„A central bank is exposed to permanent pressures. The dilemma is that one is always in a conflict between the long-run perspective of monetary policy and the short-run wishes of the economy and politics."
Markus Lusser)

Neue Zürcher Zeitung, 27. /28. 4. 1996, 31

Acknowledgments

„Political Economy of the Swiss National Bank“ is my habilitation thesis written at the University of Freiburg/Switzerland. Thanks to Henner Kleinewefers, University of Freiburg, and Friedrich Schneider, University of Linz, for supervising my research work and for providing valuable comments. I am particularly grateful to Henner Kleinewefers for granting the academic freedom while working at his Institute. I also benefited from constructive criticism and support from faculty members at the University of Freiburg/Switzerland.

This study was conceived during my stay as research fellow at the Center for Study of Public Choice, George Mason University, in Fairfax/Virginia. There I was influenced by 'Virginia Political Economy' of James M. Buchanan, Robert D. Tollison, Charles K. Rowley and Viktor J. Vanberg. Moreover, I had the opportunity to expose myself to the intellectual ideas of Mancur Olson and Dennis C. Mueller at the University of Maryland. Thanks to Viktor J. Vanberg and Charles K. Rowley for acting as supervisors during this research stay. I am especially grateful to Charles K. Rowley for guiding my interest towards empirical research and for encouraging me with his principle 'keep your nose down'. Financial support was granted by the Swiss National Science Foundation.

Parts of this study were presented at research seminars. Thanks to the participants for their comments. I appreciate the discussions with Alan Pitts on technical issues. Thanks for providing data for chapter 2 to Yves Ammann of the 'Bundesamt für Konjunkturfragen' and to Beat Schwab of the Union Bank of Switzerland. The Swiss National Bank, the Swiss 'Bundesamt für Statistik', the Swiss 'Bundesamt für Konjunkturfragen', the Swiss 'Bundesamt für Industrie, Gewerbe und Arbeit', the 'Konjunkturforschungsstelle Eidgenössische Technische Hochschule Zürich', and the 'Eigenössische Finanzverwaltung' also made available their data. Thanks for compiling the legislative ratings for chapter 5 to Tobias Hohl.

Financial support for publication is provided by the 'Hochschulrat' Freiburg/ Switzerland.

The usual caveat applies.

Freiburg/Switzerland, December 1998 Bruno Jeitziner

Contents

CHAPTER 4

CHAPTER 5

Introduction

From a public-choice perspective, there are two myths on central banking. (Havrilesky 1988) The first myth is that monetary (and fiscal) policy systematically attempt(s) to maximize social welfare. The second myth is that a central bank is an independent, politically neutral institution.

Most contemporaneous monetary policy research implicitly or even explicitly assumes that monetary authorities pursue the public interest. The central bank is modeled as an unitary actor formulating monetary policy to maximize social welfare subject to constraints. The conduct of optimal monetary policy becomes a purely technical question, a straightforward exercise in applied welfare economics. The more adequate the economic models of how monetary policy truly works, the better are central banks able to bring about the combination of inflation and unemployment that society most prefers. The central bank's principal problems are informational: quantification of goals and restraints. (Kane 1980 200) The question of how the central bank arrives at its particular conception of social welfare is not addressed. (Beck 1988 368) The paradigm of utility maximization is (wrongly) applied to society as a whole. (Frey/Schneider 1981 292) The central bank is regarded as a benevolent social planner.[1]

This 'public-interest' or 'social welfare' approach to central bank behavior has been challenged by the 'private-interest' or 'political' perspective. This theory of government behavior builds on private interests of decision makers. The focus may be either on the central bank's internal politics or on its relationship to other political actors. „The question is not whether monetary policy is political, but how politics affects policy." (Beck 1988 368)

Bureaucratic theories focus on the monetary authority's internal politics. Although the central bank is an agent of elected politicians, central bank officials will enjoy considerable leeway because there are costs of monitoring the agent's behavior.[2] Traditional bureaucratic theories treat the central bank as autonomous. Central bank officials maximize their own private welfare, which may be a function of discretion, power, prestige, amenities, budget, staff, chance of a lucrative job in the private sector, preservation of the organization ... Private and social welfare are unlikely to coincide. To predict central bank behavior, the incentives faced by central bank officials need to be studied. The resulting behavior is not the socially optimal policy. This bureaucratic theory is the antidote to the public-interest approach to central bank behavior.

The other branch of the political approach to central bank behavior focuses on the relationship of the central bank to other political actors. It is assumed that the central bank is not independent of the political processes that are dominated by

---

1 For literature in this social welfare tradition see e.g. Cukierman 1992 43; Dwyer 1985 664.

2 For literature that treats the central bank as a bureaucracy see e.g. Toma/Toma 1986.

distributional considerations. The monetary authority is modeled as the agent of elected politicians in both the executive and legislative branch of government, as well as of other private interest groups (e.g. the financial services industries). As other government agencies, the central bank redistributes wealth in order to generate private gains for itself and its agents.[3]

The impact of distributional and other political considerations depends on the degree of central bank independence. The higher the level of independence accorded to a central bank, the smaller will be these impacts. Three central banks are commonly considered as politically independent: the Federal Reserve Board, the German Bundesbank, and the Swiss National Bank (SNB).

Whether redistribution among groups of private agents is an important determinant of the policy of these formally independent central banks ultimately is an empirical question. Empirical work on the Federal Reserve has shown that the notion of an independent, politically neutral institution is a myth. „The Fed is often heavily influenced by pressures from Congress, the executive branch, and private interests, but it is not a simple captive of any of these groups; nor are all political pressures partisan ones.“ (Dillon/Willett 1988 30) Evidence on political influence has also been reported for the German Bundesbank. (e.g. Lang/Welzel 1992) There remains the third of the allegedly independent central banks, the SNB. Is the SNB politically independent in the sense that no systematic political influence on its monetary policy can be measured?

This study attempts to provide answers to this question by investigating a variety of domestic political factors that might influence Swiss monetary policy. The goal is to provide a detailed analysis of Swiss monetary policy that may complement the existing studies of the 'autonomous' central banks in the US and Germany. Stated differently: the intention is to find out whether (changes in) monetary policy must be modeled in dependence of domestic political forces, even for the case of Switzerland. At the same time it is also questioned which theory of government behavior serves best to explain the SNB's behavior.

Chapter 1 starts with a purely economic model. A standard linear reaction function for the SNB relating the monetary base and the money supply M1 to some key economic variables measuring the state of the economy is estimated. Analysis of the stability of the regression equation over the time period from 1973 to 1995 suggests a structural break for 1980. For the subperiod before 1980 econometric results for quarterly data identify the consumer price index and the nominal DM/SFr exchange rate as highly significant regressors. While the monetary base and the money supply M1 contract in response to inflation, their response to exchange rates is accommodative. For the subperiod after 1980 much less reactive behavior is found.

It is tempting to interpret the SNB's response to the economic variables - especially to the exchange rate - as evidence of political dependence. But it can be ar-

---

3 For literature in this political approach to central bank behavior see e.g. Cukierman 1992 43; Dwyer 1985 667.

gued that the SNB's reaction to exchange rates is purely in the public interest, since it serves to prevent negative effects on the Swiss economy. In this sense, the reaction function presented in chapter 1 can be interpreted as the public-interest model of Swiss monetary policy.

Starting from this purely economic model, the question now is: Does Swiss monetary policy also have political causes? To answer this question, the model is extended to the political sphere.

Indirect political influence on central banks is investigated by testing for effects of fiscal policy on monetary policy. Direct political influence on monetary policy is analyzed in the framework of elections, parties, and administrations. Chapters 2 to 5 address the impact of deficits, elections, administration (parties), and the legislature (committees and committee leaders) on Swiss monetary policy.[4]

The impact of fiscal policy on monetary policy is frequently studied in the context of a *budget deficit* (or surplus) money supply relationship. Chapter 2 examines the relationship between fiscal policy as measured by different fiscal variables and changes of the monetary base and the money supply M1 for Switzerland. Estimation results using quarterly data for the time period from 1973.2 to 1995.2 differ for the two dependent variables investigated.

With the money supply M1 as dependent variable fiscal variables have no impact on monetary policy. The only exception is a negative relationship found between the growth rate of the money supply M1 and the growth rate of gross federal debt.

With the growth rate of the monetary base as dependent variable a significant and positive relationship with the actually measured total deficits as well as with the structural components of the federal and total deficits (with and without social security) can be found for the time period before 1980. Following the conventional interpretation the positive sign on these deficit measures implies accommodating behavior and is consistent with political dependence of the central bank. A negative response to the cyclical component of the total deficit including social security might indicate offsetting behavior and is rather consistent with political independence of the central bank. If insignificant coefficients on deficit variables are interpreted as a sign of benign neglect, estimation results clearly support the hypothesis that Swiss monetary authorities act independently of the fiscal authorities for the time period after 1980.

Politico-economic models of business cycles argue that politicians have an incentive to manipulate economic policy - including monetary policy - in order to win *elections*. Chapter 3 examines in detail the evidence on political monetary cycles for Switzerland. While a comparison of economic conditions for election and nonelection years yields results that are consistent with the predictions of opportunistic business cycle theory, more rigorous tests do not support this finding. It is

4 The chapters are written such that they can easily be read independently of each other.

concluded that Swiss money growth does not follow an election cycle. This supports the hypothesis of political independence of the SNB.

Executive influence on central banks is widely recognized. Chapter 4 questions whether the Swiss executive exerts any systematic influence on Swiss monetary policy. From the analysis of the legal framework of the SNB some executive influence could be predicted, especially because the executive controls the appointment process. But this does not result in a higher variability and level of inflation. The structure of the executive (the commission government) and the characteristics of the Swiss political market for monetary policy (especially the privileged access of the financial sector to the central bank) help the SNB to achieve its inflationary record. In empirical tests some association between variables that are supposed to measure preference changes in the executive and money growth rates can be found. But the conclusion that the executive does in fact influence Swiss monetary policy is not warranted. Not only the theoretical, but also the empirical analysis remains inconclusive.

The *legislature* is usually not considered to be important in monetary policy, despite the fact that the central bank is a creation of the legislature and ultimately is accountable to it. The conventional wisdom is that legislators lack incentives to monitor and influence monetary policy. This view has been challenged by the theory of legislative influence (also referred to as the 'new' theory of bureaucracy). This theory predicts that specialized legislative committees control government agencies. Chapter 5 reviews the application of the theory of legislative influence to the Federal Reserve and presents an application to the SNB. Empirical results do not support the hypothesis of legislative influence on Swiss monetary policy.

Although we clearly expect politics to play a role also in Swiss monetary policy, the investigation of these domestic political sources for pressure is unable to identify signs of de facto political dependence. Empirical results rather support the hypothesis of political independence of the SNB. This implies that in the case of Switzerland, (changes in) monetary policy can be modeled independently of these political forces.[5]

Does this absence of hard evidence mean that there exists no such political influence? This conclusion may not be warranted for several reasons.

---

[5] It can be argued that an analysis of direct political influence on SNB behavior must include bank-internal decisionmakers such as the Bank Council, the Bank Committee, or even the Board of Directors. (See e.g. Vaubel 1993 for the German Bundesbank.) Political influence from these bank-internal decisionmakers is not investigated here. The *theoretical* argument is that - since political authorities (the executive) basically control(s) who gets appointed to these bodies - only those changes in political preferences can occur that are also preferred by the political authorities. Or as Weingast/Moran (1983 769 Fn. 6) state, „new and different managers are the means but not the cause of agency policy change." The *empirical* argument is that in the case of the SNB party composition and interest-group affiliation of these bank-internal authorities does hardly change, violating the comparative statics condition. Alternative measures of political preferences that would eventually allow for a measurement of some variation cannot easily be constructed because of a lack of voting records or popularity measures.

First, the Swiss political market (in general and for monetary policy, too) shows an enormous *stability*. In the executive, for instance, party composition did not change since 1959. The executive is composed according to the 'magic formula'. This is the most basic reflection of the stability in the Swiss political market. The party composition of parliament shows only minor shifts. As to the interest groups, changes in their relative importance also seem to occur only very slowly. The stability of the political market affects the comparative statics condition and makes it very difficult to measure any influence from political variables.

A second reason may be the *quality* of the data. As Bomhoff (1985) argues, US monetary data are of much better quality than their European counterparts. Quality (and availability) of data may even be a more serious problem for Swiss political variables. Legislative ratings for instance are available for a much shorter time period, are based on less numerous roll call votes, and are plagued by the problem of abstentions.

Third, each political variable has its specific problems:

- Fiscal policy tended to be rather conservative in Switzerland. Hence, *deficits* are relatively small. On average they are even balanced for the period from 1980 to 1990. Inflation as a result of an aggregate demand stimulus generated by deficit spending is unlikely. Only in the nineties did deficits increase dramatically. But that time period is too short to have much impact on the regression results. This might change if fiscal authorities do not manage to regain control over fiscal spending.
- The problem with the *electoral* variable is that empirical tests for partisan models of business cycles are not viable, since Switzerland had no change in government during the period under investigation. Only the predictions of the opportunistic models can be tested. More recent international evidence suggests that partisan models are superior to the opportunistic models. Hence, only the less promising models can be analyzed in the case of Switzerland.
- The main difficulty with the measurement of *executive* influence is the lack of any variation in the party composition of the executive. But in addition, commission government per se affects the ability to test for executive influence.
- In empirical tests for *legislative* influence, party affiliation cannot be used as an independent variable because it is not a reliable preference measure for Swiss legislators, and because it shows only little variation. Alternative measures of legislative preferences (ratings) are not readily available and have to be constructed. The assumption of a negative relationship between positive ratings and preferred money growth rates that needs to be introduced is problematic.

For these reasons, the fact that no systematic political influence on Swiss monetary policy can be detected does not preclude the existence of such influences. The problem might just be one of measurement.

Still, several theoretical considerations weaken the case for central bank dependence in the Swiss case:

- Given the institutional setting, a political influence (if any) is most likely to come from the *executive* branch of government. But the theoretical argument is confronted with an institutional peculiarity, commission government. Commission government tends to isolate the central bank from short-run political pressures.
- The characteristics of the Swiss political market (the political system and the constellation of parties in power) make it difficult to rationalize an *electoral* manipulation of monetary policy.
- And *legislative* influence is rather unlikely because of the institutional setting. The central bank is not directly accountable to the legislature. This constitutes a double-layer principal agent relationship. There are no oversight and confirmation hearings. The only control mechanism available to the legislature is the threat of changing the legal status of the central bank. But because of the stability of the political market this threat may not be very credible. The committee system, which is the most important feature in the theory of legislative control, is not specialized enough.

Overall, the extensions to a political model do hardly improve the explanatory power of the 'economic' model. But this does not yet imply that the SNB pursues the public interest. Maintaining the assumption of privately interested decision-makers, the traditional theory of bureaucracy predicts that an independent agency will use its discretion to pursue its own private goals. Before it is claimed that Swiss monetary authorities pursue the public interest, this possibility needs to be investigated. This opens up new avenues for research on the 'Political Economy of the SNB'.

CHAPTER 1

A Reaction Function Study for the Swiss National Bank

1.1 Introduction

How does the Swiss National Bank (SNB) react to the state of the economy? There exists almost no quantitative evidence on this question. Moreover, the little existing empirical work provides conflicting results. This chapter presents some further evidence on SNB behavior. For this purpose a standard linear reaction function relating the change in the monetary base and in the money supply M1 to a set of economic stabilization goals is estimated. Since central banks are generally expected to respond to inflation, growth, unemployment, exchange rates and interest rates, variables representing these basic economic pressures are employed as regressors.

Section 1.2 starts with some general remarks on the concept of reaction functions. Section 1.3 discusses the results of previous reaction function studies for the SNB and develops the money supply function estimated in this chapter. Section 1.4 offers a detailed discussion of the data used. Section 1.5 presents the empirical results. Section 1.6 concludes with a summary of the major results and suggestions for future studies.

1.2 The Concept of Reaction Functions

Reaction functions are very popular for investigating how some policy instrument changes in response to some other variables. In the *standard form*, instrument y at time t is a linear function of its own past values and the contemporaneous values of the economic targets x_i of which there are k (Alt/Chrystal 1983 127; see also Harvey 1990 265):

$$y_t = a + by_{t-1} + \sum_{i=1}^{k} c_i x_{ti} . \qquad (1.a)$$

Applied to *monetary policy* changes in a monetary policy instrument are explained as a function of its own lagged values and a set of variables representing (changes in) the state of the economy.

Formally, reaction functions have to be interpreted as single-equation solutions of constrained optimization problems. They are derived by maximizing an objective function (utility or welfare function) reflecting preferences subject to an economic constraint, whereas the economic constraint contains a set of equations representing the structure of the economy.[1]

Solving the optimization problem requires knowledge of the objective function and the structural model of the economy used by the relevant decision makers at the central bank. The difficulties involved in this usually lead researchers to postulate some *ad hoc* reaction functions. This is also the approach followed here. It is not intended to develop a model of the macro-economy. Instead an equation relating a dependent variable measuring the conduct of monetary policy to a set of widely accepted monetary policy objectives is postulated. The behavioral model underlying this equation is outlined in section 1.3.2a.

The problem with the empirical *estimation* of single-equation reaction functions is that preferences and constraints are estimated simultaneously from one piece of information. Estimated coefficients involve parameters of both the objective function and the constraints. They give no direct evidence about policymakers' preferences. Inferences about preferences of the central bank authority can only be drawn after disentangling the underlying economic structural elements within the coefficients. (Alt/Chrystal 1983 141)

The formal *optimizing model* assumes that the policymaker chooses the values of a set of instrument variables y in order to maximize some objective function W which depends upon the instruments and some target variables x, subject to the constraints determined by the general structure of the economy: (Alt/Chrystal 1983 132)

$$\text{Choose } y \text{ to maximize } W = w(x,y) \tag{1.b}$$
$$\text{subject to } c(x,y) = 0 \tag{1.c}$$

A solution for optimal instrument values y^* can be expressed as a function of the targets x:

$$y^* = f(x) \tag{1.d}$$

The decisive point is that this function depends on the parameters of both w and c, the objective function and the constraints.

To *illustrate* the problem consider the following example presented by Alt/Chrystal (1983 132-135). Suppose there is only one target P and one instrument R. The central bank's preferences are represented by the amount of distress they feel at the differences between prevailing values of the target P and the instrument R and their ideal values P* and R*. Assume that the central bank's objective function can be set up as a quadratic loss function:

---

1 For an outlining of this procedure see Wood 1967; Alt/Woolley 1982; Alt/Chrystal 1983 chap. 6; Missong/Herrault 1990; Schultes 1994.

$$W(P,R) = a(R^* - R)^2 + b(P^* - P)^2 \quad (1.e)$$

For simplicity, assume that the ideal values for P* and R* are both equal to zero. Then the objective function is

$$W(P,R) = aR^2 + bP^2 \quad (1.e')$$

Assume further that the constraint is given by the following linear equation

$$P = c - dR \quad (1.f)$$

Constrained optimization involves maximizing welfare, which in the present case is minimizing the loss function (1.e') subject to the constraint (1.f). The problem is to choose R to minimize

$$W = aR^2 + b(c^2 + d^2R^2 - 2cdR)$$

Differentiating with respect to R and setting equal to zero yields

$$\frac{dW}{dR} = 2aR + 2bd^2R - 2bcd = 0$$

and by rearranging

$$R = \frac{bcd}{a + bd^2}.$$

The optimal choice of the instrument R depends on both the parameters a and b of the objective function (1.e') *and* the parameters c and d of the constraint (1.f).

Therefore, coefficients estimated from single-equation reaction functions contain, at least implicitly, a structural *and* a preference component. Unless the researcher fully knows the structural model of the economy employed by the authority making the policy decisions, he cannot assign unambiguously policy reactions to changes in preferences versus changes in parameters of the authorities' structural model. (Hodgman/Resek 1983 147; Cecco 1983 204; Frey/Schneider 1981 292) Only under the restrictive assumption that the structural model of the economy remains unchanged over the period of estimation will all changes in the coefficients of the reaction function reflect changes in the monetary authority's preferences. (Havrilesky et al. 1975 838) Otherwise it is not legitimate to interpret the coefficients as characterizing the preferences or intentions of the policymakers involved. (Missong/Herrault 1990; Alt/Woolley 1982; Beck 1984 793) The coefficients do not show „why the policy instrument responded, failed to respond, or responded differently at different times.“ (Abrams et al. 1980 31) Therefore, inferences about the policymakers' preferences are avoided in this study.[2]

Despite these *limits of interpretation*[3], reaction function studies are a useful approach for the present purposes, since the intention is not to make inferences about the policymakers' preference function, but to test for systematic changes in policy behavior in response to changes in the economic (and political) environment. Reaction functions do tell how a policy instrument changes as other factors change. „In other words, reaction functions are useful for finding changes in economic conditions which are associated with changes in monetary policy.“ (Beck 1984 793; see also Abrams et al. 1980 31.)

1.3 Reaction Functions for the SNB

1.3.1 Existing Studies

Reaction function studies for central banks abound.[4] This is especially the case for the Federal Reserve. However, there is very little quantitative evidence as to the behavior of the SNB. Though Swiss monetary policy is frequently analyzed, most studies do not provide any direct empirical tests of SNB responses to the economy. Up to now there exist (to the best of my knowledge) only three reaction function studies for the SNB.[5] Table 1.1 summarizes their basic results.

In a first paper *Parkin* (1987) studies the relationship between deficits and central bank laws for twelve countries including Switzerland[6]. In order to explain the money growth process he regresses the percentage growth rate of base money on the nominal deficit expressed as a percentage of nominal GNP and lagged one period, the percentage growth rate of base money lagged one period, and the current

2 A different approach is chosen by Camen et al. 1990, who explicitly seek to reveal the SNB's preferences.

3 There are even more problems inherent in reaction function studies that are well known in the literature. For a discussion see especially Alt/Woolley 1982; Alt/Chrystal 1983 chap. 6.

4 The empirical literature is far too extensive to be cited here. Early contributions are Reuber 1964 and Wood 1967. More recent examples are Burdekin/Langdana 1992, Grier 1991, and Missong/Herrault 1990. For an early summary of major studies see Barth et al. 1982.

5 Three more empirical studies on SNB behavior are discussed in section 2.3. Since they are not single-equation reaction functions, they are not included in table 1.1. Also excluded is the vector autoregression model proposed by Camen et al. 1990. A recent working paper by Landmann/Jerger (1997) presents estimates of reaction functions with short-term interest rates as dependent variable. This study is not summarized here either.

6 The other eleven countries are Australia, Belgium, Canada, France, Germany, Italy, Japan, Netherlands, Sweden, United Kingdom, and the United States.

Table 1.1: Existing Reaction Function Studies for the SNB with Authors' Evaluation of the Results

	Parkin 1987	*Burdekin/ Langdana 1992*	*Sheehan 1992*
Sample	annual 1955-83	quarterly 1966.2-1983.4	quarterly 1959.1-1990.2
Dependent Variable	percentage growth rate of base money	growth rate of monetary base	growth rate of money stock M1
Independent Variables and Results:			
Lagged Dependent Variable	negative and significant	negative and significant	insignificant
Inflation Rate	-	negative and significant under flexible exchange rates	insignificant
Exchange Rate DM/SFr (Index)	-	positive and significant	-
Exchange Rate US$/SFr	-	-	insignificant
Growth Rate of Real Government Purchases	-	positive and significant under flexible exchange rates	-
Deviation of Real GNP from Trend	positive and significant	-	-
Unemployment (in thousands)	-	insignificant	-
Interest Rate on Long-Term Government Bonds	-	-	negative and significant under floating exchange rates
Three-Month Deposit Rate	-	insignificant	-
Balance of Trade	-	insignificant	-
Federal Budget Deficit/GDP	positive and significant	negative and significant under fixed exchange rates	-
Various US Variables	-	-	some significant under fixed exchange rates

- not included in the reaction function.

cyclical state of the economy measured as deviations of real GNP from trend. Estimating this equation using annual data from 1955 to 1983 for the twelve countries it turns out that Switzerland is the only case where the previous year's deficit has a significant positive influence on the current year's money supply growth rate. Even though the significance attaching to the coefficient is weak, Parkin comments on this that „it has to be recorded that the Swiss money supply growth process has this unique feature and a feature which would be expected to be associated not with an independent central bank such as that of Switzerland but with one that is heavily dominated by the government and encouraged to accommodate past deficits." (Parkin 1987 325) Switzerland is also one of four countries (the other countries are Belgium, the United Kingdom, and the United States) with a significantly autoregressive money supply growth process, and it is one of four countries (the other countries are Canada, Japan, and the United Kingdom) with a money supply growth process that responds to the cyclical state of the economy. Another interesting finding is that Switzerland has the largest variance in the money supply growth rates among all twelve countries for the period under investigation. (Parkin does not comment on this. But the high variance can be explained with the fact that Switzerland is a small open economy with large transactions of capital.)

A second study by *Burdekin/Langdana* (1992 105-113) stands in the context of international evidence on the relationship between central banks and governments. They present an explicit case study of Swiss monetary policy[7] which is supposed to complement the existing studies of the autonomous central banks in the U.S. and West Germany. The reaction function approach is used to assess the empirical importance of a range of pre-selected stabilization goals and fiscal policy variables. The focus is on the response of the SNB to changes in the inflation rate. The growth rate of the monetary base is regressed on the federal budget deficit divided by gross domestic product, the growth rate of real government purchases (real government and social security consumption), the growth rate of consumer prices, the three-month deposit rate, unemployment (numbers unemployed in thousands), the exchange rate between the SFr and the DM, the balance of trade, and lagged values of the growth rate of the monetary base. All regressors enter as lagged values. The specific lag lengths are determined using Akaike's minimum final prediction error.

Ordinary least squares (OLS) estimation results over quarterly data from 1966.2 to 1983.4 indicate the deficit, inflation and exchange rate variables to be significant at the 5 percent level. The response to the deficit is strongly negative implying an offsetting monetary policy. The negative coefficient of the inflation variable evidences the antiinflationary policy of the SNB. The positive response of the monetary base growth to the exchange rate probably reflects attempts to suppress upward pressure on the SFr. Government purchases are significant only at the 10 percent level, and the positive coefficient might suggest monetary accom-

---

[7] The case study is based on an earlier publication by Burdekin (1987).

modation of increases in spending. The three-month deposit rate, unemployment and the balance of trade did not turn out to be significant. The failure of the unemployment variable to be selected is explained with the extremely favorable unemployment figures, also due to the importance of immigration policy as an instrument to control the large migrant labor force.

Allowing for a possible structural break corresponding with the adoption of floating exchange rates in January 1973, two separate reaction functions were reestimated over the fixed exchange rate (1966.2 to 1973.1) and floating exchange rate (1973.2 to 1983.4) subsamples. In the fixed exchange rate subsample, only the lagged monetary base, the deficit and the exchange rate are significant at the 10 percent level or higher. For the floating exchange rate subsample, government purchases, the inflation rate and the exchange rate are significant, but the deficit is not. Overall, the countercyclical response to inflation (reflecting the emphasis given to the price-stability objective) and the offsetting response to fiscal policy is interpreted as evidence supporting the hypothesis of formal independence of the SNB.

A third reaction function study for the SNB is presented by *Sheehan* (1992). Although the focus is on the impacts of U.S. variables including U.S. monetary policy on the monetary policy of the G7 countries[8] and Switzerland, the monetary authorities' reaction to domestic variables is also investigated. The money stock M1 is regressed on inflation (measured by the consumer price index during the fixed exchange rate period and the GNP deflator for the floating exchange rate period), the interest rate on long-term government bonds, the US$/SFr exchange rate, the lagged money growth rate, and several U.S. variables. Interest rates and exchange rates enter the regression as simple first differences, all other variables are first differences of logarithms. Alternative statistical criteria[9] are used to determine the optimum lag length of the regressors, with the maximum lag length set at four quarters. Separate estimates for quarterly data are presented for the period of fixed exchange rates (1959.1 to 1971.3) and the floating rate period (1973.1 to 1990.2). Swiss monetary policy under fixed exchange rates reacts to U.S. money growth, U.S. real output growth and U.S. inflation. However, consistent with fixed exchange rates, the SNB does not respond in the long run[10] to any domestic variables. Estimates for the floating exchange rate regime differ dramatically. All U.S. variables are insignificant, but domestic interest rates are significant. „The Swiss results are the first that are consistent with a monetary authority taking full advantage of the insulating properties of floating exchange rates." (Sheehan 1992 458) According to Sheehan the results for the floating exchange rate period should be interpreted with caution because of the relatively poor performance of the equation.[11]

---

8 These countries are Canada, France, Germany, Italy, Japan and United Kingdom.

9 See Fn. about finding the appropriate lag structure in section 1.3.2g.

10 The long run response equals the sum of the estimated coefficients.

11 The R^2 of the money growth equation for the floating exchange rate regime is 0.48.

With respect to the *deficit*, the first two cited studies present conflicting results. (However, see the qualifications offered for Parkin's study in section 2.3.) While Parkin (1987) finds a significantly positive response to the lagged deficit indicating accommodating behavior, Burdekin/Langdana (1992) detect a strongly negative response implying offsetting behavior of the SNB. These differences may well be due to the different model specifications, sample periods, and periodicity of the data.[12] In Parkin's model, neither exchange rate nor inflation variables are included. Does the deficit variable remain significantly positive if these additional variables are included? Sample periods and periodicity of the data are also known to have impacts on estimation results. (Thieme 1993 177)

Parkin's study may have more *weaknesses* in addition to leaving out such important arguments as inflation and exchange rates. The impact of fixed versus floating exchange rate regimes, for instance, is not investigated. However, the case study by Burdekin/Langdana is quite sophisticated, also showing knowledge of institutional background and of existing literature on Swiss monetary policy. Somewhat puzzling is the fact that they find a strongly negative response to the deficit and a positive coefficient for government purchases in the regression over the whole sample. Several arguments may help to explain these conflicting results. First, the significance level attaching to the coefficient for government purchases is low. Second, the regressions over subsamples reveal that the deficit is only significant under fixed exchange rates, while government purchases are only significant under flexible exchange rates. Third, the authors note that the fiscal policy variables have to be interpreted with care, since the federal budget has on the average been balanced over the sample period.

The studies by Parkin and Burdekin/Langdana stop their samples at 1983. Since then, the deficit variable, but also the unemployment figure changed drastically, increasing these pressures on monetary policy. What happens to the estimation results if the sample is *extended* to these periods with substantial deficits and relatively high unemployment figures?

In Sheehan's study M1 is employed as dependent variable to maintain comparability across the countries. Other monetary aggregates, especially the monetary base, are not investigated as dependent variables. The growth rate of real output is excluded from the regression because quarterly data for real GNP provided by the International Monetary Fund begin in 1967. The exchange rate used is the US$/SFr exchange rate. For the floating rate period the DM/SFr exchange rate probably is a better choice. These factors may help to explain the differences in the results between his and the other two studies.

---

12 Time series analyses always vary with choice of exact specification and sample period. Beck 1987 200.

1.3.2 Reaction Functions for the SNB

The goal of this section is the specification of a simple and parsimonious reaction function for the SNB that helps to assess the empirical importance of a range of pre-selected macroeconomic stabilization goals. The focus is on choice and measurement of the variables. First the behavioral model underlying the reaction function is presented. In a second step the choice of the dependent variable is carefully elaborated. The third step explains the choice of the regressor variables. Steps four to seven discuss the choice of the time period, periodicity of data, measurement of the variables (levels versus changes), and lag structure. Step eight offers a critical note on the problem of predicting signs for the coefficients. Step nine concludes with a summary of the equation and some general remarks on the postulated reaction function.

1.3.2a The Behavioral Model Underlying the Reaction Functions

An economic justification for the standard form of the reaction function (equation 1.a) is provided by the partial (stock) adjustment or habit persistence model. In this model it is assumed that the *desired* rather than the actual value of the dependent variable is determined by the independent variable(s).

If y_t^* denotes the optimal or equilibrium value of y in period t, the equation for optimal y is

$$y_t^* = \alpha + \beta x_t \tag{1.g}$$

Applied to the reaction function approach the dependent variable represents the equilibrium or optimal value of the policy instrument as a function of some exogenous variable(s).

Equation (1.g) cannot be estimated directly because the desired level of the dependent variable is not observable. To resolve this dilemma an assumption about the relationship between actual y and y^* must be made. It is generally assumed that the actual value of the dependent variable adjusts or is adjusted to the desired level according to some simple rule.

The so-called 'adjustment equation' states that the actual change in the dependent variable, $y_t - y_{t-1}$, is proportional to the discrepancy between the desired value and the previous value, $y_t^* - y_{t-1}$:

$$y_t - y_{t-1} = \lambda(y_t^* - y_{t-1}) + u_t \tag{1.h}$$

where $y_t^* - y_{t-1}$ = desired change
$y_t - y_{t-1}$ = actual change
λ = adjustment coefficient

and $0 < \lambda < 1.$

The adjustment coefficient λ denotes the rate at which the desired change in y occurs in each period. This value is restricted so that $0 < \lambda < 1$.

If $\lim_{\lambda \to 0}, y_t = y_{t-1}$. In this case no adjustment in y occurs. When $\lim_{\lambda \to 1}, y_t = y_t^*$; the entire adjustment of actual y to its optimal level occurs in a single period.

The larger is λ, the more rapid is the adjustment of y to y^*. (Lardaro 1992 570)

The partial adjustment model says that the actual change is only a fraction of the desired change. An economic explanation for this partial adjustment to the desired level is as follows. (See Kmenta 1986 530; Maddala 1992 419; Nickell 1985.) The decision maker faces two costs: costs of making the adjustment and costs of being in disequilibrium. Assuming that the two costs are quadratic and additive, total costs C_t can be written as

$$C_t = a(y_t - y_t^*)^2 + b(y_t - y_{t-1})^2 \tag{1.i}$$

The first term on the right-hand side of (1.i) represents the cost of being in disequilibrium and the second represents the cost of making the adjustment.

Given y_{t-1} and y_t^*, y_t must be chosen so that total cost C_t is minimum. The cost minimizing rule is

$$\frac{dC_t}{dy_t} = 2a(y_t - y_t^*) + 2b(y_t - y_{t-1}) = 0.$$

This yields (after subtracting ay_{t-1})

$$y_t - y_{t-1} = \frac{a}{a+b}(y_t^* - y_{t-1}) \tag{1.j}$$

or

$$y_t - y_{t-1} = \delta(y_t^* - y_{t-1}) \tag{1.j'}$$

where

$$\delta = \frac{a}{a+b}$$

and

$$0 < \delta < 1.$$

δ is close to 1 if the costs of being in disequilibrium are much higher than the costs of adjustment. δ is close to 0 if the costs of adjustment are much higher than the costs of disequilibrium.

Letting $\delta = \lambda$ and allowing for a stochastic disturbance in achieving cost minimization yields the 'adjustment equation' (1.h).

Equation (1.h) may be rewritten as

$$y_t = \lambda y_t^* + (1-\lambda)y_{t-1} + u_t \tag{1.k}$$

This shows that actual y is a weighted average of its optimal and last period's actual values, where the adjustment coefficient is the basis for the weights.

Substituting (1.g) into (1.k) yields an expression for y in terms of observable variables:

$$\begin{aligned} y_t &= \lambda(\alpha + \beta x_t) + (1-\lambda)y_{t-1} + u_t \\ &= \alpha\lambda + \beta\lambda x_t + (1-\lambda)y_{t-1} + u_t \end{aligned}$$

so that

$$y_t = \beta_0 + \beta_1 x_t + \beta_2 y_{t-1} + u_t \tag{1.l}$$

where $\beta_0 = \alpha\lambda$, $\beta_1 = \beta\lambda$, and $\beta_2 = (1-\lambda)$.

The parameters α and β of the behavioral model (1.g) and the adjustment coefficient λ of equation (1.h) can be estimated by regressing y_t against x_t and y_{t-1}. The coefficient of y_{t-1} yields an estimate of $(1 - \lambda)$ and hence of λ. The coefficient of x_t divided by the estimate of λ yields an estimate of β. And the constant term divided by the estimate of λ yields an estimate of α.[13]

Mathematical manipulation of the relationship (1.g) determining the desired level and the equation (1.h) determining the adjustment of the actual level creates an estimating equation that is autoregressive.

The error term u_t in (1.l) is spherical, since it is not affected by this mathematical manipulation. (Of course, serial correlation might still be present if u_t itself suffers from this problem.) Equation (1.l) contains the stochastic explanatory variable y_{t-1}, but it is not contemporaneously correlated with the disturbance term u_t. Under these conditions, OLS yields estimates that are asymptotically unbiased and efficient, but the estimates will not possess these properties in small samples.

---

13 Note that equation (1.l) is the short-run expression for y, „since it is stated in terms of actual y and the entire adjustment of actual to optimal y does not occur in a single period." (Lardaro 1992 570) Equation (1.g) is stated in terms of the optimal or equilibrium level of y and provides an expression for the long-run level of that variable.

A reaction function usually includes several explanatory variables. (See equation 1.a.) The partial adjustment model must be extended to a model with more explanatory variables. This extension is straightforward, since no lags must be added for these regressors in equation (1.l). (Lardaro 1992 570) Therefore, this is not presented here.[14]

Nothing has been said so far about the specific variables appearing in the equations (reaction functions). This is discussed in detail in the next two sections.

1.3.2b Choice of the Dependent Variable

In order to measure the SNB's actual response to the economic environment, an adequate indicator of the use of its control instruments has to be chosen as dependent variable. The list of *potential candidates* includes monetary aggregates (adjusted or unadjusted monetary base, M1, M2, M3)[15], individual monetary policy instruments (foreign exchange reserves, discount rate etc.), or other indicators such as interest rates (e.g. three-month deposit rate, government bond yield, lending rate[16]) or exchange rates.[17]

The choice among these candidates can be based on several *desirable criteria:*[18] (i) The dependent variable should measure the aggregate effect of the control instruments; (ii) it should be under the effective control of the central bank; (iii) it should have the character of a (intermediate) target variable; (iv) observations should be available as a consistent series for the period under investigation; (v) if it corresponds with the variable chosen in other existing studies, comparisons of the results can be made.

---

14 The partial adjustment model can be criticized because it is backward looking. It can also be criticized as being ad hoc.

„The desired level y^*_t is derived independently by some optimization rule and then the adjustment equation is tagged on to it. However, the costs of adjustment and the costs of being in disequilibrium should be incorporated in the optimization rule. There have been many attempts along these lines but they have not resulted in any tractable estimable equations." (Maddala 1992 420)

15 For a definition of these monetary aggregates see SNB 1975 1-6, 1985 51-56, and 1995a 61-69.

16 Rate of interest on first mortgages.

17 For the Federal Reserve nonborrowed reserves and the Federal Funds rate are frequently used instruments (Beck 1987; see also McCallum 1989 65).

18 Availability of policy instruments can be added to this list as a further criterion. Availability of a policy instrument does not mean that the instrument is actually used. Selection of one policy instrument may effectively remove some other instruments from use. „A decision to control exchange rates effectively excludes the domestic money supply from consideration as an intermediate target. Floating exchange rates mean that the domestic money supply is available for use as an intermediate target of monetary policy." (Alt/Woolley 1982 732)
This can be considered as an argument for limiting the sample to the period of fixed or flexible exchange rates!

(i) Instead of estimating a separate reaction function for every individual monetary policy instrument, one single reaction function using an aggregate indicator of monetary policy is estimated. The dependent variable should therefore be a variable reflecting the *aggregate effect* of all important policy actions. Since every single policy measure is reflected in changes of the monetary base, it satisfies this criterion especially well. To a lesser extent this is also true for the other monetary aggregates, since they build on the monetary base. Indicators such as interest rates also measure aggregate effects of monetary policy and are, therefore, suitable as dependent variable.[19] However, with respect to this criterion individual monetary policy instruments are rather ill-suited dependent variables. (See also Schultes 1994 14 and 38.) Their relative importance would have to be evaluated and changes thereof would have to be accounted for. Moreover, different instruments might even signal conflicting policies. Some instruments might not show much variation.

(ii) The response variable should be a variable actually *controlled* by the SNB. „The less a variable is controlled ..., the less useful that variable will be as an indicator of policy.“ (Beck 1984 794) The control criterion would definitely favor the choice of some individual policy instruments, since these can be directly and effectively manipulated by the central bank. Monetary aggregates, also called intermediate target variables, differ in their degree of controllability by the SNB.[20] It is generally agreed that the monetary base can be directly controlled by the SNB. (SNB 1975 3 and 1995 7; Hoffmann 1990 73)[21] In a regime of flexible exchange rates this aggregate can therefore also be considered as a monetary instrument. (Rich 1989 349) A lot of con-

---

[19] In their reaction function study for the German and French central banks Missong/Herrault 1990 573 argue that interest rates and monetary aggregates both measure the aggregate effects of monetary policy and that they are equivalent as dependent variable.

[20] As to the controllability of monetary aggregates three points should be noted:

1. Monetary aggregates can effectively be controlled only under a floating exchange rate regime, but not under a fixed exchange rate regime. As Schiltknecht (1983) states, the switch to a floating exchange rate gave the SNB virtually full control over the monetary base. (Schiltknecht 1983 83; cited in Burdekin/Langdana 1992 190 Fn. 7.)
2. The impacts of financial innovations on the controllability of monetary aggregates (such as the monetary base) are not completely clear yet. Empirical evidence suggests that these financial innovations affect the money multiplier, but not the monetary base. Therefore, though the control of monetary aggregates becomes more difficult, it is not getting impossible. See Thieme 1993 176. The discussion about the controllability of monetary aggregates is once again induced by financial innovations.
3. The controllability of a variable and its usefulness as a target variable are closely related.

[21] As Wasserfallen/Kürsteiner 1993 209 point out, the SNB can only control the monetary base but not its composition.

troversy exists on the controllability of M1. (See e.g. Beck 1982 419, 1984 795, 1987 202, and Grier 1989 377 on the Fed.) M1 does not only depend on the behavior of the central bank, but also on decisions of private actors on the demand side of the market. In this sense, M1 is not under direct control of the central bank. Still, the central bank might be able to hit M1 targets if it chose to do so and thus control M1. According to monetarists, the central bank can do so even in the short run.[22] Others argue that M1 cannot be controlled in the short run, since the multiplier which links M1 to the monetary base is not stable in the short run. In the long run, the multiplier follows a trend which is known, while in the short run, it can sometimes move against the trend. (Beck 1987 203 Fn. 14)[23] Therefore, M1 can be controlled in the long run, even though it does not only depend on the behavior of the central bank. If a stable relationship between the monetary base and M1 can be assumed it matters little whether the monetary base or M1 is used as a policy measure. The rationale for preferring the monetary base is that the SNB can manipulate the base more directly, while M1 is a much more indirect policy measure. Moreover, even if the central bank is trying to control M1, its policy actions will also be reflected by changes in the monetary base.

If both the monetary base and M1 can be controlled by the SNB, which one does it actually control? This question will be addressed when discussing the target criterion.

If there is already a potential control problem with M1, it will even be more so with M2 and M3. With respect to controllability the monetary base and M1 are preferred to M2 and M3 as dependent variables.

Other indicators such as interest rates or exchange rates are determined by supply and demand factors. They can certainly be influenced by the central bank, but they can't be controlled directly.[24] This is especially the case with exchange rates. Therefore, they are not good measures of what policy the central bank is pursuing.

(iii) The dependent variable should also be a variable actually *targeted* by the SNB. These targets could be market interest rates, the price level, nominal GNP, or a monetary aggregate. There is an ongoing academic discussion about which monetary target variables should be preferred by a central

---

22 Monetarists argue that the base is controlled by the central bank, and that the money supply M1 is stably related to the monetary base. See e.g. Friedman 1982.

23 Empirical evidence for Switzerland shows that the money multiplier is relatively stable, though not constant, since it depends on interest rates, rates of return, political and other factors. Changes in the money multiplier reflect both decisions of banks and the public on the composition of their portfolios as well as the central bank's monetary policy actions. SNB 1975 4. See Kästli 1995 460 on the development of the money multiplier for the period from 1973 to 1994.

24 See Grier 1989 377 Fn. 2 on the controllability of the federal funds rate by the Federal Reserve. Havrilesky et al. 1975 839 assume that the federal funds rate is controlled by the monetary authority, even though the rate itself is influenced from the demand side.

bank.[25] For the purposes at hand this discussion is not really relevant. The issue is not what the optimal control variable would be for measuring the real thrust and appropriateness of monetary policy but estimating how the SNB actually reacted to various pressures from the environment.[26] Therefore, it suffices to find out which variable was actually chosen as the intermediate target. The SNB started with publicly announcing targets for annual growth rates of M1 in 1975. In 1978 the value of the SFr rose dramatically. The SNB gave up the 5 percent growth rate target for M1 and shifted to an exchange rate policy. In 1979 no monetary target was set. In late 1979 the SNB returned to announcing monetary targets for 1980. But it switched from M1 to a monetary base target.[27]

If it is assumed that the SNB actually pursues the targets that are publicly announced,[28] the monetary base should be selected as dependent variable. This is obvious for the period after 1980. Already for the period from 1975 to 1978 the monetary base was officially adopted by the SNB as an instrument for controlling the growth of M1. SNB emphasis on the monetary base has a much earlier origin, however, and Schiltknecht (1983; cited in Burdekin/Langdana 1992 190 Fn. 7) states that even in the fixed exchange rate era the trend in the monetary base was regarded as the best indicator of monetary ease or tightness.

There exists a close relationship between controllability and target character of a variable. Only those variables controllable by the central bank can be regarded as target variables.[29] If the central bank is able to control several variables, which one is it actually trying to control? This question is relevant for the discussion about monetary base versus money supply M1 as dependent variable. It can be answered by looking at the variable selected as target. If we are willing to accept that the SNB can control both the monetary base

---

25 Rich/Béguelin (1985; cited in Burdekin/Langdana 1992 Fn. 6 190) for instance focus primarily on the monetary base and M1 as competing intermediate targets. See also Kästli 1995, Dueker/Fischer 1996, and Landmann/Jerger 1997.

26 As Havrilesky et al. 1975 839 Fn. 9 note these two issues have frequently been confused in the reaction function literature.

27 Laney 1985 99 and Fischer/Peytrignet 1990 505 cite difficulties in predicting the money multiplier that caused this shift. Capitelli/Buomberger (1990 540) argue that the demand for M1 had become very unstable, mainly because of changing expectations with respect to exchange rates. According to Rich 1985 64 demand for base money was expected to be less sensitive to expectations with respect to exchange rates than M1. This was one of the reasons for the switch from M1 to monetary base targets.

28 Of course, this assumption may not be justified. See e.g. Landmann/Jerger 1997. This holds especially for the period since 1988. The announcement of a target for the monetary base in the form of an average growth rate over a period of three to five years since 1991 may indeed signal that the SNB does no longer pursue this target.

29 „Had the central bank not been reasonably confident that the specified aggregate could be controlled with some degree of precision, that aggregate presumably would not have been chosen as a target." Laney 1985 104.

and M1, its targeting policy suggests that it tried to control M1 between 1975 and 1978, and the monetary base since 1980. The SNB's shift from an M1 to a monetary base target in 1980 may indicate that it found it increasingly difficult to control M1.

In october 1978 the SNB formulated an exchange rate target for the first time after giving up fixed exchange rates. It explicitly stated that the SFr/DM exchange rate should be above 80 SFr per 100 DM. Implicitly a target range of 80 to 85 was adopted for this exchange rate. By the end of 1979 the SNB returned to its policy of targeting monetary aggregates. There is a debate about whether the SNB missed its monetary base targets because of exchange rate considerations in the following years, especially in 1980-81 and in 1987. (See Capitelli/Buomberger 1990 and Rich 1990.) Exchange rate considerations are explicitly acknowledged by the SNB for 1987. (Rich 1990 557-558) Some critics even argue that the SNB - instead of targeting the monetary base - was guided by exchange rate considerations from 1989 to 1992. (Wild 1992) Announcements of the monetary base targets usually are accompanied by a caveat: The SNB will deviate from the monetary base target if unexpected developments at exchange rate and financial markets endanger price stability.[30] Hence, under this criterion the SFr/DM exchange rate could eventually also serve as a dependent variable. Notice that a central bank in a small open economy cannot target monetary aggregates and exchange rates simultaneously. (Rich 1990 561)

According to SNB officials other indicators such as interest rates have never been used as intermediate target variables. The only exception is 1988, when the SNB temporarily used short-term interest rates as its main policy indicator. (Rich 1995 10 and 14) The reason was a serious indicator problem caused by a temporary instability in money demand. (See also SNB 1988 271-272.) Landmann/Jerger (1997) argue, however, that instabilities in the money demand were more frequent during the period of flexible exchange rates and that the SNB switched to an interest rate target. For this reason they choose the short-term interest rate as dependent variable in their reaction function approach.

(iv) The choice of the dependent variable can also be influenced by the *availability of data.* Data on monetary policy instruments and on other monetary indicators such as interest rates and exchange rates are readily available. Data on monetary aggregates are published by the SNB since 1973. The published series start in 1950. A frequent problem with monetary aggregates is a change in definition, or the use of a different adjustment procedure. Monetary aggregates were revised a first time in May 1975 (SNB 1975), a second time

---

30 According to Rich 1995 the SNB tends to adjust its policy to three types of stochastic disturbances: unanticipated shifts in the demand for money, unanticipated shifts in the aggregate demand for goods and services, and unanticipated exchange rate shocks. The supply of base money is adjusted „provided these shifts are permanent or, if transitory, at least persistent." Rich 1995 40.

in November 1984 (SNB 1985), and a third time in January 1995 (SNB 1995a). In addition, computation of the monetary base was revised in 1982. (SNB 1982a) However, for M1 there is a series available which links the series from June 1975 to November 1984 with the series from December 1984 until today. (This series on M1 is provided by the Konjunkturforschungsstelle KOF at the Eidgenössische Technische Hochschule ETH in Zürich.) For the unadjusted monetary base a consistent series is available from 1950 until today. With respect to the criterion of data availability, the unadjusted monetary base or the consistent series on the money supply M1 provided by KOF are the preferred monetary aggregates.

(v) Finally, in choosing the dependent variable *existing studies* can be consulted. The reason is not just to make the choice consistent with other studies. It offers as an additional advantage the possibility of comparisons. This criterion again suggests the choice of the monetary base as the dependent variable.[31]

To sum up this discussion: The *unadjusted monetary base* is probably the best single measure of SNB behavior. It reflects the aggregate effects of all important policy actions. It can be controlled by the SNB and is explicitly targeted since 1980. Data for the unadjusted series are readily available from 1950 until today. And two of the three reaction function studies cited above use the monetary base as dependent variable. The important assumption being made is that movements in the monetary base reflect the central bank's use of its control instruments.

The *money supply M1* also measures aggregate effects of policy instruments. It can be controlled by the SNB and actually was target variable from 1975 to 1978. A consistent series on M1 is also available. So though the monetary base is the primary candidate M1 should not be excluded a priori from the analysis. Since M1 represents the money supply and since it was originally the target variable regressions with M1 as dependent variable are also run. The results for the two measures are then compared.[32]

1.3.2c Choice of Independent Variables

The idea of a reaction function is that the central bank reacts with its control instruments to actual or expected undesirable states or developments of the economy.[33] What are these undesirable states or developments, and how can they be measured?

---

31 Especially in cross-country studies the monetary base is the preferred dependent variable. Lothian (1976) for instance favors this monetary measure because of the relative constancy of the characteristics of high-powered money across countries and across time. See Burdekin/Langdana 1992 189.

32 The Pearson correlation coefficient for the quarterly growth rates of the monetary base and the money supply M1 for the period from 1973 to 1995 is 0.60.

33 Hence, the existence of a discretionary monetary policy regime is assumed. Notice that a central bank that has adopted an orthodox monetarist policy would not react

There is no theory which states upon which variables a central bank really focuses. It probably considers a whole range of economic variables. Hence, many different independent variables could be used in a reaction function study.

A simple idea is to start from a public-interest model for the central bank[34]. According to the SNB law the Swiss central bank is supposed to conduct monetary policy in the interest of the Swiss economy. What does this interest of the Swiss economy mean? The law does not stipulate this any further (as is done for instance for the Deutsche Bundesbank, where price stability is prescribed by the law, or, more recently, for the central bank of New Zealand). So one possible departure is to relate the dependent variable to the *economic stabilization objectives* postulated for economic policy in general.[35] These include price stability (maintain internal value of the national currency), employment, economic growth, and exchange rate stability (maintain external value of the national currency). These goals relate to various dimensions of economic activity. Price stability, employment, and economic growth represent the internal state of the economy. Exchange rate stability reflects its international standing. All goals are strongly affected by monetary policy. Hence, they all can be regarded as key variables influencing the conduct of the SNB's monetary policy. (See for instance Rich 1989; Fürstenberg 1980 10.)

Among these macroeconomic objectives of central banks long-term *price stability* is attributed a paramount position. This priority of the objective of price stability is a result of the dominant influence of monetary policy on the price level. It is generally agreed that inflation ultimately is a monetary phenomenon, „in the sense that inflation cannot occur in the long term without monetary accommodation or validation of the various pressures exerting themselves on the authorities.“ (Laney 1985 103; see also Baltensperger/Böhm 1984 1.) The central bank is the authority ultimately responsible for price stability. For the SNB price stability is achieved if the annual inflation rate (measured with the consumer price

---

at all. It would simply set a target for the monetary base or the money supply M1 according to the expected mid-term growth rate of GDP.

34 An alternative approach is the interest-group model of the central bank, typically used in the public-choice perspective of central banking.

35 „Monetary policy responsibilities of central banks today go far beyond the role originally seen for central banks, which involved ensuring the stability of the banking system and the convertibility of deposits, especially in times of financial panics. Early in their history, central banks assumed the role of 'the lender of last resort' ... it has been joined in this century by a responsibility for overall macroeconomic stabilization.“ Lindsey/Wallich 1987 510.
According to Issing (1983) the goals of monetary policy and economic policy in general are identical today. The dispute, however, is about the priority of the goal of price stability. See also Fischer/Zurlinden 1994, 67-68.
The choice of the general economic stabilization goals as regressor variables is very common in reaction function studies. See e.g. Missong/Herrault 1990 574.

index) is between zero and one percent. (Rich 1992 73)[36] An inflation rate of slightly above zero takes into account the quality bias in the CPI. (Rich 1995 4)

Inflation can be measured with different variables: consumer price index CPI, wholesale price index WPI (producer price index), GDP deflator, or the percentage change in the yield of AAA corporate bonds as a measure of future inflation. Which is the best measure in the present context? Asked differently: Which inflation variable is the SNB most likely to pay its attention?

The CPI is without any doubt the most important measure of inflation. For the public, it is *the* indicator of inflation. Although the CPI is periodically revised it is made available as a consistent monthly series. Data once published are not revised. For several reasons, the CPI is likely to overestimate actual inflation. (Fischer/Zurlinden 1994 71; Rich 1995 4) Still, it can be considered as a relatively reliable measure of current inflation.

The WPI is an interesting measure because of its function as a leading indicator of inflation. It has the advantage of resembling an economic forecast for inflation. However, the index introduced in 1963 has not been revised until 1993. It might therefore be considered as a rather poor measure of inflation.

The GDP deflator is published on a quarterly basis with a longer time lag than the CPI and the WPI. Because of this longer time lag it is not expected to be a good measure of inflation in a reaction function study. Moreover, the GDP deflator does not account for imported goods.

CPI, WPI, and GDP deflator all measure current (or even past) inflation. But the central bank will primarily be interested in future inflation. One interesting measure of future inflation is the percentage change in the yield of AAA corporate bonds. „In standard Fisherian interest rate theory the yield on long-term AAA bonds consists of a real return and returns to cover risk, inflation, and loss of flexibility. In the short run, changes in bond yields should be caused primarily by changes in the expected rate of inflation“. (Beck 1984 796) The percentage change in the yield of long-term AAA bonds, or, in the case of Switzerland, the percentage change in government bond yield, can therefore be used as a measure of expected inflation.

While price stability might be the priority *real economic activity* also is constantly on the monetary authorities' minds. (Laney 1985 110; Rich 1985 62) The impact of monetary policy on real economic activity such as production and employment is subject to an ongoing academic discussion (transmission theory). According to Rich, the SNB assumes that production and employment react to monetary policy actions only in the short run. (Rich 1989 348) Despite this widely shared insight it is frequently argued that monetary policy should try to

---

36 Notice that causation is usually running from changes in the money supply to inflation rather than vice-versa. Inclusion of inflation as an independent variable is justified on the hypothesis that some endogenous central bank response to changes in inflation rates is possible as a result of concerns voiced by the central banks (financial market) 'constituency'. See Laney/Willett 1983 56.

stabilize production and employment (at least) in the short run.[37] Economic activity variables are therefore included in the reaction function to see whether the SNB is responsive to changes in real economic activity, and whether it reacts in a countercyclical or accommodative way.

Production can be measured in several ways: gross domestic product GDP, index of industrial production (manufacturing production), orders inflow, order books, finished goods stocks, retail sales, rate of capacity utilization. GDP seems to be the best overall measure of economic activity.[38] Orders inflow is an interesting variable because of its characteristics as a leading indicator.

Initially, *employment* variables were also included in the reaction function. They are a measure of slack in the economy. Employment variables are the unemployment rate, rate of capacity utilization, employment index, or the manpower index[39]. The unemployment rate (registered unemployed as percentage of total labor force) certainly is the most common measure. However, for the reasons already stated by Langdana/Burdekin (1992) the unemployment rate usually is considered as a poor measure of economic slack in the Swiss economy. (See also Rich 1995 6.) It is therefore not expected that this variable is of importance. This has only changed in the recessions of the nineties, where Switzerland had peak unemployment rates of five percent. Instead of the more common unemployment rate the index of capacity utilization can be used. This variable is a less lagging indicator of the state of the economy than the unemployment rate. The index of capacity utilization has already been proposed as a measure of production, which indicates that a reaction function with production and employment variables might be plagued by multicollinearity. The employment index, based on the number of people employed, probably measures economic slack with a significant time lag. It is therefore not expected that this variable will be a significant regressor. The manpower index established itself only more recently as a leading indicator of economic activity. The SNB is not likely to react to this variable.

For small open economies like Switzerland with relatively large foreign sectors *international influences* are very important. Exchange rates and the balance of trade (or the balance of payments, if data were available on a quarterly basis) are two variables to measure foreign pressure on monetary policy.

Exchange rate considerations always played a prominent role in SNB policy. The central bank perceives stabilization of exchange rates not as a goal per se, but as a policy instrument to alleviate fluctuations in inflation, production, and employment. (Rich 1989 349) Despite the transition to flexible exchange rates in 1973 and the decision to follow a money supply rule in 1975 the SNB continued to intervene in the exchange rate markets. (Lusser 1984 and 1992 66) In the fall of

---

37 See for instance the recent controversy on Blinder's proposition that fighting unemployment is a legitimate goal for central banks. Caspar 1994; Tzermias 1994.

38 Instead of GDP, the GDP gap which is the percentage deviation of GDP from trend can be used. (Grier 1989 379).

39 The manpower index is a monthly measure of employment offers in the Swiss economy, calculated from the number of job offers advertised in Swiss newspapers.

1978 the SNB even set a target for the SFr/DM exchange rate. (Rich 1989 347) In 1987 it again intervened in the exchange rate market to prevent the SFr from rising too much, thus hurting the export industry and tourism. (See e.g. AB 1987 1027.)

Monetary policy certainly has an impact on exchange rates. But the relationship between money supply and exchange rates is complex. (See Rich 1989 351 and the literature cited there.) According to SNB publications Swiss monetary authorities are very skeptical about their abilities to control exchange rates. (This may, of course, be part of a strategy to respond to political pressure for exchange rate policy.) Wasserfallen/Kürsteiner (1993) find no systematic effects of Swiss monetary policy actions on exchange rates during the period since the breakdown of the Bretton Woods System (1974-1991). Zurlinden (1996) analyzes the impact of the SNB's interventions in the exchange rate market for the period from 1986 to 1994. He concludes that the interventions constitute a relatively weak and less than reliable instrument for conducting exchange rate policy.[40] However, this does not necessarily imply that the SNB is not responding at all to developments in the foreign currency markets.

It is important to remember that price stability and exchange rate stability (internal and external price stability) can be conflicting goals. (See Rich 1989 347, 349; Schiltknecht 1977 16.) In order to avoid a too strong SFr an expansionary monetary policy is necessary. This usually leads to higher inflation rates.

Which exchange rates should be chosen: DM, US$, or the export weighted (effective) exchange rate? Should several exchange rates be included in the regression? Should they be measured in nominal or real terms? The SFr/DM probably is the most important exchange rate for the Swiss economy. Germany is the most important trading partner, with about one quarter of Swiss exports going to Germany and about one third of Swiss imports coming from Germany. Moreover, Swiss industrial goods, for instance chemicals and machinery, compete actively with German ones on world markets. SNB officials frequently made statements about what the desired level of the SFr/DM exchange rate would be. These statements usually refer to the nominal exchange rate.[41]

Exchange rate variables can be constructed in different manners. One possibility is to use the readily available exchange rates, measured in units of domestic currency per 1 (or 100) unit(s) of foreign currency. A second possibility is to work with index numbers. The construction of these indices implies that a rising index indicates a stronger SFr and vice versa, i.e. DM/SFr. (Bohley/Jans 1990 265) A third possibility is to focus on the deviations from some desired level or simply

40 International evidence on the effectiveness of foreign exchange intervention is also unclear, although some recent studies do suggest a significant link between official intervention and exchange rates. See Taylor 1995 section V.

41 According to Fürstenberg 1980 8 the SNB „seems to attach some importance to the nominal level of bilateral exchange rates irrespective of relative price trends in Switzerland and the corresponding other country".

from trend. The latter can be accomplished by using a detrended exchange rate.[42] Finally, changes in exchange rates can be splitted up in devaluation and valuation to analyze whether the central bank reacts symmetrically or not.[43]

The *balance of trade* might be measured as a proportion of GDP.

Should the exchange rate or the balance of trade variable be included as a measure of international pressure on monetary policy? The balance of trade certainly gives a direct measure of the foreign equilibrium. The balance of payments would even be a better measure, but there are no quarterly data available for this variable. The DM/SFr exchange rate index is preferred here to capture the foreign considerations in monetary policy decisions of the SNB.[44]

In addition to the inflation, production, unemployment, exchange rate, and balance of trade variables discussed several other variables are also investigated as *potential regressors,* including the three-month deposit rate representing short-term interest rate stability, government bond yield (interest rate on long-term government bonds) or mortgage rate representing long-term interest rate stability, index of consumer confidence, and the leading indicator for the economy provided by KOF.

Interest rates represent the general goal of stability in financial markets. The traditional function of banks is to transform short-term liabilities into longer-term loan assets. That is, banks typically commit to loan contracts that stretch over longer periods than the term for which deposits are committed to them. Because of this asymmetry in the structure of bank contracts, bank's profits are negatively related to the level of interest rates in the short run. For this reason, they dislike large unexpected swings in interest rates, particularly if they are upward. If the central bank is concerned about the stability of the financial system, it will engage in interest rate smoothing. (See Cukierman 1992 chap. 7.) Technically the SNB is able to completely control short-term interest rates. (Bernegger/Ettlin 1991) However, in practice this ability is constrained by the effects of the DM/SFr exchange rate on Swiss production and inflation. In Switzerland the stabilization of interest rates (at a low level) may be additionally motivated by the fact that rents are tied to the lending rate.

As is explained in section 1.3.2a the partial adjustment model leads to an equation with a lagged dependent variable. Hence, a *lagged dependent variable* is also included in the regression equation in order to account for the use of the monetary policy instrument(s) in the preceding period(s). Following common practice, the dependent variable will enter with several lags to whiten the errors.

---

42 The deviation from trend can also be standardized. See Laney 1985 107.

43 In their reaction function for the period from 1975 to 1996 with short-term interest rates as dependent variable Landmann/Jerger (1997) find that the SNB reacts only to valuation, suggesting that the SNB is concerned about exports, but not about imported inflation.

44 Fluctuations of the exchange rates are at the same time also a measure of inflationary expectations. See Missong/Herrault 1990 574.

(See section 1.5.1a.) More generally, effects from omitted variables can operate through these terms. (See e.g. Barro 1977 104; Laney/Willett 1983 55.)

Since most of the data are not seasonally adjusted, three *seasonal dummies* are included in the regressions with nonseasonal differences to control for seasonal factors. (See also Burdekin 1987 458.) Instead of including seasonal dummies more sophisticated seasonal adjustment procedures could be used. (See for example Demopoulos et al. 1987 1034 Fn. 13.)

What *signs* can be predicted for the regressors? As pointed out in section 1.2 reaction functions have to be interpreted as single-equation solutions of constrained optimization problems. For these reduced-form equations interpretation of signs of the coefficients is not valid without presentation of a structural model of the economy. Statements about expected signs of the coefficients can only make sense if the reaction function is interpreted as some simple behavioral equation. But even in this case interpretation of signs can be very difficult because of the lag problem. (See the discussion in section 1.3.2h.)

Despite these difficulties most researchers hypothesize signs for the coefficients of their reaction functions, obviously having a very simple behavioral model in mind. The following discussion of expected signs of coefficients basically serves to *summarize* the arguments typically made in the reaction function literature. But the reader should keep in mind that ad hoc reaction functions can only tell whether a regressor is significant and whether the coefficient is positive or negative. However, it can be difficult to explain why the coefficient is positive or negative. Hence, the reader should be cautious when so-called 'unexpected' signs show up.

It also has to be noted that *differing theories* of how the central bank should be operating imply differing signs for the various coefficients. (Beck 1984 796) Especially monetarist and Keynesian theories lead to opposite signs for some of the coefficients. Estimation results may therefore indicate which theory was guiding monetary policy in a distinct period. This probably is an important motivation for predicting signs of the reaction function coefficients.

For the *inflation* variables a negative sign is hypothesized. The higher the (current or future) inflation rate the more restrictive monetary policy should be. This interpretation is also valid for the percentage change in the yield of AAA corporate bonds (percentage change in government bond yield) as a measure of expected inflation. However, Beck notes that under alternative theories of monetary policy it is possible for the sign of the yield variable to be reversed. (Beck 1984 797) He also states that the sign of the inflation coefficient might not be that easy to predict. „(U)nder high inflation, some growth in nominal supply of money is required to keep the real supply from falling; reserves should show some accommodation to inflation, and the sign on the inflation coefficients should be positive. However, in comparing differing time periods, which is of interest here, a smaller coefficient on inflation indicates an increased anti-inflationary posture." (Beck 1984 796)[45]

Hypothesized signs for the *production* variables depend on accommodating or countercyclical reactions of monetary policy. On the one hand the central bank will deem it necessary to accommodate changes in economic activity. On the other hand it might be motivated to react in a countercyclical fashion, reversing the sign on this variable. (Laney 1985 105) The actual results are expected to tell which policy the SNB is pursuing.[46]

The sign of the *unemployment rate* is expected to be positive. The sign of the index of *capacity utilization* should be positive for accommodating policy and negative for a countercyclical response. The actual results are again supposed to indicate the type of monetary policy pursued by the SNB.

Predicted signs for the *exchange rate* variables obviously depend on the construction of these variables. (And it depends on which interests the SNB is pursuing). If the SNB tries to stabilize the exchange rate, a rise in the exchange rate - which implies a weakening SFr - induces a contractionary monetary policy. Falling exchange rates, however, lead to an expansionary reaction by the SNB. Hence, a negative sign is anticipated. For exchange rate indices a positive sign is expected: a rising index induces an expansionary monetary policy, and a falling index leads to a contractionary monetary policy. For a detrended exchange rate positive deviations imply a weaker SFr and a contractionary monetary response, and negative deviations indicate a stronger SFr, thus inducing an expansionary monetary reaction. Hence, the detrended exchange rate should show a negative sign.

Stabilizing *interest rates* means that the SNB reacts to rising interest rates with an increase in money supply and vice versa. This would imply a positive sign on the coefficient.

The coefficient of the *lagged dependent variable* is interpreted as an adjustment speed parameter. (Alt/Chrystal 1983 127; see also section 1.3.2a.) Its value is expected to be between zero and one. Values close to zero mean that the current value of the dependent variable is not related to the last period's value. A coefficient close to one means that the instrument does not change much from period to period. A significant positive coefficient is usually perceived as an indicator of inertia in the policy making process. (Chappel et al. 1993 201; Lang/Welzel 1992 76)[47]

---

45 Beck works with the level of bank reserves as dependent variable. The prediction on the sign of the coefficient will be the same for bank reserves and the monetary base.

46 Laney/Willett 1983 55 address this problem by including two variables measuring real economic activity, one for assessing an accommodative response, the other for finding a countercyclical reaction.

47 „The sign on the lagged dependent variable might have been negative, indicating a contraction in the money supply in the year following an expansion. The fact that it is positive but less than one is evidence of a stationary money growth process,

A somewhat different approach from the one presented here would be the departure from *deviations* from stabilization goals.[48] While this wouldn't be a problem with the inflation variables, the desired levels of the other regressor variables are not easily defined. Therefore, this approach is not investigated here.

Once the dependent variable and the regressors are identified, a few more questions regarding the reaction function have to be discussed:

- Which time period should be considered?
- What about the periodicity of the data?
- Should the variables enter the regression equation as levels or changes?
- What is the appropriate lag structure for the reaction function?

1.3.2d Time Period

The reaction function is estimated using quarterly data for the period of flexible exchange rates from 1973.2 to 1995.2. The basic reason for this limitation to the *flexible* exchange rate era is to avoid the problems of structural instability caused by the transition from fixed to floating exchange rates.[49] A second and more special reason is the inclusion of an exchange rate variable (the DM/SFr exchange rate index) as a regressor. (For a similar argument see Missong/Herrault 1990 575.) A third reason is the choice of the monetary base as the primary dependent variable. Under fixed exchange rate regimes the monetary base cannot effectively be controlled by a central bank. Only under flexible exchange rate regimes is the monetary base a viable monetary policy instrument. The transition from fixed to floating exchange rates is therefore an important precondition for the controllability of the monetary base. This also holds for the other monetary aggregates.[50]

The period of flexible exchange rates starts in 1973. On January 23, 1973 the SNB stopped buying US$ to maintain the US$/SFr exchange rate. This decision was made after large speculative demands for SFr against US$ had led to annual growth rates of the monetary base of almost 50 percent during the early seventies, with subsequent inflation rates at about 10 percent per year.

---

with a persistence effect similar to that found by Barro ... (A coefficient greater than one would have indicated a nonstationary process ...)" Laney/Willett 1983 57.

48 Beck 1982 uses monetary target deviations as regressors to measure whether the Fed is sensitive to recent target misses. In his monthly model he uses the difference between the previous month's M1 growth and the target for M1, as well as the deviation of M1 averaged over the prior six months.

49 Given the impacts of regime changes (such as the shift from fixed to floating exchange rates) Alt/Chrystal 1983 145 recommend the analyst to estimate a different function before and after the regime change.

50 Burdekin 1987 457 lists as another argument the additional balance of payments constraints imposed under the fixed exchange rate era.

The *major events* in the period since 1973 include the following:[51] In 1975, the SNB starts to follow a money supply rule. Until 1978, annual targets for the money supply are set in terms of M1.[52] Except for an interruption in 1979[53] annual targets are publicly announced at the end of the previous year. In February 1978 the so-called 'Konjunkturartikel' is accepted in a popular vote. Intervention by the Federal Council (the executive) into monetary policy now rests on a constitutional basis. In October 1978, after all attempts to reduce a strong upward pressure on the SFr by administrative means had more or less failed, the SNB formulates an exchange rate target. The SFr/DM exchange rate should be more than 80 SFr for 100 DM.[54] In the second half of 1978, massive intervention in the foreign exchange rate markets by buying large amounts of US$ is aimed at countering the considerable appreciation of the SFr against most other currencies. The annual growth rate for the money supply M1 reaches 17 percent. In December 1979 the SNB returns to monetary targeting. For 1980 a monetary base target of four percent is set. Since then, monetary base targets were set for each year until 1991.

By the end of 1987 Swiss monetary policy was complicated by several developments. (Blancpain 1987 33; for an account from the perspective of the SNB see Rich 1992 and 1995.) In 1987 an expansionary monetary policy is conducted to prevent the SFr from rising too much. (Rich 1990 557) In June 1987 the electronic Swiss Interbank Clearing System (SIC) is introduced.[55] In October 1987 follows the crash in the stock markets. In January 1988 new and lower liquidity requirements for banks are introduced. The introduction of the SIC and the new liquidity requirements resulted in a substantial decrease in the demand for base money. This had been expected (Rich 1985 61) and the SNB reacted to this structural shift in money demand with a reduction of the monetary base. However, the SNB probably was surprised by the quick adjustment process and the amount of the decline. The fall in demand was larger than the reduction in supply.[56] Moreover, after the crash in the stock markets in October 1987 widespread fears of a

---

[51] For a more detailed account of monetary policy in this period see Landmann/Jerger 1997 (for the period from 1975 to 1995), Dueker/Fischer 1996 (for the period from 1977 to 1995), Rich 1995 (for the period from 1973 to 1994), SNB 1982b (for the period before 1982), Schiltknecht 1977 (for the first three years after the shift from fixed to flexible exchange rates), Baltensperger 1985 (for the period from 1973 to 1983), Capitelli/Buomberger 1990 (for the eighties), Spörndli 1994 (for the period from 1986 to 1992), and Nilles 1994 (for the period after 1987).

[52] The target periods were set from fourth quarter to fourth quarter or from December to December.

[53] „The SNB did not announce a money supply target for 1979, presumably because events were too turbulent.“ Wasserfallen/Kürsteiner 1993 214.

[54] According to Capitelli/Buomberger 1990 540 the SNB ceded to pressure from the Swiss export industry.

[55] Compared to the previous arrangement, the Swiss Interbank Clearing (SIC) is a much more efficient interbank funds transfer system.

[56] „Under these circumstances, monetary growth and interest rates become positively correlated in the short run due to the systematic reaction of the monetary authorities.“ Wasserfallen/Kürsteiner 1993 212.

liquidity crisis in the banking system, rising interest rates and recession caused the SNB to respond with an expansionary monetary policy. But the financial markets quickly recovered and the economy did not fall into a recession. Due to the instabilities in the money demand the monetary aggregates could no longer serve as useful targets. Temporarily the SNB used short-term interest rates as its main policy indicator. Since 1991 the target for the monetary base is an average growth rate of one percent per year over a period of three to five years.[57]

The appreciating value of the SFr in 1987, the unusually high inflation and interest rates, and the recession with a dramatic increase in unemployment rates in the early nineties increased political pressure on the central bank.

These events may justify a distinction of the following *subperiods:*[58] subperiod from 1973 to 1979 (flexible exchange rates including interventions in currency markets and targeting of M1); subperiod from 1980 to 1987 (targeting of the monetary base); subperiod from 1973 to 1987 (before changes in liquidity requirements and introduction of SIC); subperiod after 1988 (after changes in liquidity requirements and introduction of SIC).

It has to be expected that parameters are not constant over the period under investigation. Addressing the problem of structural breaks will help to answer the following questions: Did the SNB react to the regressor variables representing the state of the economy in the same way throughout the period from 1973 to 1995? Or did its reaction change? If its reaction changed, when did it change, and to which regressors did it respond differently?

1.3.2e Periodicity

The use of quarterly data is consistent with the idea of the reaction function. Quarterly data are probably best suited to pinpoint and estimate the *relevant shifts* in monetary policy. Monthly data might pick up too many short-term fluctuations,[59] and annual data may not show relevant fluctuations in some variables. Quarterly data, however, allow for some of the monthly aberrations to average out (see also Beck 1984 798) but still pick up mid-year fluctuations.

Too long time periods may lead to a serious *identification problem* in ascribing one-way causality to the coefficients of the reaction function. Especially with annual data it can become difficult to separate one flow of causation (from the state of the economy to the dependent variable) from the reverse flow of causation (from

---

57 See Landmann/Jerger 1997 for a criticism of this concept. It can indeed be argued that the SNB ceased to target monetary aggregates in the nineties.

58 See Wasserfallen/Kürsteiner 1993 213 for a similar distinction of subperiods for the Swiss money supply process.

59 However, quarterly data do not pick up monthly and daily fluctuations. It is conceivable that a central bank is quite active in foreign exchange rate markets on a daily basis. But these activities may not show up in quarterly regressions because of cancellation of daily activity over a quarter. See for example Demopoulos et al. 1987 1043 Fn. 21.

the dependent variable to the state of the economy). Quarterly data make it easier to attribute unilateral causality to the reaction function from the regressors to the dependent variable.[60]

Quarterly data are employed also because most variables measuring production (e.g. estimates on GDP) are not *available* on a monthly basis, excluding the use of a monthly model. However, quarterly data are available for all variables.

The use of quarterly data also ensures a sufficient *number of observations* (and, hence, degrees of freedom and 'quality' of hypothesis testing). Quarterly data for the time period from 1973.2 to 1995.2 yield 89 observations.

1.3.2f Levels Versus Changes

Should the variables be measured in *levels or* as *changes?* Firstly, the answer to this question depends on whether it can be assumed that the SNB reacts to levels or changes. Here it is argued that the SNB concentrates on changes rather than levels. Secondly, the answer depends on statistical properties of the series. Variables measured in levels are often not stationary, and this can lead to serious problems with traditional statistics such as R^2, Durbin-Watson and the t statistic. Stationarity can usually be achieved by differencing the series. Thirdly, the answer also depends on whether levels or changes are a better predictor of policy. This can only be answered by looking at the data. Several of the level variables (expressed as natural logarithms) show very high simple correlation coefficients indicating problems of multicollinearity. For all these reasons, it is decided to work with changes and not to pursue the level approach any further. Details on measurement of the data are discussed in section 1.4.

The concept of cointegration has prompted a reconsideration of the problem of regression using variables measured in their levels. Differencing leads to a loss of all long-run information in the data. Cointegration allows for an evaluation of models which combine both short-run and long-run properties and which at the same time maintain stationarity in all of the variables. (See e.g. Charemza/ Deadman 1997 for a textbook exposition.) These error-correction models are closely related to the partial adjustment model which is used here. (See e.g. Nickell 1985.) However, error-correction models are not without problems (see e.g. Kennedy 1992 259), and the underlying theory is still immature.

1.3.2g Lag Structure

The central bank sets its instruments as a function of where it expects the economy to be in the (near) future. It reacts to forecasted values of the levels or changes

---

60 According to Havrilesky et al. 1975 839 the identification problem also exists for quarterly data. For this reason they prefer to work with monthly data.

of the regressors available at the time decisions are made. The difficulty is that the forecasts that condition SNB policy actions usually are *not observable.*[61]

Forecasts from other Swiss institutions[62] or the semiannual forecasts from the OECD could be used as a proxy for the expectations of the monetary authority. One problem is that these forecasts vary considerably, so that one of these forecasts would have to be chosen or some aggregate measure of several forecasts would have to be constructed. Another problem is that it is still not known how the central bank's own expected values deviate from these forecasts.

Researchers have therefore circumvented this problem in a number of ways. (See also Demopoulos et al. 1987 1033.)

One alternative is to work with *own forecasted values.*[63] Here, at least three methods can be distinguished: (i) autoregressive forecasting, (ii) perfect foresight assumption, and (iii) consistent predictions.

(i) The method of *autoregressive forecasting* assumes that the forecast of a variable in time period t is a function of the values of that variable in periods prior to t. Since past values of the regressor variable are the only information employed, however, this method is likely to err in the direction of assuming that the forecast is based on too little information. (Abrams et al. 1980 33)

(ii) The *perfect foresight* assumption is implied when actual current-period values of the target variables appear in the reaction function. (Abrams et al. 1980 33; Laney 1985 105) It is implicitly assumed that the central bank sets its instruments as a function of the current state of the economy, also assuming that the information on this state is readily available. This may be true for some variables such as exchange rates and interest rates with the data being available contemporaneously, but not for other variables such as inflation rates or growth rates where the actual values are available only after a time lag. This assumption errs in ascribing to the central bank a prescience not possessed.

Both the method of autoregressive forecasting and the perfect foresight assumption are likely to result in inconsistent estimates of the reaction-function coefficients. (For details see Abrams et al. 33 and Beck 1984 795.) Using contemporaneous actual values of the regressor variables implies that there will almost certainly be simultaneous equation bias in the estimates. (Beck 1984 793)

---

61 The correct solution would be to use the central bank's forecasted values. However, Lombra and Moran (1980) show that the current state of the economy is a better predictor of monetary policy than are the Fed's own forecasts. The reason they cite is that the Federal Open Market Committee often ignores staff forecasts.

62 These institutions are the „Konjunkturforschungsstelle der Eidgenössischen Technischen Hochschule Zürich“ (KOF), the „Konjunkturforschung Basel AG“ (BAK), the „St.Galler Zentrum für Zukunftsforschung“ (SGZZ), the „Centre de recherches économiques appliquées“ (Créa), all major commercial banks (especially Union Bank of Switzerland, Credit Swiss, Swiss Bank Corporation), and the „Kommission für Konjunkturfragen“.

63 The use of forecasted values diminishes the reversed causality problem. See Havrilesky 1988 93 and 1987 321 with reference to Froyen 1974.

(iii) The method of *consistent predictions* is applied by Abrams et al. (1980 33; see also Chappell et al. 1993 197.) By a 'consistent' prediction they mean a forecast that takes into account information that does improve upon the prediction made solely on the basis of the past values of a variable. According to Beck (1984 793 Fn. 2) „it is not obvious that the use of optimal linear forecasts is superior to the use of simple lagged variables" in representing the state of the economy.

As an alternative to forecasted values *leading* (rather than 'coincident' or 'lagging') *indicators* resembling economic forecasts can be employed. Examples are the wholesale price index which leads the consumer price index, or the rate of capacity utilization which leads the unemployment rate. SNB publications reveal that the monetary authority is sensitive to leading indicators.

Another alternative would be to use *actual values* as *leads* in order to proxy forecasted values. But this would amount to the unrealistic assumption that the future state of the economy corresponds with its actual state, and that the central bank doesn't even account for the effects of its own policy actions. Moreover, this would create severe problems of reversed causality.

Finally, as the most common alternative researchers simply use *lagged values* of the target variables. (See e.g. Grier 1991 215.) This involves the implicit assumption that the policymakers set their instruments as a function of where the economy was in the recent past. (Beck 1984 793 Fn. 2) Ex post data do not measure the forecasts to which the policymaker has reacted. But the assumption that current policy depends on prior information does not seem completely untenable given that it takes the authority some time to collect the data and act on them (Beck 1984 793 Fn. 2); the SNB does not have current information on the state of the economy. In addition, the use of lagged actual values is at least an attempt to make the independent variables predetermined in the model. (Laney/Willett 1983 56; Laney 1985 105)[64]

This study simply works with lagged values of the target variables. Using lagged values certainly does not give the central bank enough credit. But the 'consistent' predictions procedure used by Abrams et al. (1980) to calculate forecasted values might give it too much credit. The use of lagged values is consistent with the view that the central bank reacts more to the current state of the economy than to forecasts of its future. A position somewhere between this naive approach (working with lags) and the very sophisticated one taken by Abrams et al. (using forecasted values calculated by a special procedure) is probably correct. (Beck 1982 424)

If lagged actual values of the target variables are used, the *appropriate lag structure* has to be found out. Theory provides little guidance for this problem. Given the rather small number of observations no attempt is made to model a

64 Moreover, Laney 1985 105 Fn. 11 reports that the outcomes for the Federal Reserve when using semiannual forecasts of the OECD were not significantly different from simply using lagged actual values.

gradual response of the central bank with a distributed-lag function. The approach taken here is to work with lags of one quarter for the regressor variables. Higher order lags are hard to justify theoretically. Experiments with various other lags did not generally help to improve the fit.[65]

1.3.2h Lag Structure and Expected Signs of the Coefficients

According to Friedman's famous dictum monetary policy works with long and variable lags. (Friedman 1982) A central bank which takes the monetary policy lag seriously will react to values forecasted for the next one to three years. These forecasts must also account for the effects of the central bank's own policy actions. If lagged values for the regressors are proxy variables for these forecasted values, statements about *expected signs* of the estimated coefficients become very difficult (even if the reaction function is interpreted as a simple behavioral equation). Depending on the assumed current cyclical state of the economy and the assumed length of the monetary policy lag any sign on the coefficients can be hypothesized. This is especially the problem with the inflation variable - where a lag of two to three years must be anticipated[66] - and the production variables. It might be less serious with exchange rates and interest rates because of much shorter time lags.

The lag problem discussed in the previous section also affects the ability of making inferences about the policymaker's *preferences*. As Alt/Chrystal (1983 145) point out reaction function studies „inevitably rely on ex post measurements of how things turned out". However, actual outcomes do not only reflect deliberate discretionary choice. Many large changes in targets and instruments of policy arise 'automatically', i.e. without central bank interference. The fact that reaction

---

65 Adding lags may result in a loss of efficiency due to multicollinearity. But this has to be set against the omitted variable bias likely associated with a more spartan specification. Burdekin/Wohar 1990 537 Fn. 10.
In order to determine the lag values, Burdekin/Langdana 1992 apply Akaike's minimum final prediction error criterion to the model with a maximum lag length set at six and four quarters. See Burdekin/Wohar 1990 537 for an exact description of their application of the final prediction error criterion.
In the lag selection process Sheehan 1992 uses the Bayesian information criterion (BIC), Mallow's C_P, and Amemiya's prediction criterion (PC). He also employs the subset procedure for choosing lags proposed by Haggan/Oyetunji. His results indicate that the choice of the lag selection criterion matters primarily for the selection of the lag lengths rather than for the variables included. Only in two cases alternative criteria yield opposite conclusions.

66 „In Switzerland the monetary policy lags are particularly long due to important rigidities in price setting behavior ... It may take up to three years until a change in the growth of the monetary base (or M1) significantly affects Swiss inflation." Rich 1995 17. One important rigidity is due to an institutional feature of the Swiss housing market that links housing rents and mortgage rates. Rich 1995 12 Fn. 11.
However, some critics argue that SNB policy is too much concerned about fighting existing inflation and not enough about preventing future inflation. See Brenner 1993 31.

function studies cannot always distinguish between the two further hampers inferences about intentions and preferences of policymakers.

1.3.2i Summary of the Model and Comments

The preceding discussion results in the postulation of the following standard linear[67] *reaction function* for the SNB with the monetary base as dependent variable and all variables measured as nonseasonal differences (see section 1.4.1 for definition and measurement of the variables and section 1.4.3 on the problem of seasonality):

$$\Delta \ln(MB)_t = \beta_0 + \beta_1 \Delta \ln(MB)_{t-1} + \beta_2 \Delta \ln(CPI)_{t-1} + \beta_3 \Delta \ln(DMN)_{t-1}$$
$$+ \beta_4 \Delta \ln(GDP)_{t-1} + \beta_5 \Delta DR_{t-1} + \beta_6 SD1_t + \beta_7 SD2_t + \beta_8 SD3_t + \varepsilon_t$$

The growth rate of the unadjusted monetary base MB is regressed on a lagged dependent variable (which may enter with additional lags), the lagged change in the consumer price index CPI, the lagged change in the nominal DM/SFr exchange rate index DMN, the lagged growth rate of real and seasonally unadjusted gross domestic product GDP, the lagged change in the three-month deposit rate DR, and three seasonal dummies SD1, SD2 and SD3.[68] ε_t is a random variable representing all other influences. The unemployment rate is not included because it is never significant. An analogous equation is postulated for the money supply M1 as dependent variable.

As pointed out there are obviously many different measures for the economic key variables represented in this regression equation. Though the foregoing discussion serves to work out the most important measures, experiments are also made with other variables found to be less relevant from a theoretical perspective. Exact specification is inevitably somewhat arbitrary.[69]

There are several things to note on the postulated reaction function:

1. It contains only *economic* variables as regressors. Other potentially influential (fiscal and political) variables are not considered at this point.
2. In this reduced-form reaction function money becomes *endogenous*. It appears as a function of exogenous economic variables representing the state of the economy. Thus the more intuitive macroeconomic causation that extends from money to the state of the economy in general and to prices in the longer run in particular is reversed. Money becomes endogenous „not because it cannot be controlled but because its movements reveal the authorities' response to various pressures included as independent variables in the equation.“ (Laney 1985 103)

---

67 For a criticism of the linearity assumption see Barth et al. 1982 67.

68 Inflation and real output growth are the two variables most frequently used in reaction function studies. Interest rates and exchange rates are also often included.

69 „As Leamer (1978) argues, we should make sure that the coefficients of interest are not the result of atheoretical arbitrary choices.“ (Beck 1987 205 Fn. 19).

3. The central bank is likely to respond to changes in the regressor variables over several time periods and not just to those for the most recent period.[70] This *gradual adjustment* is captured by the lagged dependent variable(s).
4. The central bank's response does not change depending on the *severity of economic conditions*. It can be argued, however, that the response of the monetary authority will not be the same, if the inflation rate is two percent and seven percent, for instance. To capture this sort of structural change in the reaction function a less restrictive functional form in which the marginal response is permitted to vary with economic conditions would have to be estimated.[71]

1.4 The Data

1.4.1 Definition and Measurement

Table 1.2 gives exact definitions and sources of all variables reported in this chapter.

Table 1.2: Variable Definitions and Data Sources

Variable	Definition	Source
	dependent variables	
MB	unadjusted monetary base	SNB[a]
M1	money supply M1, including Liechtenstein	KOF[b]
	regressor variables	
CPI	consumer price index, 1977=100	BFS[c]
DMN	DM/SFr exchange rate index, nominal; Nov. 1977=100	SNB
DR	deposit rate: rate of interest on three-month deposits with large banks	SNB
GDP	gross domestic product, seasonally unadjusted, real	BFK[d]

[a] Swiss National Bank, Monthly Bulletin
[b] Konjunkturforschungsstelle Eidgenössische Technische Hochschule Zürich
[c] Swiss Bundesamt für Statistik
[d] Swiss Bundesamt für Konjunktur

---

[70] Barth et al. 1982 52, working with monthly data, use a four-month moving average of past values of the regressors to capture this effect. Other studies employ a lag function to account for the gradual response.

[71] Barth et al. 1982 use spline functions to permit the marginal response of the central bank to vary with the severity of economic conditions. They find that the Federal Reserve responds somewhat uniformly to unemployment rate changes regardless of the level of the rate or the severity of the unemployment problem. However, the Federal Reserve seems to react to inflation rate changes only when inflation is most severe.

The data are quarterly and cover the time period from the second quarter of 1973 to the second quarter of 1995, yielding 89 observations. Interest rates (DR) are in fractions. All other variables are expressed in natural logarithms (e.g. ln(MB)).

The data are not seasonally adjusted. Seasonally unadjusted series are preferred because estimated dynamic relationships between variables may be distorted by the seasonal adjustment. (See e.g. Hylleberg 1992 10, 21 and 249 Fn. 1; Bell/ Hillmer 1992 104).[72]

The common practice to (implicitly) seasonally adjust the data is to take seasonal differences, i.e. the differences between a given quarter of the current year and the same quarter of the preceding year. Seasonal differences are denoted as Δ_4, where $\Delta_4 = 1 - B^4$ with B as the lag operator. Taking differences of logarithms is equivalent to using rates of growth as long as the changes in the variables are only small. (Mills 1992 50) Seasonal differences of natural logarithms, e.g. $\Delta_4\ln(MB)$, yield annual growth rates.

Accordingly, first or nonseasonal differences are denoted as Δ, with $\Delta = 1 - B$. First differences of natural logarithms, e.g. $\Delta\ln(MB)$, give quarterly growth rates. In the graphs Δ is replaced with D, and L denotes ln.

1.4.2 Data Plots

Figures 1.1 to 1.6 present graphs for exploratory data analysis. For each variable, the actual values (in logarithms), the nonseasonal and seasonal differences (quarterly and annual growth rates), as well as the correlogram, the spectrum, and the density for the seasonal differences are given.

The plots of the *actual values* show the variation of the series over time. They inform about salient features such as trends, structural breaks, outliers, and seasonality. Together with the discussion of the major events during the period under investigation (see section 1.3.2d) this may facilitate the subsequent interpretation of the results.

The *correlogram* provides information on the time dependence and the stationarity of a variable. Two forms of time dependence can be detected: (remaining) seasonality and serial correlation. A significant autocorrelation coefficient at every fourth value of lag k would suggest a seasonal influence. (Kennedy 1992 261) The correlogram also informs about whether there is serial correlation or not, and whether this may be an AR(p) or a MA(q) process. (See e.g. Maddala 1992 542 or Kennedy 1992 260 for typical patterns.)[73] However, the correlogram cannot be used to determine the order of an AR(p) process, because it does not give 'net contributions'. (Kennedy 1992 261) For this the partial autocorrelation function is needed.

---

[72] Reasons for seasonal adjustment of data are discussed in Bell/Hillmer 1992 100-102.

[73] In practice, time series often exhibit both types of processes. A pure AR(p) or MA(q) process may be too restrictive to model them.

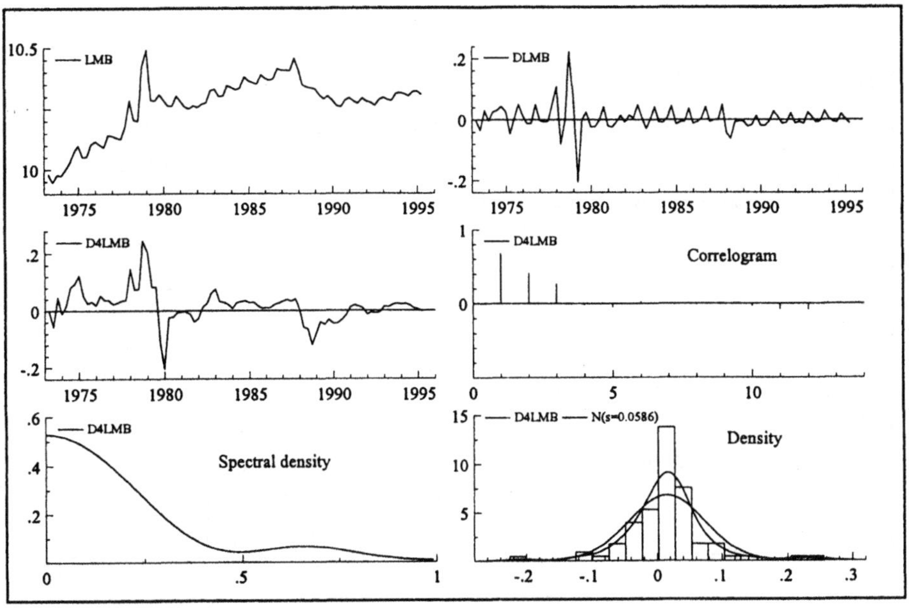

Figure 1.1: Unadjusted Monetary Base

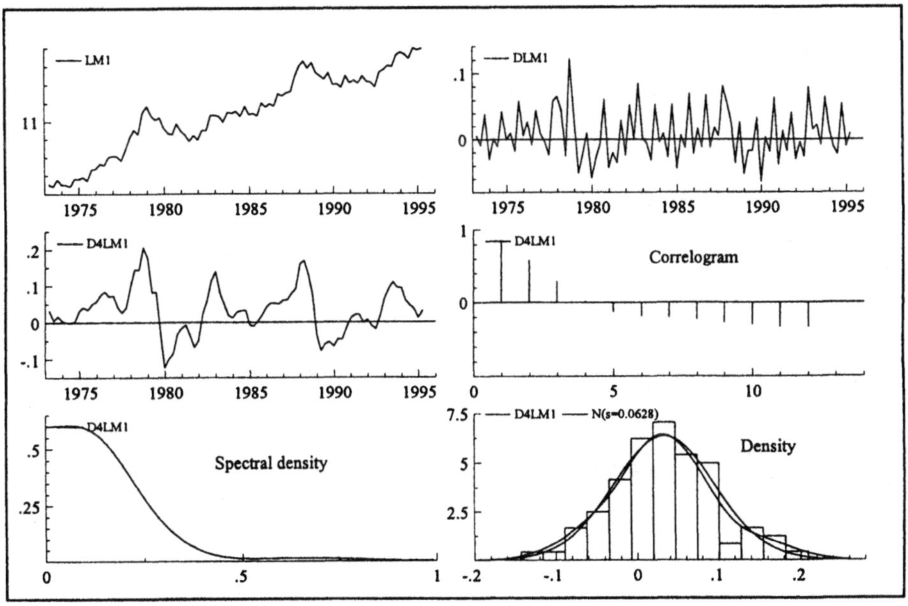

Figure 1.2: Money Supply M1

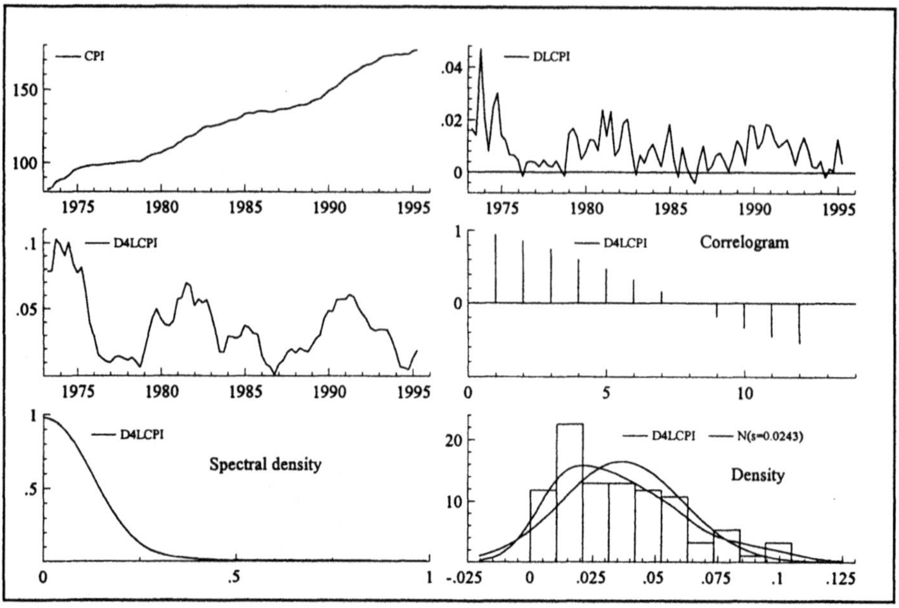

Figure 1.3: Consumer Price Index (1977 = 100)

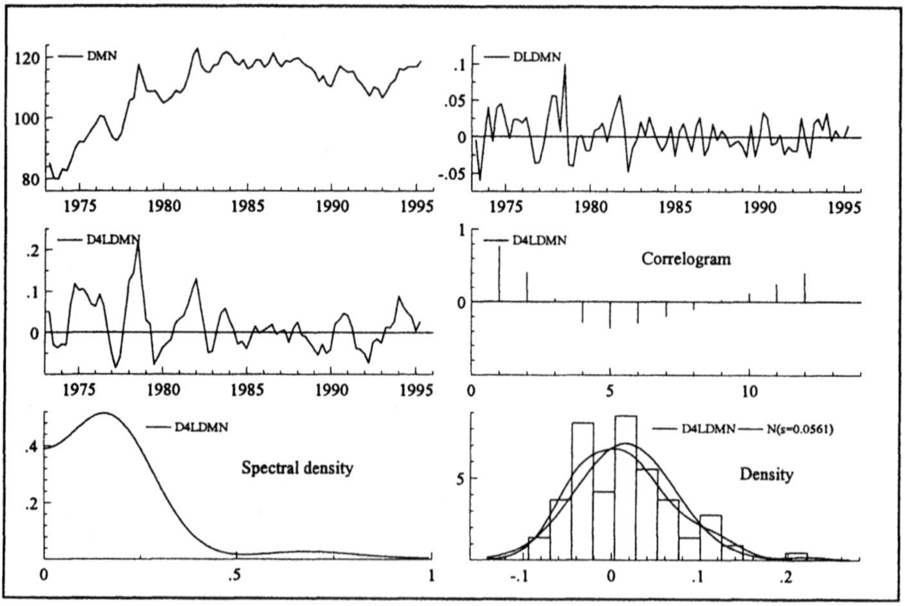

Figure 1.4: Nominal DM/SFr Exchange Rate Index (1977 = 100)

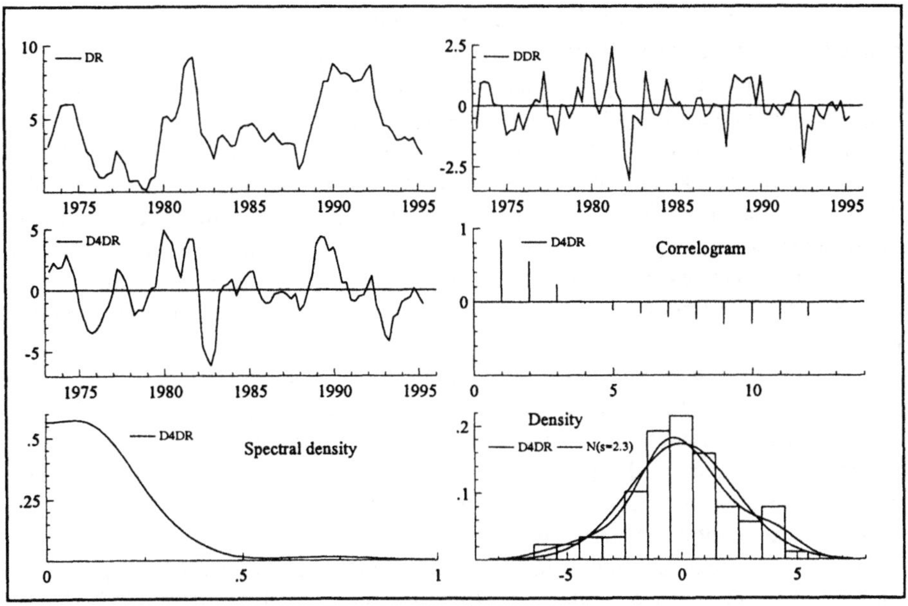

Figure 1.5: Deposit Rate - Rate of Interest on Three-Month Deposits

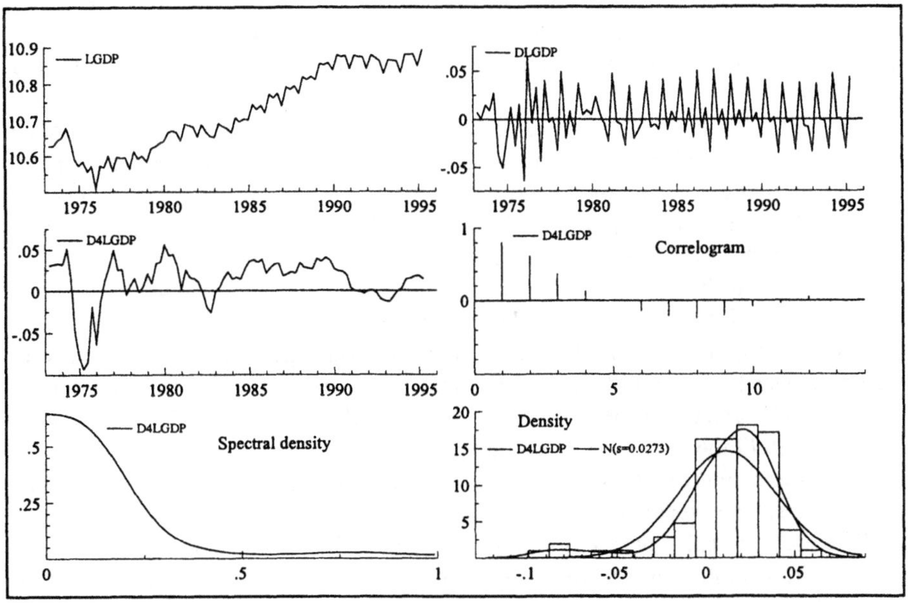

Figure 1.6: Seasonally Unadjusted, Real Gross Domestic Product

The visual inspection of the correlogram helps to decide whether or not a series is stationary. For a stationary variable the correlogram should show autocorrelations that die out fairly quickly as k becomes large. A correlogram which does not damp indicates a long-memory process and nonstationarity.

The *spectrum* serves to analyze the (seasonal) cyclical behavior of a series. „A typical spectrum for an economic time series is high at low frequencies, falls steeply, and becomes flat at high frequencies, with an occasional peak at seasonal frequencies." (Kennedy 1992 262) A flat spectrum results if there are no cyclical elements (regularities) in the series, suggesting that the series is white noise. For quarterly data the frequency $\pi/2$ corresponds with an annual cycle, the frequency π with a semiannual cycle.

The spectrum also informs about stationarity. For a nonstationary series the spectrum has an infinite value at a particular frequency. (Engle et al. 1993 276).

The *density* summarizes the distributional shape of the data.

At this stage, only the plots of the *actual values* (in logarithms) are commented. The other plots are discussed together with the descriptive statistics, especially in the context of stationarity.

The plot of the actual values for the unadjusted monetary base MB (figure 1.1) shows a distinct seasonal pattern, a structural break at the end of 1987 (introduction of Swiss Interbank Clearing System, new and lower liquidity requirements for banks, crash in the stock market), outliers for 1978.4 and especially 1979.1 (exchange rate experiment), and different trends before and after 1988.

Seasonality is also evidenced in the plot for the money supply M1 (figure 1.2). This series follows a rather regular trend, except for the two peaks around 1979 and 1988.

The salient features of the series for the consumer price index CPI can best be observed with the plot on the annual growth rates (seasonal differences of logarithms) in figure 1.3. Inflation rates are above 10 percent before 1975. They are again high in the early eighties and nineties. The three periods of disinflation - beginning with 1975, 1982, and 1992 - are also clearly visible.

The plot on the exchange rate variable DMN (figure 1.4) shows the general trend of the Swiss franc - but with high fluctuations - towards strength during the seventies and early eighties. In the eighties the exchange rate remains relatively stable. Towards the end of the eighties and in the early nineties the Swiss franc weakens. The impact of the German monetary unification after 1990 is also visible. Since 1993 the Swiss franc is again gaining strength.

Short-term interest rates DR (figure 1.5) peak in the early seventies, eighties and nineties. They reach very low values in 1979.

The plot on real, seasonally unadjusted GDP (figure 1.6) evidences the crisis in the mid seventies and in the early eighties, as well as the general stagnation since 1990.

1.4.3 The Problem of Seasonality and Stationarity

Time series usually have seasonal patterns, trends and variances that change. These features must be adequately modeled. Often some transformations of the data may be required.

There is little consensus on how *seasonality* should be treated in empirical research.[74] Only few researchers provide an explicit justification for their handling of seasonal variation (Beaulieu/Miron 1993 305). Usually seasonal differencing is applied mechanically to get rid of seasonality (and nonstationarity). It is implicitly assumed that there are seasonal unit roots (Hylleberg et al. 1992 426). This transformation is not based on a statistical test and might or might not be correct. „Since the statistical properties of different seasonality models are distinct, and since seasonality is quantitatively important in many aggregate series, the imposition of one kind when another is present can result in serious biases or loss of information. It is therefore useful to establish what kind of seasonality is present in the data" (Beaulieu/Miron 1993 305-306). In the following it is tested whether or not there are any seasonal unit roots in the univariate series in order to decide whether taking seasonal differences is the appropriate method to remove the seasonal component.

Figures 1.1 to 1.6 show that the series on CPI, DMN and DR do not exhibit seasonal movements. For these variables the usual Augmented Dickey-Fuller (ADF) test is appropriate. The series on MB, M1 and GDP show a distinct seasonal pattern. For these variables the test for seasonal integration proposed by Hylleberg, Engle, Granger and Yoo (1990, 1992) (HEGY) is applied. (For a textbook exposition see Charemza/Deadman 1997 107-109.)

The HEGY test is a more general test than the ADF test. It allows for cyclical movements at different frequencies and thus gives a richer insight into the nature of the seasonal pattern of a variable. Tests for stationarity can be performed individually at all the seasonal frequencies as well as the zero (long-run) frequency. That means with quarterly data we test for the existence of unit roots of the long-run (π_1), semi-annual (π_2), and annual frequencies (π_3 and π_4). Each negative π_i has a different interpretation. (Charemza/Deadman 1997 108). If only π_1 is negative, then there is no nonseasonal stochastic stationary component. If only π_2 is negative, there is no semi-annual cycle. If both π_3 and π_4 are found to be negative in a joint test, there is no annual cycle. Hence, processes that may be integrated at only some of the seasonal frequencies can be distinguished (Beaulieu/Miron 1993 309).

---

[74] Hendry (1995 560-561) distinguishes four main approaches. „First, dummy variables for the seasons are often added to models to parametrically adjust for seasonality: a constant (or steadily evolving) pattern is assumed ... Secondly, endogenous dynamics are used to model the seasonality: for example, Box and Jenkins (1976) use annual differences ... Thirdly, an evolving pattern has been proposed ... Finally, filters are applied to seasonal time series to remove components at seasonal frequencies."

Test results for unit roots at zero and seasonal frequencies are presented in table 1.3.

Table 1.3: Tests for Unit Roots at Zero and Seasonal Frequencies (HEGY-test)

	Auxiliary Regression:		t value π_1	t value π_2	t value π_3	t value π_4	F statistic $\pi_3 \cap \pi_4$
Variable	Determi-nistic part	Augmen-tation	zero	biannual	annual	annual	
ln(MB)	SD	-	-2.26	-8.32***	-3.18	-5.45	24.54***
ln(M1)	SD, TR	1, 2, 4	-3.03**	-3.95***	-3.90	-4.09	18.42***
ln(GDP)	SD, TR	1	-3.08**	-3.19**	-3.64	-4.14	15.64***

The time period for all variables is 1973.2 to 1995.2 (89 observations).
SD = seasonal dummies, TR = linear trend.
Critical values for both the t test and F test are from tables 8 and 9 in the appendix of Charemza/Deadman 1997. *** and ** denote significance at the 1 and 5 percent level.

For variables that show trending and seasonal behavior a linear trend (TR) and seasonal dummies (SD) are included in the auxiliary regression. The inclusion of seasonal dummies represents the hypothesis that the variable contains both deterministic and stochastic seasonal components.[75] In addition, lagged values of the dependent variable are included to whiten the errors. The power and size of the test may depend critically on the 'right' augmentation being used (Engle et al. 1993 279). In the augmented regressions the number of lags is determined using the Schwarz Criterion, the Hannan-Quinn Criterion and the Final Prediction Error. In cases where the three criteria lead to conflicting results, the criterion which selects the least parsimonious model is preferred, because the consequences of overspecification are less serious than the consequences of underspecification. The order of augmentation is presented in the column headed with augmentation, and 'holes' are allowed in the lag distribution. In the testing procedure Hendry's general-to-specific modeling strategy is applied. The initial estimation equations include seasonal dummies, a linear trend, and five lags of the dependent variable.

A first null hypothesis states that there exist nonseasonal and seasonal unit roots. It is accepted if unit roots are found at the zero ($\pi_1 = 0$), biannual ($\pi_2 = 0$), and annual frequencies ($\pi_3 = \pi_4 = 0$). The corresponding alternative hypothesis is that the series has *no unit roots at all* and is therefore stationary. This is the case if each of the π_i's are different from zero (save possibly either π_3 or π_4).

A second null hypothesis states that there exists stochastic seasonality, which means that the variable is seasonally integrated. The alternative hypothesis is that there exist no *seasonal* unit roots. This occurs if π_2 and either π_3 or π_4 are different

[75] „We allow for seasonal dummies in all tests, because the loss of power that results from their inclusion when unnecessary is insignificant compared to the bias that results from their omission when necessary." Beaulieu/Miron 1993 318.

from zero. It requires the rejection of both a test for p_2 and a joint test for π_3 and π_4 (Hylleberg et al. 1992 433). For the joint test an F-type of statistic (Wald test for linear restrictions) is computed.

The presence of deterministic components (seasonal dummies, trend) in the regression changes the distributions of the statistics.[76] Critical values are from Table 8 and 9 in the appendix of Charemza/Deadman (1997).

Test results in table 1.3 show that the data reject a *seasonal* unit root (biannual and annual frequency) at the 1 percent level for MB and M1 and at the 5 percent level for GDP. The hypothesis of a unit root at the zero frequency (long run) is also rejected for M1 and GDP at the 5 percent level. However, the test fails to reject the hypothesis of a unit root at frequency zero for MB. This suggests that MB contains a stochastic trend and needs to be differenced.

It should be noted that these test results are not sensitive to the augmentation being used. Moreover, the (deterministic) seasonal dummies included in the regressions are always significant.

What do these test results imply for the method to deseasonalize the data? Seasonally integrated series have 'long memory'. Shocks last forever and may in fact change permanently the seasonal patterns. (Hylleberg et al. 1992 428). „As the existence of a seasonal unit root in the data-generating process implies that summer may become winter in the sense that the seasonal pattern may change dramatically, the finding of a seasonal unit root is best interpreted as an indication of a varying and changing seasonal pattern and against a constant seasonal pattern.“ (Hylleberg 1992 11) This suggests that the seasonal pattern is not deterministic, but stochastic. Then taking seasonal differences is the correct procedure to handle seasonality, because it annihilates all the roots. (Hylleberg 1992 7).

However, from table 1.3 it follows that the null hypothesis of stochastic seasonality can be rejected in all cases. This is consistent with the general observation that seasonal unit roots are not encountered very often (Osborn 1993 300). „A deterministic seasonal pattern, superimposed on a conventional I(1) process, seems to be a better description of the 'typical' observed macroeconomic variable“ (Osborn 1993 300). This is even more the case given the fact that the deterministic seasonal dummies in the auxiliary regressions are always significant.

To sum up: The problem is to choose between seasonal differencing and an I(1) process with deterministic seasonals.[77] In practice, it is extremely difficult to choose between the two possibilities. (See e.g. Hylleberg 1992 394). „At one end is the seasonal dummy model which allows some variation but no persistent change in the seasonal pattern, and at the other end the seasonally integrated process, which allows a very changing seasonal pattern.“ (Hylleberg 1992 395). The appropriateness of applying the seasonal difference filter depends on the series be-

---

76 The addition of augmentation terms does not affect the distributions of the statistics and the critical values used. Charemza/Deadman 1997 109.

77 The two possibilities are extensively discussed in Beaulieu/Miron 1993 for the US and Osborn 1990 for the UK. Osborn (1993 300-301) mentions as a third possibility a nonstationary periodic AR(1) process, also referred to as periodic integration.

ing integrated at zero frequency and all of the seasonal frequencies (Beaulieu/Miron 1993 321). In the absence of seasonal integration - which is the case here - a conventional I(1) process with deterministic seasonal effects is preferred to seasonal differencing.[78] This has the additional advantage that the two main drawbacks of the seasonal difference filter - introduction of an MA(3) error process and implied loss of information - can be avoided.[79]

From a statistical point of view - i.e. following the results of the HEGY test - models with nonseasonal differences (assuming an I(1) process) and seasonal dummies are preferred.[80] Still, regressions with seasonal differences are also presented here for the following reasons:

First, the power of these tests is never perfect, and it is possible that seasonal unit roots are not detected. A sensible strategy would be to ask also whether the economic problem under consideration suggests mechanisms that would plausibly give rise to seasonal unit roots. (Beaulieu/Miron 1993 322)

Second, the use of dummy variables for the seasonal components also seems to be problematical in that the seasonality of the series apparently changes over time. (See e.g. Dickey 1993 329) It is the fact that seasonal patterns evolve over time that makes the handling of seasonality less than straightforward. (Hendry 1995 560) The plots for the nonseasonal differences of MB, M1 and GDP in figures 1.1, 1.2 and 1.6 show how the seasonal pattern changes. Especially for MB and GDP the pattern seems to shift around 1980. These shifts will be modeled. (See section 1.5.1c.)

Third, taking seasonal differences is the common practice to deseasonalize the data. In the existing literature both seasonal and nonseasonal differences are being used. Both methods are applied in order to allow for a comparison of the results. Moreover, results can also be compared with previous studies.

A different argument is put forward by Kirchgässner/Savioz (1997 4). They note that for Germany, the politically relevant variables used in public discussions and published in the official statistics are always the growth rates over one year. For this reason they work with seasonal differences, although they admit that from a statistical point of view, if the data are not seasonally integrated (which is the case) one might prefer to use nonseasonal differences and to model the seasonal structure explicitly. This argument may be questionable, however, and is not adopted here, because the problem is one of statistical inference.

„As noted by many authors in the context of zero frequency, there are potentially serious problems of statistical inference when one or more series contains a unit root. For example, the variance of a series with a unit root is infinite, the distribution of the estimated first-order autocorrelation changes when the true autocor-

---

78 See e.g. Barsky/Miron 1989, Beaulieu/Miron 1992 and 1993, Miron/Zeldes 1988, Miron 1994. See also Wolters 1996 279 and Nautz 1997 5 Fn. 7.

79 The MA terms that are present in seasonal differences are a sign of overdifferencing. Nautz 1997 5 Fn. 7.

80 However, the use of seasonal dummy variables is not appropriate if the observed seasonality is generated by an integrated process. (Beaulieu/Miron 1993 321).

relation equals one, and two independent integrated series can display spurious correlation ... These problems are not alleviated by blind differencing to ensure stationarity." (Beaulieu/Miron 1993 321). Therefore, it is important to make sure that the transformed data, i.e. the seasonal and nonseasonal differences, are stationary.

The next step is to find out whether the *seasonal differences* can be assumed to be stationary. Since the data plots for the seasonal differences show no seasonal patterns (see figures 1.1 to 1.6), the standard augmented Dickey-Fuller test (denoted conventionally as ADF test) is applied. (For a textbook exposition see e. g. Charemza/Deadman 1997 104-105.) ADF test results are displayed in table 1.4.

Table 1.4: Results of the ADF Tests for Variables Expressed as Seasonal Differences (Annual Changes or Growth Rates)

Variable	Period	*Auxiliary Regression:* Deterministic part	Augmentation	t value = ADF test statistic
$\Delta_4 \ln(MB)$	1973.2-1995.2	C, TR	1, 2, 3, 4	-3.57**
$\Delta_4 \ln(M1)$	1973.2-1995.2	C, TR	1, 2, 3, 4	-3.06
$\Delta_4 \ln(M1)$	*1973.2-1995.2*	*C, TR*	*1, 2, 3, 4, 5, 6, 7*	*-4.68****
$\Delta_4 \ln(CPI)$	1973.2-1995.2	C, TR	1, 2, 3, 4, 5	-2.95
$\Delta_4 \ln(CPI)$	*1974.4-1995.2*	*C, TR*	*1, 2, 3, 4, 5*	*-3.88***
$\Delta_4 \ln(DMN)$	1974.2-1995.2	C, TR	1, 2, 3, 4	-3.93**
$\Delta_4 DR$	1973.2-1995.2	C, TR	1, 2, 3, 4, 5	-4.35***
$\Delta_4 \ln(GDP)$	1973.2-1995.2	C, TR	1, 2	-3.88**

C = constant, TR = linear trend.
Critical values used are -3.46 for the 5 percent level and -4.06 for the 1 percent level.
*** and ** denote significance at the 1 and 5 percent level.

Since overspecification has less serious consequences than underspecification, the equations include not only lagged dependent variables, but also a constant (C) and a deterministic linear time trend (TR). (See case 4 in Hamilton 1994 529). Augmentation serves to account for the possibility of an ARMA process in the errors. The use of the 'correct' augmentation (order of autoregressive model) is of paramount importance for the size and the power of this test in finite samples. (Hylleberg 1992 393). Here the general to specific procedure is applied: The initial specification includes five lagged dependent variables as regressors. The number of augmentations is systematically reduced by imposing and testing zero restrictions and testing for autocorrelation in the restricted model (Charemza/Deadman 1997 105). The ADF test is parametrized such that the t tests are asymptotically valid. Hence, the decision about the lag length can also be based on the t values (see Hendry/Doornik 1996 42).

The null hypothesis is that of a unit root. A significant ADF test statistic rejects that hypothesis and suggests stationarity.

Test results in table 1.4 show that the data reject a unit root at the 1 percent level for DR, at the 5 percent level for MB, DMN and GDP. However, these initial ADF tests fail to reject the hypothesis of a unit root for M1 and CPI.

The correlogram for CPI (see figure 1.3) clearly suggests stationarity.[81] It is well known that structural breaks can cause I(0) variables to appear I(1) in ADF tests. (See e.g. Perron 1989.) The plot for the seasonal differences of CPI (see figure 1.3) suggests the presence of structural breaks. Assuming a structural break around 1975, the starting observations are dropped from the sample, and the null hypothesis can be rejected at the 5 percent level (see the row for CPI printed in italic).

From the correlogram for M1 (see figure 1.2) it is not clear whether the series is stationary or not. For a stationary series the autocorrelations should tend towards zero. This is not the case, because the autocorrelations start to grow again. However, without further testing it is not known whether the high order autocorrelations are significantly different from zero at all. In any case the correlogram does not contradict stationarity. The spectrum does not suggest nonstationarity either (see figure 1.2).

Unit root tests over various subsamples for M1 suggest that structural breaks are not a problem here[82] (see also the plot of the original series in figure 1.2).

Another reason might be that the residuals are not white noise even with 4 lags added. (This may be indicated by the fact that the series can clearly be assumed to be stationary at the 1 percent level if only 1, 2, or 3 lags are included.) If the ADF test starts with an equation with nine lagged terms added to whiten the residuals, the general-to-specific testing procedure leads to an equation with seven lagged terms.[83] For this equation, the errors are white noise, and the null hypothesis of a unit root can be rejected at the 1 percent level (see the row for M1 printed in italic).

Overall, it is concluded that all series can be assumed to be stationary when expressed as seasonal differences (annual changes or growth rates).

Finally, it is analyzed whether the *nonseasonal differences* can be assumed to be stationary. The ADF test is applied to the series expressed in nonseasonal differences. Test results are displayed in table 1.5.

---

81 „In the Box-Jenkins approach, whether or not there is a unit root is decided by visual inspection of the correlogram ... The unit root tests are just a formalization of this visual inspection.“ Maddala 1992 585.

82 For an analogous strategy with respect to the effects of German unification on the money supply M1 and real GNP see Brüggemann/Wolters 1997 5. Another strategy would be to apply the unit root test proposed by Perron (1989) which allows for a structural break in the alternative model. See Charemza/Deadman 1997 115-122 for a textbook exposition.

83 The high order of lags is probably caused by the two peaks at the end of the seventies and after 1987. See the plot of the original series (in log levels) in figure 1.2.

Table 1.5: Results of the ADF Tests for Variables Expressed as Nonseasonal Differences (Quarterly Changes or Growth Rates)

		Auxiliary Regression:		t value = ADF
Variable	Period	Deterministic part	Augmentation	test statistic
Δln(MB)	1973.2-1995.2	C, TR, SD	1, 2	-5.64***
Δln(M1)	1973.2-1995.2	C, TR, SD	1, 2, 3, 4	-4.61***
Δln(CPI)	1973.2-1995.2	C, TR, SD	1, 2, 3	-2.26
Δln(CPI)	*1975.1-1995.2*	*C, TR, SD*	*1, 2, 3*	*-3.34**
Δln(DMN)	1973.2-1995.2	C, TR, SD	1, 2, 3	-5.57***
ΔDR	1973.2-1995.2	C, TR, SD	-	-5.99***
Δln(GDP)	1973.2-1995.2	C, TR, SD	1	-6.28***

C = constant, TR = linear trend, SD = seasonal dummies.
Critical values used are -3.46 for the 5 percent level and -4.06 for the 1 percent level.
*** and * denote significance at the 1 and 10 percent level.

All equations include a constant (C), a linear time trend (TR), and seasonal dummies (SD). Again, the general-to-specific strategy is applied to identify the augmented terms. The starting equation included nine lags of the dependent variable as regressors.

Test results show that all series can be assumed to be stationary at the 1 percent level, with the exception of CPI. Again, the nonstationarity of CPI may be caused by structural breaks. If the sample starts with the first quarter of 1975 only, the null hypothesis of nonstationarity is rejected at the 10 percent level (see the row for CPI printed in italic). The choice of the smaller sample period is based on the plot of the series (see figure 1.3). The ADF test is not very robust and it is only asymptotically valid, so that small sample problems may arise. But without simulation the direction of a small sample bias is not known. Hence, the evidence on CPI is inconclusive.[84]

1.4.4 Summary Statistics

Tables 1.6 and 1.7 list the summary statistics for all transformed variables for the time period from 1973.2 to 1995.2. The tables include the first four moments, as well as the smallest (minimum) and the largest (maximum) values. The skewness statistic measures the deviation from symmetry, and the excess kurtosis measures how 'fat' the tails of the distribution are. For a standard normal distribution - denoted by N(0, 1) - the mean, skewness and excess kurtosis are all equal to zero, and the standard deviation is one.

---

84 If the nonsignificant trend is removed from this regression, a unit root is rejected at the 1 percent level.

Table 1.6: Summary Statistics for Variables Expressed as Seasonal Differences (Annual Growth Rates and Changes) 1973.2 - 1995.2 (89 observations)

Variable	Mean	Standard Deviation	Skewness	Excess Kurtosis	Minimum	Maximum
$\Delta_4 \ln(MB)$	0.01514	0.05861	0.34380	4.65059	-0.20593	0.24576
$\Delta_4 \ln(M1)$	0.03309	0.06276	0.19567	0.21100	-0.12242	0.20647
$\Delta_4 \ln(CPI)$	0.03676	0.02426	0.80129	0.03035	0.00074	0.10254
$\Delta_4 \ln(DMN)$	0.01553	0.05612	0.80598	0.81228	-0.08595	0.21916
$\Delta_4 DR$	0.02360	2.30290	-0.12423	0.06801	-6.19000	4.92000
$\Delta_4 \ln(GDP)$	0.01177	0.02736	-1.76596	4.07538	-0.09399	0.05578

Table 1.7: Summary Statistics for Variables Expressed as Nonseasonal Differences (Quarterly Growth Rates and Changes) 1973.2 - 1995.2 (89 observations)

Variable	Mean	Standard Deviation	Skewness	Excess Kurtosis	Minimum	Maximum
$\Delta \ln(MB)$	0.00362	0.04262	0.32148	12.32489	-0.20612	0.22243
$\Delta \ln(M1)$	0.00839	0.03758	0.51167	-0.25379	-0.06467	0.12181
$\Delta \ln(CPI)$	0.00892	0.00802	1.50031	4.34377	-0.00421	0.04692
$\Delta \ln(DMN)$	0.00368	0.02546	0.52616	1.37922	-0.05977	0.10010
ΔDR	-0.01652	0.87862	-0.23125	1.78250	-3.09000	2.44000
$\Delta \ln(GDP)$	0.00287	0.02696	0.15974	-0.46061	-0.06468	0.06493

1.5 Results: How the SNB Behaved

1.5.1 Outlining of the Estimation Procedure

1.5.1a The General-to-Specific Strategy

The most appropriate strategy for dynamic model selection is to begin with a very general specification and then 'testing down' until a more specific model is identified. (See e.g. Harvey 1990 section 8.4.)[85] Maddala summarizes this strategy (which is originally due to Sargan, but has been popularized by Hendry) as „intended overparametrization with data-based simplification." (Maddala 1992 494) The initial specification takes the form of a very generous lag length on the

[85] In 'testing down', the size of the overall test (the overall probability of a type I error) can be determined and controlled. Kennedy 1992 89; see also Maddala 1992 495.

lagged dependent variable (or on all explanatory variables, in the case of an autoregressive distributed lag model). „This is done to reflect the fact that economic theory typically has very little to say about the nature of the dynamics of a relationship.“ (Kennedy 1992 89)

The basic reason for starting with a high order lag is to avoid specification errors that lead to biased and inconsistent parameter estimates. More specifically, a high order lag has to be assumed in order to maintain an equation where the errors are not serially correlated, so that OLS estimates are consistent (though inefficient) and F tests that serve to simplify the model are (asymptotically) valid. Common sense is used to choose the initial lag length. (Kennedy 1992 89) For quarterly data expressed in seasonal differences five lags of the dependent variable are initially specified. Equations for nonseasonal differences start with 9 lags.

If too many lags are included, the 'irrelevant' regressors will not produce bias or inconsistency, but they will potentially contribute to a multicollinearity problem since current and lagged regressors are likely to be correlated. At least some of the parameters will not be estimated with much precision if the OLS estimator is used. (Judge et al. 1988 723; Lardaro 1992 546). Nonsignificant regressors are therefore eliminated to gain a more parsimonious model. Several criteria have been suggested in the literature to address the problem of selection of regressors. (See Maddala 1992 496-500 for an overview). They imply different F-ratios. (Maddala 1992 500-502). Here the Schwarz Criterion, the Hannan-Quinn Criterion and the Final Prediction Error are used. In cases where the three criteria lead to conflicting results, the criterion which selects the least parsimonious model is preferred, because the consequences of overspecification are less serious than the consequences of underspecification.[86] (The sequence of lags eliminated, the F statistics and associated p values, and the values of the information criteria are not reported. They could be listed in tables, as is proposed by Judge et al. 1988 727, or Lardaro 1992 550).

Estimation results of the resulting equations as well as a series of diagnostic tests which are surveyed in table 1.8 are reported. These equations are termed 'homogeneous', because all coefficients are assumed to be constant over the sample period. (See section 1.5.1c for the terminology).

1.5.1b Testing and Evaluation

Absence of *serial correlation* is not only important for the validity of the F tests. The reaction functions contain a lagged dependent variable. A lagged value of the dependent variable is a stochastic regressor, because it is in part determined by a disturbance. (See e.g. Lardaro 1992 577.) One assumption of the classical linear regression model is violated. The OLS estimators of the coefficients will be biased in small samples.

---

86 It is important that the sample size is held constant in the testing procedure. Judge et al. 1988 725.

Whether or not further estimation problems arise depends on whether the error term is serially correlated:

- If the errors are not serially correlated, the OLS estimators are biased but consistent. In this case the normal distribution is asymptotically valid for statistical inference. (Lardaro 1992 578)
- If the equation has serially correlated errors, the OLS estimators are both biased and inconsistent (asymptotically biased). (For a proof of this see e.g. Koutsoyiannis 1977 307.) With two assumptions of the classical linear regression model being violated simultaneously - a lagged dependent variable as a regressor and serial correlation of the errors - the application of OLS breaks down completely. It is necessary to discard the estimated coefficients because they are invalid, even asymptotically. The normal distribution is not a proper basis for statistical inference. (Lardaro 1992 578)

Given the possibly deleterious effects of this simultaneous violation of the two assumptions for the linear regression model it is critical to test whether the errors are themselves autoregressive. And although the partial adjustment model leads to an estimating equation with spherical errors (see section 1.3.2a), serial correlation may still be present because the original error term is nonspherical (Lardaro 1992 570), or because of data transformations (Greene 1990 429). The detection of serial correlation is therefore a major concern in the present context. If the tests for serial correlation would indicate the presence of this violation, special estimation methods would have to be applied.

A standard test for serial correlation is the Durbin-Watson test. But this test is not valid when an equation contains a lagged dependent variable, since the test statistic is biased towards the value of 2, giving the impression that serial correlation is absent when this might not be the case. Usually, Durbin's t test is recommended to test for first-order serial correlation. (See e.g. Kmenta 1986 333.)

Serially correlated errors are not always first-order autoregressive. This may especially be the case when working with quarterly data (however defined). To test for higher-order serial correlation the Lagrange multiplier (LM) test for serial correlation is employed. (See e.g. Greene 1990 452 or Maddala 1992 250 for textbook expositions.) Since the LM test is a generalization of Durbin's t test, it is also used here to detect first order serial correlation. The test is calculated by regressing the residuals on all the regressors of the original model and the lagged residuals. Since the LM test is a large sample test, the χ^2 test rather than the F test is used traditionally. The conventional F statistic multiplied with p (the number of the lagged residuals) is used as χ^2 with p degrees of freedom. (See e.g. Maddala 1992 250.)[87] But Hendry/Doornik (1996 193) cite research which indicates that F-forms suggested by Harvey (1981 and 1990) have more appropriate significance levels and that χ^2 versions reject acceptable models too often. They recommend the F-form. Hence, only the F-form of this diagnostic test is reported. For the equations

[87] In the literature different ways for calculating the χ^2 statistic are proposed. See e.g. Kennedy 1992 128.

with seasonal differences this LM test is performed for five lags. For the estimations with nonseasonal differences tests up to nine lags are carried out. In order to preserve space only a subset of these tests is reported.

Heteroskedasticity causes the OLS estimates to be inefficient. Models that take into account the changing variance can make more efficient use of the data. To test for the presence of heteroskedasticity results of three tests are reported:

The first is the LM test for autocorrelated squared residuals proposed by Engle (1982; for a textbook exposition see e.g. Kmenta 1986 296.) This test, commonly referred to as the ARCH (autoregressive conditional heteroskedasticity) test, checks whether the residuals have an ARCH structure. The squared residuals are regressed on a constant and lagged squared residuals. An F statistic is reported. The null hypothesis is that there are no ARCH effects. It is rejected if the test statistic is too high. Test statistics and significance p values are calculated for conditional heteroskedasticity at lag windows ranging from 1 through 12. In order to preserve space only the test result for four lags (denoted ARCH 4) is reported.

The second is the test for heteroskedasticity using squares. This test is based on White (1980). It tests whether the errors have constant variance (null hypothesis) against the alternative that the squared residuals depend on the original and squared regressors. The squared residuals are regressed on a constant, the original regressors, and the original regressors squared. For this test (denoted with X_i^2) an F statistic is reported. The null hypothesis is rejected if the test statistic is too high. (Hendry/Doornik 1996 240 and 268).

The third is the test for heteroskedasticity using squares and cross-products. This is the White (1980) test. The squared residuals are regressed on a constant, the original regressors, the original regressors squared, and all the cross-products. For this test (denoted with X_i*X_j) an F statistic is reported, too. The null hypothesis (absence of heteroskedasticity) is rejected if the test statistic is too high. (Hendry/Doornik 1996 240 and 268). The test is not calculated if there are not enough degrees of freedom.[88]

There exist several approaches for improving the efficiency of the parameter estimation in the presence of heteroskedastic errors:

- If the error variance at different times is known, weighted regression is a good method. If weights are proportional to the reciprocals of the error variances, then the weighted least squares (WLS) estimates are best linear unbiased estimators (BLUE).
- If the form of the heteroskedasticity is unknown, the heteroskedasticity consistent estimator of the variance-covariance matrix due to White (1980), or the heteroskedasticity and autocorrelation consistent estimator (HAC) proposed by Newey/West (1987) can be used to determine parameter estimates that are as-

[88] The portmanteau test - sometimes referred to as the Q test - is another test for heteroskedasticity. (For a textbook exposition see e.g. Kmenta 1986 332.) According to Maddala (1992 540) the Q test is not appropriate in autoregressive models (or models with lagged dependent variables). Therefore, it is not reported.

ymptotically more efficient than the OLS parameters. (See e.g. Greene 1990 439 for a textbook exposition.)

- If it can be assumed that the changing variance follows an autoregressive conditional heteroskedasticity model estimation of a GARCH model provides another means of correcting for the changing variability of the data. (See e.g. Hamilton 1994 chap. 21.)

In those cases where the diagnostic tests indicate the presence of heteroskedasticity, heteroskedasticity consistent standard errors (HCSEs) are estimated and the corresponding t values are reported.

Also reported is a χ^2 statistic for normality. (Hendry/Doornik 1996 209-210) It tests whether the skewness and kurtosis of the residuals correspond to that of a normal distribution. The null hypothesis states that the residuals are from a normal distribution. It is rejected at the 5 percent level if the test statistic is larger than 5.99. The number in brackets is the probability of getting a number at least as large if the residuals would really have a normal distribution. The smaller this value, the less likely it is that the residuals are generated by a normal distribution.

Finally, the RESET test (regression specification test) proposed by Ramsey (1969) tests the null hypothesis of correct specification of the functional form against the alternative that powers of the fitted values have been omitted. The null hypothesis of no functional misspecification is rejected if the reported F statistic is too high. (Hendry/Doornik 1996 241 and 268)

Table 1.8 provides a survey of the diagnostic tests that are reported together with each regression equation.

Table 1.8: Survey of Diagnostic Tests Reported

Alternative	Statistic	Sources
qth-order residual autocorrelation	AR 1-q $\chi^2[q]$; AR 1-q F[q, T-k-q]	Box/Pierce (1970); Godfrey (1978); Harvey (1981, p. 173)
qth-order ARCH	ARCH 1-q $\chi^2[q]$; ARCH 1-q F[q, T-k-2q]	Engle (1982)
Heteroskedasticity quadratic in regressors (q quadratic terms)	X_iX_j F[q, T-k-q-1]; X^2_i F[q, T-k-q-1]	White (1980), Nicholls/Pagan (1983); Hendry (1989)
Skewness and excess kurtosis	Normality $\chi^2[q]$	Jarque/Bera (1980)
qth-order RESET	RESET F[q, T-k-q]	Ramsey (1969)

The table is adopted from Hendry/Ericsson (1991 849) (modified). „There are T observations and k regressors in the model under the null. The value of q may differ across statistics, as may those of k and T across models and samples". (Hendry/Ericsson 1991 849).

These formal tests are complemented with a visual inspection of the residuals for each equation, including plots of actual and fitted values, cross-plots of actual and fitted values, scaled residuals, residual correlograms, residual spectra, residual densities with histogram and normal distribution, and residual QQ plots. In order to preserve space this graphic analysis is not reported.

1.5.1c Analysis of Parameter Stability

One major objective of the chapter is to examine the stability of the reaction function. *Instability* of the reaction function may have several causes: the set of available instruments changes over time, the working of an actual instrument adapts or changes, the policymaker becomes aware of new theoretical developments ... (Alt/Chrystal 1983 144) Based on the discussion of the major events during the period of flexible exchange rates (section 1.3.2d) it could be assumed that parameter values may shift at a priori determined epochs which divide the sample period into subperiods of different 'regimes'. This procedure can be criticized as being somewhat arbitrary. Therefore, the preferred strategy is to let the data determine whether or not there are any structural breaks and identify specific points within the sample period where such a break in the model may have occurred. This evidence can then be compared with the a priori information.

The issue of parameter (in)stability is addressed in two steps. First, the equation (with homogeneous coefficients) is estimated with recursive least squares and the graphical output is screened for existence and dates of structural breaks. If structural breaks are identified, formal F tests are performed in a second step to decide on which particular coefficients are unstable.[89]

Recursive Least Squares Estimation

Recursive least squares (RLS) estimation is used to find out whether or not there are any structural breaks. At the same time, possible break dates can be determined. RLS is OLS where coefficients are estimated sequentially. The sample starts from a minimal number of observations and statistics are recalculated adding observations one at a time. „That is, starting from the small subsample of $t = 1, 2, ..., n$, where $n \geq k$, estimate the k parameters of the model by OLS. Then extend the sample period by one observation to $t = 1, 2, ..., n+1$, and re-estimate the model. Continue this procedure until the estimation period is the complete sample $t = 1, 2, ..., T$." (Charemza/Deadman 1997 47). The output generated by the recursive procedures is a powerful tool to study parameter constancy. (Hendry/Doornik 1996 58 and 256) Parameter constancy, or its absence, is most easily studied graphically. This includes graphs of the RLS coefficients, the associated t values, the one-step residuals, the one-step Chow test, the break-point Chow test, and the forecast Chow test.

---

89 For a more rigorous procedure to identify parameter instability and structural change with unknown change point see Andrews 1993.

Graphs of the RLS *coefficients* show the time paths of the coefficients in the model. The values of the coefficients - together with their approximate 95 percent confidence intervals (+/- 2 standard errors shown on either side) - are plotted against the latest time period in the sample used for the estimation of that regression. (Charemza/Deadman 1997 47). The graphs show whether or not the coefficients remain relatively stable over the sample period. „The initial instability of the parameter estimates for all the variables simply reflects the small number of observations used to estimate them at the start of the recursions." (Charemza/ Deadman 1997 48) A structural break is indicated if the coefficient „lies outside of the previous confidence interval which an investigator .. would have calculated as the basis for forecasting." (Hendry/Doornik 1996 59)

The graphs of the *t values* show whether the estimates are significantly different from zero and how their significance changes over the sample period.

The graphs of the *one-step residuals* (one-step ahead residuals or forecast errors, denoted 'Res1Step') are plots of the residual for the last period in the sample used for the recursion against time. The graphs also include an approximate 95 percent confidence interval (+/- 2 standard errors shown on either side). Residuals which are outside of the error bars are either outliers or are associated with some alteration in the structural parameters of the model. (Hendry/Doornik 1996 59 and 232). Instability of parameters is indicated for the following reason: At each recursion the OLS residual for the last period in the sample is calculated. In the absence of structural breaks this residual should be of the same order of magnitude as those that preceded it. „Once the break point is reached, however, the residual calculated for this period is likely to appear abnormal compared with the other residuals, as the model will provide a poor fit for the break period." (Charemza/Deadman 1997 49) The confidence bands also yield information on potential heteroskedasticity: A reasonably constant confidence band suggests homoskedasticity. An increasing or decreasing confidence band indicates heteroskedasticity.

The *one-step Chow test* ('1up CHOWs') is a one-step forecast test. (See Charemza/Deadman 1997 50-51 for a textbook exposition). The initial model is estimated from a minimal number of observations at the beginning of the sample period (t-1). The model is extended by one observation to the sample period t and re-estimated. The test statistic is calculated from the residual sum of squares for the two models fitted. This procedure is repeated until the estimation period is the complete sample T. The forecast period is always one period, that is, the two models compared differ only with respect to one observation. The test statistic and the critical values of F are functions of t. Therefore, it is useful to divide the Chow value by its 5 percent critical value from the tables of F. This yields a scaled recursive Chow test. (Charemza/Deadman 1997 50) The critical value is a straight line at unity independent of t and the changing degrees of freedom. (Hendry/ Doornik 1996 266) The null hypothesis is that there is no structural change in the model between periods t-1 and t. Under the null hypothesis the scaled recursive Chow test should be less than unity. „Values of this statistic greater than unity imply that the null of no structural change between periods t-1 and t would be rejected at the 5 percent level of significance." (Charemza/Deadman 1997 51) The test can be performed for other probability levels, too.

The *break-point Chow test* ('Ndn CHOWs') compares the minimal model at the end of the sample period against all other models up to the whole sample period. The forecast horizon is decreasing from left to right, hence the name Ndn tests. (Hendry/Doornik 1996 59) Each point in the plot is the value of the Chow F-test for that date against the final period. The test statistic is again scaled by its critical value, which becomes the line at unity. The value shown at t tests for parameter constancy from t to T. (Hendry/Doornik 1996 266) The null hypothesis of parameter constancy is rejected if the scaled test values are greater than unity. This test is closely related to the CUSUMQ statistic. (Hendry/Doornik 1996 233)

The *forecast F test* ('Nup CHOWs') is analogous to the break-point Chow test just described. It compares the minimal model at the beginning of the sample period including observations from 1 to M-1, with all alternative models including observations M to the whole sample T. The forecast horizon increases from left to right, i.e. from M to T (hence the name Nup tests).

The one-step Chow test, the break-point Chow test and the forecast F test are all variants of Chow (1960) tests. As such they are closely related to each other. The first value of the one-step Chow test is equal to the first value of the forecast F test, and the last value of the one-step Chow test is equal to the last value of the break-point Chow test. (Hendry/Doornik 1996 233).

Two additional recursive graphics are reported: a graph of the *residual sum of squares* (RSS) which may also help to confirm breaks, and the *standardized innovations* (standardized recursive residuals) which often highlight outliers. (Charemza/Deadman 1997 51)

The graphical output from RLS estimation of the money supply equations clearly suggests a structural break for 1980. The evidence is less clear for the monetary base equations. For comparison, a structural break for 1980 is assumed (and modeled) in all equations.

Most reaction function studies do separate estimations over different subperiods to examine whether the significance of the variables depends on the sample period and to test for the stability of the reaction function. This approach is not followed here, since it implies hypothesis testing on the basis of rather small samples. Instead of running separate regressions, the data are pooled, and the break is modeled using products of the variables and the dummies for breaks. The implied discontinuity at the selected epoch (1980) and stability during the two subperiods are taken as approximations to a more complete model of parameter instability. Shifts in parameter values are referred to as *heterogeneity*.

Allowing for heterogeneous coefficients means that intercepts and slope coefficients are allowed to be different for each period. For the coefficient estimates the results are exactly the same as if one separate regression is fit for each subperiod. However, the estimates are not efficient, because the error variance σ^2 is not estimated on the basis of all observations, but only for each separate subperiod, consisting of much fewer observations. Pooling the data leads to more efficient estimates of the variance, and, hence, more efficient standard errors.

Heterogeneity may affect the coefficients of the regression function as well as the variance of the error term. The latter is called *heteroskedasticity.* The problem is that with short time series it is difficult to distinguish shifts in regression function parameters and changes in variance. Large errors which occur at shifts of the regression function can often suggest increased error variance and vice versa. Heterogeneity and heteroskedasticity can be confounded. This problem can make the use of a priori information concerning the nature of the shifts quite important.

F tests for Continuous-by-Class Effects

RLS estimation serves to determine whether or not and when structural breaks occur. But it is also of interest to find out which particular coefficients are unstable. Therefore, the stability of the intercept and slope coefficients is tested with the dummy variable method of structuring the Chow test,[90] also called *analysis of covariance test.* This test is performed by running a dummy variable regression which includes the dummy variables for each regime, interaction terms between dummy variables and quantitative variables, as well as the original quantitative variables (continuous-by-class specification).

Hence, for J levels the following regression equation with the last level J omitted is estimated:

$$Y_i = a_1D_{1i} + a_2D_{2i} + ... + a_{J-1}D_{J-1i} + a_J + b_1D_{1i}X_i + b_2D_{2i}X_i + ... + b_{J-1}D_{J-1i}X_i + b_JX_i + e_i$$

(D = dummy variable).

F tests for continuous-by-class effects are used to test for the homogeneity of the coefficients. In these F tests, the null hypothesis H_0 for testing the homogeneity of the slope coefficients is: $b_1 = b_2 = ... = b_{J-1} = 0$ (homogeneity). Accordingly, the alternative hypothesis H_a is: At least one of these coefficients of the interaction terms is significantly different from zero (heterogeneity). The F test for testing the homogeneity of the intercepts is analogous.

It might be argued that for this F test a significance level larger than the traditional 5 percent should be used to reduce the risk of committing a type II error

---

[90] This test was developed by Gujarati 1970. For a textbook exposition see Maddala 1992 318-319 and Kennedy 1992 224-225.
Laney 1985 108 also uses the interactive binary variable technique, with a dummy set equal to unity for the sub-interval under investigation and zero otherwise, to test for shifts in the reaction function coefficients. Abrams/Froyen/Waud 1980 37 use the random-coefficient regression technique (RCR). Beck 1982 (427, 435, 437) addresses the problem of shifts in reaction functions with Quandt's likelihood ratio test.

(i.e. accepting the hypothesis of homogeneity although there is heterogeneity). The reason is that committing a type II error when testing for homogeneity may have more serious implications (biased estimation) than committing a type I error (loss of efficiency). But since the goal is to formulate a parsimonious equation, the traditional significance level of 5 percent is applied here.

If the continuous-by-class effect is insignificant, the effect can be removed so that the response with respect to the regressor variable is the same for all regimes (i.e. homogeneity of the coefficient can be imposed). If the continuous-by-class effect is significant, the coefficient is allowed to be heterogeneous across the regimes.

Thus, this test helps to formulate a more parsimonious model which takes into account the structural break. (These models will be used in the regressions with the political variables included.)

1.5.2 Estimation Results

In this section the estimation results of the regression equations with the monetary base and the money supply M1 as dependent variables, measured in nonseasonal and seasonal differences, are presented.[91] For each of the four equations, the choice of the initial model, the (non)sphericalness of the errors, the question of structural breaks and homogeneity of the regression coefficients is discussed in detail.

1.5.2a Nonseasonal Differences with the Monetary Base as Dependent Variable

Starting from an initial model with nine lags of the dependent variable added (and absence of serial correlation), sequential testing down allows for the deletion of all lags except for the second. The resulting equation 1.1 is reported in the second column of table 1.9, headed with 'homogeneous coefficients' (because the coefficients are constrained to be constant over the whole sample period). Since the diagnostic tests (second column in table 1.10) clearly indicate the presence of heteroskedasticity, the heteroskedastic-consistent standard errors HCSEs (see Eicker 1967 and White 1980) are estimated. These estimates are consistent even if the residuals are heteroskedastic in an unknown way. Reported t statistics are calculated with the HCSEs. (Note that the corresponding t values based on the OLS standard errors are the final observations plotted in the recursive graphs in figure 1.8).

Next, the equation is estimated with RLS to study parameter stability. Figures 1.7 to 1.9 present the graphical output. The graphs of the RLS coefficients (figure 1.7) do not suggest parameter instability, perhaps with the exception of DMN and DR. The plots of the t statistics (figure 1.8) exhibit considerable variation for

91 All equations are estimated with SAS release 6.08 on a VAX model 4000-400 at the University of Fribourg/Switzerland and recomputed with PcGive for Windows.

Table 1.9: Regression Results for Nonseasonal Differences with Monetary Base ($\Delta\ln(MB)$) as Dependent Variable

Variables	Equation 1.1: Homogeneous Coefficients	t values	Equation 1.2: Heterogeneous Coefficients	t values	Equation 1.3: Partly Homogeneous Coefficients	t values
Constant						
73.2-95.2	0.027***	3.51			0.034***	4.52
73.2-79.4			0.053***	3.76		
80.1-95.2			0.029***	6.54		
$\Delta\ln(MB)_{t-2}$						
73.2-95.2	-0.381*	-1.82			-0.275*	-1.89
73.2-79.4			-0.311*	-1.66		
80.1-95.2			0.080	0.42		
$\Delta\ln(CPI)_{t-1}$						
73.2-95.2	-0.372	-0.96				
73.2-79.4			-2.232***	-2.82	-1.860***	-3.41
80.1-95.2			-0.129	-0.45	-0.563	-1.34
$\Delta\ln(DMN)_{t-1}$						
73.2-95.2	0.349	1.37				
73.2-79.4			0.824***	2.89	0.875***	2.72
80.1-95.2			-0.058	-0.75	-0.172*	-1.66
$\Delta\ln(GDP)_{t-1}$						
73.2-95.2	-0.425*	-1.83			-0.689***	-2.69
73.2-79.4			-0.716*	-1.88		
80.1-95.2			-0.493***	-2.75		
ΔDR_{t-1}						
73.2-95.2	-0.0005	-0.17				
73.2-79.4			0.033*	1.93	0.032**	2.39
80.1-95.2			-0.002	-0.67	-0.003	-1.06
R^2	0.51		0.75		0.70	
F statistic	F(8,80) = 10.29		F(17,71) = 12.23		F(12,76) = 14.56	
σ	0.0316		0.0241		0.0254	

All three regression equations include three seasonal dummies. They are also allowed to change across the two subperiods in the heterogeneous equation 1.2. In the partly homogeneous equation 1.3 only the dummy for winter is allowed to change across the two subperiods. To correct for the inefficiency of OLS in the presence of heteroskedasticity, all t statistics are calculated on the basis of HCSEs.
***, ** and * denote significance at the 1, 5 and 10 percent level.

Table 1.10: Diagnostics for Equations with Monetary Base ($\Delta ln(MB)$) as Dependent Variable (Nonseasonal Differences)

Diagnostics	Equation 1.1: Homog. Coefficients	Equation 1.2: Heterog. Coefficients	Equation 1.3: Partly Homog. Coeff.
AR 1	F(1,79)=0.05 [0.8326]	F(1,70)=0.30 [0.5881]	F(1,75)=0.13 [0.7195]
AR 1-5	F(5,75)=0.49 [0.7803]	F(5,66)=0.39 [0.8546]	F(5,71)=0.72 [0.6089]
AR 1-9	F(9,71)=0.32 [0.9653]	F(9,62)=0.59 [0.7980]	F(9,67)=0.70 [0.7064]
ARCH 4	F(4,72)=10.79 [0.0001]	F(4,63)=5.66 [0.0006]	F(4,68)=7.63 [0.0001]
X_i^2	F(13,66)=20.8 [0.0001]	F(27,43)=3.76 [0.0001]	F(20,55)=5.30 [0.0001]
X_i*X_j	F(38,41)=7.37 [0.0001]	-	-
Normality	$\chi^2(2)$=34.64 [0.0001]	$\chi^2(2)$=12.05 [0.0024]	$\chi^2(2)$=14.12 [0.0009]
RESET	F(1,79)=1.38 [0.2441]	F(1,70)=0.15 [0.7010]	F(1,75)=0.02 [0.8944]

Numbers in brackets [] are p values.

most variables. They need to be interpreted with care, however, because the t values are biased due to the presence of heteroskedasticity. The graph of the one-step residuals (figure 1.9) illustrates the nonconstant variance: The confidence band narrows as the sample increases.

The one-step Chow test and the Nup-step Chow test suggest a structural break for 1980. (The Nup-step Chow test is even significant at the 1 percent level). Variation of the number of observations for initialization (i.e. changing the size of the minimal sample) helps to make clear that the break point should be set at this date. A structural break is not confirmed by the break-point Chow test, however. Hence, the evidence on structural breaks is mixed. To avoid the risk of biased estimation (as a result of committing a type II error), and to allow for a comparison with the money supply equations, a break is implemented for the first quarter of 1980. Estimation results of this (heterogeneous) equation are presented in the third column of table 1.9. T values are again calculated with HCSEs. (Note that the values of the coefficients and the associated t statistics based on the OLS standard errors for the first subperiod can be read from the RLS graphs).

A visual inspection of the heterogeneous equation shows that some coefficients (CPI, DMN, DR) differ considerably in size and significance among the two subperiods, while others (e.g. GDP) remain rather stable. To gain formal evidence on which particular coefficients are stable and which are unstable, the analysis of covariance test is performed. Test results are displayed in table 1.11.

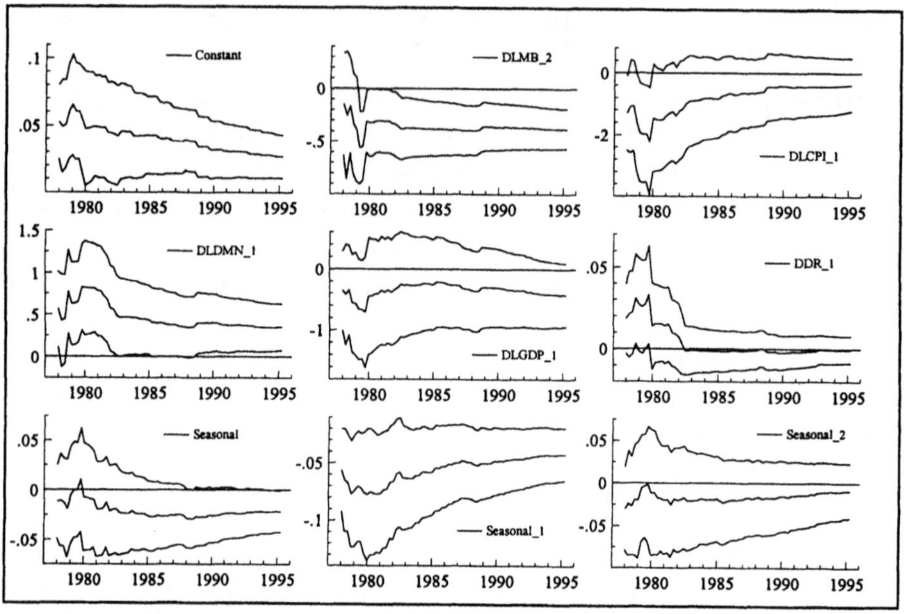

Figure 1.7: Recursive Least Squares Coefficients for Monetary Base Equation Measured in Nonseasonal Differences

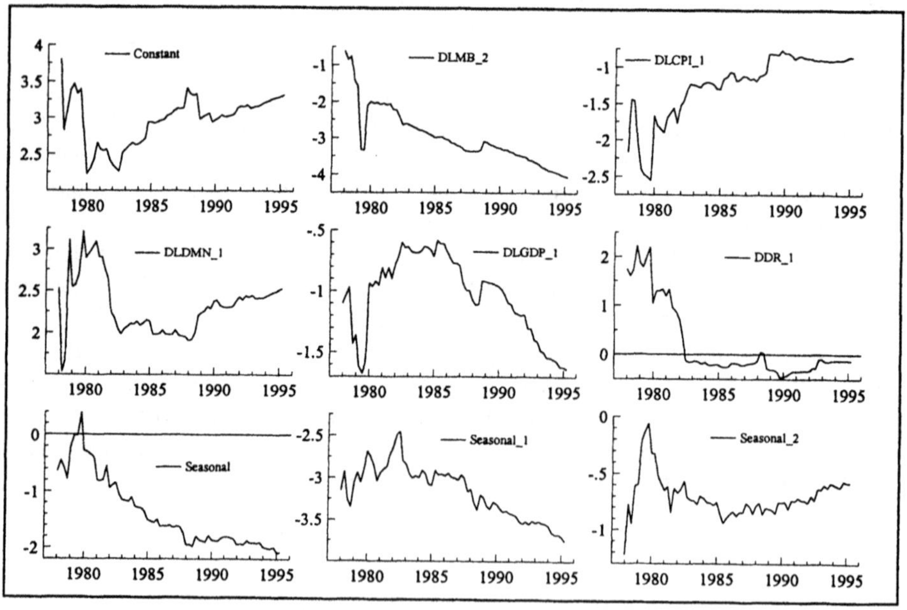

Figure 1.8: Recursive Least Squares t Statistics for Monetary Base Equation Measured in Nonseasonal Differences

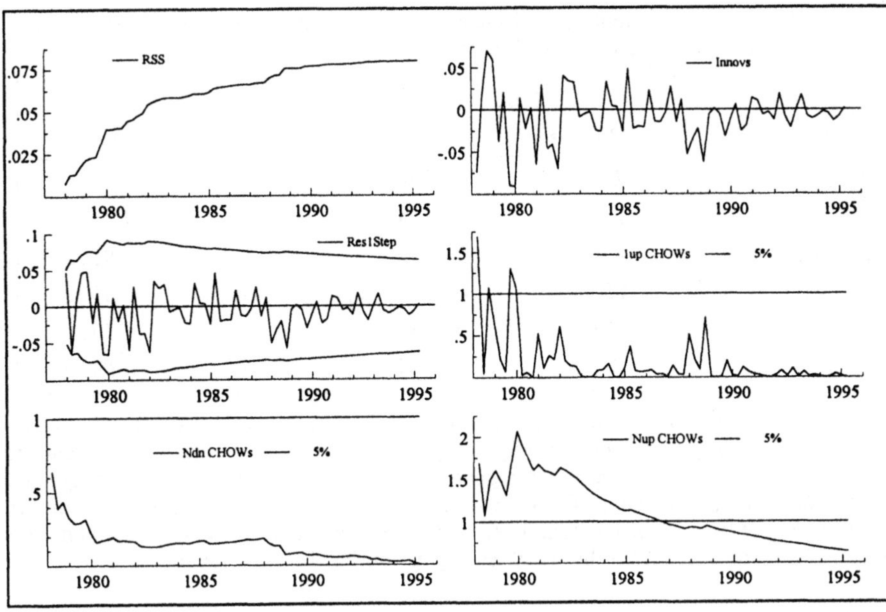

Figure 1.9: Recursive Least Squares Graphical Constancy Statistics for Monetary Base Equation Measured in Nonseasonal Differences

Table 1.11: F Tests for Continuous-by-class Effects Assuming a Structural Break for 1980 in Nonseasonal Monetary Base Model

Variables	OLS F statistics[a]	OLS p values	*WLS F statistics*[a]	*WLS p values*
Constant	2.85	0.0958	*1.60*	*0.2094*
$\Delta\ln(MB)_{t-2}$	2.46	0.1214	*2.46*	*0.1211*
$\Delta\ln(CPI)_{t-1}$	8.31	0.0052	*6.11*	*0.0158*
$\Delta\ln(DMN)_{t-1}$	15.51	0.0002	*15.96*	*0.0002*
$\Delta\ln(GDP)_{t-1}$	0.24	0.6248	*0.22*	*0.6368*
ΔDR_{t-1}	13.63	0.0004	*7.96*	*0.0062*

[a] In the F tests for homogeneity of the slope coefficients the null hypothesis H_0 is: $b_1 = b_2 = ... = b_{J-1} = 0$ (homogeneity). H_a is: At least one of these coefficients is significantly different from zero (heterogeneity). The F test for testing the homogeneity of the intercepts is analogous. The OLS column contains F statistics from the ordinary least squares regression of the completely heterogeneous model. The WLS column lists F statistics recomputed from the weighted regression for the same model.

At this stage attention is restricted to the test results for the OLS regression. The F tests for continuous-by-class effects indicate that the SNB reacted differently to the consumer price index CPI, the nominal exchange rate index DMN, and the three-month deposit rate DR. Moreover, heterogeneity is also found for the seasonal dummy representing the first quarter. (F statistics for seasonal dummies are not reported in table 1.11.) At the 10 percent level the intercept is also found to be heterogeneous, indicating shifts in the constant monetary base growth rate. No significant continuous-by-class effects are detected for the coefficients on the lagged dependent variable, the real unadjusted gross domestic product GDP, and the other two seasonal dummies.

The final equation reported in the last column of table 1.9 incorporates the results of these formal tests. The coefficients for CPI, DMN, DR, as well as the seasonal dummy for winter are allowed to be heterogeneous across the two regimes. For all other coefficients, homogeneity is imposed. T values are again calculated with HCSEs. This is the reaction function for the monetary base as dependent variable - measured in nonseasonal differences - that will be used in the remaining chapters of this work.

The F tests for structural breaks reported in the column headed with OLS in table 1.11 are not valid because the errors are nonspherical (heteroskedastic). In the following it is demonstrated how the reliability of these F tests is further investigated. The goal is to get an estimate of σ^2 in order to perform WLS regression and to recompute the F tests for the WLS regression estimates. These F tests are valid, since σ^2 is known. The question is whether the tests for the OLS und WLS regressions lead to the same conclusions with respect to the homogeneity of the coefficients.

The error variances are unknown and must be estimated from the data. A simple GARCH(1,1) model is estimated on the residuals of the completely heterogeneous equation.[92] The conditional standard errors of this regression are retrieved and plotted in figure 1.10.

Figure 1.10 serves to determine the weights to be employed in the WLS regression. For observations before 1979.4 and between 1988.1 and 1989.3 the conditional standard errors are approximately three times larger than for the other observations. In WLS the weights are proportional to the reciprocals of the error variances.[93] Hence, a weight of 1/9 is given to these observations to reduce their influence. All other observations have weight one. This weighting scheme is chosen after experimenting with various weights and different selections of observations with a subsequent analysis of the standardized residuals. The results of this WLS regression (not reported) are very similar to the OLS estimates of the heterogeneous equation.

Next the F tests for continuous-by-class effects are recomputed for the WLS regression. They are reported in table 1.11. The comparison of the results shows that the homogeneity tests for the OLS regression are all confirmed by those for the WLS regression.

The lagged dependent variable in the regression equation is a stochastic regressor. It is in part determined by the disturbance. In the present case the regressors are *contemporaneously* uncorrelated with the disturbance vector because of the absence of serial correlation. (Kennedy 1992 140; Lardaro 1992 577) The OLS estimator is biased, but retains its desirable asymptotic properties.[94] „In

---

92 The generalized autoregressive conditional heteroskedasticity (GARCH) model combines the mth-order autoregressive error model with the GARCH(p,q) variance model. It is also denoted as the AR(m)-GARCH(p,q) regression model. This model can be written as

$$y_t = x_t'\beta + \upsilon_t$$

$$\upsilon_t = \varepsilon_t - \rho_1 \upsilon_{t-1} - \dots - \rho_m \upsilon_{t-m}$$

$$\varepsilon_t = \sqrt{h_t}\, e_t$$

$$h_t = \omega + \sum_{i=1}^{q} \alpha_i \varepsilon_{t-i}^2 + \sum_{j=1}^{p} \gamma_j h_{t-j}$$

$$e_t \approx IN(0,1).$$

The conditional variance of the errors h_t depends on the size of the preceding errors ε_{t-i}, and it is also a function of past conditional variances h_{t-j}. For a simple GARCH(1,1) model, $m = 0$, $p = 1$, and $q = 1$.

93 Greene 1990 405-407. The normal equations for WLS are

$$\beta = (\mathbf{X'WX})^{-1}\mathbf{X'WY}$$

where $\mathbf{W}$ is a diagonal matrix containing the values of the weight variable.

94 See e.g. Greene 1990 568 on the two requirements that are sufficient to ensure that the OLS estimates retain their desirable asymptotic properties.

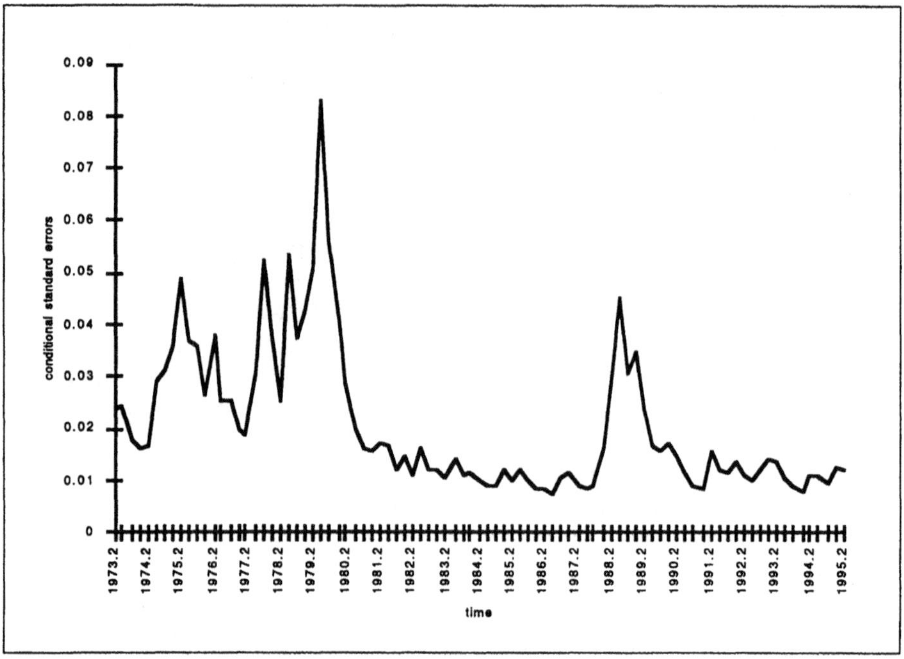

Figure 1.10: Conditional Standard Errors of GARCH(1,1) Model Estimated on Residuals of Heterogeneous Equation Assuming a Structural Break for 1980

general, no alternative estimators are available with superior small-sample properties, so the OLS estimator is retained on the basis of its desirable asymptotic properties." (Kennedy 1992 135)[95]

As an alternative to OLS Koutsoyiannis (1977 320) recommends instrumental variable estimation (IVE). For comparison, the equation was also estimated with the instrumental variable technique. The main problem is to find a suitable 'instrument', i.e. a new independent variable, for the regressor which is (contemporaneously) correlated with the error. This new independent variable must be contemporaneously uncorrelated with the error. And it should be correlated (preferably highly so) with the 'problem' variable.[96]

In the case of a lagged dependent variable there is an obvious choice of an instrumental variable. „The lagged value of an exogenous regressor appearing in this equation, say x_{t-1}, will not be correlated with the error (because x_{t-1} is an exogenous variable), but will be correlated with the lagged value of the dependent variable y_{t-1} (because x_{t-1} appears as an explanatory variable when the equation for y_t is lagged)." (Kennedy 1992 143) If several exogenous variables that are uncorrelated

---

95 Nothing is gained by maximum likelihood estimation in this case. See e.g. Schneeweiss 1990 210.

96 See e.g. Kmenta 1986 532 on the conditions that the instrumental variable should satisfy in order to produce a consistent estimator.

with the error appear in the equation, they are all eligible to serve as an instrument for y_{t-1}. Any linear combination of these variables will be uncorrelated with the error. The linear combination that is most highly correlated with the 'problem' variable y_{t-1} is chosen, because the higher this correlation, the smaller the variance of the IVE. Therefore, the lagged dependent variable is regressed on all exogenous regressors lagged one (additional) period. The estimated, or predicted, value of the lagged dependent variable obtained from this regression serves as the instrument for the lagged dependent variable. „This procedure is called generalized instrumental variable estimation (GIVE)." (Kennedy 1992 137; see also Harvey 1990 78.) Least squares estimation of this equation yields two-stage least squares (2SLS) estimates. A maximum likelihood estimation of the same equation produces limited-information maximum likelihood (LIML) estimates. (See e.g. Theil 1971 503.) The comparison of the OLS and LIML estimates showed that nothing is gained by this instrumental variable technique in the present case.

1.5.2b Nonseasonal Differences with the Money Supply M1 as Dependent Variable

As with the monetary base model for nonseasonal differences, the initial equation includes nine lags of the dependent variable. The errors are spherical, and sequential testing down leads to the elimination of all lags of the dependent variable. The resulting regression estimates are reported in the second column of table 1.12, headed with 'homogeneous coefficients'. The diagnostic tests in table 1.13 (second column) show - in addition to mild departure from normality - some signs of heteroskedasticity. Therefore, the HCSEs are estimated and compared with the OLS standard errors. Since the HCSEs are very close to the OLS standard errors, „there is little evidence of distortion of inference from untreated heteroskedasticity." (Hendry/Doornik 1996 138). Hence, the p values for the t statistics calculated with the OLS standard errors are reported.

Next the stability of the estimated coefficients is analyzed. Figures 1.11 to 1.14 display the graphical output of RLS for equation 1.4 with homogeneous coefficients. The graphs of the RLS coefficients (figure 1.11) indicate parameter instability only for the DR. The plots of the t statistics (figure 1.12) exhibit considerable variation for most variables. (Note that the entry for the last observation is the t statistic for equation 1.4). The graph of the one-step residuals (figure 1.13) identifies outliers in 1981 and 1988. The confidence band remains reasonably constant and suggests homoskedasticity. The one-step Chow test detects outliers and/or structural breaks for 1980, 1981 and 1988. The Nup-step Chow test clearly confirms a structural break for 1980. A structural break is also evidenced by the break-point Chow test, but the timing is not obvious from this graph. Overall, the graphical output clearly indicates a structural break for 1980.

Table 1.12: Regression Results for Nonseasonal Differences with Money Supply M1 ($\Delta ln(M1)$) as Dependent Variable

Variables	Equation 1.4: Homogeneous Coefficients	p value	Equation 1.5: Heterogeneous Coefficients	p value	Equation 1.6: Partly Homogeneous Coefficients	p value
Constant						
73.2-95.2	0.057***	0.0001			0.060***	0.0001
73.2-79.4			0.057***	0.0001		
80.1-95.2			0.059***	0.0001		
$\Delta ln(CPI)_{t-1}$						
73.2-95.2	-0.595**	0.0304			-1.085***	0.0001
73.2-79.4			-1.423***	0.0002		
80.1-95.2			-0.645*	0.0918		
$\Delta ln(DMN)_{t-1}$						
73.2-95.2	0.256***	0.0036				
73.2-79.4			0.444***	0.0001	0.400***	0.0001
80.1-95.2			0.043	0.7226	0.025	0.8340
$\Delta ln(GDP)_{t-1}$						
73.2-95.2	-0.096	0.5466			-0.237	0.1136
73.2-79.4			-0.192	0.2929		
80.1-95.2			-0.449*	0.0959		
ΔDR_{t-1}						
73.2-95.2	-0.012***	0.0001				
73.2-79.4			0.001	0.8116	0.00001	0.9896
80.1-95.2			-0.013***	0.0001	-0.013***	0.0001
R^2	0.75		0.84		0.81	
F statistic	F(7,81) = 34.26		F(16,73) = 23.21		F(10,78) = 34.30	
σ	0.0198		0.0172		0.0173	

All three regression equations include three seasonal dummies. They are also allowed to change across the two subperiods in the heterogeneous equation 1.5 to account for changes in seasonality. In the partly homogeneous equation 1.6 only the dummy for winter is allowed to change across the two subperiods.

***, ** and * denote significance at the 1, 5 and 10 percent level.

Table 1.13: Diagnostics for Equations with Money Supply ($\Delta\ln(M1)$) as Dependent Variable (Nonseasonal Differences)

Diagnostics	Equation 1.4: Homog. Coefficients	Equation 1.5: Heterog. Coefficients	Equation 1.6: Partly Homog. Coeff.
AR 1	F(1,80)=0.08 [0.7753]	F(1,72)=0.04 [0.8402]	F(1,77)=0.03 [0.8699]
AR 1-5	F(5,76)=0.43 [0.8281]	F(5,68)=0.06 [0.9971]	F(5,73)=0.16 [0.9756]
AR 1-9	F(9,72)=0.47 [0.8886]	F(9,64)=0.34 [0.9599]	F(9,69)=0.44 [0.9080]
ARCH 4	F(4,73)=0.98 [0.4215]	F(4,65)=0.05 [0.9957]	F(4,70)=0.07 [0.9898]
X_i^2	F(11,69)=2.42 [0.0130]	F(23,49)=0.30 [0.9988]	F(16,61)=0.42 [0.9725]
X_i*X_j	F(29,51)=1.03 [0.4556]	-	F(47,30)=0.34 [0.9996]
Normality	$\chi^2(2)$=7.65 [0.0219]	$\chi^2(2)$=27.96 [0.0001]	$\chi^2(2)$=23.46 [0.0001]
RESET	F(1,80)=0.19 [0.6682]	F(1,72)=0.72 [0.3998]	F(1,77)=0.12 [0.7269]

Numbers in brackets [] are p values.

The question is whether 1988 should be interpreted as a break or an outlier. To answer this question, the number of observations for initialization is changed so that the minimal model includes all observations up to the first quarter of 1980. Now the effects of the break in 1980 do not interfere with the effects after this date. The resulting graphs are displayed in figure 1.14. The break-point Chow and the Nup-step Chow tests do not find any signs of a break. It can be concluded that the observation for 1988 in the graph of the one-step residuals indicates an outlier, but not a structural break.

A structural break is modeled for the first quarter of 1980. Estimation results of this (heterogeneous) equation are presented in the third column of table 1.12. The diagnostic tests in the third column of table 1.13 do not detect any heteroskedasticity, so that OLS standard errors and t statistics are used and the associated p values are reported.

The comparison of the coefficients for the two regimes reveals major differences in size and significance for some coefficients (especially for DMN and DR). Formal evidence on specific coefficients is provided by the F tests for continuous-by-class effects in table 1.14. These tests - which are valid because of the absence of serial correlation and heteroskedasticity - indicate heterogeneity for DMN and DR, as well as for the seasonal dummy representing the first quarter. All other coefficients can be assumed to be homogeneous. Estimates of the resulting equation are reported in the last column in table 1.12 headed with 'partly homogeneous coefficients'. This is the equation that will be employed in the subsequent chapters.

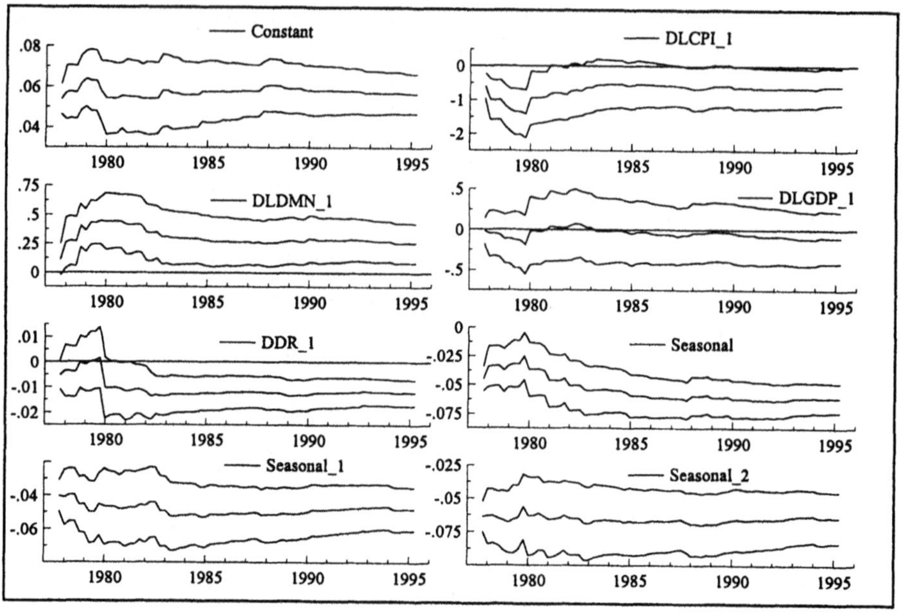

Figure 1.11: Recursive Least Squares Coefficients for Money Supply Equation Measured in Nonseasonal Differences

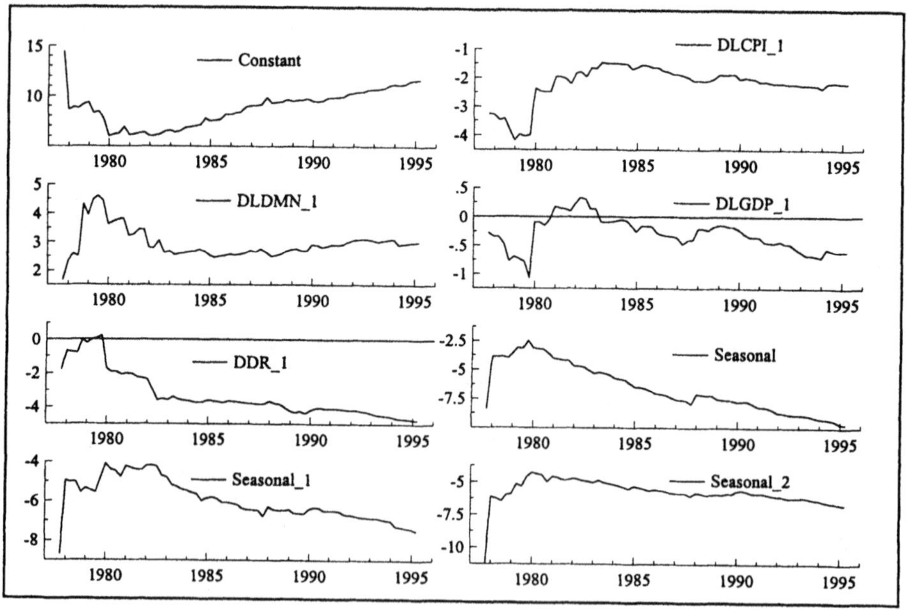

Figure 1.12: Recursive Least Squares t Statistics for Money Supply Equation Measured in Nonseasonal Differences

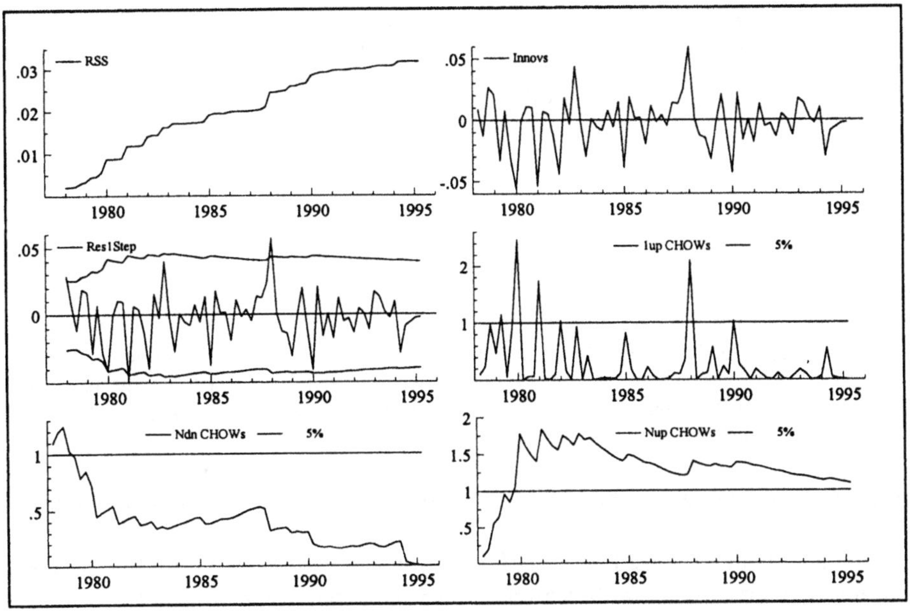

Figure 1.13: Recursive Least Squares Graphical Constancy Statistics for Money Supply Equation Measured in Nonseasonal Differences (n=20)

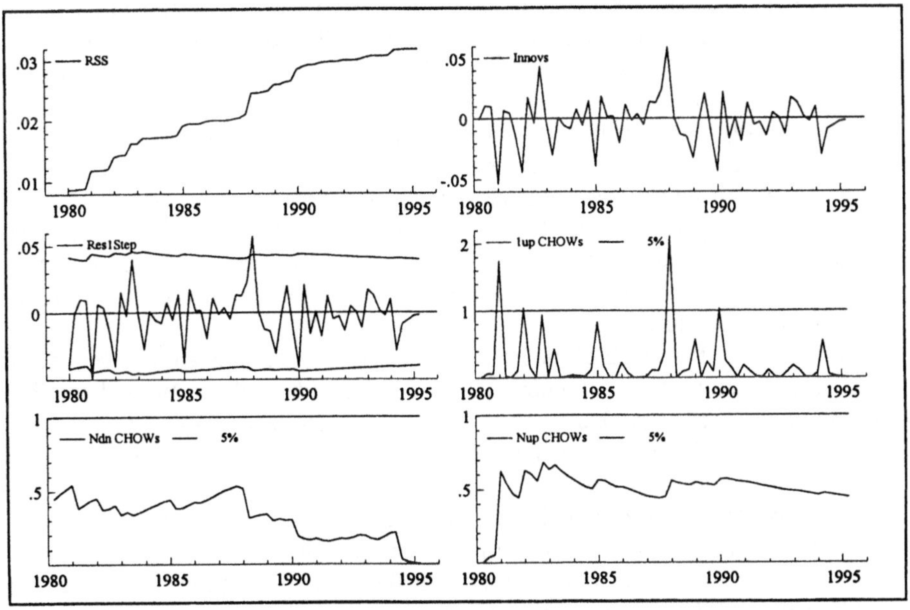

Figure 1.14: Recursive Least Squares Graphical Constancy Statistics for Money Supply Equation Measured in Nonseasonal Differences (n=28)

Table 1.14: F Tests for Continuous-by-class Effects Assuming a Structural Break for 1980 in Nonseasonal Money Supply Model

Variables	F statistics[a]	p values
Constant	0.02	0.9013
$\Delta\ln(CPI)_{t-1}$	2.22	0.1404
$\Delta\ln(DMN)_{t-1}$	6.51	0.0128
$\Delta\ln(GDP)_{t-1}$	0.63	0.4281
ΔDR_{t-1}	4.56	0.0361

[a] In the F tests for homogeneity of the slope coefficients the null hypothesis H_0 is: $b_1 = b_2 = ... = b_{J-1} = 0$ (homogeneity). H_a is: At least one of these coefficients is significantly different from zero (heterogeneity). The F test for testing the homogeneity of the intercepts is analogous.

1.5.2c Seasonal Differences with the Monetary Base as Dependent Variable

Following common sense five lags of the dependent variable are initially specified for this quarterly model with seasonal differences. (See Kennedy 1992 89). Diagnostic tests suggest absence of serial correlation (at the 5 percent level) but presence of heteroskedasticity. Since none of the lags can be eliminated the estimation results for this equation are reported in the second column of table 1.15. Because of the presence of heteroskedasticity (see table 1.16), HCSEs are estimated and the corrected t statistics are reported (although the differences between HCSEs and OLS standard errors are rather small). In order to preserve space the coefficients on the five lagged dependent variables are not reported.

The stability of the parameters is investigated using RLS estimation. RLS graphical output is presented in figures 1.15 to 1.17. The graphs for the coefficients and associated t values of the lagged dependent variables are not reported.

The graphs of the RLS coefficients (figure 1.15) reveal no obvious parameter instabilities. The graphs of the t statistics (figure 1.16) exhibit major fluctuations. For most variables 1980 seems to represent some kind of 'turning point' with respect to the t statistics.

In figure 1.17 the graph of the RSS suggests (parameter) instability, but without clear indication of a break point. The one-step residuals detect no outliers. But the narrowing confidence band shows distinct heteroskedasticity. The one-step Chow test and the break-point Chow test clearly indicate structural breaks, but the break points are not obvious. It could be 1979, 1980, or 1981. Variation of the number of observations for initialization does not help to clarify this issue. However, the Ndn-step Chow tests detect no break. Overall, the evidence on whether or not there exists a structural break and on the exact break point is mixed. To avoid the risk of biased estimation, and to allow for a comparison with the equations for the money supply as dependent variable, a structural break is assumed for 1980.

Table 1.15: Regression Results for Seasonal Differences with Monetary Base ($\Delta_4\ln(MB)$) as Dependent Variable

Variables	Equation 1.7: Homogeneous Coefficients	t values	Equation 1.8: Heterogeneous Coefficients	p value	Equation 1.9: Partly Homogeneous Coefficients	p value
Constant						
73.2-95.2	0.006	0.51				
73.2-79.4			0.052***	0.0052	0.051***	0.0034
80.1-95.2			0.014	0.3675	0.015	0.1892
$\Delta_4\ln(CPI)_{t-1}$						
73.2-95.2	-0.075	-0.29				
73.2-79.4			-0.870***	0.0064	-0.855***	0.0037
80.1-95.2			-0.261	0.3612	-0.278	0.2763
$\Delta_4\ln(DMN)_{t-1}$						
73.2-95.2	0.275**	2.21				
73.2-79.4			0.520***	0.0001	0.522***	0.0001
80.1-95.2			0.101	0.3289	0.099	0.3300
$\Delta_4\ln(GDP)_{t-1}$						
73.2-95.2	-0.021	-0.08			-0.333	0.2060
73.2-79.4			-0.355	0.2569		
80.1-95.2			-0.288	0.5021		
Δ_4DR_{t-1}						
73.2-95.2	-0.001	-0.52				
73.2-79.4			0.015**	0.0286	0.014**	0.0196
80.1-95.2			-0.004	0.2025	-0.003	0.1154
R^2	0.64		0.79		0.80	
F statistic	F(9,79) = 15.28					
σ	0.0376		0.0312		0.0310	

Equation 1.7 includes five lags of the dependent variable as additional regressors. Equations 1.8 and 1.9 include nine lags of the dependent variable which are constrained to be homogeneous for the two subperiods.
*** and ** denote significance at the 1 and 5 percent level.

Table 1.16: Diagnostics for Equations with Monetary Base ($\Delta_4 \ln(MB)$) as Dependent Variable (Seasonal Differences)

Diagnos-tics	Equation 1.7: Homog. Coefficients	Equation 1.8: Heterog. Coefficients	Equation 1.9: Partly Homog. Coeff.
AR 1	F(1,78)=3.11 [0.0816]	F(1,69)=1.81 [0.1830]	F(1,70)=1.70 [0.1972]
AR 1-3	F(3,76)=1.07 [0.3666]	F(3,67)=0.65 [0.5863]	F(3,68)=0.62 [0.6042]
AR 1-5	F(5,74)=0.87 [0.5086]	F(5,65)=0.41 [0.8368]	F(5,66)=0.41 [0.8428]
ARCH 4	F(4,71)=3.67 [0.0090]	F(4,62)=1.54 [0.2028]	F(4,63)=1.58 [0.1908]
X_i^2	F(18,60)=2.52 [0.0039]	F(35,34)=1.33 [0.2012]	F(33,37)=1.57 [0.0918]
X_i*X_j	F(54,24)=2.52 [0.0076]	-	-
Normality	χ^2(2)=13.02 [0.0015]	χ^2(2)=9.28 [0.0096]	χ^2(2)=9.29 [0.0096]
RESET	F(1,78)=0.09 [0.7682]	F(1,69)=0.74 [0.3938]	F(1,70)=0.70 [0.4053]

Numbers in brackets [] are p values.

To save degrees of freedom, and since the main interest is in the 'behavior' of the variables measuring the state of the economy, homogeneity is imposed for the coefficients on the lagged dependent variables. All other variables are allowed to change across the two regimes. Diagnostic tests indicate that now, with the structural break for some of the variables introduced - there is serial correlation. Several strategies are pursued to get rid of this violation. Introducing heterogeneity for all lagged dependent variables does not solve the problem. So additional lags are added to whiten the errors. Nine lags of the dependent variable are needed.

This is unusual for annual growth rates. The question arises whether the events in 1988 might be responsible for this high order lag and whether explicit modeling may help to reduce the number of lags in order to get a more parsimonious equation.[97] Hence, an (additional) intercept shift is modeled for 1988. (For an analogous strategy see Brüggemann/Wolters 1997 21). But even now none of the lags can be eliminated. So the third column of table 1.15 reports the estimation results for the equation which assumes heterogeneity for all coefficients except for the nine terms of the lagged dependent variable. The diagnostics for this equation (third column of table 1.16) show that not only serial correlation, but also heteroskedasticity has disappeared, so that OLS results are filed. (Absence of heteroskedasticity is also suggested by the comparison of HCSEs with OLS standard errors.)

97 Another possibility is that the high order lag is caused by some other missing regressor(s).

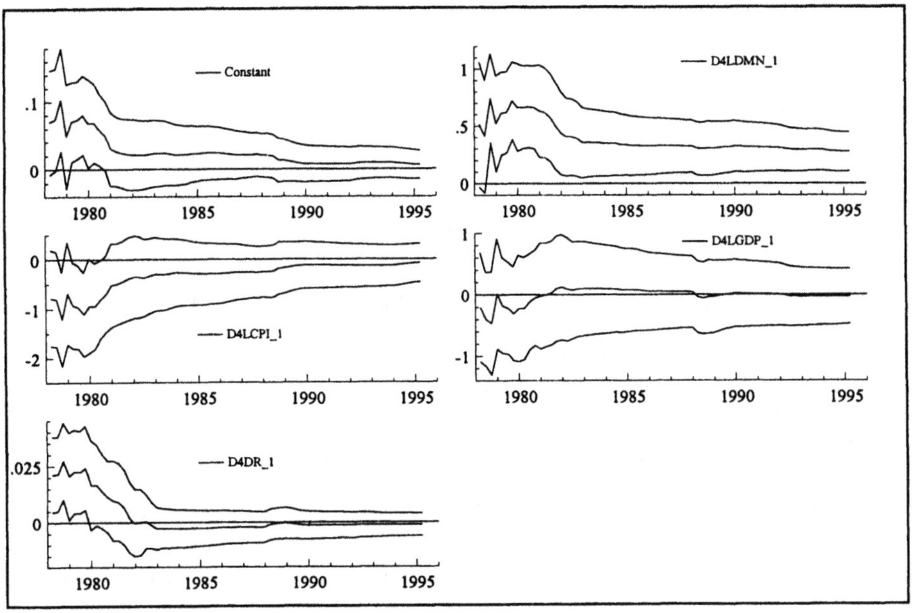

Figure 1.15: Recursive Least Squares Coefficients for Monetary Base Equation Measured in Seasonal Differences

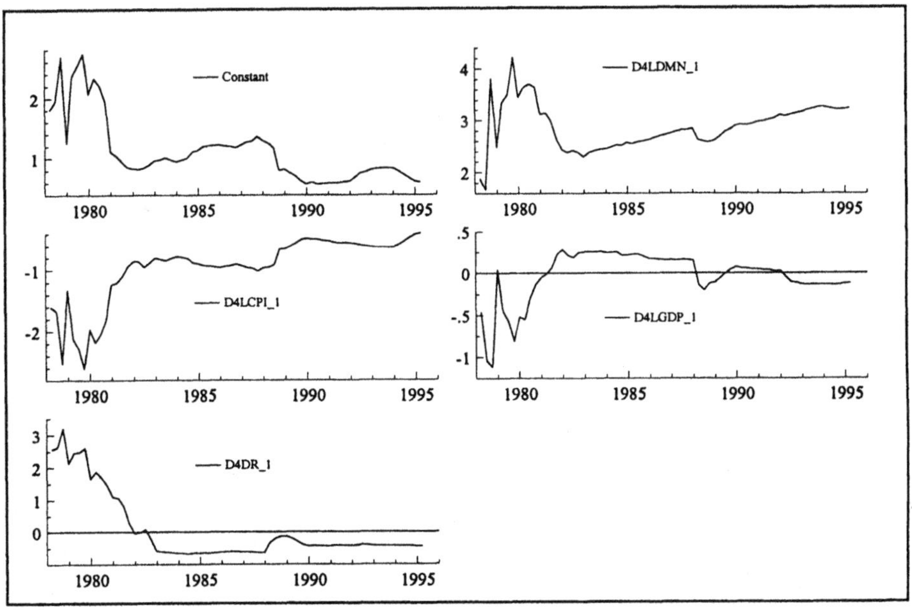

Figure 1.16: Recursive Least Squares t Statistics for Monetary Base Equation Measured in Seasonal Differences

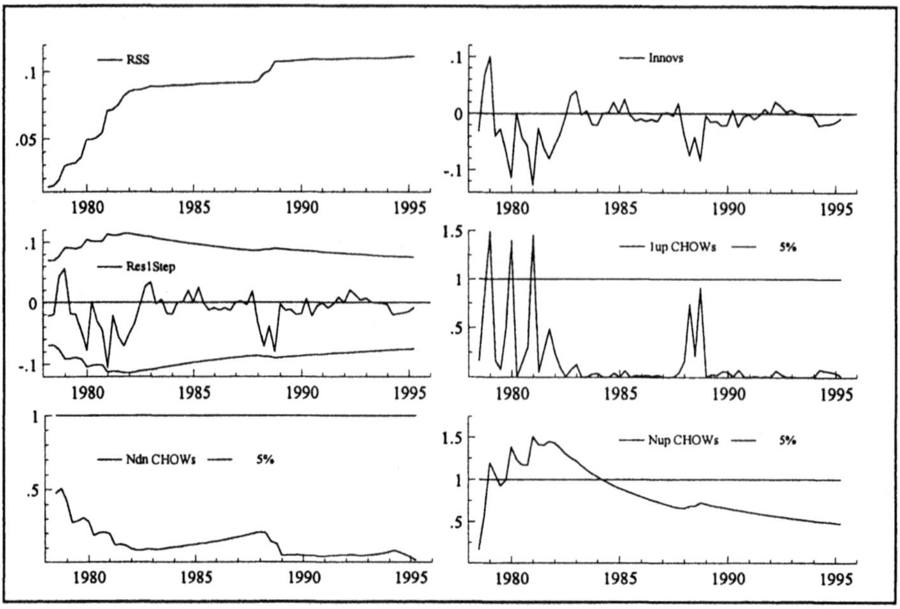

Figure 1.17: Recursive Least Squares Graphical Constancy Statistics for Monetary Base Equation Measured in Seasonal Differences

Table 1.17: F Tests for Continuous-by-class Effects Assuming a Structural Break for 1980 in the Seasonal Monetary Base Model

Variables	F statistics[a]	p values
Constant	8.58	0.0046
$\Delta_4 \ln(CPI)_{t-1}$	7.19	0.0092
$\Delta_4 \ln(DMN)_{t-1}$	17.51	0.0001
$\Delta_4 \ln(GDP)_{t-1}$	0.02	0.8972
$\Delta_4 DR_{t-1}$	12.59	0.0007

[a] See note on table 1.14.

Next it is formally tested whether coefficients differ in sign and significance. The results of the F tests for continuous-by-class effects are reported in table 1.17. They are valid because the equation is not plagued by heteroskedasticity. The test results suggest that the SNB changed its reaction to all variables except for GDP. Hence, the only difference between the heterogeneous (third column) and the partly heterogeneous equation (fourth column) in table 1.15 is that in the latter homogeneity is imposed for GDP. The partly homogeneous equation 1.9 will be used in the subsequent chapters.

1.5.2d Seasonal Differences with the Money Supply M1 as Dependent Variable

As with the monetary base model measured in seasonal differences, an equation with 5 lags of the dependent variable is initially specified. But this equation is plagued by serial correlation. Starting with nine lags of the dependent variable, the errors are not serially correlated, and sequential testing down leads to an equation which includes lags one to five and lag eight. The high order lag is probably due to the peaks in the M1 series (see figure 1.2) which introduce a long-memory process. No serial correlation and no heteroskedasticity is found for this equation (see table 1.18), and OLS results are filed in the second column of table 1.19.

Next the stability of the coefficients is investigated using RLS. The graphical output is presented in figures 1.18 to 1.21. The graphs of the RLS coefficients (figure 1.18) clearly indicate structural breaks for the intercept, DMN and CPI for 1980. For DR a change of sign is evidenced. No break appears for the coefficient on GDP (which does hardly differ from zero). Given the small sample at the beginning, all coefficient estimates show a remarkable stability before 1980. In the graphs of the t statistics (figure 1.19) the break for 1980 is even more pronounced. Now a structural break is suggested even for GDP.

The plot of the one-step residuals (figure 1.20) detects an outlier for 1988. The constant confidence band indicates homoskedasticity. The three versions of the Chow test clearly identify a structural break for 1980 (at the one percent level). The question is whether 1988 should be interpreted as an outlier or a structural break. Figure 1.21 answers this question: The number of observations for initialization is set at the beginning of 1980, so that the break for 1980 does not mask the effects for the period since 1980. The break point and the forecast Chow tests are not significant at the five percent level. It can be concluded that the peak for 1988 in the plot of the one-step Chow test is an outlier.

Implementing the break for 1980 for all variables including the lagged dependent regressors yields the estimates filed in the third column of table 1.19. Unlike the monetary base model measured in seasonal differences, the lagged dependent variables also have to be assumed as heterogeneous. (This means that the adjustment pattern is allowed to shift.) Otherwise, this regression would be plagued by serial correlation. The estimates of the coefficients support the interpretation which is gained by the plots of the RLS coefficients. Most coefficients differ substantially in size and significance across the two subperiods. This is also formally confirmed by the F tests for continuous-by-class effects reported in table 1.20. Heterogeneity is found at the five percent level for all variables except for GDP. In addition, homogeneity can be assumed for lags three, four and five of the lagged dependent variable (not reported). The equation with homogeneous coefficients for GDP and lags three, four and five, and heterogeneity for all other coefficients, can be further simplified, because lag three can now be deleted. Estimation results of this partly homogeneous equation are presented in the last column of table 1.19. This equation could further be simplified by eliminating the nonsignificant GDP variable.

Table 1.18: Diagnostics for Equations with Money Supply M1 ($\Delta_4 \ln(M1)$) as Dependent Variable (Seasonal Differences)

Diagnostics	Equation 1.10: Homog. Coefficients	Equation 1.11: Heterog. Coefficients	Equation 1.12: Partly Homog. Coeff.
AR 1	F(1,77)=3.00 [0.0873]	F(1,66)=0.22 [0.6428]	F(1,71)=1.53 [0.2198]
AR 1-3	F(3,75)=1.69 [0.1764]	F(3,64)=0.45 [0.7168]	F(3,69)=0.57 [0.6386]
AR 1-5	F(5,73)=1.66 [0.1540]	F(5,62)=1.01 [0.4221]	F(5,67)=1.51 [0.1985]
ARCH 4	F(4,70)=0.67 [0.6168]	F(4,59)=0.52 [0.7241]	F(4,64)=0.45 [0.7688]
X_i^2	F(20,57)=0.68 [0.8295]	F(41,25)=0.11 [1.0000]	F(31,40)=0.21 [1.0000]
X_i*X_j	F(65,12)=0.19 [1.0000]	-	-
Normality	$\chi^2(2)$=8.67 [0.0131]	$\chi^2(2)$=37.05 [0.0001]	$\chi^2(2)$=24.73 [0.0001]
RESET	F(1,77)=0.19 [0.6627]	F(1,66)=4.12 [0.0463]	F(1,71)=10.22 [0.0021]

Numbers in brackets [] are p values.

Table 1.19: Regression Results for Seasonal Differences with Money Supply M1 ($\Delta_4\ln(M1)$) as Dependent Variable

Variables	Equation 1.10: Homogeneous Coefficients	p value	Equation 1.11: Heterogeneous Coefficients	p value	Equation 1.12: Partly Homogeneous Coefficients	p value
Constant						
73.2-95.2	0.019**	0.0113				
73.2-79.4			0.078***	0.0001	0.065***	0.0001
80.1-95.2			0.034***	0.0079	0.045***	0.0001
$\Delta_4\ln(CPI)_{t-1}$						
73.2-95.2	-0.233*	0.0840				
73.2-79.4			-1.533***	0.0001	-1.151***	0.0001
80.1-95.2			-0.576**	0.0216	-0.774***	0.0010
$\Delta_4\ln(DMN)_{t-1}$						
73.2-95.2	0.188***	0.0013				
73.2-79.4			0.415***	0.0001	0.401***	0.0001
80.1-95.2			0.072	0.3400	0.062	0.4133
$\Delta_4\ln(GDP)_{t-1}$						
73.2-95.2	0.025	0.8708			-0.147	0.3930
73.2-79.4			-0.413*	0.0619		
80.1-95.2			0.056	0.8453		
Δ_4DR_{t-1}						
73.2-95.2	-0.005*	0.0729				
73.2-79.4			0.005	0.2288	0.002	0.5616
80.1-95.2			-0.006**	0.0362	-0.004*	0.0664
R^2	0.87		0.94		0.93	
F statistic	F(10,78) = 52.47		F(21,67) = 48.89		F(16,72) = 60.33	
σ	0.0241		0.0198		0.0202	

Equations 1.10 and 1.11 include lags one to five as well as lag eight of the dependent variable as additional regressors. In equation 1.11 these lags are all allowed to be heterogeneous, too. In equation 1.12 lag three is eliminated, and lags four and five are constrained to be homogeneous for the two subperiods.

***, ** and * denote significance at the 1, 5 and 10 percent level.

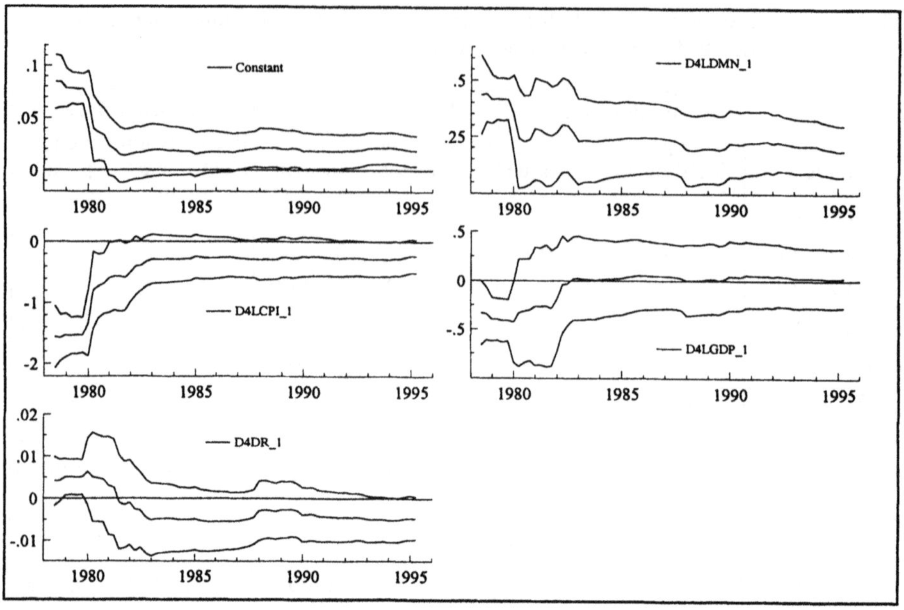

Figure 1.18: Recursive Least Squares Coefficients for Money Supply Equation Measured in Seasonal Differences

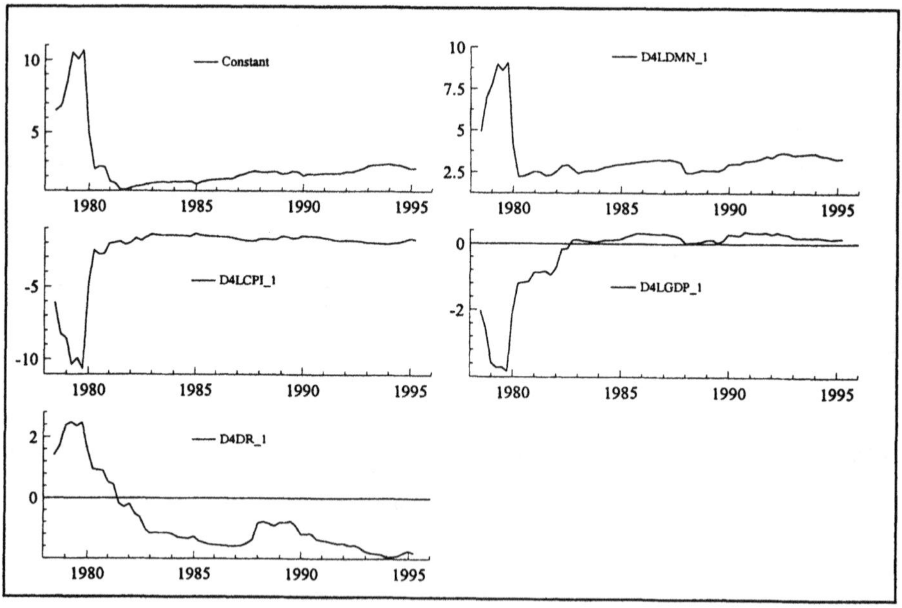

Figure 1.19: Recursive Least Squares t Statistics for Money Supply Equation Measured in Seasonal Differences

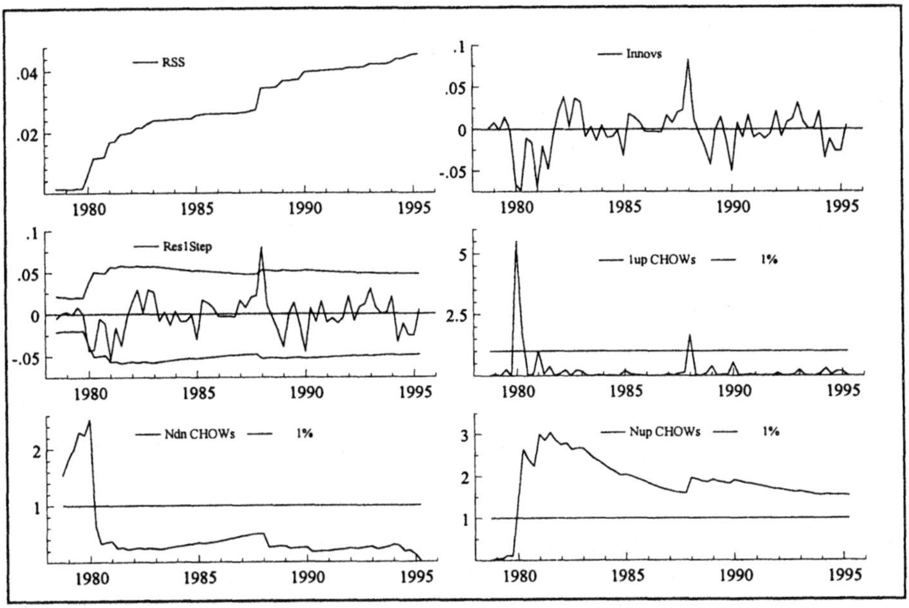

Figure 1.20: Recursive Least Squares Graphical Constancy Statistics for Money Supply Equation Measured in Seasonal Differences (n=20)

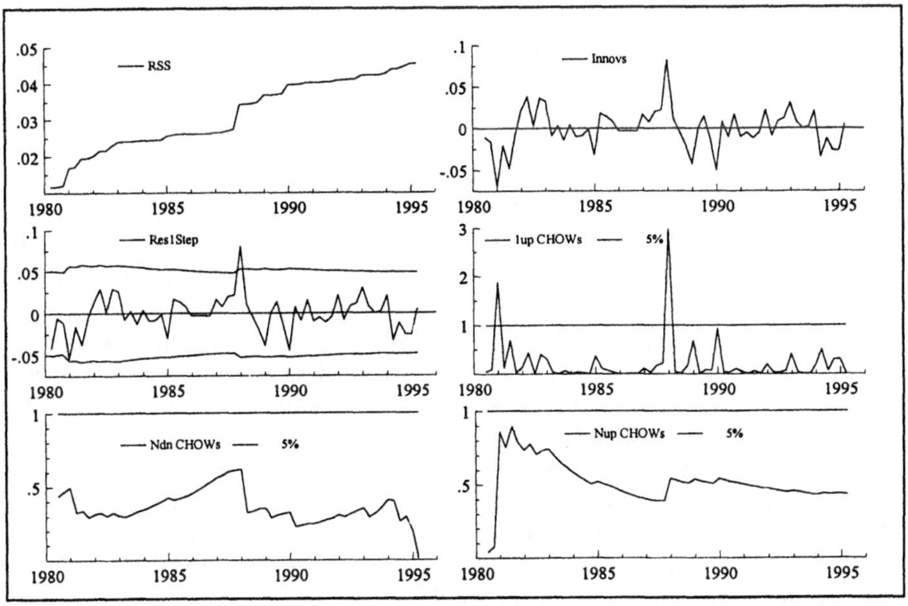

Figure 1.21: Recursive Least Squares Graphical Constancy Statistics for Money Supply Equation Measured in Seasonal Differences (n=28)

Table 1.20: F Tests for Continuous-by-class Effects Assuming a Structural Break for 1980 in the Seasonal Money Supply Model

Variables	F statistics[a]	p values
Constant	5.19	0.0259
$\Delta_4 \ln(CPI)_{t-1}$	6.30	0.0145
$\Delta_4 \ln(DMN)_{t-1}$	8.32	0.0053
$\Delta_4 \ln(GDP)_{t-1}$	1.70	0.1972
$\Delta_4 DR_{t-1}$	4.75	0.0328

[a] See note on table 1.14.

Estimation with a Lagged Dependent Variable and Serially Correlated Errors

Both equations with seasonal differences require a high order lag to whiten the errors. This could be a sign of overdifferencing due to the application of the (inappropriate) seasonal difference filter. (See section 1.4.3). The question arises whether more parsimonious models with corrections for serial correlation and heteroskedasticity would lead to the same qualitative results. To answer this question, both seasonal equations were also estimated with only one lag of the dependent variable added - as is postulated by the reaction function.

Diagnostic tests for the 'parsimonious' *money supply* equation do not detect heteroskedasticity, but clearly indicate the presence of serial correlation. This creates an estimating problem with two assumptions of the classical linear regression model being violated simultaneously - autocorrelated errors and a lagged dependent variable as a regressor.

In the presence of these two problems the OLS estimator is even asymptotically biased, because the lagged dependent variable is *contemporaneously* correlated with the autocorrelated disturbance.[98] The OLS estimates have to be discarded. And F tests (e.g. for structural breaks) are not valid.

As pointed out in section 1.5.1a special estimation methods must be applied in this situation. Since alternative estimators with desirable small-sample properties cannot in general be found, the search for appropriate estimators is conducted on the basis of their *asymptotic* properties. (Kennedy 1992 136)

The most common approach to estimation problems of this kind is provided by the method of instrumental variables. (Kennedy 1992 136; Harvey 1990 76) Applying the generalized instrumental variable estimation (GIVE) as described in section 1.5.2a yields limited-information maximum likelihood (LIML) estimates (or two-stage least squares estimates 2SLS).

98 An intuitive explanation for this is provided by Kmenta 1986 340.

The basis for the instrumental variable technique is to salvage at least the property of consistency. And it is the fact that the 'instrument' is not correlated with the error term that allows the IVE to avoid asymptotic bias. (Kennedy 1992 149) If the two conditions cited in section 1.5.2a are satisfied, the IVE „is consistent regardless of the type of autocorrelation“ in the errors. (Greene 1990 569) The drawback of this method is that it provides only a 'cure' for the presence of the lagged dependent variable, but does not account for the autocorrelated errors. (Koutsoyiannis 1977 323) For this reason the IVE generally lacks efficiency.[99]

Two-step linearized maximum likelihood estimators are proposed to improve efficiency.[100] One frequently cited example is the method suggested by Hatanaka (1974) for the case of AR(1) errors. However, inspection of the sample autocorrelation function suggests a more complicated form of serial correlation, and the properties of the estimator are not clear when applied to this more complex situation. Moreover, Hatanaka raises some questions about the small-sample performance of the estimator. (Greene 1990 569) Another estimator proposed by Wallis corrects the estimate of the correlation coefficient for bias (See Koutsoyiannis 1977 325.) This estimator is reported to possess a better small-sample performance. But again, it is only discussed in the context of an AR(1) process, and its properties when applied to a more complex setting are unclear.

A standard approach to correct for autocorrelation is to estimate an autoregressive error model.[101] Because of the presence of a lagged dependent variable, either a grid-search or a ML procedure must be applied.[102] For the money supply equation an AR(1,4) model is chosen on the basis of the Akaike information criterion

---

99 „... the variance-covariance matrix of the IV estimator is larger than that of the OLS estimator, by an amount that is inversely related to the correlation between the instrument and the regressor ... This is the price paid for avoiding the asymptotic bias of OLS; the OLS estimator could be preferred on the MSE criterion.“ Kennedy 1992 137.

100 The idea is to start with a consistent estimator of the correlation coefficient. Since OLS is inconsistent, the residuals are likewise inconsistent and any estimator of the correlation coefficient based on these residuals will also be inconsistent. A consistent estimator, such as the IVE, produces consistent residuals and a consistent estimate of the correlation coefficient. See Greene 1990 571.

101 The regression model with autocorrelated errors AR(m) is

$$y_t = \mathbf{x}_t'\beta + \upsilon_t$$

$$\upsilon_t = \varepsilon_t - \rho_1\upsilon_{t-1} - \ldots - \rho_m\upsilon_{t-m}$$

$$\varepsilon_t \approx \mathrm{IN}(0, \sigma^2).$$

The regression estimates are corrected for serial correlation by simultaneously estimating the regression coefficients β and the autoregressive error model parameters ρ_i.

102 The Cochrane-Orcutt procedure should not be used in this context. Since it relies on a single solution for ρ, it might give a local minimum, and even when iterated might converge to a local minimum. Maddala 1992 239.

(AIC) and the Schwartz Bayesian criterion (SBC). Application of a grid-search procedure produces almost identical results.[103]

The comparison of LIML and AR(1,4) estimates (not reported) for the 'parsimonious' money supply equation with the result for equation 1.11 in table 1.19 reveals that coefficient estimates do not differ dramatically and that the pattern of significance is almost the same.

Things are even more complicated with the 'parsimonious' *monetary base* model measured in seasonal differences. The diagnostic tests do not only detect serial correlation, they also indicate the presence of heteroskedasticity. Serial correlation is the more serious problem, because it affects consistency of the estimates, while heteroskedasticity 'only' leads to a loss of efficiency. To produce consistent estimates the equation is estimated using the instrumental variable technique yielding LIML estimates. Again, the IVE lacks efficiency, because it does not account for serial correlation and heteroskedasticity.

A different approach is to estimate a model that combines autoregressive errors and GARCH-type heteroskedasticity. An AR(2,4)-GARCH(1,1) model - where the order of the autoregressive model is chosen on the basis of the MSE criterion - is also estimated.

The comparison of the LIML and AR(2,4)-GARCH(1,1) estimates for the monetary base model (not reported) with the result for equation 1.8 in table 1.15 reveals that coefficient estimates do not differ dramatically and that the pattern of significance differs only for the GDP variable.

Serial correlation might be caused by omitted variables. (See e.g. Maddala 1992 253.) More specifically, it might be due to misspecification of the dynamic process, for instance the noninclusion of lagged values of the explained variable. (See e.g. Maddala 1992 255; Harvey 1990 288.) For this reason a significant serial correlation in the estimated residuals does not necessarily imply that a serial correlation model should be estimated.[104] High autocorrelation in the residuals can be interpreted as a symptom of lack of fit. And it is frequently warned that an autoregressive error model should not be used as a nostrum for models that simply do not fit. (See e.g. Mizon 1995.)

In the present equations the serial correlation can be eliminated with the inclusion of lagged values of the dependent variable. Therefore, it can be argued that the dynamic process in the 'parsimonious' equations is misspecified. For this reason the estimation results which are obtained from the general-to-specific strategy are preferred.

---

[103] Grid-search and ML are not the same! But „if the number of observations is large ... the ML procedure and the Hildreth-Lu procedure will give almost the same results." Maddala 1992 240.

[104] The transformed regression equation when estimating a serial correlation model involves new variables. „The question then arises whether the problem is one of autocorrelation or one of incorrect specification of the regression equation in the first place." Kmenta 1986 334.

1.5.3 Interpretation of the Regression Results

1.5.3a Overview of the Results

Does the SNB respond in any systematic way to the macroeconomic stabilization goals? Table 1.21 summarizes the results for the four models investigated. For each dependent variable, the partly homogeneous equation which is reported in the last column of the tables is chosen.

Table 1.21: Summary of Regression Results

		Dependent Variables			
Regressors	Period	Δln(MB)	$\Delta_4$ln(MB)	Δln(M1)	$\Delta_4$ln(M1)
Constant	73.2-95.2	+++		+++	
	73.2-79.4		+++		+++
	80.1-95.2				+++
CPI	73.2-95.2			---	
	73.2-79.4	---	---		---
	80.1-95.2				---
DMN	73.2-79.4	+++	+++	+++	+++
	80.1-95.2	-			
GDP	73.2-95.2	---			
DR	73.2-79.4	++	++		
	80.1-95.2			---	-

+++ (---), ++ (--) and + (-) denote positive (negative) and significant at the 1, 5 and 10 percent level.

The multiple correlation coefficients (tables 1.9, 1.12, 1.15 and 1.19) show that the chosen specification explains between 70 and 80 percent of the variation in the growth rates of the monetary base and between 81 and 93 percent of the growth rates of the money supply M1. These R^2's are reasonably high given the fact that the dependent variables are changes, not levels.

1.5.3b The Difference in Behavior Before and After 1980

The general result of these equations including a structural break for 1980 (partly homogeneous coefficients) is that the SNB reacted very strongly to some variables representing macroeconomic stabilization goals during the period from 1973 to 1980. It showed much less reactive behavior since 1980.

To Which Variables Did the SNB Change Its Reaction?

The findings with respect to *parameter stability* can be summarized as follows: While the coefficient on GDP is found to be homogeneous in all equations, coefficients on the exchange rate variable and on short-term interest rates are always heterogeneous. Results are mixed for the remaining two regressors. The coefficient on CPI is shifting except for the money supply equation measured in nonseasonal differences. For the intercept parameter stability can be assumed only in the equations measured in nonseasonal differences.

Parameter stability is found for the GDP measure throughout all equations. The sign is always negative, implying that the SNB reacts countercyclically to real economic growth. But it is only significant (at the 1 percent level) in the monetary base equation measured in nonseasonal differences.

Regression Results for the Period from 1973.2 to 1979.4

During this period the change in the *consumer price index* lagged one quarter turns out to be highly significant in all equations, and it always has a negative sign. Higher inflation rates induce a contractionary response by the SNB. The relative size of this coefficient indicates the high priority of the price stability goal.

As expected the SNB shows much susceptibility to *exchange rate* considerations. The change in the nominal DM/SFr exchange rate index lagged one quarter is a highly significant (at the one percent level) predictor of SNB monetary policy in all equations. It always shows a positive sign. The higher this index, the stronger the SFr, and the more expansionary the SNB's policy to meet the increased demand for SFr. These findings for the consumer price index and the exchange rate confirm Burdekin/Langdana's results.[105]

The monetary base indicates a significant response to changes in *short-term interest rates* lagged one quarter in both equations. The positive sign suggests that the SNB expands the monetary base as short-term interest rates rise, thus trying to stabilize them. In the M1 equations short-term interest rates are not significant for this subperiod.

---

[105] Grier 1987 examining models of the Fed including lagged inflation rates and real income growth as predictors of money growth found these variables to be consistently insignificant. Amazingly, the lagged inflation rate rarely turns out to be a significant predictor of money growth in studies on the Fed (even if both levels and first differences of inflation are used! See Grier/Neiman 1985 209.) See also Laney 1985 109: the lagged inflation variable does not perform very robustly, except for Germany, which has a reputation as an inflation-conscious society. Frey/Schneider 1981 308 argue that insignificance of the inflation variable (for Germany) may suggest a misspecified equation.

Regression Results for the Period from 1980.1 to 1995.2

Regression results evidence a dramatic *shift in the behavior* of the SNB for the period after the beginning of 1980. The overall impression is that the SNB does no longer seem to react to the state of the economy.

A significant response to inflation can be found only for the money supply equations. The comparison of the coefficients in the corresponding equations headed with „heterogeneous coefficients“ shows that these are very similar numerically, but that the coefficient in the seasonal equation is more significant.

A significant (at the 10 percent level) reaction to the exchange rate variable DMN is indicated in the monetary base equation measured in nonseasonal differences. The coefficient is much smaller than it is before 1980 and it switched sign. The SNB does not seem to pay much attention to exchange rates in this period. The reason may be that in the eighties changes in exchange rates occurred primarily vis-à-vis the US$, while the DM/SFr exchange rate remained rather stable. In 1986 and 1987 the SNB even bought US$ and sold Yen to support the US$. (AB 1987 1027) The present model does not capture these effects.

The coefficients on short-term interest rates changed to a negative sign in all equations, but they are significant only in the equations with M1 as dependent variable.

While constant money growth for the nonseasonal M1 equation shows no marked shift, a decrease is indicated in the seasonal M1 equation.

It is tempting to conclude that the SNB adopted some *monetarist rule* in 1980. However, especially the negative signs for the real growth rate (in the nonseasonal monetary base equation) and short-term interest rates (in the M1 equations) still raise some questions. A central bank that has adopted a monetarist policy wouldn't react at all. It would expand the monetary base or the money supply M1 at a rate equal to the expected mid-term growth of potential output. The countercyclical response may reveal that the SNB continued to pursue a discretionary monetary policy.

The empirical finding of less responsive behavior in the eighties may also simply reflect the fact that the SNB was exposed to much less pressure from changes in the economic conditions compared to the seventies. This is certainly true for the fluctuations of the DM/SFr exchange rate. (Lusser 1984 62) As already noted, the formation of the European Monetary System in March 1979 may have played an important role here.

1.5.3c Comparing Nonseasonal and Seasonal Equations

As explained in section 1.4.3 regressions in nonseasonal differences are preferred, but for comparison regressions in seasonal differences are also presented. For each dependent variable, signs, significance, and numerical values of the coefficients are compared. Moreover, the findings on parameter stability are of interest.

In the regressions with the *monetary base* as dependent variable (equations 1.3 and 1.9 in tables 1.9 and 1.15) most coefficients show the same pattern of signs and significance. With respect to signs the only difference is the coefficient on DMN for the period after 1980. This is at the same time the first case where a difference in significance is detected. The second case with a different result for significance is the coefficient on GDP. Test results for structural breaks differ only for the intercept. In the equation for seasonal differences heterogeneity is suggested, while homogeneity can be assumed with nonseasonal differences. Numerically most coefficients for the equation in nonseasonal differences are approximately double size of those in the equation in seasonal differences.

Regression results with the *money supply M1* as dependent variable measured in nonseasonal and seasonal differences (equations 1.6 and 1.12 in tables 1.12 and 1.19) show an identical pattern of signs and significance. However, different homogeneity conditions exist for the intercept and CPI. The constant M1 growth rate can be assumed to be the same in the nonseasonal equation. In the seasonal equation it is lower for the second subperiod. The coefficient on CPI can be assumed to be homogeneous in the nonseasonal equation. The heterogeneous coefficients for the same variable in the seasonal equation suggests that the SNB changed its reaction to inflation rates.

The equations in nonseasonal and seasonal differences reflect different assumptions about the type of seasonality in the data (see section 1.4.3). Regression results show that the different treatment of seasonality (i.e. the method to deseasonalize the data) and the implied differences in the dynamic structure of the equations do not lead to different conclusions with respect to the patterns of signs and significance of coefficients in the present example. However, most coefficients differ numerically. It is unclear how these differences have to be interpreted. The comparison between nonseasonal and seasonal equations only illustrates whether and how measurement of the variables affects regression results.

1.5.3d Comparing Monetary Base and M1 Equations

Comparing the equations for the monetary base and the money supply M1 measured in *nonseasonal* differences (tables 1.9 and 1.12) similar qualitative results are suggested. However, some differences can be observed:

In the monetary base equation the coefficient on CPI is found to be heterogeneous, while the same coefficient can be constrained to be homogeneous in the money supply equation. A significant negative reaction to exchange rates for the time period since 1980 is evidenced only in the monetary base equation. GDP is significant in the monetary base equation, but fails to be significant in the money supply equation. And the positive reaction to short-term interest rates in the first subperiod is significant in the monetary base equations, while the negative reaction to this variable in the second subperiod is significant in the M1 equation.

The comparison of the same equations, but measured in *seasonal* differences (tables 1.15 and 1.19), shows that the same homogeneity assumptions are imposed on both regressions. While estimation results for some coefficients are very similar (DMN and GDP), they differ for others. In the monetary base equation the intercept fails to be significant for the subperiod after 1980. The negative response to inflation rates in the second subperiod is significant only in the M1 equation. And for the short-term interest rates the analogous difference as with the nonseasonal equations can be observed.

1.5.4 Other Model Specifications

In section 1.3.2c it is pointed out that different measures for the economic key variables can be used as regressors. Experimenting with various other measures shows that the regression results do not depend on a particular specification of the regression equation. Hence, the general conclusions of the previous analysis remain valid.

Replacing the nominal DM/SFr *exchange rate* index by the same index in real terms, or by the nominal or real effective exchange rate index yields basically the same results. The nominal US$/SFr exchange rate index is significant for the period before 1980 if it enters the equation as the only exchange rate variable. Its significance disappears as soon as the DM/SFr exchange rate index is added.

Regression results for alternative measures for *production, employment, and interest rates* can be summarized as follows. Replacing the real unadjusted domestic growth rate by other variables measuring economic activity increases the effect of the consumer price index for the period before 1980. The overall reaction to the long-term interest rates, measured by the nominal government bond yield, is significantly negative for both dependent variables. Interpreting the change in long-term interest rates as a measure of expected future inflation, this result is consistent with a countercyclical response by the SNB. The lending rate was not found to be significant, even when used as the only interest rate. Domestic orders inflow is not a significant regressor, too. Replacing domestic orders inflow with total orders inflow (domestic and abroad) makes very little difference. In the regressions on the monetary base the rate of capacity utilization indicates a significant negative response for the period before 1980. In the regressions on the money supply M1 the employment index can be assumed to be homogeneous and turns out to be significant. The coefficient for the rate of capacity utilization can also be assumed to be homogeneous. It suggests a significant negative response by the central bank.

Using different measures for the *gross domestic product* (seasonally adjusted, trend adjusted) in nominal or real terms gives the same qualitative results.

Among the *inflation variables*, the consumer price index performs best throughout the regressions. The GDP deflator is also found to be a good predictor of monetary policy for the period before 1980. However, the wholesale price index, though always negative, is never significant.

1.6 Conclusions

This chapter presents estimates of the systematic reaction of the SNB, measured with nonseasonal and seasonal differences in the monetary base and the money supply M1, to the state of the economy, as reflected by inflation, real growth, interest rates, and exchange rates.

A prime interest is the stability of the regression coefficients over time. For the period from 1973.2 to 1995.2 formal tests confirm a structural break for 1980. F tests for continuous-by-class effects identify the variables to which the SNB changed its reaction.

Regression results evidence a highly significant response to inflation and exchange rates over the subperiod before 1980. While the monetary base and the money supply M1 contract in response to inflation, their response to exchange rates is accommodative. The assurances of the SNB that its main concern is price stability do not appear to be mere public relations pronouncements. For the period after 1980 much less reactive behavior can be observed. Evidence on short-term interest rates is mixed: Significant coefficients in the monetary base equations are positive for the subperiod before 1980; they are negative in the money supply equations for the subperiod after 1980. As expected the unemployment rate is never significant and is dropped from the equations. Several alternative models show that these general conclusions do not depend on a particular specification of the reaction function.

Regression results for the time period before 1980 evidence substantial discretionary monetary policy. Even for the period after 1980 the finding of some significant responses to changes in the state of the economy indicates discretionary monetary policy. This probably reflects the problem that a country with a small open economy cannot simply start to impose a monetarist monetary policy on its own without incurring the risk that shocks originated abroad have significant negative effects for the economy. Other major central banks would have to stabilize their policy, too.

There are some *limitations* to note for this chapter. Although a behavioral model underlying the reaction function is presented, the postulated reaction function is ad hoc, since it is not derived from the preference function of the central bank's authority and its structural model of the economy. Regressing the monetary aggregates on the independent variables simply lagged one quarter is rather naive. Using forecasted values instead of lagged values of the regressors appears to be a more realistic model. Another idea would be to use not just changes in the environment, but prior target misses as regressors. Finally, fiscal and political variables are excluded from the analysis. Including fiscal and political variables may help to improve the analysis. This is explored in the following chapters.

CHAPTER 2

Deficits and Money Growth: Empirical Evidence for Switzerland

2.1 Introduction

Direct political influence on monetary policy is analyzed in the framework of elections, parties and administrations. Indirect political influence is investigated by testing for effects of fiscal policy on monetary policy. (Laney/Willett 1983 54; Alesina/Sachs 1988 67 Fn. 6; Lang/Welzel 1992 73) The impact of fiscal policy on monetary policy is frequently studied in the context of a budget deficit (or surplus) money supply relationship. The basic argument is that fiscal policy controls macroeconomic variables, for instance the deficit, that influence monetary policy. The way the central bank reacts to these variables is interpreted as evidence on the (in)dependence debate.

This chapter investigates the budget deficit (or surplus) money supply relationship for Switzerland. The purpose is twofold: (1) to test for the significance of fiscal variables using various deficit measures, and (2) to test for the structural stability of these coefficient estimates for the period of flexible exchange rates.

Estimation results using quarterly data for the time period from 1973.2 to 1995.2 differ for the two dependent variables investigated. With the *money supply M1* as dependent variable fiscal variables have no impact on monetary policy. The only exception is a negative relationship found between the growth rate of the money supply M1 and the growth rate of gross federal debt.

With the *growth rate* of the *monetary base* as dependent variable a significant and positive relationship with the actually measured total deficits as well as with the structural components of the federal and total deficits (with and without social security) can be found for the time period before 1980. Following the conventional interpretation the positive sign on these deficit measures implies accommodating behavior and is consistent with political dependence of the central bank. A negative response to the cyclical component of the total deficit including social security might indicate offsetting behavior and is rather consistent with political independence of the central bank. If insignificant coefficients on deficit variables are interpreted as a sign of benign neglect, estimation results clearly support the hypothesis that Swiss monetary authorities act independently of the fiscal authorities for the time period after 1980.

However, these interpretations cannot directly be inferred. It can only be argued that the results are consistent with these interpretations. They could be consistent with other arguments, too. Depending on the assumed cyclical state of the economy and the assumed length of the monetary policy lag a negative sign on the coefficient of the cyclical deficit could also be consistent with political dependence (and vice versa). Or it could simply be the result of the central bank's own stabilization plan and have nothing to do with political dependence.

The chapter is organized as follows. Section 2.2 discusses the theoretical background of the linkage between fiscal and monetary policy. Section 2.3 reviews existing work on this relationship for Switzerland. Section 2.4 develops the money growth equation estimated in this chapter. Section 2.5 contains some comments on the fiscal data. Section 2.6 presents the estimation results. Section 2.7 offers some concluding remarks.

2.2 Budget Deficits and Money Growth

A central bank is not concerned with deficits per se, but with deficits as they affect macroeconomic variables that the central bank is trying to control. Since the central bank is the authority ultimately responsible for price stability, the potential impacts of deficits on *inflation* are of special interest.[1] Two possible links are usually discussed in the literature:[2]

Keynesians argue that budget deficits are inflationary because they stimulate *aggregate demand*. This theory suggests a linkage between the full-employment deficit[3] and inflation, but not between the actual deficit and inflation. Actual deficits can be high either because the full-employment deficit is high or because the economy is in a recession. In a recession the rate of capacity utilization is low so that deficit spending will affect quantities rather than prices. The inflation rate will not be high, even though the deficit will be high. The higher the rate of capacity utilization the more likely will increased deficit spending feed inflation.

Monetarists emphasize the relationship between *deficits, money growth, and inflation*. The central question is whether government deficits cause money growth. A government can finance its budget deficit by selling bonds to the central bank (printing money), or by selling bonds to the private sector (borrowing from the public).[4] Formally independent central banks are not required to pur-

---

1 For a more general discussion of the macroeconomic consequences of deficits with an explicit application to Switzerland see Buomberger/Schwab 1993 and Schwab 1994a 11-16. For international evidence on the macroeconomic effects of budget deficits see Karras 1994.

2 Following Parkin 1987 these might be called mechanical links and 'behavioral' links. „By mechanical links I mean the links between the deficit and the price level with unchanged settings of policy instruments. By 'behavioral' links I mean those links that arise as a result of actions taken by those who set policy instruments.“ Parkin 1987 317.

3 The full-employment or structural deficit measures the deficit that would prevail at some trend level of potential output. It removes the effects of the business cycle from the measured deficit. Perry 1987 762.

4 Another possibility of financing budget deficits is to run down foreign exchange reserves.

chase bonds from the government, so that a direct monetization[5] can be excluded. Borrowing from the public *can* lead to excessive money growth and cause inflation. This argument is generally based on the assumptions that (1) deficits tend to drive up nominal and real interest rates and that (2) the central bank takes efforts to smooth interest rates. (Hamburger/Zwick 1981 147; Levy 1981 351; Joines 1990 414) While the assumption that central banks try to avoid substantial interest rate escalation and variability is plausible,[6] the question whether deficits lead to higher interest rates is complex and remains controversial.

2.2.1 Deficits and Interest Rates

A positive relationship between *deficits and interest rates* seems a trivial application of supply and demand. (Dwyer 1985 656) As the deficit rises, the supply of government bonds increases and, ceteris paribus, the interest rate rises. However, budget deficits need not always place upward pressure on interest rates.

According to the *capital-inflow hypothesis* rising interest rates caused by budget deficits attract foreign capital and thereby attenuate any relationship between deficits and interest rates. (Dwyer 1985 674) This hypothesis may be especially plausible for small open economies. In the limiting case of an infinitely elastic demand for government securities a government deficit does not affect the interest rate. However, the capital inflow may ultimately lead to interest rate increases if the government seeks to maintain the exchange rate by selling domestic currency to meet foreign demand. This inflationary policy encourages a subsequent rise in the interest rate.

Ricardian equivalence[7] is another argument which weakens the link between budget deficits and interest rates. If individuals are indifferent between paying taxes in the present and paying taxes in the future the present generation will increase saving to cover the liability of a bond financed deficit.[8] If the increase in saving is approximately the same amount as the rise in the deficit, then aggregate demand does not change and interest rates are not affected.[9]

Interest rate effects also depend on the *cyclical state* of the economy. When the economy is contracting, the private sector demand for funds is falling, and deficit spending should cause negligible financial market pressure. Upward pres-

---

5 The government sells bonds to the central bank rather than to the private sector, thereby increasing the money supply.

6 However, for a criticism of this proposition see Niskanen 1978 597.
According to Cagan (1985 215) the Federal Reserve for instance conducted monetary policy with an interest-rate target in one form or another, except for a brief period from late 1979 to mid-1982.

7 A modern version of this theorem is presented by Barro 1974.

8 Therefore, the effects of budget deficits and taxation are the same, because both result in a reduction in consumption by the present generation.

9 For a criticism of the Ricardian equivalence theorem see for instance Buchanan 1976; Jordan 1993 93-100.

sure on interest rates is more likely when the economy is near full employment and when the private demand for funds is high.

Whether deficits lead to higher interest rates is an *empirical* question.[10] Evidence for some countries with high budget deficits suggests the existence of a positive relationship. (Münster 1994; Uhlig 1994) So far, there is no evidence that government deficits are associated with higher interest rates in Switzerland, except for Buomberger/Schwab (1993 11) and Schwab (1994a 15). These authors find a significant positive relationship between their measure of the structural component of the total deficit (i.e. the sum of federal, cantonal, and communal deficits) and the government bond yield.

Interest rate effects and aggregate demand effects are *not independent.* Rising interest rates will tend to induce crowding out of private investments. This reduces aggregate demand and thus lowers the upward pressure on prices. Hence, in the short run crowding out effects will operate in the other direction and thus help to dampen these price effects. But in the long run crowding out has negative effects on potential production and retards growth. (See e.g. Karras 1994 191.)

2.2.2 Deficits and Central Bank (In)Dependence

With a formally independent central bank any relationship between deficits, money growth and inflation is a result of decisions made by the monetary authority. It has the discretionary power to accommodate, not to accommodate, or even to offset the fiscal disturbance. In deciding whether to accommodate a deficit or not the central bank may face a *dilemma.* If it decides not to accommodate fiscal policy, interest rates *may* rise and thus crowd out private investment and consumption. If it decides to accommodate fiscal policy, it will buy government bonds to keep interest rates from rising, and a crowding out of private expenditures can be prevented (at least in the short run). By doing this, however, the central bank is in effect allowing the government to finance itself by printing money - the deficit is monetized. And if money growth is excessive it will lead to inflation.

The way the central bank 'solves' this dilemma is considered as being evidence on the *(in)dependence debate.* Monetization of the deficit may eventually increase aggregate demand. This will raise the real interest rate and induce crowding out. Monetizing the deficit ultimately fails to prevent crowding out. But it leads to inflation. A politically independent central bank that tries to control inflation should therefore not monetize the budget deficit. (Demopoulos et al. 1987 1023) It may even attempt to neutralize (offset) the fiscal expansion by tightening monetary policy. If a central bank is observed to monetize the deficit, it is concluded that it is yielding to political pressure to expand the money supply.[11] No-

[10] According to Dwyer (1985 656) the most noticeable omission in this area of research is any review of evidence concerning the relationship between deficits and interest rates.

[11] If central banks are targeting interest rates, they are „pressured into monetizing deficits to defend the interest rate targets; the resulting inflation is the 'price' they pay." Demopoulos et al. 1987 1025.

tice that it is the preoccupation with the stabilization of interest rates (i.e. the targeting of interest rates) that pressures the central bank into monetizing the deficit.

Political pressure on monetary policy may arise for various reasons. (See e.g. Tietmeyer 1993; Thieme 1993 174.) The effectiveness of fiscal policy measures often depends on the behavior of the monetary authority. Fiscal authorities will therefore pressure the central bank to 'coordinate' monetary policy with their own fiscal policy actions. Fiscal authorities can pressure the central bank to keep interest rates low in order to reduce the burden of interest payments (easy money policy). Rising interest rates, caused for instance by deficit financing, may attract foreign capital and lead to an appreciation of the exchange rates. This may induce political pressure to stabilize exchange rates. Or the central bank may simply be pressured to increase the money supply in order to raise revenue through its right to create money (seignorage).

Whether a formally independent central bank cedes to these political pressures is an *empirical* question. It is frequently argued that central banks owe their appearance of independence to the tacit cooperation with the goals of elected fiscal authorities. (Kane 1980; see also section 5.3.1.)

2.2.3 Cyclical and Structural Deficits

When testing the hypothesis whether a central bank monetizes the deficit the manner in which a deficit is generated may matter. Deficits can arise either through the automatic revenue losses and expenditure increases that occur when the economy is in a recession (cyclical deficits), or through legislated changes in spending and taxation (structural deficits). There are at least two reasons why this distinction between *cyclical and structural deficits* is important. (Grier/Neiman 1987 202; see also Laney/Willett 1983 57.)

First, inflationary effects of deficits - either as a result of the increase in aggregate demand or in the context of the money-growth relationship (accommodation by the central bank) - depend on the cyclical state of the economy. Since cyclical deficits occur when the economy is in a recession, they are unlikely to cause significant *upward pressure on interest rates* and inflation. However, structural deficits at or near full employment may generate financial market pressures. If a central bank is only concerned with stabilizing interest rates, it should respond to the structural deficit rather than to the cyclical deficit.

Second, the central bank may pursue a countercyclical monetary policy designed to *smooth out the business cycle.* If this is its only concern, then the cyclical deficit will be a significant determinant of monetary policy because of its high correlation with the business cycle. The structural deficit should have little or no impact in this case.

A central bank may respond to both financial market pressures and the business cycle. „But unless the response to interest rate pressures caused by structural deficits is somehow the same as the response to the business cycle as proxied by the cyclical deficit, it is not correct simply to use the measured deficit as an independent variable in a regression explaining money growth." (Grier/Neiman 1987 202) In any empirical investigation of the relationship between deficits and money growth in the framework of political dependence the actually measured deficit should be divided up into *cyclical and structural* components. This reduces the danger of spurious correlation which might result from corresponding cyclical variations in both monetary and fiscal policy. (Hamburger/Zwick 1981 146 Fn. 5; Laney/Willett 1983 57; Cagan 1985 215)

However, the *actual deficit* would seem to be the correct measure if *seignorage* is the explanation for the deficit-money link. (Grier/Neiman 1987 202) The (politically dependent) central bank deliberately increases money stock as a means of raising government revenue. (Klein/Neumann 1990; Lange 1995; Maennig/Hunger 1996)

There are regular attempts to increase the amount of central bank profits to be transferred to the fiscal authorities (Confederacy and cantons).[12] (See the discussion in section 5.4.2 and table 5.6.) The seignorage argument cannot be completely excluded for the SNB.[13] Hence, the relationship between the actual deficit and money growth is also investigated.

Still, the theoretical case for the seignorage argument may be rather weak in the case of the SNB. In addition, a recent study concludes that the SNB's management of the country's seignorage profits have been disappointing, suggesting that the central bank is not much interested in earning seignorage income on its assets. (See Ungern-Sternberg 1996a.) Therefore, the actually measured deficit is divided up into cyclical and structural components to find out whether any response of the central bank to the deficit may be due to the business cycle argument or to the market pressure argument.

2.2.4 Deficits and Central Bank (In)Dependence Revisited

Usually it is argued that an accommodating response of monetary policy to the *structural* component of the deficit is consistent with political dependence of the central bank, while an offsetting response to the structural deficit suggests political independence.

It could be argued that the coefficient on the *cyclical* component of the deficit also yields information on the political (in)dependence debate. Generally, the SNB is not held responsible for the trend in long-term interest rates (since these are rather determined on the international level). However, the SNB is regularly

12 See e.g. Nedwed 1992 233-237 and Ungern-Sternberg 1996b on the financial interests of the cantons.

13 Before 1990 the SNB delivered a rather symbolic amount to the government: 5.016 millions SFr annually between 1971 and 1980, 5.093 millions SFr annually between 1981 and 1990. Since 1991 an additional 600 millions SFr are handed over to the Confederacy and the cantons each year. Even this amount is rather modest. In Spring 1998 the SNB and the Federal Council agreed that the SNB shall deliver 1.5 billions SFr annually from 1999 to 2003. For a more detailed review (and criticism) of the SNB's policy towards central bank profits see Ungern-Sternberg 1996a and especially 1996b.

pressured to take an (more) active role in the business cycle, especially when the economy is in a recession.

If the cyclical deficit is a measure of the business cycle,[14] the reaction to the cyclical component of the deficit represents the central bank's response to the business cycle. A rise in the cyclical deficit (defined as expenditures minus revenues, so that the deficit is a positive number) means that the economy is moving into a recession. Hence, a positive sign on the cyclical deficit could suggest countercyclical monetary policy at first glance. However, it is well known that monetary policy works with long (and eventually also variable) lags. Accepting the proposition that this lag is two years for Switzerland and the business cycle is four years on average, this monetary policy is likely to work procyclically. Since the central bank is aware of this, it should not accommodate cyclical deficits. If it is, then it can be argued that it is yielding to political pressure. Hence, a positive sign on the cyclical component of the deficit suggests accommodating behavior and political dependence. A negative coefficient would be rather consistent with political independence.

It must be emphasized that this argument for the cyclical deficit critically depends on the underlying lag structure. This *caveat* applies whenever coefficients on the cyclical deficit variables are interpreted as evidence on the political (in)dependence of the central bank.

Of course, it can only be argued that an accommodating behavior of the central bank to the cyclical deficit is *consistent* with political dependence. But it could be consistent with other arguments as well. It could for instance be part of the central bank's own stabilization plan and have nothing to do with political dependence.

Insignificant coefficients on (actual, cyclical and structural) deficit variables also yield evidence on political independence of the central bank, if they are interpreted as a sign of benign neglect. A politically independent central bank authority may simply not care about fiscal deficits.

Table 2.1 summarizes this discussion about the relationship between different deficit measures and the type of evidence provided on the political (in)dependence debate.

---

14 In Switzerland taxes are filed every two years and paid on the basis of the average income earned in the past two years. This implies that the deficit reacts with a lag to the business cycle. Correlation analysis of the growth rates of gross domestic product, government revenues and expenditures does not yield a clear answer.
The cyclical deficit measures employed in this chapter try to account for this particularity of the Swiss tax system. But see the correlation analysis in section 2.5.

Table 2.1: Origin of the Deficit and Evidence on Political (In)Dependence

Deficit Measure[a]	Theoretical Argument	Political Independence	Political Dependence
actually measured deficit	seignorage	negative sign (offsetting) or insignificant (benign neglect)	positive sign (accommodation/ monetization)
structural component of deficit	financial market pressure	negative sign (offsetting) or insignificant (benign neglect)	positive sign (accommodation/ monetization)
cyclical component of deficit	business cycle argument	negative sign[b] or insignificant (benign neglect)	positive sign[b]

[a] defined as expenditures minus revenues, so that the deficit is a positive number
[b] critically dependent on underlying lag structure

2.3 Previous Studies on the Impact of Fiscal Policy Variables on Swiss Monetary Policy

Evidence on the effects of fiscal policy on monetary policy is most frequently reported in the context of reaction function studies. Two types of reaction function approaches can be distinguished in the literature. (See e.g. Landon/Reid 1990 382.)

Most studies estimate a central bank reaction function within a *single-equation framework.* Usually the change in the money supply is regressed against a set of explanatory variables that includes some measure of the government's budget position. (Examples are cited in Landon/Reid 1990 and Dwyer 1985.)

In some studies the central bank's reaction function is imbedded within a *system of equations* describing the macroeconomy, and the reduced form reaction function is derived from some optimizing model. (Examples are Levy 1981; Turnovsky/Wohar 1987; Landon/Reid 1990.)

As an alternative[15] to reaction function studies some authors employ *autoregressive* model specifications. The growth rate of the money supply is regressed on several lagged dependent variables, a constant, and the variable(s) measuring fiscal policy. (An example is Grier/Neiman 1987.)

Numerous *empirical* studies attempt to determine whether federal budget deficits lead to higher money growth in the US. The quantitative evidence remains mixed, however; a consensus does not exist. „In fact, recent empirical studies

15 As a third category Landon/Reid (1990 382) list causality studies examining the linkages between money growth and a variety of macro variables. Examples are Dwyer 1982 and McMillin 1986.

have found this connection to be either positive and significant or zero, and stable or unstable over time." (Grier/Neiman 1987 201; see also Burdekin/Wohar 1990 534; Joines 1990 413; Karras 1994 190.) For other central banks a smaller number of studies is available, but here too, results are mixed. (Demopoulos et al. 1987 1027)[16] The deficit money growth relationship estimated is sensitive to the specification of the regression equation, the periodicity of the data,[17] and the time period considered.[18] Studies differ considerably from one another in the type of equations, monetary aggregates (as dependent variables), deficit measures, and other control variables used. They also vary by choice of data periodicity and sample period. Therefore, it is not surprising that results also vary. (Grier/Neiman 1987 204) However, Dwyer (1985 677) sees the underlying problem with these conflicting estimates in the fact that there is little underlying theory to impose constraints on the estimates.

There is some quantitative evidence on the relationship between fiscal and monetary policy for *Switzerland,* too. Table 2.2 offers a summary of these papers.

Giannaris/Kolluri (1985) analyze the effects of budget deficits on money supply growth and inflation for ten industrialized countries including Switzerland over the period 1950-81. They specify and estimate a two-equation econometric model consisting of the money supply growth and inflation equations. The growth rate of the money stock M1 is assumed to depend on the growth rate of the expected money supply as predicted by lagged dependent variables and the lagged nominal budget deficit (national income account basis) as a percentage of nominal GNP. Estimation results using annual data reveal that the budget deficit is not a significant determinant of the money supply growth in Switzerland (the coefficient reported is 0.001134 with a t-value of 1.00). Alternative model specifications and the use of other fiscal variables (nominal government expenditures divided by the GNP deflator multiplied by trend real GNP lagged one year) produce similar results.

Also of interest in the present context are the results of their inflation equations. Assuming that inflation is a function of the current and the lagged money supply growth rates and the lagged budget deficit a significant (at the ten percent level) direct effect of the budget deficit on inflation is reported. And the estimated

---

16 More recent empirical evidence on Germany is provided by Lang/Welzel 1992. Using annual values for the period from 1962 to 1989 they find some accommodating behavior for the German Bundesbank.

17 As Joines (1990 413) points out evidence of monetization appears stronger in studies using quarterly data than in those using annual data. He cites two possible reasons. First, it is possible that quarterly data contain more information than annual data, resulting in an increased power to reject the null hypothesis of no relation between deficits and money growth. Second, the apparent relation between deficits and money growth in quarterly data is an artifact of seasonality that has not been adequately modeled. Joines 1990 414.

18 In general estimates are unstable over time. Dwyer 1985 677.

Table 2.2: Existing Studies on the Relationship between Deficits and Money Growth for Switzerland

Author(s)	Dependent Variable	Sample	Deficit Measure (Source)	Results
Giannaros/Kolluri (1985)	growth rate of the money supply M1	annual 1950-1981	lagged nominal deficit (revenues minus expenditures) in percent of nominal gross national product (IFS[a] Yearbook line 80)	positive (0.001134) and not significant (t = 1.00)
Parkin (1987)	percentage growth rate of base money	annual 1955-1983	lagged nominal deficit (revenues minus expenditures) in percent of nominal gross national product (IFS line 80)	positive (4.48) and significant (t = 2.34)
Burdekin/Wohar (1990)	growth rate of the monetary base	quarterly 1967.1-1985.4	lagged government budget surplus (IFS line 80) divided by gross domestic product and multiplied by -1	negative (-1.769) and not significant
Burdekin/Langdana (1992)	growth rate of the monetary base	quarterly 1966.2-1983.4	lagged government budget surplus (IFS line 80) divided by gross domestic product and multiplied by -1	negative and significant
		subsample 1966.2-1973.1		negative and significant
		subsample 1973.2-1983.4		negative and not significant
Karras (1994)	growth rate of the money supply M1	annual 1958-1989	contemporaneous federal deficit (expenditures minus revenues) as a percentage of gross domestic product (IFS line 80)	negative (-3.42) and not significant (t = -1.76)

[a] International Financial Statistics

coefficient (-0.000917 with a t-value of -1.66) has the expected negative sign, suggesting that the deficit contributes to a higher rate of inflation. However, this result is not confirmed in an alternative specification where inflation is regressed on lagged money supply growth rates, lagged inflation, and the lagged budget deficit.

Estimation results for *Parkin's* (1987) model of the money growth process for Switzerland indicate that the previous year's deficit has a significant positive influence on the current year's money supply growth rate.[19] (See the discussion in section 1.3.1.) Parkin comments on this that „it has to be recorded that the Swiss money supply growth process has this unique feature and a feature which would be expected to be associated not with an independent central bank such as that of Switzerland but with one that is heavily dominated by the government and encouraged to accommodate past deficits.“ (Parkin 1987 325) However, a closer look at his data appendix suggests that the deficit is defined as the difference between revenues and expenditures (so that the deficit is a negative number). With this definition a positive coefficient is not consistent with accommodating policy. It rather indicates offsetting behavior and independence.[20]

Burdekin/Wohar (1990) estimate monetary growth, budget deficit and inflation equations jointly as a three-equation system for eight countries, including Switzerland. Using quarterly data for the period of 1967.1 to 1985.4 they find a negative response of the monetary base growth to budget deficits for Switzerland. Their coefficient reported for the sum of all lags included is -1.769, but it fails to be significant. Since their deficit measure is the domestic government budget surplus divided by gross domestic product and multiplied by minus one, a negative coefficient suggests offsetting behavior. Combined with findings obtained by Burdekin (1987) for Switzerland, and Demopoulos et al. (1987) for West Germany they conclude that „it does seem very difficult to argue that deficit accommodation is a feature of the two countries with the most fully autonomous central banks. (Rather the relationship, if anything, appears to be negative in these two cases.)“ (Burdekin/Wohar 1990 545 Fn. 14)[21]

Again of interest are the results of their inflation equations. In these equations the inflation rate is regressed on the deficit and a series of other variables. „In Japan, Switzerland and the United Kingdom budget deficits actually appear to be deflationary - leaving perhaps relatively little support for taking deficits to be an important independent cause of inflation across the present sample of countries.“ (Burdekin/Wohar 1990 546)

---

19 „If, however, the other two variables - the lagged money supply growth rate and the cycle are excluded from the equation, the coefficient .. drops in value and becomes insignificant at the 5 percent level.“ Parkin 1987 325.

20 Unfortunately, I was unable to contact Parkin to clarify this point.

21 Because of the number of right-hand-side variables no separate estimation is made for fixed and floating exchange rate regimes. The potential effects of changes in the exchange rate regime are controlled with exchange rate regime dummies. Burdekin/ Wohar 1990 538.

In their reaction function study of Swiss monetary policy *Burdekin/Langdana* (1992) find a strongly negative response of the growth rate of the monetary base to the deficit implying an offsetting monetary policy. (See the discussion in section 1.3.1.) Allowing for a possible structural break corresponding with the adoption of floating exchange rates in January 1973, two separate reaction functions were reestimated over the fixed exchange rate (1966.2 to 1973.1) and floating exchange rate (1973.2 to 1983.4) subsamples. While the deficit is significant at the 10 percent level or higher in the fixed exchange rate subsample, it fails to be significant in the floating exchange rate subsample. Overall, the offsetting response to fiscal policy is interpreted as evidence supporting the hypothesis of formal independence of the SNB.

Karras (1994) investigates macroeconomic effects of budget deficits on money growth, inflation, investment and real output growth for 32 countries including Switzerland. To test for effects on money growth he regresses the growth rate of the money supply M1 on a constant, a lagged dependent variable, the contemporaneous federal deficit (measured as the difference between government expenditures and revenues and expressed as percentage of gross domestic product), and the real growth rate of gross domestic product lagged one period. Using annual values for the time period from 1958 to 1989 he finds a negative coefficient for the deficit variable (-3.42) which fails to be significant at the 5 percent level ($t = -1.76$) for Switzerland. But his equation explains only a small part of the total variation in the dependent variable, suggesting a poor specification. (The R^2 is 0.14.) Still, the negative sign suggests offsetting behavior. Among the 32 countries, Japan is the only country where a negative and statistically significant relationship between deficits and money growth is found. Since the sample includes both fixed- and flexible-exchange rate regimes a binary variable equal to 0 (1) before (since) 1973 is used interactively with the slope coefficients to allow for potentially different effects. The results are generally unaffected by this modification.

Adopting the same definition for the deficit variable - and accepting the qualifications offered for Parkin's study - there exists a *consensus* in that all authors find a negative (though in most cases insignificant) response of the money growth rate to the deficit. Still, there remains the question what the negative sign could imply. Does it suggest that the SNB is really trying to offset potentially harmful effects generated by the deficit? Or does it rather reflect a response of monetary policy to the business cycle? These questions are addressed in this chapter by distinguishing between structural and cyclical components of the deficit. The sample only extends over the period of flexible exchange rates, but it includes data until 1995.2. The structural stability of the coefficient estimates is tested. The significance of different fiscal measures is tested while controlling for various other variables. Different versions of money growth equations are employed.

2.4 The Money Growth Equations

To test for the impact of fiscal deficits on Swiss money growth the reaction function developed in chapter 1 is *extended* to fiscal variables DEF.[22] The stance of monetary policy is proxied by two monetary aggregates, the unadjusted monetary base MB and the money supply M1. (See the discussion in section 1.3.2a.) The regression equation for the monetary base as dependent variable with all economic variables expressed as nonseasonal differences is

$$\begin{aligned}\Delta\ln(MB)_t &= \beta_0 + \beta_1\Delta\ln(MB)_{t-2} + \beta_2\Delta\ln(CPI)_{t-1} + \beta_3\Delta\ln(DMN)_{t-1} \\ &+ \beta_4\Delta\ln(GDP)_{t-1} + \beta_5\Delta DR_{t-1} + \beta_6 SD1_t + \beta_7 SD2_t + \beta_8 SD3_t \\ &+ \beta_9 DEF_{t-1} + \beta_{10} DEF_{t-2} + \beta_{11} DEF_{t-3} + \beta_{12} DEF_{t-4} + \varepsilon_t\end{aligned}$$

(For dependent variables and the other control variables used as regressors refer to table 1.2. See table 2.3 for a complete list of all fiscal variables reported in this chapter, as well as their definitions and sources.)

The monetary base is preferred as dependent variable for at least two reasons. First, it is considered to be under direct control of the monetary authority. A control of the money supply M1, however, can be complicated by the possibility of an endogenous money multiplier. Second, whether the central bank targets M1, interest rates, or an exchange rate, the control of these variables is achieved through policy operations that affect the monetary base as well. So even for the time period before 1980 policy actions will be measured by changes in the monetary base, although the SNB was not explicitly targeting the monetary base. But for comparison, equations with the growth rates of both the unadjusted[23] monetary base and the money supply M1 as dependent variables are estimated.[24]

A central bank probably responds to a wide variety of interacting objectives, and it considers those objectives within the context of a structural model of the economy. (Levy 1981 352) Here the central bank is assumed to respond to inflation, exchange rates, production, interest rates, and - for the reasons discussed in section 2.2 - it is also alleged to respond to deficits.

---

22 Here we choose the single-equation approach. The formulation of a theoretical model is beyond the scope of this chapter. This has been extensively done elsewhere. See Dwyer 1985; Protopapadakis/Siegel 1987; De Haan/Zelhorst 1990. For an explicit model see Niskanen 1978.

23 The use of the unadjusted monetary base helps to avoid data limitations caused by changes in definition and adjustment procedures of this monetary aggregate. (See section 1.3.2a.) Moreover, „using a monetary base data series not seasonally adjusted, complemented by quarterly seasonal dummy variables, avoids estimating biases that may occur with seasonally adjusted data." Levy 1981 362. See also section 1.4.

24 „In this view the money supply is endogenous, not because it cannot be controlled to a reasonable approximation, but because the authorities have incentives to respond to various pressures in the economy such as wage push or central government deficit finance." Laney/Willett 1983 53.

Table 2.3: Fiscal Variable Definitions and Data Sources

Variable	Definition	Source
	deficit variables DEF[a]	
FDEF	federal deficit, quarterly series with seasonal pattern, including extrabudgetary transactions (mainly the railways and postal communications system)	IFS[b] line 80
FDEFE	federal deficit, as reported annually in Compte d'Etat	EFV[c]
FDEFC	federal deficit, cyclical component	BFK[d]
FDEFS	federal deficit, structural component	BFK
SETOT	total deficit (federal, cantonal, communal) including social security	BFK
SATOT	total deficit (federal, cantonal, communal) including social security, cyclical component	BFK
SSTOT	total deficit (federal, cantonal, communal) including social security, structural component	BFK
TDEF	total deficit (federal, cantonal, communal)	UBS[e]
TDEFC	total deficit (federal, cantonal, communal), cyclical component	UBS
TDEFS	total deficit (federal, cantonal, communal), structural component	UBS
	debt variable	
FDBT	gross federal debt (first differences of natural logarithms)	EFV

[a] All deficit variables are defined as the difference between expenditures and revenues. All are divided by nominal trend gross domestic product.
[b] International Financial Statistics
[c] Eidgenössische Finanzverwaltung
[d] Bundesamt für Konjunkturfragen (Y. Amman)
[e] Union Bank of Switzerland (B. Schwab)

Since the focus here is on political (in)dependence of the central bank, fiscal deficits at the federal level appear to be the appropriate measures. However, cantons too might pressure the central bank to monetize deficits. Therefore, measures of the total deficit (the sum of federal, cantonal and communal deficits) with and without social security are also used.

In all regressions the budget deficit is *defined* as the difference between government expenditures and revenues,[25] so that a deficit is a positive number. This definition makes it more convenient to discuss the estimation results for the defi-

25 Despite some well-founded and constructive criticism of these conventional deficit measures (see e.g. Jordan 1994), this standard definition remains the one most frequently used, also because of data availability. Karras 1994 208 Fn. 2.

cit. (See e.g. Dwyer 1985 669 Fn. 19.) Following common practice the deficit measures are expressed as a proportion of the trend component of nominal gross domestic product. Since the money growth is a function of the relative budget deficit, a correlation between money growth and the deficit-GDP ratio might result from the division by the GDP measure. The trend component is preferred to other GDP measures because it adds less variation to the deficit measure.

The actually measured deficit is divided up into a cyclical and a structural component. Significance of the *structural* component can be interpreted as evidence on the (in)dependence debate. (Refer to the overview in table 2.1.) A politically independent central bank that is preoccupied with price stability will try to offset any inflationary effects of fiscal deficits. Therefore, a negative sign for the coefficient of the structural deficit is hypothesized. A significant positive coefficient would indicate monetization and suggest political dependence, however.[26]

Significance of the *cyclical* component suggests (positive or negative) correlation of monetary policy with the business cycle. Following the argument offered in section 2.2 - while being aware of the critical role of the underlying lag structure - a negative correlation implies offsetting behavior that suggests political independence. A positive correlation implies accommodating behavior and can be interpreted as a sign of political dependence.

A politically independent central bank may simply not care about fiscal deficits. *Insignificant* coefficients on (actual, cyclical and structural) deficit variables may be interpreted as a result of this benign neglect.

However, predictions of signs for coefficients estimated from a single-equation reaction function have to be interpreted with care. (See section 1.2.) Coefficient estimates combine information on policymakers' preferences along with parameters of the reduced-form equations that describe the economy. Inferences about policymakers' preferences could only be derived if the central bank's objective function and its structural model of the economy were identified. A significant coefficient on a deficit variable means that this variable helps to explain money growth. But no unique meaning can be ascribed to it. Therefore, it can only be argued that the sign is *consistent* with political (in)dependence, thus emphasizing the fact that it can be consistent with other arguments that are not even related to political (in)dependence.

While all other regressors are simply lagged one quarter, the deficit variables enter with *four lags*. Adding more lags for the deficit variables does not change the estimation results. A contemporaneous measure of the deficit is not included because of a possible simultaneity bias. Including only one lag (the one that performs best) may not be appropriate, because the central bank may distribute its response to the fiscal stimulus over a longer time period.

---

26 If the central bank „decides to monetize all or some portion of the fiscal authority's deficit, then the growth of nominal high-powered money would be, at least partially, determined by the growth of nominal government debt and the deficit variable would have a significant positive impact on monetary expansion." Landon/Reid 1990 383.

Lagged dependent variables are also included to pick up elements of serial dependence and effects from omitted variables. (See section 1.3.2b.) They are dropped if they are not found to be significant in both the regressions with and without the fiscal variables.

Models with quarterly rates of change are estimated. Hence, all equations include a set of dummy variables (SD1, SD2, SD3) to capture seasonal variation.

Money growth is also regressed on the growth rate of the gross federal debt.[27] (See e.g. Landon/Reid 1990 388.) Here, the question of cyclical versus structural component cannot be addressed.

2.5 The Fiscal Data

In an empirical investigation of the relationship between deficits and money growth there are at least three reasons why the data might produce the *appearance* of a positive correlation between the two series. None of them implies monetization of the deficit. When testing the hypothesis whether the central bank monetizes the deficit allowance must be made for these features of the data.

First, both series might simply *reflect the business cycle* and may in fact not be directly related. This problem can be addressed by splitting the actual deficit in its cyclical and structural components and - since the structural component is not correlated with the business cycle - testing for the significance of the structural component. Data on the cyclically adjusted deficit for Switzerland are available only since recently. Series for the federal government and total government including social security ('general government') are provided by the Swiss Bundesamt für Konjunkturfragen.[28] The structural component does not exactly correspond to the definition of the full-employment deficit (which is usually used in studies for the Federal Reserve), since it is not calculated on the basis of potential gross domestic product, but on the basis of the trend growth of gross domestic product. The cyclical component which measures the changes in the deficit caused by the business cycle accounts for particularities of the Swiss tax system, too. Series for the total of federal, cantonal and communal deficits without social security are provided by Schwab (1993, 1994b).

Second, spurious correlation between deficits and money growth may arise because of a *common upward trend* in both series over the sample period. But this rise in monetary growth does not necessarily reflect a decision to monetize the increasing deficits either. There are other plausible interpretations. (Joines 1990 429; Cagan 1985 215) One possibility is that of reversed causality: The fiscal authority increases nominal budget deficits in response to higher rates of money growth and inflation, e.g. because it seeks to keep the real value of the public debt

---

27 Calculating the first difference of gross federal debt and comparing it with the federal deficit shows that these series are very different.

28 See Amman 1995.

from being affected by inflation. Another possibility is that the upward drift in the two series occurred for totally unrelated reasons.[29] The inclusion of a time trend in a regression of the money growth rate on the deficit reduces this tendency of spurious results. But as Nelson/Kang (1984) showed it does not eliminate the problem.

Spurious estimation can be avoided if the series are *stationary*. Augmented Dickey-Fuller tests (not reported) indicate that some deficit series are not stationary. (See section 1.4.3 on the stationarity of the money growth rates and the other control variables used as regressors.) Since regressions with first differences of the fiscal variables are difficult to interpret, all fiscal variables (except for the debt variable) enter the equations as ratios (i.e. deficit divided by GDP).[30]

Third, an apparent positive relationship between deficits and money growth in quarterly data[31] could be an *artifact of seasonality* in the two series. (See Joines 1990 on this.) Similarity of the two seasonal patterns could result in high correlation of the deficit and money growth even if these patterns arise for completely different reasons. Moreover, a seasonal pattern in money growth that is entirely due to accommodation of seasonal variation in the deficit need not imply that monetization of the deficit is an important economic phenomenon, since the seasonal variation in the two series can be purely transitory and sum to zero over the course of a year.[32] Including seasonal dummy variables in the regression of money growth on the deficit will not adequately remove the seasonal correlation if the seasonal patterns in the two series shift over time.[33] To remove all correlation due to seasonality, the seasonal patterns in deficits and money growth would have to be modeled explicitly.[34] The quarterly series on Swiss federal deficits provided by IFS and the growth rates of the unadjusted monetary base both exhibit seasonal patterns, so that seasonality could indeed cause spurious correlation between deficits and monetary base growth. The problem is indirectly addressed in this chapter by using deficit variables with and without a seasonal pattern, and by allowing seasonal patterns to shift over time.

---

29 The tendency for two independent, integrated time series to appear related has been pointed out by Granger/Newbold 1974.
As Joines (1990 436) reports, Monte Carlo simulation results indicate that, given the time-series properties of the two variables, an apparent relation as strong as that found in his paper could easily result by chance even if the two series were independent.

30 Lang/Welzel (1992 75) and Beck (1987) use first differences for the deficit variables.

31 This problem obviously does not affect studies using annual data.

32 For this reason the deficit variables enter the regression with several lags.

33 „There are two very general reasons why the seasonal pattern of an economic time series may change. First, the seasonal pattern of one or more components of the series may change. Second, the components of a series may have different seasonal patterns (each of which may remain constant over time) and the shares of these components in the total may change." Joines 1990 420.

34 Joines (1990 422) models several components of the deficit separately, decomposing each into a seasonal factor and a nonseasonal portion. The seasonal factors and the nonseasonal portion of the deficit enter the money growth equations separately.

One objective of this chapter is to test for structural breaks in the deficit money growth relationship. Since the ability to test for structural stability of a model is limited by the use of annual data (Allen/Smith 1983 606), *quarterly* data are used.[35] Except for the series provided by IFS, all deficit variables are available on an annual basis only. Quarterly estimates are interpolated from these annual series using three conversion methods, cubic spline interpolation (by fitting a cubic spline curve to the annual series), linear interpolation (producing a linear spline), and discontinuous piecewise constant curve fitting (resulting in a step function). Experimenting with all three conversion methods yields very similar results, so that it is decided to limit the analysis to cubic splines (though in some cases a step function or a linear spline performs better than the cubic spline).

Table 2.4 reports *summary statistics* for all quarterly fiscal variables.[36]

Table 2.4: Summary Statistics for Fiscal Variables

Variable	N	Mean	Std. Dev.	Minimum	Maximum
FDEF	88	0.00581	0.02101	-0.03183	0.06592
FDEFE	89	0.00497	0.00718	-0.00977	0.02519
FDEFC	89	0.00038	0.00375	-0.00790	0.01297
FDEFS	89	0.00460	0.00636	-0.00906	0.01511
TDEF	89	0.01123	0.01443	-0.01280	0.04877
TDEFC	89	-0.0019	0.00506	-0.00947	0.01018
TDEFS	89	0.01313	0.01456	-0.00699	0.04784
SETOT	89	0.00673	0.01529	-0.01775	0.03996
SATOT	89	0.00035	0.00751	-0.01744	0.01982
SSTOT	89	0.00638	0.01624	-0.02139	0.04474
FDBT	89	0.01973	0.01899	-0.00895	0.06130

For variable definitions see table 2.3.

Table 2.5 contains the correlation coefficients for all regressor variables used in this chapter. Since *correlation analysis* is the equivalent to a bivariate regression with the intercept set equal to zero correlation coefficients provide rather limited information. Nevertheless, they can be used as benchmarks for the strength of the *linear* relationship between a pair of variables.

The federal deficit measure FDEFE is positively correlated with all other fiscal variables. All three cyclical measures (FDEFC, TDEFC, SATOT) are positively correlated with each other. High correlation is also measured among the three structural components (FDEFS, TDEFS, SSTOT). Cyclical and structural meas-

---

35 There exist other arguments for using quarterly instead of annual data. Annual data for instance do not capture short-run variations in monetary and fiscal policy and in economic conditions. Annual data can make it more difficult to ascribe one-way causality to the estimated coefficients. See section 1.3.2e.

36 Numbers for 1995 are based on estimates as they were available at the end of November 1995.

ures are not correlated with each other, except for TDEFC and TDEFS, as well as for SATOT and SSTOT. The federal debt variable FDBT is positively correlated with all deficit variables except for the cyclical component of the federal deficit FDEFC and the cyclical component of the total deficit including social security SATOT. The deposit rate DR and GDP are always negatively correlated with total deficits TDEF and SETOT, with the structural components of total deficits TDEFS and SSTOT, and with the federal debt variable FDBT. All three cyclical deficit measures (FDEFC, TDEFC and SATOT) are negatively correlated with the consumer price index CPI. But they show no correlation with the other control variables, especially with GDP. This raises some doubts about these cyclical deficit measures. The growth rate of GDP should be used as an indicator of the business cycle, while the CPI can (at best) be considered as a lagging indicator of the business cycle. The lack of correlation with the GDP measure can be explained with the lag caused by the fact that taxes are filed every two years and paid on the basis of the average income earned in the past two years. This means that the cyclical measures do not successfully account for this particularity of the Swiss tax system. The negative correlation with the CPI is difficult to interpret.

Figure 2.1 presents a plot of two *federal deficit* series, the annual deficit provided by IFS (FDEF) and the annual deficit as reported in the Compte d'Etat (FDEFE). The difference in these two annual series arises from the fact that the IFS data include extrabudgetary transactions, mainly the railways and postal communications system. The Pearson correlation coefficient between these two annual series is 0.90. (The corresponding correlation coefficient for the quarterly measures in table 2.5 is only 0.35, because the two quarterly measures exhibit very different seasonal patterns.) As can be seen the federal deficit decreases during the second half of the seventies (with the exception of 1979) and is small during the first half of the eighties. A period of budget surpluses between 1986 and 1990 is followed by a dramatic rise in the size of the federal deficit after 1990.

Figure 2.2 shows that the *total deficit* with (SETOT) and without social security (TDEF) follows a very similar pattern. The Pearson correlation coefficient between the annual series of the federal deficit FDEFE and SETOT (TDEF) is 0.92 (0.89). This coefficient is 0.98 between SETOT and TDEF.

Figures 2.1 and 2.2 help to interpret the regression results. In both figures the annual deficit is defined as revenues minus expenditures, so that the deficit is a negative number.

Table 2.5: Correlation Matrix for Regressor Variables (Quarterly Measures)

	FDEF	FDEFE	FDEFC	FDEFS	TDEF	TDEFC	TDEFS	SETOT	SATOT	SSTOT	FDBT	CPI	DMN	DR
FDEFE	0.348													
	(0.001)													
FDEFC	0.176	0.468												
	(0.101)	(0.001)												
FDEFS	0.289	0.853	-0.062											
	(0.006)	(0.001)	(0.567)											
TDEF	0.304	0.832	0.216	0.812										
	(0.004)	(0.001)	(0.042)	(0.001)										
TDEFC	0.122	0.420	0.332	0.278	0.149									
	(0.259)	(0.001)	(0.002)	(0.008)	(0.164)									
TDEFS	0.259	0.678	0.099	0.708	0.939	-0.200								
	(0.015)	(0.001)	(0.356)	(0.001)	(0.001)	(0.060)								
SETOT	0.306	0.864	0.233	0.839	0.973	0.227	0.885							
	(0.004)	(0.001)	(0.028)	(0.001)	(0.001)	(0.033)	(0.001)							
SATOT	0.074	0.358	0.848	-0.096	0.049	0.553	-0.144	0.114						
	(0.494)	(0.001)	(0.001)	(0.369)	(0.649)	(0.001)	(0.179)	(0.286)						
SSTOT	0.252	0.648	-0.173	0.834	0.893	-0.043	0.900	0.888	-0.355					
	(0.018)	(0.001)	(0.105)	(0.001)	(0.001)	(0.691)	(0.001)	(0.001)	(0.001)					
FDBT	0.193	0.718	0.051	0.782	0.766	0.192	0.692	0.793	0.031	0.732				
	(0.072)	(0.001)	(0.637)	(0.001)	(0.001)	(0.070)	(0.001)	(0.001)	(0.773)	(0.001)				
CPI	0.162	-0.011	-0.278	0.152	0.092	-0.297	0.195	-0.002	-0.506	0.232	-0.023			
	(0.131)	(0.918)	(0.008)	(0.155)	(0.391)	(0.005)	(0.068)	(0.983)	(0.001)	(0.029)	(0.828)			
DMN	-0.041	0.057	0.074	0.021	0.012	0.143	-0.038	0.019	0.062	-0.010	0.123	-0.132		
	(0.703)	(0.596)	(0.489)	(0.848)	(0.912)	(0.180)	(0.723)	(0.857)	(0.566)	(0.924)	(0.251)	(0.219)		
DR	0.112	-0.118	-0.102	-0.073	-0.202	0.079	-0.227	-0.237	-0.090	-0.181	-0.283	0.082	-0.120	
	(0.297)	(0.271)	(0.343)	(0.497)	(0.058)	(0.464)	(0.032)	(0.026)	(0.402)	(0.090)	(0.007)	(0.446)	(0.261)	
GDP	0.020	-0.127	-0.003	-0.141	-0.197	0.115	-0.235	-0.205	0.132	-0.254	-0.237	-0.200	-0.233	0.316
	(0.850)	(0.236)	(0.976)	(0.187)	(0.064)	(0.283)	(0.026)	(0.054)	(0.218)	(0.016)	(0.025)	(0.061)	(0.028)	(0.003)

For variable definitions see tables 1.2 and 2.3. Numbers in parentheses are p values (significance probability of the correlation under the null hypothesis that the statistic is zero).

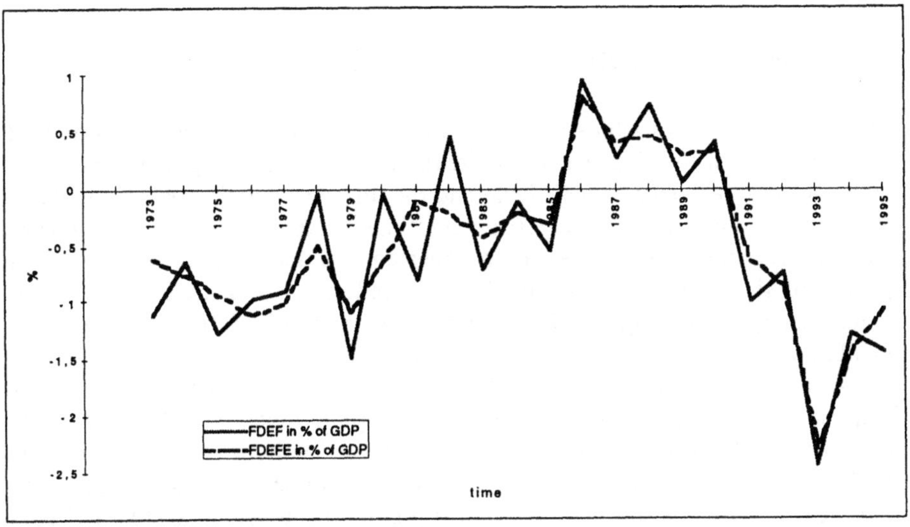

Fig. 2.1: Federal Deficit in Percent of GDP
Source: See table 2.3.

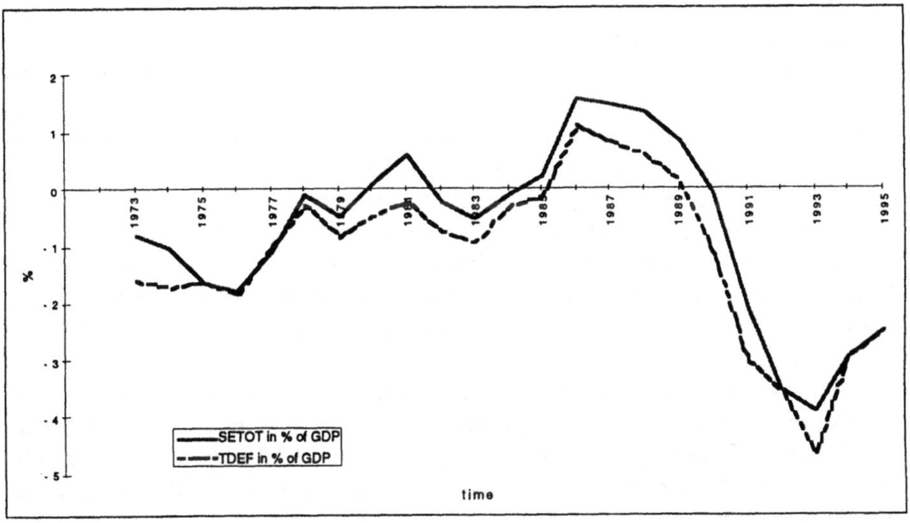

Fig. 2.2: Total Deficit with (SETOT) and without (TDEF) Social Security
Source: See table 2.3.

2.6 Estimation Results

The various fiscal variables are added to the equations 1.3 (table 1.9) and 1.6 (table 1.12) with four lags each.[37] Regression results with the growth rate of the monetary base as dependent variable and the different deficit variables included are reported in tables 2.7 to 2.9. (The coefficient estimates for the other control variables reported in table 1.9 are not repeated in order to preserve space. Their pattern of significance remains unaffected. And the size of the coefficient estimates changes only slightly.) FDEF (table 2.7) is the IFS deficit variable which exhibits a distinct seasonal pattern (and which includes extrabudgetary transactions). FDEFE is the actually measured federal deficit, as it is reported in the Compte d'Etat. It is interpolated from a cubic spline function. TDEF is the total deficit for federal, cantonal and communal levels without social security, and SETOT is the total deficit including social security. In table 2.8 the actually measured federal deficit is split into its cyclical (FDEFC) and structural (FDEFS) components. Table 2.9 reports regression results with the total deficits (with and without social security) split into cyclical and structural components, too.

The different deficit measures are used not only to check the generality of the results, but to *test several hypotheses*. For all equations the null hypotheses presented in table 2.6 are tested.

All equations are first estimated with the fiscal variables constrained to be homogeneous. Then the fiscal coefficients are also allowed to change across the two subperiods that were identified in chapter 1. (See section 1.5.1c). In both cases, the estimated sum of the coefficients of the lagged deficit variables is reported, along with the corresponding F statistic (and the associated p value) which tests whether this sum is equal to zero for the time period considered (H1, H3, H4).

Several tests serve to find out whether all coefficients of the lagged deficit variables are equal to zero (H_0), or whether at least one of them is significantly different from zero (H_a). H2 (H5) covers the whole sample period from 1973.2 to 1995.2 for the equation with homogeneous (heterogeneous) coefficients. H6 and H7 apply to the two subperiods for the equations with heterogeneous coefficients.

For the equations with heterogeneous coefficients it is also tested whether the coefficients of the lagged deficit variables are equal for the two subperiods (H_0: homogeneity of the coefficient estimates) or whether they are different (H_a: heterogeneity) (H8).

For all equations where the deficit variable is split into its cyclical and structural components three additional null hypotheses are tested: The coefficients for the cyclical and structural components of the deficit variables are equal for the

[37] A reaction function that includes fiscal variables only could also be estimated. This would imply that all of the growth rate of the monetary aggregate is either related to the deficit or is due to the error term. „While this is possible, such a simple specification does not seem particularly plausible." Dwyer 1985 670.

whole sample period (H9), for the subperiod from 1973.2 to 1979.4 (H10), and for the subperiod from 1980.1 to 1995.2 (H11).

Test results for the *monetary base* as dependent variable (tables 2.7 to 2.9 and second column of table 2.10) can be summarized as follows:

For the equations with fiscal coefficients constrained to be *homogeneous*, significant coefficients can only be found for the cyclical and structural components of the total deficit SATOT and SSTOT including social security (H2 in table 2.9). The sum of the coefficients is significant only for the cyclical component SATOT (H1 in table 2.9). Accepting the interpretation (and the caveat) proposed in section 2.2 the negative sign is consistent with the hypothesis of political independence of the SNB.

Results differ for the regressions with *heterogeneous* coefficients. For *actually measured* deficits (table 2.7) the F tests for H5 to H7 show that at least one significant coefficient can be found for all variables in the period before 1980, and that no significant coefficients can be identified for the period after 1980. Accordingly, the entries under H8 confirm heterogeneity of the coefficients. For the period before 1980, the sum of the coefficients is significant for the two measures of total deficits TDEF and SETOT (H3). The positive signs suggest accommodating behavior. This is consistent with the hypothesis of political dependence of the SNB. For the two federal deficit measures FDEF and FDEFE the sum of the coefficients fails to be significant, suggesting a transitory response by the central bank.

Table 2.6: Overview of Hypotheses Tested for Fiscal Variables

Hypothesis (Number and Abbreviation)	Explanation
	Fiscal Coefficients Homogeneous
H1 sum lag 1-4	$\beta_9 + \beta_{10} + \beta_{11} + \beta_{12}$ Sum of the coefficients of the lagged deficit variables
sum=0	$H_0 : \beta_9 + \beta_{10} + \beta_{11} + \beta_{12} = 0$ The sum of the coefficients of the lagged deficit variables for the period from 1973.2 to 1995.2 is equal to zero.
H2 all=0	$H_0 : \beta_9 = \beta_{10} = \beta_{11} = \beta_{12} = 0$ All coefficients of the lagged deficit variables for the time period from 1973.2 to 1995.2 are equal to zero.
	H1 and H2: The tests for fiscal variables split in cyclical and structural components are analogous. The cyclical and structural components are tested separately.

Table 2.6 continued

Hypothesis (Number and Abbreviation)	Explanation
	Fiscal Coefficients Heterogeneous
H3	
sum 70 lag 1-4	$\beta_{9;70}+\beta_{10;70}+\beta_{11;70}+\beta_{12;70}$ Sum of the coefficients of the lagged deficit variables for the subperiod from 1973.2 to 1979.4 (70)
sum 70=0	$H_0:\beta_{9;70}+\beta_{10;70}+\beta_{11;70}+\beta_{12;70}=0$ The sum of the coefficients of the lagged deficit variables for the subperiod from 1973.2 to 1979.4 (70) is equal to zero.
H4 sum 80 lag 1-4 sum 80=0	See H3 (with 70 replaced by 80): The sum of the coefficients of the lagged deficit variables for the subperiod from 1980.1 to 1995.2 (80) is equal to zero.
H5 all=0	See H2: All coefficients of the lagged deficit variables for the time period from 1973.2 to 1979.4 and from 1980.1 to 1995.2 are equal to zero.
H6 all 70=0	$H_0:\beta_{9;70}=\beta_{10;70}=\beta_{11;70}=\beta_{12;70}=0$ All coefficients of the lagged deficit variables for the subperiod from 1973.2 to 1979.4 (70) are equal to zero.
H7 all 80=0	See H6 (with 70 replaced by 80): All coefficients of the lagged deficit variables for the subperiod from 1980.1 to 1995.2 (80) are equal to zero.
H8 70=80	$H_0:\beta_{9;70}=\beta_{9;80},\beta_{10;70}=\beta_{10;80},\beta_{11;70}=\beta_{11;80},\beta_{12;70}=\beta_{12;80}$ The coefficients of the lagged deficit variables are equal for the two subperiods (homogeneity of the coefficient estimates).
	H3 to H8: The tests for fiscal variables split in cyclical and structural components are analogous. The cyclical and structural components are tested separately.
	H9 to H11: The tests for fiscal variables split in cyclical and structural components are analogous to H8. The cyclical and structural components are compared.
H9 c=s all	The coefficients for the cyclical and structural components of the deficit variables are equal for the whole sample period.
H10 c=s 70	The coefficients for the cyclical and structural components of the deficit variables are equal for the subperiod from 1973.2 to 1979.4.
H11 c=s 80	The coefficients for the cyclical and structural components of the deficit variables are equal for the subperiod from 1980.1 to 1995.2.

F tests are reported with degrees of freedom in parentheses () and p values in brackets []. The number 70 (80) after the semicolon denotes the coefficient before 1979.4 (after 1980.1).

Table 2.7: Actually Measured Deficits and Monetary Base Growth $\Delta \ln(MB)$

Hypothesis	Fiscal Variables FDEF	FDEFE	TDEF	SETOT
	Fiscal Coefficients Homogeneous			
H1 Sum lag 1-4 sum=0	0.135 F(1,72)=0.13 [0.7184]	0.449 F(1,72)=0.94 [0.3350]	0.160 F(1,72)=0.54 [0.4644]	0.287 F(1,72)=1.83 [0.1806]
H2 all=0	F(4,72)=1.01 [0.4087]	F(4,72)=0.61 [0.6596]	F(4,72)=0.50 [0.7355]	F(4,72)=1.52 [0.2061]
	Fiscal Coefficients Heterogeneous			
H3 Sum 70 lag 1-4 sum 70=0	-1.092 F(1,68)=1.65 [0.2037]	1.600 F(1,68)=2.56 [0.1139]	1.673** F(1,68)=6.50 [0.0131]	2.095*** F(1,68)=8.68 [0.0044]
H4 Sum 80 lag 1-4 sum 80=0	0.113 F(1,68)=0.09 [0.7643]	0.352 F(1,68)=0.59 [0.4457]	0.067 F(1,68)=0.10 [0.7486]	0.163 F(1,68)=0.65 [0.4237]
H5 all=0	F(8,68)=2.68** [0.0128]	F(8,68)=1.78* [0.0962]	F(8,68)=1.91* [0.0727]	F(8,68)=2.70** [0.0121]
H6 all 70=0	F(4,68)=3.32** [0.0152]	F(4,68)=3.17** [0.0189]	F(4,68)=3.54** [0.0111]	F(4,68)=4.85*** [0.0017]
H7 all 80=0	F(4,68)=0.79 [0.5328]	F(4,68)=0.37 [0.8270]	F(4,68)=0.30 [0.8738]	F(4,68)=0.66 [0.6254]
H8 70=80	F(4,68)=4.17*** [0.0045]	F(4,68)=2.89** [0.0285]	F(4,68)=3.26** [0.0167]	F(4,68)=3.66*** [0.0093]

The dependent variable is $\Delta \ln(MB)$. For the exact form of the reaction function used see equation 1.3 from table 1.9. For hypotheses being tested see table 2.6. F tests are with degrees of freedom in parentheses () and p value in brackets [].* significant at 10 percent level, ** significant at 5 percent level, *** significant at 1 percent level.

Table 2.8: Cyclical and Structural Measures of the Federal Deficit and Monetary Base Growth $\Delta\ln(MB)$

Hypothesis	Fiscal Variables FDEFC	and FDEFS
	Fiscal Coefficients Homogeneous	
H1 Sum lag 1-4 sum=0	-1.345 F(1,68)=0.71 [0.4009]	0.976 F(1,68)=2.68 [0.1064]
H2 all=0	F(4,68)=0.76 [0.5530]	F(4,68)=0.98 [0.4210]
	Fiscal Coefficients Heterogeneous	
H3 Sum 70 lag 1-4 sum 70=0	-4.549 F(1,60)=2.21 [0.1421]	2.633** F(1,60)=5.73 [0.0198]
H4 Sum 80 lag 1-4 sum 80=0	0.789 F(1,60)=0.15 [0.6980]	0.246 F(1,60)=0.11 [0.7419]
H5 all=0	F(8,60)=1.78* [0.0996]	F(8,60)=2.38** [0.0267]
H6 all 70=0	F(4,60)=3.24** [0.0180]	F(4,60)=3.96*** [0.0065]
H7 all 80=0	F(4,60)=0.36 [0.8348]	F(4,60)=0.57 [0.6848]
H8 70=80	F(4,60)=3.02** [0.0245]	F(4,60)=2.31* [0.0678]
H9 c=s all	F(8,60)=1.30 [0.2588]	
H10 c=s 70	F(4,60)=1.89 [0.1238]	
H11 c=s 80	F(4,60)=0.69 [0.6042]	

See Note on table 2.7. Test results for FDEFC and FDEFS are based on one regression.

Table 2.9: Cyclical and Structural Measures of the Total Deficit and Monetary Base Growth $\Delta\ln(MB)$

Hypothesis	Fiscal Variables TDEFC and	TDEFS	SATOT and	SSTOT
	Fiscal Coefficients Homogeneous			
H1 Sum lag 1-4 sum=0	-0.778 F(1,68)=1.12 [0.2942]	0.341 F(1,68)=1.65 [0.2036]	-1.127* F(1,68)=2.96 [0.0898]	0.374 F(1,68)=2.64 [0.1088]
H2 all=0	F(4,68)=0.71 [0.5866]	F(4,68)=0.89 [0.4728]	F(4,68)=2.35* [0.0625]	F(4,68)=2.74** [0.0356]
	Fiscal Coefficients Heterogeneous			
H3 Sum 70 lag 1-4 sum 70=0	-0.061 F(1,60)=0.001 [0.9762]	1.494* F(1,60)=3.05 [0.0858]	0.608 F(1,60)=0.16 [0.6933]	2.053** F(1,60)=4.52 [0.0375]
H4 Sum 80 lag 1-4 sum 80=0	-1.118 F(1,60)=1.40 [0.2411]	0.215 F(1,60)=0.54 [0.4637]	-0.073 F(1,60)=0.004 [0.9529]	0.087 F(1,60)=0.11 [0.7415]
H5 all=0	F(8,60)=0.66 [0.7212]	F(8,60)=2.15** [0.0447]	F(8,60)=2.07* [0.0533]	F(8,60)=2.66** [0.0144]
H6 all 70=0	F(4,60)=0.42 [0.7954]	F(4,60)=3.93*** [0.0067]	F(4,60)=3.90*** [0.0070]	F(4,60)=4.40*** [0.0035]
H7 all 80=0	F(4,60)=0.93 [0.4530]	F(4,60)=0.70 [0.5983]	F(4,60)=0.17 [0.9568]	F(4,60)=0.38 [0.8216]
H8 70=80	F(4,60)=0.58 [0.6766]	F(4,60)=3.43** [0.0137]	F(4,60)=2.84** [0.0319]	F(4,60)=2.59** [0.0458]
H9 c=s all	F(8,60)=0.91 [0.5112]		F(8,60)=0.76 [0.6348]	
H10 c=s 70	F(4,60)=0.91 [0.4613]		F(4,60)=1.17 [0.3339]	
H11 c=s 80	F(4,60)=0.92 [0.4593]		F(4,60)=0.33 [0.8534]	

See Note on table 2.7. Test results for TDEFC and TDEFS (SATOT and SSTOT) are based on one regression.

Table 2.10: Growth of Gross Federal Debt and Money Growth

Hypothesis	Dependent Variables $\Delta\ln(MB)$	$\Delta\ln(M1)$
	Fiscal Coefficients Homogeneous	
H1 Sum lag 1-4 sum=0	0.020 F(1,72)=0.01 [0.9168]	-0.168 F(1,74)=1.80 [0.1835]
H2 all=0	F(4,72)=0.10 [0.9823]	F(4,74)=0.74 [0.5666]
	Fiscal Coefficients Heterogeneous	
H3 Sum 70 lag 1-4 sum 70=0	0.235 F(1,68)=0.64 [0.4272]	-0.301* F(1,70)=3.14 [0.0806]
H4 Sum 80 lag 1-4 sum 80=0	-0.070 F(1,68)=0.11 [0.7432]	-0.113 F(1,70)=0.65 [0.4244]
H5 all=0	F(8,68)=0.20 [0.9896]	F(8,70)=0.77 [0.6262]
H6 all 70=0	F(4,68)=0.30 [0.8793]	F(4,70)=0.84 [0.5045]
H7 all 80=0	F(4,68)=0.08 [0.9938]	F(4,70)=0.81 [0.5252]
H8 70=80	F(4,68)=0.31 [0.8718]	F(4,70)=0.82 [0.5198]

For $\Delta\ln(MB)$ as dependent variable equation 1.3 from table 1.9 is used. For $\Delta\ln(M1)$ as dependent variable see equation 1.6 from table 1.12. Hypotheses tested are surveyed in table 2.6. F tests are with degrees of freedom in parentheses () and p value in brackets []. * significant at 10 percent level.

Test results from tables 2.8 and 2.9 inform about whether the origin of the deficit matters. The deficit measures are split into their *cyclical and structural* components and enter the same regression. Except for the cyclical component of the total deficit without social security TDEFC, all measures have at least one coefficient that is significant in the time period before 1980 (H5 and H6). No significant coefficients are identified for the time period after 1980 (H7). Hence, heterogeneity is indicated for all variables except for TDEFC (H8). While the sum of the coefficients on the cyclical components FDEFC, TDEFC and SATOT is never significant, it is significant for all structural components FDEFS, TDEFS and SSTOT in the time period before 1980. Following the traditional interpretation the positive signs indicate an accommodating behavior. This is consistent with the hypothesis of political dependence of the SNB. However, these conclusions are weakened by the test results for H9 to H11. In all three cases, F tests fail to reject the null hypothesis that the coefficients for the cyclical and structural components of the deficit variables are equal. This implies that the distinction between cyclical and structural components does not matter. Therefore, using the actually measured deficit (which implicitly imposes the restriction that the effect of the two components on money growth is equal), or only the structural component (imposing the restriction that the coefficient on the cyclical component of the deficit is zero) is justified based on these test results.

With the growth rate of the *money supply M1* as dependent variable (not reported) the sum of the coefficients for the lagged deficit variables fails to be significant in all equations. Replacing the actually measured deficits with their cyclical and structural components does not improve the results. In some equations with heterogeneous coefficients at least one of the four lags included is significantly different from zero for the period before 1980 (H6). Accordingly, the coefficient estimates are found to be heterogeneous for the two subperiods (H8). But this relationship seems to be transitory since the sum of the four lags is not significant (H3). Deficits are not associated with the growth rate of the money supply M1.

Table 2.10 lists the results for the reaction function with money growth regressed on the growth rate of gross federal debt. In the regression on the money supply $\Delta \ln(M1)$ the sum of the coefficients is negative and significant (at the ten percent level) for the period before 1980. This is consistent with political independence of the central bank. But this result should not be overstated. The quarterly growth rate for the debt variable is not stationary. The correlation with the dependent variable could be due to a trend in the debt variable.

Another fiscal variable that is also tried out as regressor is *net domestic borrowing* provided by IFS (line 84a). Results are very similar to the IFS deficit variable, so that they are not reported here.

Instead of gross federal debt it might be preferable to work with *net federal* or even with *net total debt* measures. Since consistent series on net federal debt are only available since 1975 this idea was not pursued any further.

Given the development in the deficits (see figures 2.1 and 2.2) it could be argued that the relevant break to test for is 1990. But a hypothesized break for the deficit variables in 1990 is not confirmed by tests for heterogeneity (H8).

2.7 Conclusions

This chapter reexamines the relationship between various deficit measures and the rate of monetary expansion chosen by the SNB over the period of flexible exchange rates. The focus is on the sign and significance, and on the stability of the coefficients of the fiscal variables. The statistical evidence on the relationship between deficits and money growth for Switzerland can be summarized as follows:

- Except for one case, no relationship can be found if the fiscal variables are constrained to be homogeneous.
- With fiscal coefficients allowed to be different before and after 1980 (heterogeneity), significant coefficients can be found for most variables by searching through lags 1 to 4 in the time period before 1980. For the time period after 1980, no relationship between fiscal variables and money growth can be detected.
- It is argued that significant coefficients on specific lags might indicate transitory effects. Therefore, instead of picking out the coefficients that perform best, F tests are conducted for sums of coefficients over four lags.
- For actually measured deficits a positive relationship is found only for total deficit measures, but not for deficits at the federal level (for the time period before 1980).
- If actually measured deficits are split into their cyclical and structural components, only the structural components are positively associated with money growth (for the time period before 1980).

Overall, evidence for a relationship between deficits and money growth for Switzerland is rather weak. The following remarks may help to explain these results.

First, it has to be noted that fiscal policy tended to be rather conservative in Switzerland. As figures 2.1 and 2.2 show, deficits are relatively small, on average they are even balanced for the period from 1980 to 1990. Inflation as a result of an *aggregate demand stimulus* generated by deficit spending is unlikely.[38] Only in the nineties did deficits - especially the structural components - increase dramatically. But that time period is too short to have an impact on the regression results.

Second - with the exception of Buomberger/Schwab (1993) and Schwab (1994a) - there is no evidence that government deficits are associated with higher interest rates in Switzerland. One explanation is provided by the capital-inflow

[38] In this context expectations might play a role. See e.g. Baltensperger/Böhm 1984 8; Burdekin/Wohar 1990 534. The public does not expect fiscal deficits to be inflationary in Switzerland. Instead it will (rationally) anticipate monetary policy moves that will act to keep inflation at its target level.

hypothesis. Interest rates for Switzerland are mainly determined by capital flows on the international level. (Schwab 1994a 13) Another explanation may be the fact that saving is traditionally high in Switzerland. Hence, deficits do not generate *financial market pressure.*

Third, the shift toward *targeting monetary aggregates* after 1975 and especially the monetary base since 1980 may serve as an additional explanation why monetary policy is not very responsive to fiscal deficits in the subperiod after 1980. Remember that it is the preoccupation with the stabilization of interest rates (the targeting of interest rates) that pressures the central bank into monetizing the deficit. The shift toward monetary targeting was also supposed to end such a reaction by decoupling the conduct of monetary policy from interest-rate movements.[39]

How do these results compare with the *previous studies* discussed in section 2.3? The main difficulty with a comparison is the fact that the sampling periods do not correspond with each other, while results seem to be very sensitive to this. For the IFS data used in those studies at least one significant coefficient is found for the period before 1980 (H6). But the sum of the coefficients is never significant in the present investigation.

Indications of an offsetting behavior can be found in regressions of other deficit variables on the growth rate of the monetary base (SATOT in table 2.9) and in the regression of the growth rate of gross federal debt on the growth rate of the money supply M1 (Δln(M1) in table 2.10). The significant and positive response of the monetary base to total deficit measures TDEF and SETOT (table 2.7) and to all structural components of the deficit measures for the period before 1980 (H3 in tables 2.8 and 2.9) conflicts with the findings in the previous work.

How do the overall results relate to the *political (in)dependence* debate? Following the traditional approach the focus has to be on the sign of the coefficients for the *structural* component of the federal and total deficits. The M1 models (not reported) do not yield any information on this question. In the monetary base models the significant positive coefficients for this variable for the subperiod before 1980 (H3 in tables 2.8 and 2.9) imply accommodating behavior. This is consistent with political dependence of the SNB.

Following the argument presented in section 2.2 while keeping in mind the caveat with the lag structure the significant negative coefficient on the *cyclical* components of the total deficit SATOT in the regression with homogeneous coefficients suggests offsetting behavior that is consistent with political independence. Also consistent with political independence is the negative coefficient on the growth rate of gross federal debt in the regression on the growth rate of the money supply M1 (Δln(M1) in table 2.10).

If it is argued that cyclical deficits also yield evidence on the (in)dependence debate, no clear picture emerges with respect to the (in)dependence of the SNB.

---

39 In their cross-country comparison including eight countries Demopoulos et al. (1987 1047) find „that the move to monetary targeting has seemingly reduced the degree of linkage of monetary policy to government deficits.“

But if insignificant coefficients on deficit variables are interpreted as a sign of benign neglect, estimation results clearly support the hypothesis of political independence of the SNB for the period after 1980.

These interpretations *cannot directly be inferred.* (See Demopoulos et al. 1987 1045.) A negative (positive) relationship between deficits and money growth need not indicate offsetting (accommodating) behavior and independence (dependence). It can be consistent with other arguments as well. A combination of easy fiscal policy and tight monetary policy for instance could be part of the political strategy of fiscal authorities, so that a negative relationship could equally well mean political dependence. (See Beck 1984 811 and 814.) Of course, the relationship found might also depend on the construction of the series.

CHAPTER 3

Elections and Monetary Policy: Is There a Political Monetary Cycle for Switzerland?

3.1 Introduction

Indirect political influence on monetary policy is investigated by testing for effects of fiscal policy on monetary policy. Direct political influence is analyzed in the framework of elections, parties and administrations. This chapter addresses the question whether elections have any effect on Swiss monetary policy. While this question has been analyzed for most major central banks, an explicit and systematic test for the SNB is still missing.[1] This chapter intends to fill that gap.

Evidence for the existence of a political business cycle for Switzerland is reported by Soh (1986) for the period from 1960 to 1980. He does not present any significance tests, however. Here, systematic tests for political monetary business cycles are carried out for the period of flexible exchange rates (from 1973.2 to 1995.2). These tests do not confirm the existence of a political monetary cycle for Switzerland. This is consistent with the hypothesis of political independence of the Swiss central bank.

The chapter is organized as follows. Section 3.2 presents an overview of models of politico-economic cycles following the work of Alesina and his co-authors. Section 3.3 addresses the question whether the existence of a political monetary cycle for Switzerland can be explained on theoretical grounds. Section 3.4 critically reviews Soh's findings of a political business cycle for Switzerland. Section 3.5 presents various systematic tests of political monetary cycles. Section 3.6 offers a brief conclusion.

---

1 Electoral cycles for monetary policy have been investigated for the Federal Reserve and most other central banks. Applications to the Federal Reserve include Alesina 1988, Alesina/Sachs 1988, Allen 1986, Beck 1982, 1984 and 1987, Grier 1987 and 1989, Haynes/Stone 1989, Havrilesky 1987, Laney/Willet 1983. For more recent applications to the German Bundesbank see Lang/Welzel 1992 and Berger/Woitek 1995. Other applications to the Bundesbank are cited in Vaubel 1993 49. Multi-country studies are Alesina et al. 1992 and 1993, Alesina/Roubini 1992. Switzerland is also included in some of these time series cross section analyses. Country by country results are also reported for Switzerland for the period 1958-1987. (See Alesina et al. 1992 16, table 8.) They show no signs of political manipulation of monetary policy.

3.2 Models of Politico-Economic Cycles: An Overview

Do politicians manipulate economic policy in order to win elections? And more specifically: Do elections matter for monetary policy? There are basically two arguments proposed in the literature, the opportunistic and the partisan argument. Table 3.1 summarizes the respective models, following the discussion in Alesina/Roubini 1992. The models are classified along the two most important dimensions, the assumption about policymakers' motivations and the assumption about the rationality of voters and economic agents. (Alesina 1988 16)

Table 3.1: Politico-Economic Models of Business Cycles

	opportunistic models	**partisan models**
first phase: **'pre-rational expectations' models**	PBC = political business cycle models *Nordhaus 1975* *Lindbeck 1976*	PT = partisan theory *Hibbs 1977, 1987*
second phase: **rational expectations models**	RPBC = rational political business cycle models *Cukierman/Meltzer 1986* *Rogoff/Sibert 1988* *Rogoff 1990* *Persson/Tabellini 1990*	RPT = rational partisan theory *Alesina 1987* *Alesina/Sachs 1988*

Source: Alesina 1988 16 table 1 (modified).

It is assumed that the reader is sufficiently familiar with the theory of political business cycles. Therefore, only the basic arguments and the testable predictions derived from the different models are presented here.[2]

According to Nordhaus (1975) political business cycles occur because politicians stimulate aggregate demand before elections in order to create fast growth and to reduce unemployment. The inflationary consequences of this policy are eliminated by a post-electoral contraction. Voters are assumed to be retrospective and myopic so that they can be fooled. The policymakers' only incentive to manipulate the economy is to enhance their *chances of reelection.* It doesn't matter whether a right-wing or a left-wing party is in power. The Nordhaus model pre-

---

2 For a more detailed review of the theory of political business cycles see Alesina/Roubini 1992 section 2. See also Belke 1993, Berthold/Fehn 1994, Gärtner 1994a, and the papers compiled in Frey 1997. For a textbook exposition see Mueller 1989 ch. 15. For a detailed theoretical and empirical analysis of the rational partisan theory see Belke 1996.

dicts that there will be a business cycle which peaks before the elections. But it remains unclear how long before the elections the stimulus has to occur.

Empirical results for the Nordhaus model were mixed. Moreover, the rational expectations' critique damaged the theoretical argument.[3] In the late eighties a new generation of 'rational political business cycles models' emerged. Rogoff (1988 56) calls them political budget cycle models. Since these models assume rational expectations for voters and economic agents, their empirical implications differ from those of the Nordhaus model. Elections still lead to business cycles. But these cycles are much shorter, less pronounced, less regular, and not easy to predict. They can be observed on movements of fiscal and monetary policy instruments (such as taxes, transfers, government spending, and money growth). They are less likely to be observed on policy outcomes (such as output growth, inflation or even unemployment). (See also Berthold/Fehn 1994 171.)

Politicians may not only behave in an opportunistic manner and maximize their popularity or their probability of reelection. They may be *partisan* and have ideological objectives. The partisan models of political cycles assume that different parties maximize different objectives, because they represent the interests of different constituencies. When in office, they pursue policies which are favorable to these constituencies. Generally, left-wing parties are assumed to be more concerned with the problem of unemployment. Right-wing parties are relatively more willing to reduce inflation and to bear the costs of unemployment. Hence, partisan models of the 'pre-rational' (Hibbs 1977 and 1987) and the rational type (Alesina 1987, Alesina/Sachs 1988) predict systematic differences in macroeconomic policymaking between the 'unemployment averse' left and the 'inflation averse' right parties. These parties choose different points on the Philipps curve. Hence, cycles differ for the parties in power. 'Pre-rational' partisan models hypothesize that with left-wing governments in power output growth and inflation should be permanently higher and unemployment permanently lower than with right-wing governments. (Alesina/Roubini 1992 666) In rational partisan models „permanently different inflation rates across parties may result only in temporary, post-election differences in growth and unemployment." (Alesina/Roubini 1992 664)

Opportunistic and partisan models *can coexist*. „First, as suggested by the 'political business cycle' models, politicians prefer being in office rather than out, so they have an incentive to manipulate the economy in order to be reelected. In addition, as suggested by the 'partisan theory', they may also have ideological objectives. However, 'partisan' goals can be implemented only if elections are won. Thus, even partisan politicians, regardless of their ideology, may engage in opportunistic behavior if, by doing so, they can increase their chances of reelection." (Alesina et al. 1993 20; see also Alesina/Roubini 1992 683.)

---

[3] See Grier 1989 387 on early attempts to reconcile the political business cycle with rational expectations.

As a further possibility, pre-electoral opportunistic behavior may be different for left- and right-wing governments.[4]

3.3 Application to Switzerland: Why Should There Exist a Political Monetary Cycle?

Although the existence of a political business cycle ultimately is an empirical question that cannot be settled by a priori argument, the theoretical question remains: How can the existence of a political business cycle be *explained* for Switzerland? Asked more specifically: Why should the timing of elections exert a significant influence on money growth in Switzerland?

It turns out that the existence of a political business cycle for Switzerland is not easy to rationalize on the basis of the political system and the constellation of parties in power. Two possible arguments can be put forward:

A first explanation is that the right-wing dominated government tries to boost the economy in the election year in order to maximize political support for the election. But the right-wing coalition has a comfortable majority, so that an electoral manipulation of monetary policy may not be needed.

A second explanation is that this is not a strategy of incumbent *parties*, but a strategy of incumbent *politicians* in general to stay in power aimed versus those running for election for the first time. This is a purely opportunistic argument - neglecting any partisan aspects of the business cycle approach. The critical point is that this would require a big alliance among all (or at least most) politicians in office.

Both arguments are not really convincing, so that the theoretical case for the existence of a political business cycle for Switzerland is *questionable.*

The application to monetary policy meets an *additional difficulty* that weakens the theoretical argument. Theories of political business cycles typically do not distinguish between government and central bank. It is assumed that the government determines the money supply. This assumption appears inappropriate for countries with formally independent central banks. It is argued, however, that even formally independent central banks will not be able to pursue a monetary policy that conflicts with the interests of the government in the long run. (Berthold/Fehn 1994 166; see also Frey/Schneider 1981 294 on this.) Empirical results for the German Bundesbank, formally one of the most independent central banks, seem to confirm this position. Several studies report some form of political manipulation of its monetary policy. (See e.g. Alesina et al. 1992 15, Frey/

---

4 See Alesina et al. 1992 15. They account for this possibility by investigating a 'partisan/opportunistic' interaction term.

Schneider 1981, Lang/Welzel 1992, Schneider 1979.) This might suggest that the theoretical argument for the existence of a political monetary cycle has to build on the characteristics of the political market rather than the institutional arrangements that constitute formal independence of the central bank.

As stated before, characteristics of the Swiss political market make an electoral manipulation of monetary policy rather unlikely. But since the existence of a political business cycle is an *empirical* question - and since some evidence for its existence has been reported by Soh (1986) - this result should also be established by having a closer look at the data (and the econometric evidence). In addition, tests for political monetary cycles will also yield further evidence on the political (in)dependence of the SNB.

Two different approaches are pursued here. First, Soh's results are reproduced and the corresponding calculations for the period of flexible exchange rates are added. Because of the weaknesses of this approach, more rigorous tests of the political monetary cycle follow.

Empirical tests of partisan models require changes between left- and right-wing governments. Since Switzerland had no political change in government during the period under investigation (even since 1959) tests for partisan models are not viable. But the predictions of the opportunistic models of the 'pre-rational' and rational type can be tested.

Tests of political business cycles can be carried out on policy *outcomes* (e.g. output growth, unemployment, inflation), and on policy *instruments* (such as money growth, taxes, transfers, and government spending). (Alesina et al. 1992 5) Here, tests will focus on potential effects of elections on money growth. Signs for the existence of a political monetary cycle would suggest evidence for political dependence of the SNB.

Does the variable representing the political business cycle (the electoral variable) measure executive or legislative influence? This question is not of interest for parliamentary democracies where the executive cannot exist without a majority in parliament. But a separation between executive and legislative influence is of interest in the case of the US - where the Presidency does not depend on a majority in Congress - or Switzerland - where the executive's policy at times diverges from the majority in parliament. While in applications to the US the electoral variable is usually supposed to represent executive political influence, the case is less clear for Switzerland. Since the Swiss executive is nominated immediately after the election of the legislature significance of an electoral variable cannot unambiguously be ascribed to the executive or the legislature. The electoral variable can measure the political influence of both, the executive and the legislature.

3.4 Comparing Economic Conditions for Election and Nonelection Years

Political business cycle models of the opportunistic, 'pre-rational' expectations type predict that in election years we should observe faster economic growth, lower inflation rates, and less unemployment. Following Soh (1986) the *means* of these three economic indicators are calculated for election years, nonelection years, and all years for the sample period from 1973 to 1995. Then the means for election and nonelection years are compared. The ratio of election year mean to nonelection year mean can be used as preliminary evidence of political business cycles. An opportunistic government will try to please voters by increasing economic growth in election years. Hence, for economic growth this ratio should be greater than one. Inflation should be lower in election years than in nonelection years. A ratio of the average rate of inflation in election years to that in nonelection years less than one would indicate preliminary evidence for the existence of political business cycles. For unemployment, this ratio should also be less than one.

Table 3.2 reproduces Soh's results for Switzerland (for the sample period 1961-1980) and adds the same indicators calculated for the period of flexible exchange rates (from 1973 to 1995).

While Soh finds preliminary evidence of political business cycles with the unemployment rate, the indicators for the sample period 1973-1995 do not confirm his findings. Only the ratio for the inflation rate is consistent with the predictions of the opportunistic political business cycle theory. But it is very close to one (0.98).

Soh's findings for the unemployment rate should not be overstated given the small sample (from 1975 to 1980) consisting of just one election and four nonelection years! Moreover, the unemployment rate is probably not a very useful indicator in this particular case, because it was very low during the whole sample period.

Average ratios can be heavily biased by extreme values. (A good example is the growth rate of -7% in the election year of 1975.) As an *alternative* Soh proposes the following procedure. First, the number of election years in which economic growth accelerated, inflation slowed down, or unemployment reduced, are counted and the percentage of these years to total election years is calculated. Second, the same percentage is calculated for nonelection years with acceleration of economic growth, deceleration of inflation, or reduction of unemployment. Third, for each indicator the percentages for election and nonelection years are compared. The existence of a political business cycle is indicated if the percentages of election years are at least 50 percent, and if (at the same time) they are greater than the comparable percentage of nonelection years by at least 10 percentage points. If the high incidence of election year acceleration or deceleration of an indicator coincides with the hypothesized ratio of the average of election

Table 3.2: Election Year vs. Nonelection Year Economic Conditions

	Ratio[a]	Election year mean	Nonelection year mean	All year mean	All year stand. dev.
Growth rate of disposable real income (%)					
1961-1980	0.45	1.61	3.60	3.10	3.00
1973-1995[b]	-0.08	-0.13	1.72	1.24	2.32
Rate of inflation (%)					
1961-1980	1.28	5.08	3.96	4.24	2.40
1973-1995	0.98	3.72	3.79	3.77	2.51
Rate of unemployment (%)					
1975-1980	0.90*	0.30	0.42	0.38	0.17
1973-1995	1.15	1.27	1.10	1.14	1.41

[a] The ratio of election year mean to nonelection year mean; [b] growth rate of real GDP (%); * indicates preliminary evidence of political business cycles.
Source: Soh 1986 33 table 1 (modified).

year compared to nonelection year (table 3.2), strong evidence of political business cycles is assumed. Soh finds this hypothesized pattern for Switzerland with the unemployment variable.

Again, Soh's findings are displayed in table 3.3 along with the corresponding values calculated for the sample period 1973-1995. Soh's result for the unemployment rate suffers from the weaknesses stated above. And the results for the period of flexible exchange rates do not support the predictions of the opportunistic political business cycle theory.

For a small open economy realized economic conditions such as rates of economic growth, inflation and unemployment depend heavily on international factors. Domestic political authorities may have very limited influence. Therefore, it might be more appropriate to turn to economic policy *instruments*. In addition to realized economic conditions (rates of economic growth, inflation and unemployment) Soh also analyses the two most important measures of economic policy, the rate of change in government expenditures and money supply. Opportunistic political business cycle theory predicts that both will increase before elections. Their growth rates in election years are compared with those in nonelection years. To account for time lags from policy implementation to the realization of its effects the rates of one year before an election are compared with rates in other years including election years, too.

Table 3.3: Improvement of Economic Conditions During Election Years vs. Nonelection Years

	During election years	During nonelection years	Total number of occurrence	Proportion among election years	Proportion among nonelection years
Acceleration of income growth					
1961-1980	3	6	9	60*	43
1973-1995[a]	3	8	11	50	47
Deceleration of inflation					
1961-1980	3	7	10	60*	50
1973-1995	2	8	10	33	47
Reduction of unemployment					
1975-1980	1	2	3	100**	40
1973-1995	1	8	9	17	47

The 1961-1980 period has 5 election and 14 nonelection years. The 1973-1995 period has 6 election and 17 nonelection years. [a] growth rate of real GDP (%); * indicates a proportion among election years which is greater than or equal to 50% and is greater than the proportion among nonelection years by at least 10 percentage points; ** according to Soh 'strong evidence' or 'real indication of political business cycle'.
Source: Soh 1986 35-36 tables 2 and 3 (modified).

Table 3.4 lists Soh's results along with corresponding values calculated for the sample period 1973-1995. Soh finds evidence of political business cycles in the growth rates of government expenditures (one year before election), and in the growth rates of money supply (one year before election and also during the election year). The data for the period of flexible exchange rates do not confirm the finding for the government expenditures. (The one year before election ratio only marginally exceeds one.) However, results for the growth rate of the seasonally adjusted monetary base are consistent with the predictions of the opportunistic business cycle theory. Mean growth rates are much larger for election years and one year before the elections than in other years.

Although these results for government expenditures and especially for the money supply and the monetary base are interesting, the whole approach of comparing economic conditions for election and nonelection years must be *criticized* on at least two grounds. First, there is no control for other factors that might have caused these effects. Second, this approach does not present any significance tests. Two more criticisms must be added to Soh's results. His finding for the unemployment variable is very questionable for the reasons explained above. And his sample also extends over the period of fixed exchange rates where monetary growth could not really be manipulated by domestic policymakers.

Table 3.4: Growth Rates of Government Expenditures and Money Supply

	Growth rates of government expenditures		Growth rates of money supply	
	1961-1980	1973-1995	1961-1980	1973-1995[a]
Election year ratio[b]	0.57	0.75	1.25*	7.53*
Election year mean (%)	6.50	5.16	8.64	4.12
Nonelection year mean (%)	11.33	6.86	6.93	0.55
1 year before election ratio[c]	1.27*	1.02	1.10*	7.00*
1 year before election mean (%)	12.01	6.51	7.88	4.03
Other year mean (%)	9.49	6.38	7.19	0.58
All year mean (%)	10.12	6.42	7.36	1.48
All year stand. dev.	7.83	4.75	6.28	5.22

[a] growth rate of the seasonally adjusted monetary base; [b] ratio of election year mean to nonelection year mean; [c] ratio of mean in one year before election to the mean of other years; * indicates evidence of political business cycles.
Source: Soh 1986 38 and 40 tables 4 and 5 (modified).

The following section pursues the issue with the money supply further by presenting rigorous tests for the existence of a political monetary cycle.

3.5 Testing for Political Monetary Cycles

All types of political business cycles require some electoral manipulation of either, or both, of the macroeconomic policy instruments, monetary and fiscal policy. The goal of this section is to test for the existence of opportunistic political business cycles in Swiss monetary policy.[5]

Different approaches can be used to empirically investigate the relationship between monetary policy and elections. Figure 3.1 presents an overview and indicates some tests that are performed in this chapter.

Most authors work with '*fixed-effect* models', i.e. they assume constant slopes. (See Alesina/Roubini 1992 669.) One might argue that the monetary cycle takes a specific form for each election. This is in fact somewhat the prediction of rational political business cycle theory, since cycles are not only hypothesized to be

[5] As noted above, tests for the existence of political business cycles can be carried out for policy outcomes and policy instruments. Pre-electoral fiscal and monetary 'favors' to key constituencies are not only electorally very useful. They are also easy to implement, relative to an attempt to increase the rate of growth of GNP, for instance. For a test using the inflation rate (a policy outcome) as dependent variable see e.g. Alesina/Roubini 1992.

shorter, but also to be less regular. (See Belke 1993 920.) In this case it is not correct to assume fixed effects for election years. To model the *uniqueness* of each election, separate dummies are constructed for every election and entered, either one at a time, or all together, in the regression equation. (See Beck 1984 for an example.)

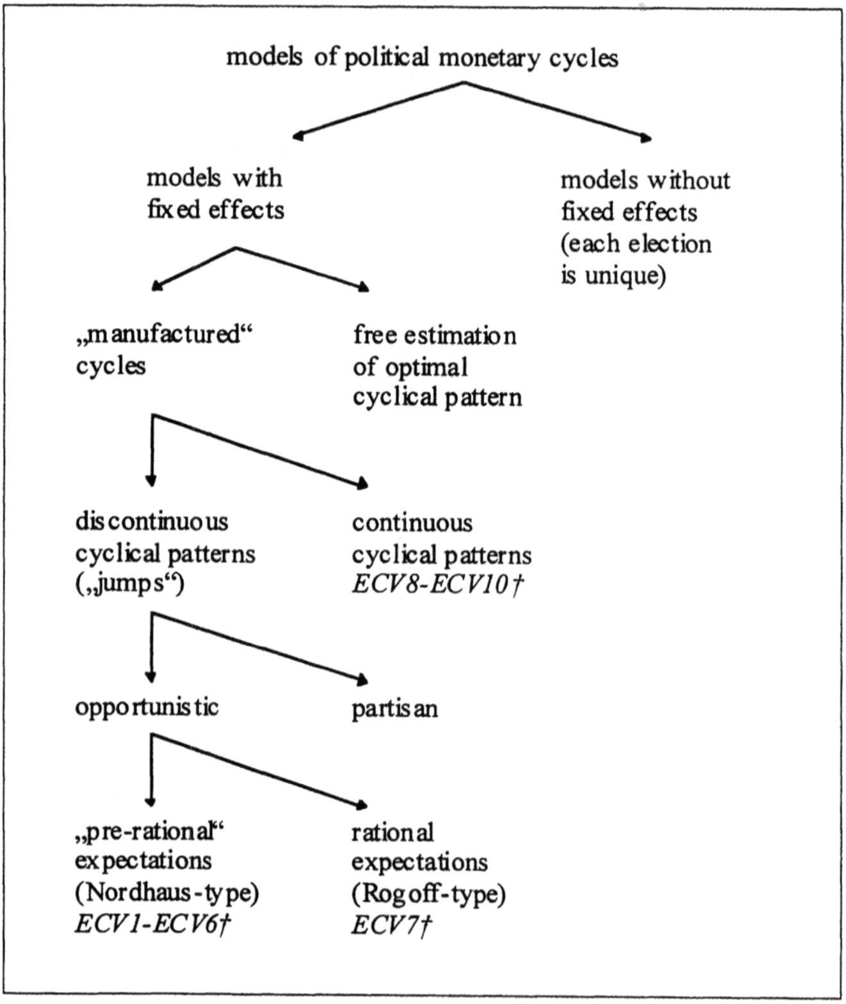

Figure 3.1: Testing for the Existence of Political Monetary Cycles
† variables tested in this section.

Within fixed-effect models there are two ways to look for cycles in monetary policy. One approach is to *'manufacture'* dummy variables that are supposed to capture the cycle. Another approach is the *free estimation* of the optimal cyclical pattern using the Almon polynomial technique. Manufactured dummy variables

„impose different prior restrictions on the pattern of the election cycle, such as piece-wise linearity, precise turning points, and a duration of 16 quarters. By using a dummy variable/polynomial distributed lag (PDL) technique this type of prior restriction can be avoided and the data can 'speak for itself' about the existence, shape, and periodicity of the electoral cycle.“ (Grier 1987 478) In the estimation with the Almon lag model the election variable takes the shape that best fits the data.

'Manufactured' dummy variables can model *'jumps'* in monetary policy or other, rather *continuous* cyclical patterns. 'Jumps' in monetary policy may have their causes in *opportunistic* or in *partisan* behavior of policymakers. And in both cases cycles may describe the *'pre-rational* expectations' or the *rational* expectations hypotheses.

The electoral variable can have many different shapes. The definitions of 'manufactured' electoral dummy variables used in this section are summarized in table 3.5.

Table 3.5: 'Manufactured' Electoral Cycle Variables

	Quarters of each electoral period															
	1	2	3	4	5	6	7	8	9	10	11	12	13	14	15	16
	Year one				Year two				Year three				Year four			
Variable	1	2	3	4	1	2	3	4	1	2	3	4	1	2	3	4
ECV1	0	0	0	0	0	0	0	0	0	0	0	0	1	1	1	1
ECV2	0	0	0	0	0	0	0	0	0	0	1	1	1	1	1	1
ECV3	0	0	0	0	0	0	0	0	1	1	1	1	1	1	1	1
ECV4	0	0	0	0	0	0	0	0	0	0	0	0	0	1	1	0
ECV5	0	0	0	0	0	0	0	0	0	0	0	0	1	1	1	0
ECV6	0	0	0	0	0	0	0	0	0	0	1	1	1	1	1	0
ECV7	-1	0	0	0	0	0	0	0	0	0	0	0	0	0	0	1
ECV8	7	6	5	4	3	2	1	0	1	2	3	4	5	6	7	8
ECV9	9	6	3	0	1	2	3	4	5	6	7	8	9	10	11	12
ECV10	8	6	4	2	0	0	0	0	0	2	4	6	8	8	8	8

The different specifications describe possible shapes of the electoral cycle and are supposed to capture the implications of different business cycle theories.

ECV1 to ECV6 represent the *Nordhaus* cycle. Nordhaus predicts a monetary stimulus before elections. The exact timing of monetary ease depends on several factors. First, it depends on how myopic voters are assumed to behave. Second, it takes some time for monetary changes to show up in the real economy. (Beck 1984 788) Because of anticipated lags the stimulus might even be hypothesized in the year before the election, with no effort in the election year itself. (Laney/

Willett 1983 59) Third, elections occur in four year intervals. Therefore, a specification of the pre-electoral period longer than eight quarters seems unreasonable. (Alesina/Roubini 1992 676-677)

Here, the general definition of the first three electoral variables representing the Nordhaus cycle is as follows: ECVN is equal to 1 in the (N-1) quarters preceding an election and in the election quarter; it is equal to 0 otherwise. The choices for N are 4 (ECV1), 6 (ECV2) and 8 (ECV3). According to ECV1 the effects of elections can be felt only in the years in which they occur. In ECV3 the electoral dummy assumes the value of 1 in the second half of each administration and zero otherwise. It hypothesizes two years of restraint to combat inflation and two following years of stimulus as the election approaches.[6]

ECV4 to ECV6 are slightly different specifications of the Nordhaus-type business cycle. In all three cases, money growth increases just prior to an election, excluding the election quarter.[7] ECV4 is the electoral dummy variable originally employed by MacCallum (1978), ECV5 is adopted from Allen (1986), and ECV6 is a specification used by Beck (1984).

ECV7 represents the *Rogoff* cycle. Because of the assumption of rational expectations, money growth must increase immediately before elections, and it must be reduced immediately after elections. Over the rest of the cycle money growth is not (electorally) manipulated, since that would be counterproductive to the reelection goals of politicians. In this model there is no need for monetary policy to show effects on the real economy (i.e. on growth and employment), because voters will anticipate these effects as soon as they learn about the money surprise (for instance in the form of interest rate reductions).[8] Therefore, the monetary expansion can take place much shorter before the election.

Originally, the Rogoff-type cycle was developed for fiscal policy. (See e.g. Rogoff/Sibert 1988.) Its application to monetary policy may not be unproblematic.[9] The SNB publishes its assets and liabilities three times a month. It must be assumed that rational voters quickly learn about monetary policy strategies. Therefore, lags must be much shorter for monetary policy than they are for fiscal policy. Here, the shortest possible lag of one quarter is employed. (Of course, it

---

6 According to Laney/Willett (1983 59) this last scenario may correspond most closely to the Nordhaus cycle for the US, since Nordhaus divides his electoral periods generally in half in this fashion.

7 Beck (1987 203) argues that voters are unconcerned with (and not even knowledgeable about) money growth. They care about its consequences, such as unemployment and inflation. Because of the monetary policy lag money growth during the electoral quarter will not show up in the variables that have an electoral impact until after the election. Therefore, it is unreasonable to assume that money will grow most rapidly on election day.

8 These cycles „may imply very little or nothing at all for a four-year cycle on employment; thus, they are consistent with the lack of empirical evidence for the Nordhaus' 'political business cycle'.“ Alesina 1988 36.

9 This point was brought to my attention by Manfred Gärtner. See e.g. Gärtner 1994b 438.

would be preferable to work with monthly data.) ECV7 is a modified version of an electoral cycle variable employed by Alesina (1988 37). In an earlier version, the unmodified version of Alesina's electoral cycle variable which specifies two quarters of expansionary monetary policy before the elections and two quarters of restrictive policy after the elections was used. Regressions for the modified and the unmodified versions yield basically the same qualitative results.

A comparison of ECV1 to ECV6 with ECV7 should allow for some discrimination between the Nordhaus-type and the Rogoff-type cycle.

The electoral variables ECV1 to ECV7 are specified to capture any 'jumps' in the monetary growth rate around (i.e. before and after) election dates. ECV8 to ECV10 represent other possible shapes of the electoral monetary cycle that are employed by Grier (1987). ECV8 is a symmetric V-shaped cycle with 8 quarters of monetary deceleration followed by 8 quarters of acceleration. (A very similar variable is already employed by MacCallum (1978) and Allen (1986)). ECV9 depicts a short and intensive period of monetary deceleration after the election followed by 12 quarters of cyclical growth. It is maximal at election quarter and minimal a year later. ECV10 „is designed to capture deceleration after an election and acceleration before, with a 5 quarter trough in the middle.“ (Grier 1987 477)

Obviously there could be many other cycle patterns constructed. The present choice of patterns inevitably involves some degree of arbitrariness. But these ten cycles should capture the most basic forms, and they should help discriminate between two things: first between the Nordhaus-type cycle and the Rogoff-type cycle, and, second, between simple 'jumps' around the elections and other shapes that imply a 16 quarter cycle.

These ten separate specifications of an electoral cycle are then tested, one at a time, first by adding to a reaction function, second by adding to an autoregressive model for money growth. A positive and significant coefficient on the electoral cycle variables is consistent with the modeled electoral cycle.

For small open economies like Switzerland the exchange rate regime decisively influences the possibility of manipulating monetary policy. (See Alesina/Roubini 1992 667 Fn. 7.) The inclusion of exchange rate dummies may not be sufficient to model these effects. For this reason the analysis is restricted to the period of *flexible exchange rates*, where this policy instrument could be manipulated in order to enhance chances of reelection.

The sample period from 1973.2 to 1995.2 includes five elections. The timing of the elections is exogenous. Elections take place every four years at the beginning of the fourth quarter.[10] This yields the following election dates: 1975:4, 1979:4, 1983:4, 1987:4, 1991:4. Parliament and executive are always dominated by a right-wing majority. Since there is no change in government (from right to left and vice versa), the partisan models cannot be tested.

---

[10] Especially for rational political business cycle models it remains unclear whether this quarter should be considered pre- or post-electoral. See also Alesina 1988 37 for the US.

Quarterly data are used because the precise timing of cyclical fluctuations in relation to elections is crucial for the theories. (Alesina/Roubini 1992 668)[11]

In a first approach the electoral variables are tested in the context of reaction functions. In a second approach, these variables enter autoregressive model specifications.

3.5.1 Evidence from Reaction Functions

In addition to the electoral variable the central bank may systematically respond to other variables, such as inflation rate, exchange rates, growth rate of GDP, and interest rates. To test for the existence of political monetary cycles the electoral cycle variables ECV listed in table 3.5 are added to the reaction functions developed in chapter 1, which control for these other factors. The regression equation for the monetary base as dependent variable with all economic variables expressed as nonseasonal differences is

$$\Delta \ln(MB)_t = \beta_0 + \beta_1 \Delta \ln(MB)_{t-1} + \beta_2 \Delta \ln(CPI)_{t-1} + \beta_3 \Delta \ln(DMN)_{t-1}$$
$$+ \beta_4 \Delta \ln(GDP)_{t-1} + \beta_5 \Delta DR_{t-1} + \beta_6 SD1_t + \beta_7 SD2_t + \beta_8 SD3_t + \beta_9 ECV + \varepsilon_t$$

(See table 1.2 for variable definitions and data sources.)

For comparison, regressions with the money supply M1 as dependent variable are also investigated. Equations with both nonseasonal and seasonal differences - i.e. quarterly and yearly rates of change - are estimated. Since most series are not seasonally adjusted regressions with nonseasonal differences include three seasonal dummies (SD1, SD2, SD3).[12] In the equations with seasonal differences seasonality is removed by the definition of the yearly rates of change. (For a similar method of seasonally adjusting the data see Alesina et al. 1992 14 and Alesina et al. 1993 12. However, see section 1.4.3 for a detailed discussion of the problem of seasonality.)

The analysis starts from the estimates presented in chapter one. The electoral cycle variables are added to the partly homogeneous equations 1.3, 1.6, 1.9 and 1.12 (see section 1.5.2) one at a time. Table 3.6 presents the estimation results for

---

11 Of course, quarterly data are preferred to annual data for other reasons, too. Quarterly data yield more observations and, hence, more robust statistical tests. See section 1.3.2e. As already mentioned, monthly data might be more appropriate to model the Rogoff-type cycle. Unfortunately, production variables used in the reaction function approach are only available on a quarterly basis. And to allow for comparisons, autoregressive model specifications also employ quarterly data.

12 The question whether seasonally unadjusted or adjusted data are used may be important. „Haynes and Stone (1987) argue that one reason they found a political business cycle when others did not is that they used unadjusted data. Since the political monetary cycle peaks in the fourth quarter of the election year, it is possible that seasonal adjustment also removes the political cycle.“ (Beck 1987 213).

all four equations. In order to preserve space only the coefficients for the electoral cycle variables and their associated t or p values are reported. Each entry is based on a separate regression. Coefficients of the other control variables do hardly change as a result of the inclusion of the electoral variables. And the overall fit of the model (measured by adjusted R^2) does not improve.

Estimation results for the reaction functions are *not supportive* of the election cycle hypotheses. The only exception is the coefficient on ECV6, which is positive and significant (at the ten percent level) in the quarterly monetary base model. No meaningful comparison between 'pre-rational' and rational expectations models, and between the 16-quarter cycle models and the ones that simply imply effects near (before) the election can be made.

Table 3.6: Estimation Results for Reaction Functions

	Dependent variables			
	$\Delta\ln(MB)$	$\Delta_4\ln(MB)$	$\Delta\ln(M1)$	$\Delta_4\ln(M1)$
Electoral cycle variable	Coefficient (t value)	Coefficient (p value)	Coefficient (p value)	Coefficient (p value)
ECV1	0.0024 (0.401)	0.0077 (0.4429)	-0.0038 (0.3925)	-0.0032 (0.6097)
ECV2	0.0079 (1.263)	0.0126 (0.1537)	-0.0029 (0.4823)	-0.0070 (0.2329)
ECV3	0.0083 (1.638)	0.0121 (0.1753)	-0.0022 (0.5677)	-0.0029 (0.6042)
ECV4	0.0029 (0.353)	-0.0001 (0.9953)	-0.0036 (0.5636)	-0.0031 (0.6891)
ECV5	0.0069 (1.008)	0.0072 (0.4802)	-0.0022 (0.6696)	-0.0020 (0.7566)
ECV6	0.0113* (1.819)	0.0128 (0.1602)	-0.0011 (0.7878)	-0.0066 (0.2908)
ECV7	0.0049 (0.609)	0.0052 (0.6198)	-0.0099 (0.1172)	-0.0103 (0.1262)
ECV8	-0.0010 (-0.868)	0.0017 (0.3995)	-0.0005 (0.5399)	0.0012 (0.3158)
ECV9	0.0003 (0.396)	0.0019 (0.1431)	-0.0001 (0.9769)	0.0006 (0.4399)
ECV10	-0.0002 (-0.202)	0.0020 (0.1417)	-0.0001 (0.8028)	0.0009 (0.2972)

The following equations are used: For $\Delta\ln(MB)$ as dependent variable equation 1.3 from table 1.9; for $\Delta\ln(M1)$ equation 1.6 from table 1.12; for $\Delta_4\ln(MB)$ equation 1.9 from table 1.15; for $\Delta_4\ln(M1)$ equation 1.12 from table 1.19. Numbers in parentheses are associated t statistics or p values; t statistics are calculated on the basis of HCSEs; * significant at 10 percent level.

3.5.2 Evidence from Autoregressive Model Specifications

For comparison the electoral variables are also tested in the context of an autoregressive model specification. (For examples see Alesina et al. 1993, Alesina/Roubini 1992, Beck 1987 and Grier 1987.)[13] In these models money growth rates are regressed on lagged dependent variables, a constant, and the variable measuring the political business cycle. All variables are defined as yearly rates of change (thus removing seasonality). Autoregressive models containing up to 12 lag lengths are investigated. The 'best' autoregressive model - excluding the electoral variables - is chosen on the basis of the following three standard criteria: Schwarz Criterion, Hannan-Quinn Criterion and Final Prediction Error. If the criteria lead to conflicting results, the criterion which selects the least parsimonious model is preferred, because the consequences of overspecification are less serious than the consequences of underspecification. For the yearly monetary base model an AR(9) is chosen. For the yearly money supply model lags 1, 2, 4, 5 and 8 of the dependent variable are selected. Formal tests do not confirm structural breaks hypothesized for 1980 and 1987 (at the ten percent level). Residual analysis for the yearly monetary base model indicates heteroskedasticity, but no autocorrelation. The inefficiency of OLS is corrected using the HCSEs. For the yearly money supply model no autocorrelation and no heteroskedasticity can be detected, so that results are OLS estimates.

Next, the electoral variables are added to the autoregressive equations one at a time, capturing the implications of the different business cycle theories. These theories predict that money growth should be higher (immediately) before elections. Hence, coefficients on the electoral cycle variables should be positive and significantly different from zero.

Estimation results for autoregressive equations using yearly rates of change for the monetary base and the money supply M1 as dependent variables are listed in table 3.7. For brevity only the coefficients on the electoral cycle variables are displayed. The autoregressive equations yield a pattern which is similar to the reaction function results from table 3.6. ECV6 is again significant (at the 5 percent level) in the monetary base equation. Also significant is ECV3 (at the 10 percent level). Both coefficients are consistent with the predictions of the pre-rational political business cycle models.

13 Autoregressive models are based upon the assumption that money growth is generated by a covariance-stationary stochastic process that can be expressed in autoregressive form. See Alesina/Roubini 1992 668-669.

Table 3.7: Estimation Results for Autoregressive Models

	Dependent variables $\Delta_4\ln(MB)$	$\Delta_4\ln(M1)$
Electoral cycle variable	Coefficient (t value)	Coefficient (p value)
ECV1	-0.0082 (-0.736)	-0.0085 (0.2203)
ECV2	0.0103 (1.268)	-0.0012 (0.8503)
ECV3	0.0122* (1.777)	0.0026 (0.6625)
ECV4	-0.0113 (-1.108)	-0.0080 (0.3739)
ECV5	-0.0006 (-0.057)	-0.0041 (0.5857)
ECV6	0.0167** (2.091)	0.0029 (0.6462)
ECV7	-0.0022 (-0.164)	-0.0120 (0.1493)
ECV8	-0.0012 (-0.680)	-0.0010 (0.4502)
ECV9	0.0003 (0.312)	0.0002 (0.8290)
ECV10	0.0004 (0.304)	0.00001 (0.9977)

The equation for $\Delta_4\ln(MB)$ is an AR(9). The equation for $\Delta_4\ln(M1)$ includes lags 1, 2, 4, 5 and 8 of the dependent variable as additional regressors. Numbers in parentheses are associated t statistics or p values. t statistics are calculated on the basis of HCSEs; * significant at the 10 percent level; ** significant at the 5 percent level.

3.5.3 Evidence from Models Without Fixed Effects

Next it is argued that the monetary cycle takes a specific form for each election. A separate dummy variable is constructed for every election, assuming the cycle patterns represented by ECV6 - an example for the Nordhaus cycle - and ECV7 - an example for the Rogoff cycle. (See table 3.5.) These dummy variables enter the regression equations, first one at a time, then all five together. (See Beck 1984 for an example.) Estimation results for reaction functions and autoregressive models are listed in tables 3.8 and 3.9. Again, coefficients for the other variables included in the regressions are not displayed.

The variable representing the Nordhaus-type cycle (ECV6) is significant for the 1979 election in the reaction function and in the autoregression with the seasonal difference of the monetary base as dependent variable. The coefficients are consistent with the predictions of the pre-rational political business cycle theory.

The variable measuring the Rogoff-type cycle (ECV7) is significant for the 1987 election in all equations except for the regression on the seasonal difference of the monetary base. However, coefficients are consistent with this theory only in the regressions on the monetary base. ECV7 shows the wrong signs in the regressions on the money supply.

Do the findings for the monetary base equations support the hypothesis of opportunistic political business cycle theories?

By the end of *1987* Swiss monetary policy was complicated by several factors: crash in the stock market in October, introduction of the Swiss Interbank Clearing (SIC), new liquidity requirements for banks, and an appreciating SFr which lead the SNB to intervene in the exchange rate markets. (See section 1.3.2d.) The reaction functions only control for exchange rate movements, but not for the other factors. It can easily be argued that the electoral variable ECV7 for 1987 simply captures aspects of these other factors. In any case, the results cannot be uniquely ascribed to elections. Hence, they cannot be interpreted as evidence supporting the hypotheses of rational political business cycle theories.

The results for the *1979* election may not just be due to the measurement of the yearly growth rates combined with the structural break imposed at the beginning of 1980. ECV6 is also significant (at the ten percent level) in the quarterly monetary base equation in table 3.6. The evidence from the models without fixed effects suggests that the significance of ECV6 is caused by the events around 1979. In late 1978, strong speculative pressure led to an appreciation of the SFr against the US$. The SNB abandoned its monetary control policy and reverted to an exchange rate target. The signal was given in the form of a SFr/DM exchange rate. This exchange rate should be 'noticeably' above 80 SFr for 100 DM. The massive intervention in the exchange rate market that followed generated a lot of controversy. Many observers agree that these interventions were not simply a mistake, but that the SNB yielded to political pressure. According to Capitelli/Buomberger (1990 540), for instance, the SNB ceded to pressure from the suffering Swiss export industry. Given the long recession that preceded it cannot be ruled out that the upcoming elections for Fall 1979 helped to increase the pressure on the central bank. At least it is interesting to note that the SNB did not return to monetary targeting before December 1979, just after the elections. However, even if it is accepted that the events from late 1978 to December 1979 illustrate the limits of the SNB's political independence, this result is not enough to suggest the existence of a Nordhaus-type political business cycle for Switzerland.

Table 3.8: Estimation Results for Reaction Functions (Without Fixed Effects)

	Dependent variables			
	$\Delta\ln(MB)$	$\Delta_4\ln(MB)$	$\Delta\ln(M1)$	$\Delta_4\ln(M1)$
Electoral cycle variable	Coefficient (t value)	Coefficient (p value)	Coefficient (p value)	Coefficient (p value)
$ECV6_{75}$	0.0189 (1.129)	-0.0016 (0.9531)	-0.0110 (0.2474)	0.0079 (0.7343)
$ECV6_{79}$	0.0300 (1.364)	0.0460* (0.0565)	-0.0004 (0.9589)	0.0299 (0.2438)
$ECV6_{83}$	0.0039 (0.816)	0.0116 (0.5462)	0.0016 (0.8522)	-0.0015 (0.9083)
$ECV6_{87}$	0.0055 (1.214)	0.0166 (0.3153)	0.0058 (0.4855)	-0.0084 (0.4918)
$ECV6_{91}$	0.0011 (0.165)	0.0032 (0.8553)	0.0014 (0.8693)	-0.0051 (0.6368)
$ECV6_{all}$	*0.818 (0.5407)*	*1.113 (0.3624)*	*0.368 (0.8692)*	*0.375 (0.8642)*
$ECV7_{75}$	0.0241 (1.596)	0.0046 (0.8482)	0.0065 (0.6280)	-0.0058 (0.7087)
$ECV7_{79}$	-0.0258 (-0.967)	-0.0150 (0.6338)	-0.0129 (0.3234)	0.0177 (0.3100)
$ECV7_{83}$	0.0013 (0.338)	-0.0040 (0.8581)	-0.0056 (0.6582)	-0.0070 (0.6331)
$ECV7_{87}$	0.0221*** (2.713)	0.0214 (0.3337)	-0.0283** (0.0243)	-0.0356** (0.0126)
$ECV7_{91}$	-0.0065 (-0.634)	0.0092 (0.6787)	0.0003 (0.9831)	-0.0121 (0.4048)
$ECV7_{all}$	*1.836 (0.1168)*	*0.276 (0.9250)*	*1.387 (0.2392)*	*1.715 (0.1432)*

See notes on table 3.6. The subscripts denote the election-year specific dummy variables. Entries for $ECV6_{all}$ and $ECV7_{all}$ are the results of F tests and corresponding p values which test whether the coefficients of the election-year specific dummies are *jointly* significant. * significant at the 10 percent level; ** significant at the 5 percent level; *** significant at the 1 percent level.

Table 3.9: Estimation Results for Autoregressive Models (Without Fixed Effects)

	Dependent variables	
	$\Delta_4\ln(MB)$	$\Delta_4\ln(M1)$
Electoral cycle variable	Coefficient (t value)	Coefficient (p value)
$ECV6_{75}$	0.0054 (0.425)	0.0011 (0.9281)
$ECV6_{79}$	0.0611* (1.781)	0.0209 (0.1338)
$ECV6_{83}$	0.0092 (1.039)	-0.0103 (0.4318)
$ECV6_{87}$	0.0063 (1.332)	0.0077 (0.5265)
$ECV6_{91}$	-0.0015 (0.138)	-0.0064 (0.6265)
$ECV6_{all}$	*2.424*** (0.0432)*	*0.697 (0.6273)*
$ECV7_{75}$	0.0128 (0.693)	0.0011 (0.9516)
$ECV7_{79}$	-0.0700 (-1.104)	-0.0024 (0.9075)
$ECV7_{83}$	-0.0046 (-1.172)	-0.0074 (0.6931)
$ECV7_{87}$	0.0222*** (3.040)	-0.0340* (0.0649)
$ECV7_{91}$	0.0069 (0.885)	-0.0169 (0.3636)
$ECV7_{all}$	*1.212 (0.3119)*	*0.874 (0.5024)*

See notes on table 3.7. The subscripts denote the election-year specific dummy variables. Entries for $ECV6_{all}$ and$ECV7_{all}$ are the results of F tests and corresponding p values which test whether the coefficients of the election-year specific dummies are *jointly* significant. * significant at the 10 percent level; ** significant at the 5 percent level; *** significant at the 1 percent level.

3.5.4 Free Estimation of the Optimal Cyclical Pattern

Instead of using 'manufactured' electoral variables (i.e. prespecifying the timing and the shape of the cycles) the data can be allowed to select a structure for an electoral cycle. This can be achieved by applying the Almon polynomial technique. (For a textbook exposition see e.g. Lardaro 1992 552-561.) Following Grier

Table 3.10: Lag Distribution for the Autoregressive Money Supply Growth Model (Yearly Rates of Change)

Lag	Coefficient	p value	Lag	Coefficient	p value
1	0.04259	0.0542	9	0.06276	0.0338
2	0.04787	0.0450	10	0.06173	0.0335
3	0.05237	0.0404	11	0.05991	0.0334
4	0.05607	0.0379	12	0.05730	0.0337
5	0.05899	0.0364	13	0.05390	0.0347
6	0.06111	0.0355	14	0.04971	0.0373
7	0.06245	0.0348	15	0.04473	0.0434
8	0.06300	0.0343	16	0.03896	0.0574

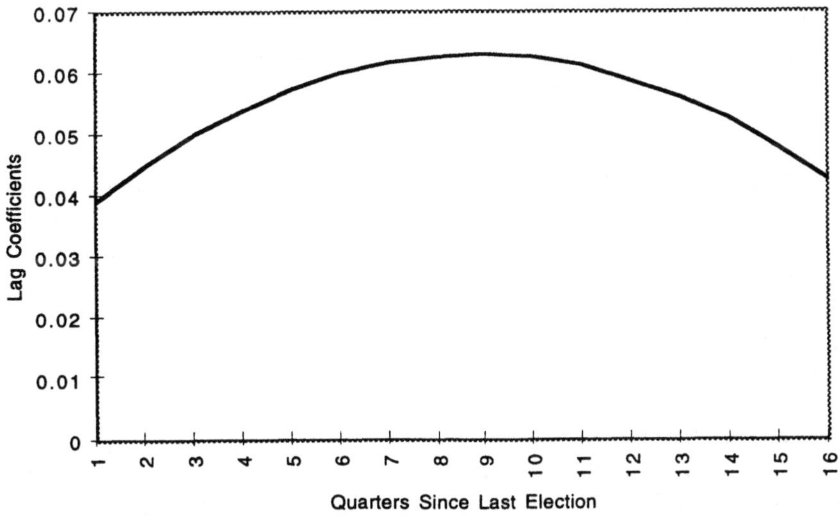

Figure 3.2: Lag Distribution for the Autoregressive Money Supply Growth Model (Yearly Rates of Change)

(1987), an electoral dummy variable that is equal to one in the quarters immediately after the elections and zero otherwise is constructed. Then a 16-quarter polynomial distributed lag is estimated on this dummy variable together with the other control variables in the reaction function or the lagged dependent variables in the autoregressive model specification. The coefficients of the lagged values of the dummy variable are assumed to lie on a polynomial of degree j. This helps to reduce the parameter space. Instead of using 16 degrees of freedom to estimate the lagged dummy variables directly, only the parameters of the polynomial function are directly estimated. (Hence, only $j + 1$ degrees of freedom are used, where j is the degree of the polynomial specified.) Then the lag coefficients for each quarter of the election cycle are derived from the estimated polynomial function. Tests for the degree of the polynomial indicate that - if at all - a second-degree polynomial may be appropriate for the models proposed in this chapter. A 16-quarter, second-degree polynomial distributed lag is estimated for all models. Significant Almon polynomial variables are found for the yearly autoregressive money supply model only. Table 3.10 lists the lag coefficients estimated along with associated p values for this model. The lag distribution is graphed in Figure 3.2. The cycle found does not look like the cycles proposed by business cycle theory.

3.6 Conclusions

The question whether monetary policy is used to help incumbents get reelected is another frequent approach to test for political influence on monetary policy. This chapter tests various electoral variables as predictors of money growth in the context of reaction function models and autoregressive model specifications. Most of these variables are consistently insignificant, and their presence or absence has no effect on the size and significance of the other variables.

One major exception is an electoral variable representing the pre-rational political business cycle. The positive and significant coefficients on this variable in regressions on the monetary base are consistent with the predictions of the Nordhaus-type business cycle theory. The evidence from models without fixed effects suggests that the events around 1979 are responsible for this result. Though it cannot be ruled out that the SNB ceded to political pressure because of the 1979 elections, this result is not enough to establish that there exists a Nordhaus-type political business cycle for Switzerland.

Significant coefficients are also found for a variable representing rational political business cycles. At least for two reasons, this cannot be interpreted as evidence for the existence of this type of political business cycle. First, results for the monetary base and the money supply M1 as dependent variables are conflicting. Second, the empirical analysis suggests that other factors that complicated the conduct of monetary policy at the end of 1987 drive these results.

Thus, the data do support what can be expected on theoretical grounds. The existence of a political monetary cycle is hard to rationalize in the case of Switzerland, mainly for two reasons. First, the central bank is formally independent. Second, the distribution of power in the political market place with a coalition government having a comfortable majority and the absence of any change in government since 1959 do not necessitate an electoral manipulation of monetary policy.

CHAPTER 4

The Executive Central Bank Relationship: The Case of Switzerland

4.1 Introduction

A central bank is usually thought - and conceives of itself as - „a nonpartisan technocratic group making nonpartisan technical decisions." (Beck 1987 199) But monetary policy is not made in a policy vacuum. And economic literature on central banking typically assumes some sort of direct and/or indirect political influence. (Havrilesky 1988 84)[1]

A fast-growing theoretical literature on politics and macroeconomic policy demonstrates that it is reasonable for a government to delegate the responsibility for price stability to an independent central bank.[2] The *theoretical rationale* for central bank independence, while not a new one, has been reformulated in the ongoing 'rules versus discretion' debate. (Eijffinger/Schaling 1995 185)[3] Both, the 'rules' and the 'discretion' approach begin from the inflationary bias that would be present in monetary policy without central bank independence. But their propositions to overcome what has been termed the 'dynamic inconsistency of policy' differ.[4] According to the conservative-central-banker approach of Rogoff (1985) entrusting monetary policy to a conservative central banker will improve overall economic performance, i.e. reduce the level and variability of inflation while at the same time taking into account the short-run trade-off between inflation and output.[5] The principal-agent-approach of Walsh (1995) and Persson/

1 The assumption of a nonpartisan central bank also conflicts with the observation that top officials of central banks regularly have to belong to a certain party. Why does party membership matter in the appointment process?

2 For a comprehensive review of the arguments for central bank independence up through 1992 see Cukierman 1992. See also Alesina 1988 40, Barro/Gordon 1983, Caesar 1980 and 1981, Fischer 1994, Kath 1995, Neumann 1991, Rogoff 1985. The seminal papers are compiled by Eijffinger 1997. For a critical assessment of the theoretical arguments (and the empirical evidence) see e.g. Carvalho 1995/1996.

3 For a textbook exposition of this debate see McCallum 1989 chap. 12.

4 Dynamic (or time) inconsistency refers to the inability of politicians to commit to and implement policies that may be best for the economy in the long run, but are politically harmful in the short run. The seminal papers are Kydland/Prescott 1977 and Barro/Gordon 1983.

5 A distinction between level and variability of inflation is of interest in a politico-economic context. The level of inflation measures the amount of 'invisible' tax used to meet the demand of rent-seeking interest groups (including bureaucrats). The variability of inflation reflects changes of monetary policy in the business cycle. It may indi-

Tabellini (1993) proposes to solve the inflationary bias problem by structuring a contract „that imposes costs on the central banker when inflation deviates from the optimal level.“ (Fischer 1995 201)

Numerous *empirical studies* support the theoretical case for central bank independence.[6] All these studies report a positive relationship between the degree of central bank independence and price stability. But there is no indication that the monetary regime systematically matters for real economic performance (i.e. growth or unemployment), as is predicted by the Barro-Gordon framework. Since central bank independence is negatively associated with inflation, but does not seem to have costs in terms of real economic performance, central bank independence is almost like having a free lunch. (Eijffinger/Schaling 1993)[7] Of course, the empirical work has correctly been criticized that the negative correlation between central bank independence and inflation does not necessarily imply a causal relationship from central bank independence to inflation or the other way around. (See e.g. Eijffinger/Schaling 1995 207; Fischer 1995 205; Goodhart 1994 112.)[8] And having an independent central bank committed to price stability has its cost, too. (Grilli et al. 1991 365; Spahn/Ziemes 1992 227)[9]

It is one thing to show that a politically independent central bank is preferable. It is another thing to ensure that a central bank can really operate autonomously. (Clausen/Willms 1993 609) Empirical analysis shows that de jure (or formal) independence of a central bank and its de facto resistance to political pressure are not perfectly correlated. (Havrilesky/Granato 1993 259 Fn. 3) This suggests that,

---

cate the central bank's responsiveness to political pressures for an anticyclical monetary policy.

6 Empirical work in this area includes Alesina 1988 and 1989, Alesina/Summers 1993, Banaian et al. 1986, Cukierman 1992 chap. 20, Eijffinger/Schaling 1993 and 1995, Grilli et al. 1991, Havrilesky/Granato 1993, Schiemann/Alshuth 1994. For a recent study see e.g. Eijffinger et al. 1998.

7 Considering the fact that central bank independence is a determinant of inflation, and assuming that inflation itself may be a determinant of unemployment and growth, these results suggest that there is no systematic empirical relationship between inflation on the one side and unemployment and growth on the other side. Why is inflation important, then? See also Gärtner 1995 422. (Of course, there still remain the distributional aspects.)

8 One related problem is the need to control for differences in underlying inflationary pressures across the countries included. See Banaian et al. 1995 179. Another problem is that the „claimed statistical association between formal measures of central bank independence and inflation is contradicted by the inflation records of two of the most important central banks in the world.“ Cargill 1995 169. These are the Bank of Japan and the Federal Reserve.

9 „Finally, there is the question of whether a central bank can be too independent. The answer is yes. As a matter of theory, both of the basic analytic models of central banking imply that the central banker can be too inflation-averse, and too insensitive to the possibilities of stabilizing output. Further, there are potential benefits from the coordination of monetary and fiscal policy that may be foregone when the central bank is independent.“ Fischer 1995 205. See also Prast 1996 for a discussion of the drawbacks of central bank independence.

while statutory autonomy is important, other institutional aspects of monetary policymaking may be important, too. To determine the degree of *de facto autonomy* these aspects must be included in the analysis.

The SNB is usually considered as one of the most independent central banks. It is the goal of this chapter to provide a detailed analysis of the de jure and de facto autonomy of the SNB that may complement the existing studies of the (formally) autonomous central banks in the US and Germany.[10] Studies of central bank independence typically focus on the relationship between the executive (the government) and the central bank. Therefore, this chapter questions if and how the SNB's monetary policy is influenced by the Swiss federal government (the Federal Council).[11] Any legislative influence is neglected here.

To determine why an *executive influence* might be expected (and also why it may not exist) the legal and institutional background is investigated. Since genuine autonomy is not only a matter of statutory rules, other aspects that determine the amount of de facto political pressures on Swiss monetary poliymakers are discussed, too. This includes the structure of the executive as the supervisory authority, but also the characteristics of the Swiss political market for monetary policy. The legal setting leaves substantial room for executive influence: The executive controls the appointment process. The stipulation of the formal relationship between central bank and executive (in terms of collaboration and supervision) is rather diffuse. There exists a general obligation of the SNB to support the government's policy. And responsibilities with respect to exchange rate regimes lie with the government. Despite these institutional shortcomings the SNB enjoys a reputation of being an independent central bank. This reputation ultimately builds on its inflationary performance. It is argued that both, the commission government and the properties of the political market for monetary policy, help the SNB to achieve this inflationary performance. Hence, the SNB's inflationary performance is not necessarily the result of its legal status. The impact of the financial community is also identified as a constraint on executive influence.

Since the question of executive influence cannot be settled by a priori argument, it is also analyzed whether any executive influence can be measured empirically. *Empirical tests* turn out to be particularly difficult in the Swiss case, not only because of the composition of the commission government, but also because of commission government per se. If it is assumed that the Federal Council decides as a body, the lack of variation in the party composition of the commission

---

[10] For a comparative analysis of the de jure independence of the German, Dutch, Austrian, and Swiss central banks see Kleinewefers 1996.

[11] Several reasons make an analysis of the political influence on monetary policy especially interesting. First, monetary policy is officially made by a rather small body, which is supposed to be nonpartisan and legally independent. Second, in this area a relatively accurate record of the conduct of the agency under investigation is available. (There exist 'good' variables to gauge agency behavior!) Third, monetary policy is important, since it affects real variables at least in the short run. Therefore, massive pressure by interest groups to influence monetary policy in their own interest can be expected. See Beck 1982 416.

government precludes a standard test of partisan theory. As an alternative, popularity measures based on national referenda are constructed. It is found that some of these measures are positively associated with Swiss money growth rates. If it is assumed that each federal councillor effectively decides on subjects concerning his department, two more tests can be performed. First, it can be tested whether partisan affiliation of the finance minister affects the conduct of monetary policy. Empirical results do not support this hypothesis. Second, it can be tested whether monetary policy depends on each individual finance minister. This hypothesis is supported by results from quarterly models.

Regression analysis does not imply causality. If shifts in monetary policy can be detected, they cannot uniquely be ascribed to changes in executive preferences. Although some association between the variables that are supposed to measure changes in executive preferences and monetary policy can be detected, it cannot be concluded that the executive does in fact influence monetary policy. Other, more convincing explanations for these shifts can be found quite easily. Not only the theoretical, but also the empirical analysis of executive influence on Swiss monetary policy remains inconclusive.

The chapter is organized as follows. Section 4.2 analyses the legal relationship between the executive and the central bank. Section 4.3 explains why commission government tends to reduce the variability of inflation, and also the ability to test for executive influence. Section 4.4 discusses the role of the Swiss political market for monetary policy as a determinant of the level of inflation, and identifies the impact of the financial community as a constraint on executive influence. Section 4.5 addresses the de facto (in)dependence of the SNB and presents various hypotheses tests. Section 4.6 offers some concluding remarks.

4.2 The Legal Relationship between Executive and Central Bank

The merit of the literature on central bank independence is not just that it demonstrates the superiority of an autonomous central bank. It also identifies the institutional (legal) setting that is required to establish a politically independent monetary authority. A comparison of this institutional setting with the legal framework actually existing for the SNB serves to determine the degree of the de jure independence of the Swiss central bank. Table 4.1 presents an overview of this discussion. The left column lists the institutional requirements for an autonomous central bank that are put forward in the literature.[12] The right column adds the corresponding regulations that hold for the SNB.[13]

---

[12] The table combines arguments from the following sources: Alesina 1988, Clausen/Willms 1993, Grilli et al. 1991, Parkin/Bade 1978.

[13] Sources for this second column are the Federal Constitution FC (Bundesverfassung), the National Bank Law NBL (Nationalbankgesetz) of 1979, and Schürmann 1980. For a complete list of the legal sources regulating SNB activities see SNB 1995 23-24.

Table 4.1: Central Bank Independence: Institutional Requirements and Actual Institutional Features of the SNB

Institutional requirements for an autonomous central bank	**Institutional features of the SNB**
Functional independence *(Constitutional provisions and relationship with the government)*	
Constitutional guarantee of central bank independence	Absent
Statutory requirements that central bank pursues monetary stability amongst its goals (legislated monetary stability objective)	No explicit statement concerning price stability or any other concrete objective in Article 39 of FC Article 31^{quinquies} of FC (Konjunkturartikel): ensure balanced economic development, prevent and combat unemployment and inflation
Legal provisions that strengthen the central bank's position in conflicts with the government are present	Absent (Article 60 of NBL: possibility of dismissal; government has the final say)
No mandatory participation of government representative on the board	*
No government approval of monetary policy formulation is required (central bank is final authority)	Article 2(2) of NBL: Consultation (information and coordination) Article 63 of NBL: Supervision by Federal Council
No obligation to support the government's policy	Article 31^{quinquies} of FC (Konjunkturartikel): obligation to support the government's policy
No democratic control by legislature	Article 63(2k) of NBL: Annual report
Personal independence *(Rules for appointments and dismissals of governor and board)*	
Governor (Board of Directors) not appointed by government	Article 53(2) of NBL: All three members of the Board of Directors appointed by the Federal Council Article 60 of NBL: possibility of dismissal by the same authority
Governor (Board of Directors) appointed for at least 5 years (term length)	* Term of 6 years
Reappointment of governor (Board of Directors) excluded	Reappointment possible

Table 4.1 continued

***Personal independence** (continued)* *(Rules for appointments and dismissals of governor and board)*	
All the board (Bank Council) not appointed by government	Bank Council counting 40 members, 25 appointed by Federal Council (proportion appointed by government is 5/8)
Board (Bank Council) appointed for at least 5 years (term length)	Term of 4 years
Reappointment of the board (Bank Council) excluded	Reappointment possible
Instrumental independence *(Control of monetary policy instruments)*	
Central bank responsible for exchange rate policy	Federal Council responsible for exchange rate regime
No requirement for monetary financing of budget deficits	*
Banking supervision not entrusted to central bank	* Federal Banking Commission in charge of bank supervision
Financial independence	
Budgetary autonomy	*
Accounts verified by nonpolitical institution	Audit committee verifies annual accounts. Written report to general meeting of shareholders, but before Federal Council is informed and has to approve this report
No pressure to earn profits	Pressure to earn profits cannot be excluded

* indicates that the SNB possesses that attribute.

4.2.1 Institutional Requirements for an Autonomous Central Bank

Following Clausen/Willms (1993) four dimensions of central bank independence are distinguished: functional, personal, instrumental, and financial independence.[14] Each dimension includes different attributes. And the overall degree of central bank independence is determined by a combination of these attributes.

---

14 See also Willms 1990 and 1992. A similar classification scheme is used by Neumann 1991.
Cukierman (1992 372) divides legal characteristics or 'variables' of central bank independence into four groups: „(1) variables concerning the appointment, dismissal, and term of office of the chief executive officer of the bank (usually the governor); (2) variables concerning the resolution of conflicts between the executive branch and the central bank and the degree of participation of the central bank in the formulation of monetary policy and in the budgetary process; (3) final objectives of the central bank as

Functional independence means that the central bank is the only authority responsible for monetary policy and, hence, price stability. Central bank independence should be guaranteed by the constitution. (Neumann 1991 105; Woll 1988 123) Since a constitutional amendment is usually more difficult to obtain than a change in legislation, the threat of change in central bank statute is less serious.[15] Statutes should contain an explicitly-declared general policy objective. (Parkin/Bade 1978 25) Especially the 'price stability' objective should appear in the central bank statute.[16] Explicit legal directives should describe a transparent procedure for how to resolve an eventual conflict between the government and the central bank. (Grilli et al. 1991 367) Both, the prescription of policy objectives (preferably monetary stability) and legal directives for the case of conflict „enhance the 'gate keeping' power of the monetary regime: they make it less likely that, in case of conflict, the bank's position will be overruled by the gov-

---

stated in its charter; and (4) legal restrictions on the ability of the public sector to borrow from the central bank."

Alesina 1988 and Alesina/Summers 1993 distinguish four dimensions of 'political independence': „the institutional relationship between the central bank and the executive, the procedure to nominate and dismiss the head of the central bank, the role of government officials on the central bank board, and the frequency of contacts between the executive and the bank." Alesina/Summers 1993 153.

Grilli et al. 1991 distinguish between 'political independence' and 'economic independence'. „Political independence is the capacity to choose the *final goal* of monetary policy, such as inflation or the level of economic activity. Economic independence is the capacity to choose *the instruments* with which to pursue these goals." Grilli et al. 1991 366.

Similarly, Fischer 1995 distinguishes between goal independence and instrument independence. „A central bank that is given control over the levers of monetary policy and allowed to use them has *instrument independence*; a central bank that sets its own policy goals has *goal independence*." Fischer 1995, 202. According to Fischer (1995 and 1994), a central bank should have instrument independence, but not goal independence.

Prast 1996 distinguishes between independence and commitment. „A committed central bank is bound by specific rules limiting the use of policy instruments so as to attain the prescribed goals." (Prast 1996 381) Given the drawbacks of independence, commitment is recommended.

15 The threat of changes in the central bank statute (i. e. a reduction of central bank autonomy) by the government (and/or the legislature) is frequently considered as the most important means to control 'independent' central banks. See sections 5.3.1 and 5.4.1. As Borins (1972, 185-186) states: „The Federal Reserve System nominally is the most independent central bank in the Western world, as its officials are well aware. They wish to maintain this independence. Paradoxically, to maintain this *general* independence to set monetary policy, they may well give up their *particular* independence at any one time by choosing to follow policies which Congress and the President would like." See also Frey/Schneider 1981 Fn. 4 295.

16 „In principle, independence to choose the final goals can be defined without reference to the contents of such goals. In practice, however, the main virtue of having an independent central bank is that it can provide credibility. This is why we identify independence with autonomy to pursue the goal of low inflation. Any institutional feature that enhances the central bank capacity to pursue this goal will, on our definition, increase central bank independence." Grilli et al. 1991 367.

ernment." (Grilli et al. 1991 367) Functional independence further requires that no government official participates in the board of the central bank, and that the central bank does not need any government approval of its monetary policy formulation. There should also be no obligation to support the government's policy. And the absence of democratic control[17] should exclude any pressure from legislative bodies. (Clausen/Willms 1993 609)

The degree of *personal independence* is determined by the rules for appointing the members of the central bank's governing bodies (Board of Directors and Bank Council), their term lengths, and the possibility of reappointments. To reduce the leverage which governments can exercise on central bank policy, no appointments should be made by the government.[18] Term lengths should be rather long and valid for a predetermined period of time. (Grilli et al. 1991 367) Of course, a dismissal by the government is ruled out. The possibility of reappointment should also be excluded. Otherwise, in order to further chances of reappointment, incumbents might be particularly responsive to the body making the appointments.[19]

Instrumental independence implies that the central bank has complete control of all monetary policy instruments that influence the money supply. In addition to the control of standard monetary instruments (such as setting the discount rate) the following three attributes should be fulfilled. First, all responsibilities related to exchange rate regimes and interventions into exchange rate markets should lie exclusively with the central bank. Second, any (direct or indirect) monetary financing of budget deficits should be excluded. The central bank may help the treasury in its short-term cash management operations. (Fischer 1995 203 Fn. 7) But direct credit to the government should not be automatic, at a market interest rate, explicitly stated as temporary, and in a limited amount. Moreover, the central bank should not participate as a buyer in the primary market for public debt. (Grilli et al. 1991 369) Third, the central bank should not be concerned with banking supervision. Administrative instruments such as portfolio constraints on bank intermediaries or ceilings to private bank loans „facilitate the financing of government borrowing by administratively increasing the private demand for government securities. They can weaken central bank independence by removing part of monetary control from the market." (Grilli et al. 1991 370)

---

17 There exists no unanimity on this point. According to Fischer (1995 202) „the central bank should be given a clearly defined goal or set of goals, and the power to achieve them, and should be held accountable for doing so. Accountability is needed for two reasons: first, to set incentives for the central bank to meet its goals and explain its actions; second, to provide democratic oversight of a powerful political institution." And he prefers precise accountability to elected officials to vague general accountability, because the former is more likely to be effective.

18 Instead, these appointments should be made by the bodies of the central bank, thus ensuring that the monetary authorities possess the necessary know-how. Clausen/Willms 1993 609; Grilli et al. 1991 367.

19 See Alt 1991 59-62 for a discussion of the effects of reappointment incentives for central bank governors.

Financial independence requires that the central bank has its own revenues to finance its operations. Its accounts should be verified by a nonpolitical institution. And the central bank should not be under pressure (from the government and other groups, e.g. shareholders) to earn profits. Therefore, profits should not simply accrue to the treasury. Otherwise the treasury anticipates this income in budget planning and the central bank is under pressure to distribute its profits even though this might conflict with monetary stability objectives.

4.2.2 Institutional Features of the SNB

An analysis of the *specific regulations for the SNB* reveals several deviations from this legal setting that is supposed to ensure central bank independence. The following discussion focuses on the attributes that deviate from this 'ideal' regulatory framework.

The SNB has its constitutional basis in Article 39 of the Federal Constitution FC (Bundesverfassung). Organizational details are regulated in the 'National Bank Law' (NBL; Nationalbankgesetz).[20] Also relevant for the activity of the SNB is Article 31^{quinquies} of the FC.

Article 39(2) of the FC stipulates: „The Confederation may exercise its monopoly of issuing bank-notes by means of a state bank placed under a separate management or concede its right, subject to a right of repurchase, to a joint stock central bank managed with the collaboration and under the supervision of the Confederation." Section 3 sets out the broad objective for the SNB: „The main function of the bank enjoying the monopoly of issuing bank-notes shall be to regulate the circulation of money in the country, to facilitate payment operations and to conduct within the scope of federal legislation a credit and monetary policy beneficial to the general interest of Switzerland". Article 2(1) of the NBL lists an additional general objective: „It shall advise the federal authorities in monetary matters."

The relationship between government and central bank is not clearly defined in the federal legislation (NBL). The bank is „managed with the collaboration and under the supervision of the Confederation". (Article 1 and 2 of the NBL) What is meant by 'collaboration' is specified in Article 2(2) of the NBL: Federal Council (i.e. the executive branch of the Swiss federal government) and SNB inform each other about their intentions before taking important policy decisions, and they coordinate their policy measures. „Formally this coordination takes place at periodic meetings between the federal government's delegation for general economic policy and the National Bank's governing board." (SNB 1995 17) 'Collaboration' and 'supervision' are further specified in Article 63 of the NBL. This article basically delimits the role of the federal government to supervision and approval of

---

20 The NBL was introduced in October 1905. It has been revised in June 1911, April 1921, December 1953, and August 1979. Changes in this law are usually prepared by the Federal Council. They must be approved by the legislature.

such matters as the size of the bank's capital, the denominations of bank notes, or the share of profits between Cantons. But as for most central banks there exists a general obligation for the SNB to support government policy.[21] Article 31 quinquies of the FC entitles the Confederation (i.e. the Federal Council) to „take measures to ensure balanced economic development and, in particular, to prevent and combat unemployment and price inflation." (Section 1) „In the case of measures in the monetary and banking spheres, public finances and foreign trade, the Confederation can if necessary depart from the principle of freedom of trade and industry." (Section 2) This so-called 'Konjunkturartikel' yields a more specific description of what is meant by the broad objective of „a credit and monetary policy beneficial to the general interest of Switzerland". Monetary policy has not only to pursue the price stability goal, but it also has to ensure balanced economic development and to prevent and combat unemployment. Moreover, the 'Konjunkturartikel' provides the constitutional basis for the Confederation to intervene in the monetary policy of the SNB whenever the executive deems it to be necessary. Although this article was added to the FC, after being accepted in a popular referendum in February 1978, it didn't create a new situation for the conduct of Swiss monetary policy. It only provided the constitutional basis for what had already been practice for at least a decade. (Schürmann 1980 24; Botschaft 1978 812, 814, 828 and 838)[22]

Overall, these regulations do not establish a *functionally* independent central bank. The constitution does not provide any guarantee of independence to the SNB. An explicit statement concerning price stability or any other concrete objective is absent in Article 39 of the FC. More concrete objectives are stipulated by the 'Konjunkturartikel', but without any priority for the price stability goal. There exists no provision saying that the central bank does not receive instructions from the executive or that it is the final authority in monetary policy. The emphasis is on information and coordination between executive and SNB. Annual targets for money growth rates are always announced in agreement with the Federal Council, for instance. It is also not explicitly regulated what happens in case of conflict between the government and the central bank.[23] Hence, a resolution of policy conflicts has to be done informally. (See Schmid 1979 110-119.) But, as will be discussed below, the possibility of dismissal by the Federal Council makes it obvious that in the end the government has the final say. The 'Konjunkturartikel' - which allows for any type of interference of politics with monetary

---

21 For a survey see Parkin/Bade 1978. For example, Article 12 of the German Bundesbankgesetz obliges the Bundesbank to support the general economic policy of the federal government in the course of pursuing its own duties. See Frey/Schneider 1981 294; Schneider 1979 476.

22 During the 70s the Federal Council and the SNB undertook various attempts to cut the demand for SFr by administrative means. For a discussion of these administrative measures see Botschaft 1978 824-827 and SNB 1982b. On the relationship between these administrative measures and central bank independence see Schmid 1979 61-66.

23 Apparently, such controversies do exist. See e.g. AB 1991 2285.

policy - obliges the SNB to support the government's policy. However, democratic control by the legislature is only indirect over the supervisory authority of the executive.

Procedures for appointing the SNB's top officials are rather diffused. (Parkin/Bade 1978 32) Figure 4.1 provides a survey of the SNB's organization. (For slightly different figures see SNB 1995 28-29 and Hotz-Hart et al. 1995 445.) It shows that (and how) the Federal Council dominates the appointment process.

The SNB is organized as a public corporation.[24] The *Bank Council* has the general oversight.[25] It is composed of 40 members, each serving for a term of four years. (Article 40 of NBL) There are no term limits. (Article 46(5) of NBL) Fifteen members are appointed by the general meeting of shareholders. Twenty-five members are appointed by the Federal Council. (Article 40 of NBL) This allows the Federal Council to appoint a majority (62.5 %) of members to this body. The way members of the Bank Council are appointed is precisely regulated in Article 42 of the NBL. It nicely illustrates the predominant role of the Federal Council in the appointment process. First the Federal Council appoints the president and vice-president. Then the general meeting of shareholders elects 15 members and informs the Federal Council about its decisions. After this the Federal Council appoints the remaining 23 members. From these 23, a maximum of 5 can be members of the federal legislature, and a maximum of 5 can be members of cantonal executives.

The *Bank Committee* (Articles 48 and 49 of NBL) has the detailed oversight and control over the management of the central bank. It meets at least once a month. It is composed of the president and vice-president of the Bank Council (both are appointed by the Federal Council), and eight other members of the Bank Council, appointed by that council. Terms are four years, and reappointment is possible. The different geographic regions should be represented. Usually, only one member per canton should sit in this committee. Exceptionally, two are allowed. The Bank Committee proposes candidates to the Bank Council that might be considered by the Federal Council for appointment to the Board of Directors.

---

24 Ownership is distributed in 100,000 shares, each with a nominal value of 500 SFr. Shares are 'Namenaktien': Only Swiss citizens and Swiss institutions can hold them. All stockholders have to be registered, and only registered shareholders are entitled to vote. Shares are listed on the stock exchange.

25 Article 41 of the NBL stipulates that various economic branches and the different regions, especially the more important financial, industrial and commercial centers, ought to be represented in the Bank Council. „Its quarterly meetings provide the Governing Board with the opportunity of elaborating and justifying its policy in detail and engaging in a valuable exchange of views." SNB 1995 20.

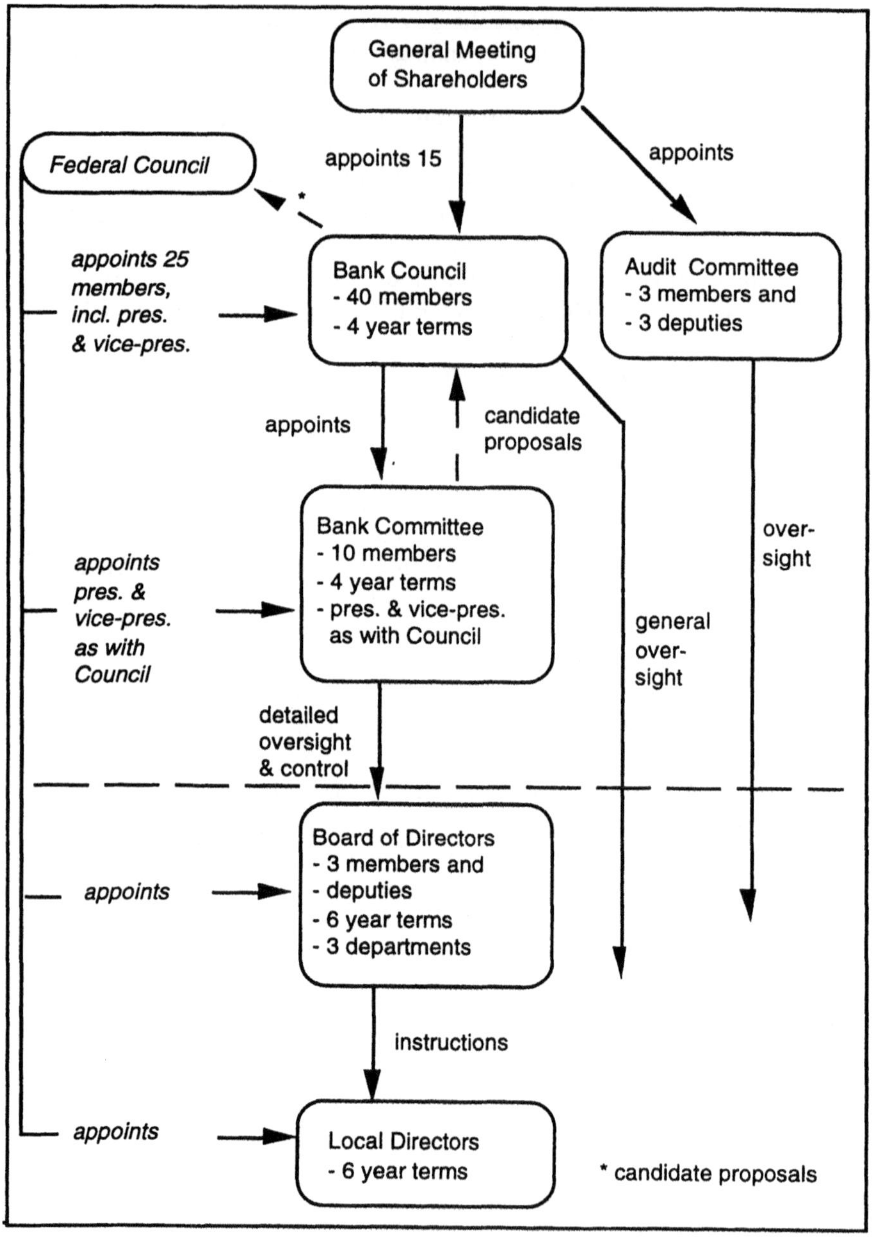

Figure 4.1: Organization of the SNB

The *Board of Directors* (Articles 52 and 53 of NBL) is the top 'executive' authority of the SNB. It counts three members, and each heads one department. Members act according to the decisions taken by the Board of Directors as a whole. They are appointed by the Federal Council for a term of six years. Nominees are proposed by the Bank Council. The Federal Council also appoints the president and vice-president of the Board of Directors, as well as the Local Directors.

Article 60 of the NBL states that all officials and employees of the bank can be recalled by the authority that appointed them. The only requirement is that reasons must be stated. This possibility of dismissal clarifies what happens (or would happen) in the case of serious conflict between government and central bank. (See also Schürmann 1980 24 Fn. 6, and 177.) The Federal Council could replace the top officials of the central bank with more compliant people. In this perspective the questions of term lengths and reappointability loose importance.

Since the executive controls the appointment process, the SNB does not enjoy *personal independence* from the federal government. The executive clearly has the possibility to exercise leverage on central bank policy over the appointment process. As Schürmann (1980 168) notes, this was also the original intention of the drafters of the NBL.

The Swiss central bank controls all standard monetary instruments. Article 15 of the NBL precludes a direct monetary financing of budget deficits. The SNB also has no obligation to indirectly finance deficits. Responsibility for banking supervision is entrusted to an independent federal authority, the Federal Banking Commission.[26] But as with other central banks (see e.g. Kath 1995 for the German Bundesbank) the authority of the SNB with respect to exchange rate policy is limited, since the responsibility for determining the exchange rate regime is entrusted to the Federal Council. This potentially weakens the *instrumental independence* of the SNB.

---

[26] For a discussion of the arguments for and against separation of the functions of monetary policy and banking supervision see Goodhart/Schoenmaker 1995.
For Fischer (1995 203) the question whether the central bank should supervise banks or not remains open and is not of much interest. More recent experiences in Switzerland show that this perception might be wrong. Economic stagnation and the crisis in the real estate market were accompanied by bank mergers and bank failures. According to Lusser, the central bank would probably not have been able to pursue the goal of price stability with the same determination had it been responsible for bank supervision, too. In addition to this potential conflict of interest the head of the SNB provides a second argument in favor of a division of labor between central bank and federal banking commission. A central bank that is in charge of both monetary policy and bank supervision would probably allocate too much power to remain independent in the long run. Calls for control of the central bank would increase and central bank independence would be endangered. This leads to the apparently paradoxical conclusion that less power tends to enhance central bank autonomy. (Brenner 1994). But the paradox is only apparent. The more power, the more numerous the stakeholders, and the greater the interests of these stakeholders to have access to this power.

The SNB enjoys budgetary autonomy. Annual accounts are verified by the Audit Committee, appointed each year by the general meeting of shareholders. (See Figure 4.1.) The three members of this committee do not need to be shareholders. They have the authority to inquire all aspects of the banks activity. The committee submits a written report to the general meeting of shareholders, but only after the report has been approved by the Federal Council. (Article 25(3) of NBL) As to the distribution of profits the FC (Article 39(4)) states that after deduction of a reasonable interest or of reasonable dividends on the initial capital or the shares and of statutory payments to the reserve fund at least two thirds of the net profits of the bank shall accrue to the Cantons. Article 42(f) of the FC also stipulates that in order to cover its expenses, the Confederation gets a share of the net profits of the bank entrusted with the monopoly of issuing banknotes. Article 27 of the NBL describes the distribution of profits in detail. (See also SNB 1995 19.) The important thing is that there is no prescription about how the SNB's profits have to be calculated. This allows the SNB the practice of reporting a constant amount of profits. (For a critical assessment of this practice see Ungern-Sternberg 1996b.) Because of the SNB's organization as a corporation pressure from shareholders to earn profits might be expected. However, shareholders play a limited role for several reasons. (See also Fn. 24.) About two thirds of stocks are owned by the Cantons and other public institutions (but not by the Confederation). The rest of stocks is distributed among private shareholders. These can allocate a maximum of 100 votes each[27] (out of a total of 100,000 votes), giving a very small weight to individual shareholders. Dividends are fixed at 6 percent of the equity capital paid in (50 millions SFr.). And as seen above, (public and private) shareholders have little influence in the appointment process. However, there are regular political attempts to increase the amount of profits to be transferred to the fiscal authorities (Confederacy and Cantons), and pressure to earn profits cannot be completely ruled out. (See section 5.4.2.) Despite these potential dangers, the SNB can be considered as being (more or less) *financially independent*.

4.2.3 De Jure Dependence of the SNB

The comparison between institutional requirements proposed for an independent central bank and the actual legal setting of the SNB reveals several features that favor executive influence on Swiss monetary policy. The conclusion that „formal government participation in monetary policy is quite minor overall“ (Banaian et al. 1986 204) may not be justified.[28] De jure the SNB is not as independent as a central bank could be. The main reasons for executive influence are

27 Though they may own more than 100 shares.

28 However, compared to other central banks the SNB is usually considered as legally independent. In a comparison of 68 central banks reported in Cukierman (1992 chap. 19) the SNB ranks first based on measures of legal independence. A closer inspection of the coding of the basic legal variables raises some question marks, however. The legal provision for dismissal for policy reasons at executive branch's discretion is not ac-

- the appointment process (which can be controlled by the executive)
- the rather diffuse relationship between executive and central bank (collaboration and supervision)
- the general obligation to support the government's policy
- the division of the responsibility for monetary policy and exchange rate regime.

As Cukierman (1992 371) notes, the legal status of a central bank suggests what degree of independence legislators meant to confer on the central bank. A discussion of the legal independence also informs about potential channels for executive influence on monetary policymaking.[29] Among these the appointment process is often considered as the primary mechanism by which the executive influences monetary policies. (Chappell et al. 1993 185) What can be observed in practice is that partisan preferences do affect the appointment process. An unwritten law calls for two radicals and one christian democrat in the Board of Directors. Since the SNB was founded in 1907, there has never been a social democrat in the Board. The 1974 appointments for instance triggered the question in the legislature whether qualification or party affiliation is relevant for becoming a member of the SNB Board of Directors. (See AB 1974 1089.) And a considerable political wrangling took place in 1984 when Meyer (who has affiliations to the right-of-centre radical democrats) had been picked out rather than Schiltknecht (a social democrat and the favorite of the social democratic finance minister Stich) mainly for party-political reasons.[30]

To sum up: From the analysis of the de jure independence of the SNB some executive influence on Swiss monetary policy can be predicted. According to the literature on central bank independence this results, ceteris paribus, in a higher level and variability of inflation.

Despite these institutional shortcomings the SNB enjoys the reputation of being one of the most independent central banks. This reputation probably builds on its record of securing price stability. How can apparent political dependence be

---

counted for, as is the diffuse relationship for monetary policy formulation. Since it is rather the executive that has the final say, the variable 'government directives and resolution of conflict' is probably marked too high. Variables related to 'limitations of lending' may have excessive weight in the overall legal index.

Prast (1996 382-383) also criticizes that - based on the legal setting - Switzerland is ranked too high in most empirical studies. Most indicators of central bank independence employ (at least partly) the classification developed by Bade/Parkin 1985. Their evaluation is based on the NBL of 1953, thus overlooking important changes in this law in 1979 (especially the impacts of the 'Konjunkturartikel'). See also Forder 1998.

29 The Bank Council regulates all bank-internal matters, such as responsibilities of bank officials, their relationships with each other, minimal and maximal salaries, and management. All these regulations, as well as the SNB's annual report, have to be approved by the Federal Council. (Article 61 of NBL) This, of course, provides additional channels for executive influence.

30 Two additional informal rules exist for the appointment process to the Board of Directors. One member always has a bank-internal career background, and one member has to be a representative of the French-speaking part of Switzerland.

reconciled with this reputation? One answer is that formal central bank independence is neither a sufficient nor a necessary condition for price stability.[31] Actual central bank behavior ultimately depends on the incentive structures. And these include more than just central bank legislation. „The basic objective difficulty in characterizing and measuring central bank independence is that it is determined by a multitude of legal, institutional, cultural, and personal factors, many of which are difficult to quantify and some of which are unobservable to the general public." (Cukierman 1992 349; see also chap. 23.) And Cukierman adds two additional arguments why the focus on legal independence may not suffice: „First, central bank laws are usually incomplete in the sense that they do not specify explicitly the limits of authority between the central bank and the political authorities under all contingencies. These voids are filled by informal practices, tradition, and the like. Second, even when the law is quite explicit, actual practice may deviate from it." (Cukierman 1992 369) Indicators of legal independence can only reflect the letter of the law.[32] Defining independence by reference to laws and statutes governing the central bank's organization and operations might even be misleading. (For an illustration see e.g. Berger 1996 on the German Bundesbank in the 1950s.)

The question arises whether there exist other factors shaping incentives that helped the SNB to achieve the record on price stability.[33] Two possible factors are discussed in the following sections, the structure of the executive (i.e. the commission government) and the properties of the political market for monetary policy in Switzerland. While the structure of the executive tends to reduce especially the variability of inflation, the properties of the political market for monetary policy help to explain the low level of inflation. And while commission govern-

---

31 Weintraub 1978, Kane 1980, Beck 1982, Woolley 1984, Stein 1985 and Havrilesky 1988 all conclude that despite the formal independence of the Federal Reserve, the US President has an important influence on monetary policy. Schneider 1979 and Frey/Schneider 1981 provide evidence that the nominally independent German Bundesbank, too, yields to government pressure. More recent evidence on the Bundesbank is cited in Hartwig 1995 85-86. Empirical results reported by Prast 1996 388 also suggest „that even independent central banks change policy according to the preferences of the government."

32 To overcome this limitation, Cukierman presents two indicators of *actual* central bank independence. The first indicator is based on average turnover rates of central bank governors and is supposed to measure actual developments. The second indicator is coded from responses to a questionnaire on central bank independence and should combine both legal and actual information on central bank independence. See Cukierman 1992 chap. 19.

33 Grilli et al. (1991 366) distinguish between institutional and behavioral features. Although they disregard behavioral indicators in their analysis, they caution: „There is no doubt that such behavioral indicators shape expectations and thus contribute to identify a monetary regime. The independence of the Bundesbank is the result of specific central bank laws but also of its reputation and a tradition of monetary discipline. Hence, by neglecting behavioral indicators we miss an important dimension of monetary regimes". See also Alesina/Summers 1993 159; Eijffinger/Schaling 1995 207.

ment per se affects the ability for empirical tests, the importance of the financial community limits executive influence.

4.3 Inflationary Performance as a Result of the Structure of the Executive

The supreme executive and governing authority of the Confederation is the Federal Council composed of seven members. (Article 95 of FC) The members of this *commission government* are elected individually and sequentially by the Federal Assembly (the legislative branch of Swiss federal government) for four years. There are no term limits, and usually members running for reelection are appointed for another term. The tasks of the Federal Council are distributed among its members according to departments (foreign affairs, interior, justice and police, defense, finance, economy, transport/communications/energy). Decisions are taken by the Federal Council as a body. (Article 103 of FC) Since 1959, the Federal Council is composed according to the 'magic formula' 2:2:2:1 (2 radicals, 2 christian democrats, 2 social democrats, and 1 centre democrat).[34] Hence, this commission government is supported by a coalition of four parties that together reach a comfortable legislative majority (between 73 and 84.5 percent of seats in the National Council or House of Representatives and between 89 and 95 percent of seats in the Council of States since 1971). However, it has to be noted that the Federal Assembly has no possibility to withdraw its confidence from the executive during interelection periods. Hence, the executive doesn't need a parliamentary majority. Actually, it often looses votes in the Federal Assembly.

There are at least three arguments put forward in the literature that help to explain why a commission government supervising a central bank enhances inflationary performance. These arguments can coexist.

4.3.1 Corporatism as Restraint on Private Rent-Seeking

Havrilesky/Granato (1993) argue that the inflationary performance of a central bank may not only depend on the de jure central bank autonomy, but also on *corporatist structures*.[35] In their perspective, corporatist structures and central bank autonomy are institutional alternatives, and their paper is aimed at testing the

---

[34] On a conventional left-right continuum these four parties can be ordered as follows (beginning on the left): social democrats, christian democrats, radicals, and centre democrats. Christian democrats, radicals, centre democrats, and some small right-wing parties form the block of bourgeois parties. The term 'radical' is used to refer to the free democratic party. It can be considered as „Switzerland's 'grand old party'„. Gruner/Pitterle 1983 35. The term 'centre democrat' is used to denominate members of the Swiss people's party.

[35] Measures of the strength of corporatist structures are frequently employed by political scientists to explain macroeconomic performance. See e.g. Cameron 1984.

relative performance of these two features with respect to inflationary performance. Although their measures of the strength of corporatism show no effect on comparative inflation performance, their reasoning is of interest in the present context.

Starting from the interest-group theory of government, their basic argument is that corporatist structures *restrain the private rent-seeking* of interest groups, which ultimately propels inflation. „Inflationary surprises frequently arise when the central bank responds to pressures on government from private rent-seeking interest groups for relief from high interest, exchange or unemployment rates." (Havrilesky/Granato 1993 250) As inflation rises and the costs in terms of a deterioration of aggregate wealth increase, either the central bank returns to monetary restraint, or a corporatist government persuades (or forces) interest groups to cooperate in order to avoid mutual disaster. The greater the loss of wealth to be avoided through cooperation, the more willing will interest groups be to forsake distributive conflict, and the easier will it be to regain price stability.[36] But the monetary policy cycle does not stop once price stability is achieved. „As memories of the inflationary phase fade, interest groups increasingly lament foregone rent-seeking opportunities. Demands for monetary relief from intermittent swings in interest rates, exchange rates, output and unemployment will grow. Corporatist constraints on distributive conflict and/or the limits of central bank autonomy will be tested. Given a sufficiently strong shock there will be a return to monetary activism, the addictive process will be resumed and inflation will once again rise." (Havrilesky/Granato 1993 251)

While Havrilesky/Granato remain rather vague on what is meant by corporatist structures, their measures of the strength of corporatism (measures of the power of organized labor and of leftist leaning in government)[37] obviously do not directly aim at the *structure of the executive.* Though they explicitly refer to Switzerland as an economy, where overt sectoral strife is not customary, polarization among interest groups is minimal, and significant corporatist restraints on political rent-seeking exist. (Havrilesky/ Granato 1993 252)

The existence of Swiss corporatism and consociational democracy - as opposed to competitive democracy - can be explained with direct democratic institutions.[38] Direct democracy, especially the referendum, gives interest groups (including political parties) a strong weapon with which to exert influence in the Swiss political market. (See also Fn. 47.) To reduce the risk that parliamentary

---

36 This is criticized by the central bank autonomy view which argues that „there are formidable organization costs associated with government forcing interest groups to cooperate to end an inflation. As a result, it is contended that it is far more efficient for central banks to be given the more or less permanent charge to resist political demands for monetary excesses." Havrilesky/Granato 1993 250-251.

37 Measures on these two institutions, unions and government, are standard indicators of corporatist arrangements in the political science literature. Havrilesky/Granato 1993 252.

38 See e.g. Lehner 1985. Lehner adds federalism as a second determinant of corporatism and consociational democracy.

decisions are defeated in a popular vote, an elaborate preparliamentary consultation procedure designed to prevent all possible opposition to new bills has developed. Highly encompassing coalitions including all groups capable of effectively using initiatives and especially referenda are formed. Such a long-term coalition is also reflected in the composition of the executive. It can be argued that the structure of the executive is *one* important institutional arrangement that allows the corporatist restraint to operate in Switzerland. The greater the strength of corporatism, the more effectively can private rent-seeking activities of interest groups be restraint, and the lower the level and variability of inflation, because (or if) interests offset each other.

Hence, corporatist structures, also institutionalized by commission government, help to explain the *inflationary performance* of the SNB, despite its shortcomings as far as formal central bank independence is concerned.

4.3.2 Supervision by a Committee to Isolate Monetary Policy from Short-Run Partisan or Electoral Pressure

To realize the advantages of an independent central bank that does not engage in partisan or electoral policymaking Rogoff (1985) proposes to appoint a central banker that is particularly inflation averse. But political parties are likely to have separate 'ideological' goals. Therefore, they will probably not be able to agree in general, on how 'conservative' (i.e. anti-inflationary) a central banker should be. For this reason, the choice of a central banker requires a compromise. According to Alesina (1988 40) this can be achieved if a bi-partisan committee, rather than an administration consisting of one person alone is in charge of supervising the central bank. „This institutional arrangement isolates monetary policy from short-run partisan or electoral pressure. On the other hand, a bi-partisan control may still guarantee some 'democratic' supervision of monetary policy and avoid the risk of a central bank developing into a bureaucratic body, unresponsive to social welfare." (Alesina 1988 40).

This argument can easily be extended to multy-party systems. Then, the case of Switzerland fits Alesina's proposal. A multi-party committee government (the Federal Council) is nominating and supervising the central bank authorities, thereby *isolating monetary policy* from short-run partisan or electoral pressure. This tends to lower the *variability* of inflation. Whether the level of inflation will also be lower compared to the case with an administration consisting of one person as oversight authority depends on the party in power. Following partisan theory, one can predict a higher level of inflation under a left-wing, but a lower level of inflation under a right-wing administration.

4.3.3 Organizational Design and Political Control of Administrative Agencies

The drafters of the Swiss Federal Constitution copied the legislature, but not the executive from the US Instead of a presidential system, a commission government or what Grilli et al. (1991 350) call a multiperson presidential system was chosen. Why did the legislature - who controls agency structure and design - choose this particular form of government? One explanation is that the *organizational design of agencies* is a major control device for legislatures in their role as principals. (Macey 1992; McCubbins et al. 1989)

Shughart et al. (1986) show that, c.p., the output of commissions will have a smaller variance than the output of agencies operating under a single department head. The larger a commission, the more accurately are preferences of the supervisory authority 'sampled', and the lower will be the variance of outcomes. This reduction in variance *facilitates legislative oversight*, and agency policy is more likely to conform to legislative preferences.[39] Thus, commission government helps to prevent bureaucratic[40] - or in the present context - executive drift.[41]

However, commission government has its cost, too. Because of the smaller variance effect, commissions will be *less responsive* to changes in the preferences of the overseer. This reduces the degree of control exercised by new members in the legislative oversight committee. Contracts between previous members of the oversight committee and interest groups will become more durable. Thus commissions are also a device to reduce legislative drift.[42]

Both effects of commission government - the reduction of bureaucratic and legislative drift - imply that legislators' contracts with interest groups become *more durable* and are enforced with little tolerance for error.[43] This parallels the role that Landes/Posner (1975) attribute to the 'independent' judiciary. It might be argued that the existence of a commission government is a substitute for an inde-

---

39 „Put in other terms, lower variance of output means that commission-type bureaucracies are less likely to nullify the political equilibrium set of policy objectives emerging from the oversight committee's struggle to reconcile each member's desire to redistribute wealth in favor of his own constituency." Shughart et al. 1986 964.

40 Bureaucratic drift exists when administrative agencies act in ways contrary to the interests of elected officials.

41 In this sense, commissions are less independent of legislative control than other types of bureaucratic organization. Shughart et al. 1986 969. This may help to explain why the Swiss executive is often considered as a weak government. (It is not supposed to be a strong government. And therefore, it is organized as a committee.)

42 Legislative or coalitional drift describes the fact that future legislators, with a different agenda than the enacting legislators, will override the original enactment. It can occur „both as a result of fluctuations in the preferences of the electorate and as a result of shifts in the preferences of the politicians themselves." Macey 1992 98.
There is a trade-off between bureaucratic and coalitional drift. See Shepsle 1992 on this drift trade-off.

43 Since the variance in commission output is a decreasing function of commission size, more valuable legislative contracts will be protected with larger commissions. Shughart et al. 1986 965.

pendent judiciary. Interestingly, Switzerland has a commission government, but no independent judiciary reviewing decisions of the Federal Council or legislative acts of the Federal Assembly.

The choice of commission government as an additional mechanism to control the agent[44] could be related to the type of the *policy mandate.* (Higgins et al. 1987 157-158) The contract between the legislature as principal and the executive as agent cannot enumerate all possible contingencies. Some (or even considerable) discretion has to be conceded to the executive to enable it to act and react on unforeseen events. This necessitates a broader policy mandate. The executive branch of a government obviously needs much more discretion than a usual government agency. Because of the broader policy mandate, commission government is chosen to facilitate control.

The control argument just set out has *implications* for the executive central bank relationship for at least two reasons.

First, the same argument carries over to the executive central bank relationship, but this time with the executive as principal and the central bank as the agency. As described in section 4.2 the central bank is also headed by a commission consisting of three members (the Board of Directors) that decides as a body. Since this *facilitates executive oversight*, deviations of central bank behavior from executive preferences - 'central bank' drift - will be reduced.

But at the same time the central bank will be *less responsive* to changing preferences of the Federal Council (caused either by adaptive preferences of federal councillors or simply by turnover). This reduces 'executive' drift and tends to generate lower variability of monetary policy and, hence, inflation. Moreover, this will make it harder to measure quantitatively the effects of preference changes of the executive on central bank behavior.

Second, since the oversight authority is a commission, it has less variation in its output than an authority administered by a single person (e.g. a president). This implies that with a commission government executive influence on monetary policy is *less variable* than with a presidential system. This tends to reduce the variability of inflation, too. Of course, lower variability of executive influence on monetary policy will also render empirical tests more difficult.

To sum up this section: All three arguments related to the structure of the executive as a commission government help to explain the relatively low *variance* in inflation[45], but not necessarily the low level of inflation.[46] The next section offers some arguments that may also help to explain the low level of inflation.

---

44 Other control mechanisms are competition among agencies, oversight activities, appointments, monitoring by interest groups, specialization in oversight committees, rules of procedure, and budgets. See section 5.2.2.

45 The variability of inflation is relatively low, given the fact that Switzerland is a small and open economy.

46 It is tempting to summarize the arguments presented in this section with „the weakness of the government is the strength of the central bank." However, the main argument is that commission government per se provides less variability.

4.4 Inflationary Performance as a Result of Characteristics of the Swiss Political Market for Monetary Policy

4.4.1 Political Market for Monetary Policy

If the interest-group model of politics[47] is adopted systematic influences from private interest groups on monetary policy must be investigated. This requires a detailed analysis of the political market for monetary policy in Switzerland. The *existence* of a political market for monetary policy can be rationalized on several grounds. First, few will deny that monetary policy has at least a short-run impact on the economy and thus has distributional effects. Second, compared to fiscal and regulatory policy, monetary policy instruments can be adjusted swiftly, and their real effects are transitory. Therefore, they are ideal instruments when quick but temporary measures are needed. (Cukierman 1992 342) Third, decisions about monetary targets and trade-offs (especially between inflation and exchange rates, but also between inflation and unemployment rates) are political decisions. Finally, it is important to note that the shift from fixed to floating exchange rates did not only strengthen the position of the SNB. (Schmid 1979 52; Bernholz 1987) It also enhanced the importance of the political market for monetary policy and probably led to increased interest-group activities and pressures on the central bank. The central bank operates in a highly politicized environment.[48]

The two most prominent *incentives* for political influence on monetary policy are reelection and redistribution.[49] Though monetary policy does not redistribute resources as overtly as fiscal policy does, it can have large distributive consequences, since it affects interest, exchange, inflation, and unemployment rates (some of them at least in the short run). (Fischer 1994 275; Grier 1991 204-205;

---

47 For several reasons the application of the interest-group model of politics may particularly well fit Switzerland. Interest groups are generally perceived as powerful actors in Swiss politics. „In addition to control over important resources which contribute to the power of economic interest groups in all Western democracies, two special factors operate in Switzerland. First, the referendum gives interest groups a strong weapon with which to exert influence over political decisions. Referenda do not require interest groups to operate through the parties, but rather allows them to act on their own. Secondly, interest groups are much more centrally organized than the parties. The result is that the interest groups are better able to speak with a single voice on the national level than are the parties.“ (Steiner 1982 321) Their right to intervene in the drafting of laws is explicitly recognized in the Federal Constitution. They are regularly invited to participate in expert commissions appointed by the Federal Council to prepare legislative bills. Interest groups are also the major actors in the preparliamentary consultation process.

48 As Bowles/White 1994 251 note: the more autonomy a central bank enjoys, the more political it becomes.

49 In Alesina's terminology, reelection corresponds with the opportunistic, and redistribution with the partisan argument.
Of course, the cost of using monetary policy as a redistributive instrument depends on the degree of central bank independence.

Bach/Stevenson 1974; Posen 1995)[50] It is generally agreed that inflation is a tax and, as such, it is a method of redistributing resources among economic groups. (Parkin 1987 318) Unanticipated inflation redistributes wealth from creditor to debtor. Therefore, individuals holding fixed rate corporate and government debt prefer price stability. (For more details on the distributional effects of inflation see Grier 1991 204-205.) Exchange rate fluctuations do not only affect the competitiveness of export industries on the world market. They also affect competition between domestic products and imports. Certain vested interests (for instance the real estate market), having an antipathy towards high and rising interest rates, prefer 'easy money'.[51] Workers with indexed labor contracts also favor expansionary monetary policy that stimulates the economy, and so on. Hence, on the *demand* side of the political market for monetary policy there will be specific, identifiable interest groups favoring either restrictive or expansionary monetary policy.

The behavior of politicians is determined by the reelection motive. (Mayhew 1974; Fiorina 1974; Fenno 1978) They have an incentive to *supply* the type of monetary policy desired by their constituency. (For details see Denzau/Munger 1986 and Grier/Munger 1991.) For instance, a politician representing holders of fixed rate corporate and government debt will favor price stability and, hence, restrictive monetary policy. Another politician representing export industry will prefer an exchange rate policy and so on. (See Grier 1991 203-204.) They all will transmit the pressure from their constituency to the monetary authorities. Depending on the relative costs, they will either choose the indirect channel over the executive, or they will try to have direct access to the central bank. Of course, interest groups (and their elected representatives) favoring restrictive or expansionary monetary policy will compete on the political market for monetary policy. And it depends on the features of this political market - or, to be more precise, on the relative strength of the competing interest groups - whether preferences for restrictive or expansionary monetary policy will prevail.

4.4.2 Privileged Access of the Financial Sector: Capture Theory

Indirect access to the central bank over elected officials, i.e. over the commission government, may not be that attractive for the reasons explained in the previous section. (Though it may be the only possibility for many interest groups.[52]) Not

---

50 The fact that resources are not distributed overtly makes monetary policy even more attractive, since overt transfers to rent-seeking interest groups are politically dangerous in a democracy. See Havrilesky 1992 13.

51 „Unfortunately while 'easy money' is often politically acceptable in the short run (e.g. during election years), in the long run it often has dire economic implications. In an overheated economy, the moderating effect of rapid money supply growth on interest rates tends to be only temporary. An increase in the growth rate of the money supply is quickly transmitted to a higher rate of price inflation and this, in turn, soon drives interest rates even higher." Havrilesky et al. 1975 837.

52 Interest groups (and also individuals) frequently address the Federal Council and ask for intervention with the SNB. In the past this was usually related to an appreciation of

only does the commission government tend to isolate monetary policy from short-run partisan and electoral pressure. (Alesina 1988 40) The fact that the same four parties form the commission (and coalitional) government since 1959 without any changes in seats reflects legislative (and eventually also interest-group) balance.[53] Chances for specific interest groups to achieve substantial (additional) benefits at the cost of other interest groups are rather small.

As to the *direct* political influence it is frequently argued that the financial sector enjoys privileged access to the central bank. (See e.g. Bowles/White 1994; Posen 1995.) The economic theory of *regulatory capture* hypothesizes that regulatory agencies are captured by their regulated constituencies. (Stigler 1971; Peltzman 1976) Though the SNB is not entrusted with banking regulation and supervision, there exists a special relationship between the central bank and the financial sector. (See e.g. Schmid 1979 57-61 on this.) The financial community has the usual resources discussed when an industry 'captures' its 'regulators'. (Alt 1991 56; see also Woolley 1984 chap. 4; Posen 1995.) This includes recruitment of personnel, frequent formal and informal contacts, provision of valuable information, but also the potential as a political ally. Moreover, the financial community has comparative advantages in monitoring central bank behavior. What does the financial community expect in exchange from the central bank? Banks are generally concerned about stability and predictability in market conditions. They are also observed to be averse to unexpected inflation. (See e.g. Posen 1995 257.) This may be related to the fact that banks anticipate that inflationary periods will be followed by periods of monetary restraint. This, of course, also affects stability and predictability in market conditions.

4.4.3 Example: The Role of Career Background

Top officials of central banks frequently come from the financial sector.[54] And empirical studies for the US show that not only partisan affiliation, but also career and background characteristics of monetary policymakers, including those who

---

the SFr. For more recent examples see Keller 1994, Marti 1994, Hayek 1995. It can be observed then that representatives of the banking sector tend to defend the SNB's restrictive monetary policy. See e.g. Brenner 1995. The situation for the central bank gets difficult in situations where it looses the support of the financial sector, too.

53 While section 4.3 focuses on the implications of the *institution* 'commission government', this section addresses the *stability* of this commission government.

54 „Furthermore, the president is more limited in making partisan appointments to the board of governors than he is in making such appointments to other economic policy-making positions. Just as it would be difficult to appoint a Supreme Court Justice without the approval of the legal community, so it is difficult for the president to appoint a member to the board without the approval of either the academic or the financial community. All recent appointees to the board (...) have come from relatively nonpartisan backgrounds. The most common rout to membership on the board recently has been through the ranks of Fed staff positions. Five of the seven current governors served at one time or another as Fed staffers. Six of the seven hold advanced degrees in economics." Beck 1982 437.

are non-politically appointed, have significant effects on their monetary policy preferences. In particular, central bank officials coming from the financial sector tend to favor more frequently a more restrictive monetary policy, since they value price stability most. (See Havrilesky/Gildea 1991 and 1995.)

Career background of the members of the Board of Directors may well establish a privileged access for the financial sector. One member is always from the staff of the central bank (e.g. Leutwiler and Meyer). Former staff members tend to favor the price stability goal: „The primary interest of Swiss monetary authorities lies in the strict control of the money supply, with the aim of achieving a stable price level and economic stability in the financial sector ...“ (Meyer 1986 190) Some Board members coming from the outside of the SNB first made a government career in the foreign department (Languetin and Zwahlen). Schürmann was a law professor. And Lusser joined the SNB in 1981 after having spent all his professional life at the Basle headquarters of the Swiss Bankers' Association. (The most recent appointments in October 1995 honor this tradition: Meyer is the new head of the SNB. The two new Board members are Roth, a former staffer of the SNB, and Gehrig, economics professor, chief economist of the Union Bank of Switzerland, and member of the Federal Banking Commission.)

The following quote may illustrate that in Switzerland the strong financial sector indeed has privileged access to the central bank.[55] „Switzerland's monetary stability has been smoothed by close collaboration between the major Swiss banks and the central bank. One Swiss banker said: 'Put us in their place and we will do exactly as they do. Put them in our place and they could play the same role.' Said another: 'We are all monetarists at heart, and we all agree that the first priority is to combat inflation, not to expand employment.'„ (Lim 1983 214) Not surprisingly, Posen (1993) argues that countries in which the financial sector is politically powerful, become effectively inflation-averse. And he adds: „This certainly fits the case of Switzerland.“ (Posen 1993, cited in Fischer 1995 205)[56]

In a recent study Posen argues that „the effectiveness of a financial sector's opposition to inflation should be seen as resulting from the unity of its interest in price stability, and of the openness of its country's political system to interest group influence.“ (Posen 1995 261) He constructs an index of effective financial opposition to inflation. In empirical tests for a set of 32 low- and moderate-inflation countries (including Switzerland) this index proves to be a significant predictor of central bank independence and inflation. This supports the hypothesis that financial sector interests are an important determinant of central bank independence. And the index captures the correlation with inflation normally associated with central bank independence. He concludes that both „central bank

55 To speak in Woolley's terminology (1984 81): Though banks do not like everything the SNB does, in comparison with other interest groups, e.g. organized labor, bankers usually sound like a SNB cheering section. This suggests that they tend to get what they expect from the central bank.

56 For an explicit test of financial sector pressures on US monetary policy see Havrilesky 1992 chap. 8.

independence and a coalition in society committed to protecting that independence are necessary to achieve the low inflation heretofore ascribed solely to central bank independence; either alone is insufficient." (Posen 1995 271)

This may yield yet another argument - perhaps the most convincing one - that helps to explain the low *level* of inflation in Switzerland. The Swiss central bank favors price stability, because it is under strong influence of the financial community.

4.4.4 Impact of Financial Sector as Constraint on Executive Influence

If the central bank is modeled in a principal-agent framework, the financial community may be considered as one of its basic principals. As such, it is also a potential competitor to the executive as principal. This is why the impact of the financial community is a constraint on executive influence. The higher the *legitimacy* that the central bank enjoys among the financial community (and among other interest groups), the more limited is the executive branch of government in the actions it can take in opposition to the monetary authority. This is especially the case if the executive also needs the support of that financial community.[57]

According to Cukierman (1992 394) central bank independence is, ceteris paribus, probably higher in countries with broad and well-developed financial markets. One reason is „that the prudential supervision of financial institutions and related intricacies are almost always under the authority of the central bank. The larger the financial sector, the wider is the span of authority of the central bank and the areas in which it is the main or even sole representative of the public sector. This raises its power and prestige vis-à-vis the treasury and other political authorities." (As an example he mentions the Bank of England.) Another reason is „that the disruptions that inflation and inflation uncertainty inflict on the process of financial intermediation between savings and investment are proportional to the size of the financial sector. As a result price stability is more valuable in countries with relatively large and well-developed capital markets." (Cukierman 1992 450)

---

[57] Beck (1982 437) for instance argues that Carter needed Volcker to give him some semblance of credibility on Wall Street. The recent reappointment of Greenspan by Clinton illustrates the same argument. Not just Congress, but also the financial markets would not have approved another candidate. The executive's appointment powers are clearly limited.

4.5 De Facto (In)Dependence of the SNB: An Empirical Test

Does the Swiss executive exert any systematic influence on SNB behavior? The theoretical arguments proposed in sections 4.2, 4.3 and 4.4 do not yield a clear answer to this question. From the analysis of the de jure independence of the SNB some executive influence can be expected. But because of commission government, the de facto use of the de jure possibilities is not attractive and rather unlikely. And the legitimacy that the central bank enjoys with influential interest groups (especially the financial sector) also operates as a constraint on executive influence. Since the question cannot be settled by a priori argument, it must be analyzed by empirical methods. Qualitative evidence basically consists of case studies.[58] Though they may yield valuable insights, there is always the danger of a judicious reading of the facts (as is well known in connection with the study of agency behavior). This is why *quantitative evidence* is preferred here. Therefore, this section turns to the data and empirical testing.

The *basic testable hypothesis* is that shifting political preferences in the executive are associated with changes in monetary policy, as measured by the growth rates of the monetary base and/or the money supply M1. The main difficulty is to measure changes in executive preferences. This problem is even further complicated by the commission government. When measuring the impacts of the Swiss executive on monetary policy, two basic approaches must be distinguished.

4.5.1 Popularity of the Executive and Monetary Policy

A first approach assumes that the Federal Council decides as a body. That is, the *principle of collegiality* effectively works. In this case, preferences of all members of the commission government are relevant and must enter the political variable used to explain monetary policy. A common measure of political preferences is party affiliation. But because of the absence of variation in a variable measuring party affiliation since 1959, the partisan argument cannot be tested empirically.

Executive pressures might be effective without being systematically partisan. (Chappell et al. 1993 207) To investigate this possibility, alternative ways of measuring the shift in preferences of the executive have to be devised. The alternative chosen here is to work with *popularity measures*, i.e. variables that are supposed to measure the popularity of the Federal Council as a whole.[59] In Swit-

---

58 Are interviews an alternative? A central bank „has an interest in perceiving itself as a neutral, nonpartisan, agency, and so it is difficult to study political motivation of the Fed by interviewing its current and former officials. It is necessary, therefore, to turn to indirect quantitative evidence.“ Beck 1987 199.

59 Popularity measures have already been employed by Schneider 1979, Frey/Schneider 1981, and Woolley 1983. Popularity measures for the Swiss executive based on outcomes of referenda are used in Schneider et al. 1981 and Schneider 1985 chap. 4.
To measure political influence on American monetary policy, Havrilesky (1988 and 1992) constructs an index of signaling. See section 5.3.4.

zerland voters regularly express their preferences via referenda. „Referenda issues are usually closely identified with the government in the eyes of most voters, regardless of what the government's actual position on the issue may be. Voting 'no' on a referendum is viewed by voters as an opportunity to indicate their discontent with the government and, moreover - as the government is a coalition of virtually all important parties - with the existing political system as a whole. Conversely, a large share of 'yes' votes is interpreted by the government as indicating support. When too large a share of proposed referenda is voted down by the electorate within a certain time period, the government becomes aware of discontent in the population with its policies as well as with general political conditions. The Bundesrat is thus induced to pursue policies which receive an adequate level of support from the voters in order to maintain its position." (Schneider et al. 1981 234) Since outcomes of national referenda influence the behavior of the Federal Council, these results are used to construct popularity measures for the Swiss executive.

A first popularity measure IR includes all national votes on popular *initiatives and referenda* that took place during the period under investigation (from 1973.2 until 1995.2). For (compulsory and optional) referenda the proportion of yes votes to all votes cast is taken. Initiatives generally propose legislation against the position of the Federal Council and the majority of the parliament. Then executive and legislature propose the electorate to reject the initiative. For initiatives where the Federal Council recommended a no vote, the proportion of no votes is calculated. Referenda and initiatives are brought up for a vote two to four times per year. Usually, several referenda issues may have to be decided per voting weekend. In these cases the arithmetic mean of the proportions is used. Values for quarters without votes are linearly interpolated.[60]

A second popularity measure AR includes all *referenda*, but no initiatives. This measure considers only votes on those topics that are initiated by government, but excludes all topics brought up by voters. (See also Schneider et al. 1981 234 Fn. 5.)

Finally, a third popularity measure ER also excludes those referenda that are judged to be of 'noneconomic' content. Since voters tend to make the government

---

60 Schneider 1979 and Frey/Schneider 1981 measure popularity surplus or deficit relative to a popularity share that is viewed by the government as being just sufficient to ensure reelection. It depends on institutional factors and the minimal safety margin that the government considers to be necessary. Their popularity share chosen is 52 percent of the total votes cast. The popularity share chosen by Schneider et al. 1981 and Schneider 1985 in their application to Switzerland is 50 percent.
In order to express the proportion of votes supporting the position of the Federal Council as a popularity surplus or deficit, the difference of the proportion to 0.5 can be calculated. If this difference is positive it is interpreted as popularity surplus. If it is negative, a popularity deficit is assumed. But this popularity surplus or deficit measure yields exactly the same information as the proportion of approving votes.
For a slightly different coding of popularity surplus and deficit see Schneider et al. 1981 243-244 and Schneider 1985 50.

responsible for economic conditions, the Federal Council is particularly sensitive to the approval rate for *'economic' referenda.* (Schneider et al. 1981 236)[61] Of course, there is no unambiguous way to decide whether a vote is on an 'economic' or 'noneconomic' topic, so that this measure can be criticized for being somewhat arbitrary.

Figure 4.2 presents a plot of the three popularity measures.

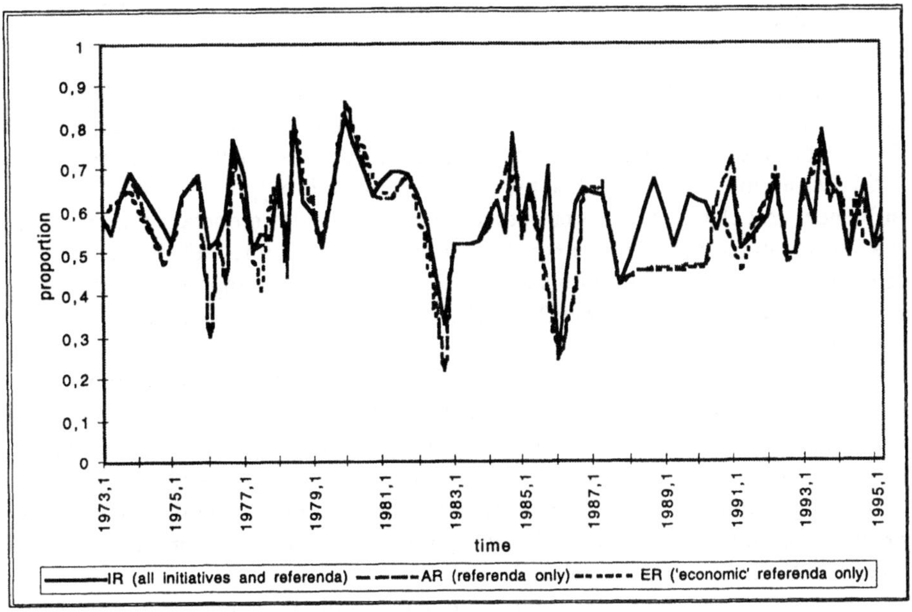

Figure 4.2: Popularity Measures for the Federal Council
See table 4.2 for definitions of variables.

Schneider et al. (1981) find that the popularity of the Federal Council has an impact on public expenditures at the federal level. „Expenditures are reduced in the case of a support deficit; they are increased (always relative to the general trend) in the case of a support surplus ..." (Schneider et al. 1981 247; see also Schneider 1985 chap. 4.) Here, it is hypothesized that the popularity of the Federal Council also affects its stance towards the central bank and monetary policy. Tests whether these popularity measures are associated with changes in monetary policy can be interpreted as *evidence on executive influence.* Predictions about whether this association should be positive or negative are not clear-cut. If it is argued that low popularity induces the Federal Council to take a more activist role in the conduct of monetary policy (i.e. a more expansionary monetary policy), a negative

61 Schneider et al. 1981 further distinguish between referenda that were 'economic in the broad sense' and 'economic in the narrow sense'.
They find empirical support for the hypothesis that „the better the state of the economy, the smaller the share of voters rejecting a referendum." Schneider et al. 1981 235.

sign should be observed. But if it is argued that the central bank enjoys greater legitimacy than the Federal Council, the opposite prediction is also plausible. In this case, the unpopular executive retreats from interference with monetary policy. This assertion is not implausible, since most Swiss voters appear to be averse to inflation. (See e.g. Schneider 1985 36.)

4.5.2 Party Affiliation or Personalities: Finance Ministers and Monetary Policy

A second approach assumes that *each federal councillor effectively decides* on matters concerning his department, and that the other members only give their formal approval (in exchange for enjoying authority within their own department). If this assumption is correct, then the finance minister is expected to have the most influence, and changes in his preferences are relevant for monetary policy. (It is the finance department that is responsible in monetary policy affairs. That is, it prepares the corresponding bills and decisions and asks for approval by the other members of the Federal Council.)[62] Within this second approach, two tests can be carried out.

First, it can be tested whether the change from bourgeois or right-wing finance ministers to social democrats affects the conduct of monetary policy. In this case it is assumed that finance ministers can usefully be grouped by party for purposes of evaluating economic policy. Partisan theory predicts, ceteris paribus, a more expansionary monetary policy under social democrats. Following the *partisan approach*, dummy variables indicating a right- or left-wing finance minister are entered into the regression equations.[63]

Second, it can be tested whether monetary policy changes as a result of changes (turnover) of the finance minister. Here, it is assumed that executive influence might not be partisan related. Instead, the nature of the executive central bank relationship may be shaped by the personalities involved.[64] To test for the

---

62 „Furthermore, the Federal Government puts forward its views on the National Bank's policy in the course of the frequent informal contacts between its members - especially the head of the Finance Department - and members of the Bank's Governing Board." SNB 1995 17.

63 Each member of the Federal Council is elected individually. The number of votes received is considered as an indicator of the popularity of the federal councillors. Still, this yields no useful popularity measure, since observations are available only every four years. Moreover, this indicates popularity in the legislature and might differ from the popularity with voters.

64 „Much of the literature discussing political pressure on the Fed concentrates on the importance of personalities in shaping the nature of Presidential-Fed interaction. Papers like Havrilesky et al. 1975, Pierce 1979, and Beck 1982 emphasize the idiosyncratic nature both of political pressure and Fed accommodation. Given this viewpoint, it is reasonable to ask whether Presidents of different parties or administrations have differing success in influencing the Fed, or whether some Fed chairmen accommodate political pressure while others hold onto Fed independence." Grier 1987 481.

idiosyncratic nature of this relationship each individual finance minister enters the regression equation as a dummy variable.

4.5.3 Regression Models and Estimation Procedure

All political variables measuring executive influence are tested in the framework of reaction functions and autoregressive model specifications. Hence, the question of executive influence is investigated in different econometric specifications to see whether results hold up in alternative models.

Assuming that the central bank does not only systematically respond to those key economic variables that are usually regarded as the most important determinants of monetary policy (inflation rate, exchange rates, growth rate of GDP, and interest rates), but also to shifts in the executive's preferences, a variable EXECUTIVE representing the different measures of changes in the executive's preferences is added to the *reaction function* developed in chapter 1.[65] The regression equation for the monetary base as dependent variable with all economic variables expressed as nonseasonal differences is

$$\begin{aligned}\Delta \ln(MB)_t &= \beta_0 + \beta_1 \Delta \ln(MB)_{t-1} + \beta_2 \Delta \ln(CPI)_{t-1} + \beta_3 \Delta \ln(DMN)_{t-1} \\ &+ \beta_4 \Delta \ln(GDP)_{t-1} + \beta_5 \Delta DR_{t-1} + \beta_6 SD1_t + \beta_7 SD2_t + \beta_8 SD3_t \\ &+ \beta_9 EXECUTIVE_{t-2} + \varepsilon_t\end{aligned}$$

(See tables 1.2 and 4.2 for variable definitions and data sources.)

As in chapter 3, models with both nonseasonal and seasonal differences (i.e. quarterly and yearly rates of change) are estimated not only for the monetary base, but also the money supply M1 as dependent variable. Since most series are not seasonally adjusted regressions with quarterly rates include three seasonal dummies (SD1, SD2, SD3). In the annual models seasonality is removed by the definition of the yearly rates of change.

---

65 This approach has been criticized. „Including a dummy variable for the party of the incumbent President in an aggregate reaction function is not likely to fully capture partisan influences by way of the appointments process.“ (Chappell et al. 1993 187). „The relationship between the central bank and government is inadequately modeled by simply introducing dummies to influence the level and slopes of a 'purely economic' behavioral equation for the central bank. It seems to us to be preferable - as done in this paper - to look at the central bank as just one actor ...“ (Frey/Schneider 1981 311).

Table 4.2: Definitions of Variables Measuring Executive Preferences[a]

Variable	Definition
	popularity measures for Federal Council
IR	proportion of voters approving the position of the Federal Council relative to all votes cast in national votes on all initiatives and referenda from 1973.2 to 1995.2; arithmetic mean of proportions for dates with votes on several topics; 26 values for quarters without votes linearly interpolated
AR	same definition as IR, but with all initiatives excluded; 34 values for quarters without votes linearly interpolated
ER	same definition as IR, but with all initiatives and 'noneconomic' referenda excluded (see appendix to chapter 4 for the list of 'noneconomic' votes dropped); 37 values for quarters without votes linearly interpolated
	dummy variables representing finance ministers
Bourgeois	dummy variable equal to one if a member of the bourgeois parties is finance minister (1973.2-1979.4) and zero otherwise
Socialist	dummy variable equal to one if a member of the social democratic party is finance minister (1980.1-1995.2) and zero otherwise
Celio	dummy variable equal to one if Celio (radical) is finance minister (1973.2-1973.4) and zero otherwise
Chevallaz	dummy variable equal to one if Chevallaz (radical) is finance minister (1974.1-1979.4) and zero otherwise
Ritschard	dummy variable equal to one if Ritschard (social democrat) is finance minister (1980.1-1983.4; died in office) and zero otherwise
Stich	dummy variable equal to one if Stich (social democrat) is finance minister (1984.1-1995.2) and zero otherwise

[a] Source: Statistisches Jahrbuch der Schweiz (Statistical Yearbook of Switzerland).

The focus is not on the observed response of the SNB to changes in the economic variables, but on its reaction to changes in variables measuring executive influences. The intention is to test for executive influence while controlling for the effects of the economic variables.[66] The use of political dummy variables basically serves to determine whether the reaction function *shifted* at politically important points. (Beck 1982 415) Of course, the main weakness of this approach (as is the difficulty with regression analysis in general) is that a significant shift of the reaction function at a politically important point need not be the result of a political change. It can be caused by some other factors. Since we cannot uniquely ascribe a cause-effect relationship, all that can be concluded is whether results are consistent or inconsistent with the hypothesis of executive influence.

---

66 Of course, a model including political variables only would be open to the criticism that the central bank reacts to other (economic) variables in addition to the political ones. Including a small set of nonredundant economic variables in the reaction function helps to decrease the possibility of spurious inference. Beck 1984 795.

Impacts of political variables are also frequently studied in the context of *autoregressive model specifications*. In applications to monetary policy money growth rates are regressed on lagged dependent variables, a constant, and the political variable(s). The autoregressive terms are included to control for changes in the economy, similar to the economic regressor variables in the reaction function approach. The autoregressive models are first estimated excluding the variables representing executive influence. (Section 3.5.2 describes in detail how the 'best' autoregressive models are identified.) Next the variables measuring changes in executive preferences are added to these autoregressive models. Significant coefficients on the political variables are consistent with the hypothesis of executive influence.

All political variables enter the regression equations with a lag of two quarters. This accounts for a reasonable interval between change in political preference (turnover) and change in monetary policy. Nevertheless, experiments with alternative lag structures (zero- and one-quarter lags) are also carried out.[67]

The sample period is restricted to the era of flexible exchange rates (from 1973.2 to 1995.2). It is pointless to test for executive influence on a central bank operating in a small open economy under the regime of fixed exchange rates, since no room is left to conduct an autonomous domestic monetary policy. (See Eijffinger/Schaling 1995 208.) The economic data are quarterly observations. The political dummy variables are constructed on the basis of the dates of changes of finance ministers. The four federal councillors that headed the finance department since 1973 (Celio, Chevallaz, Ritschard and Stich) are surveyed in table 4.2.

4.5.4 Estimation Results for Popularity Measures

Is monetary policy associated with the popularity of the Federal Council? Tables 4.3 and 4.4 present the estimation results for the three different popularity measures in the framework of reaction functions and autoregressive model specifications. In order to preserve space only the coefficients for the political variables and their associated t or p values are reported in this chapter. Entries for the popularity measures in tables 4.3 and 4.4 are based on separate regressions.

Estimated coefficients and t or p values are quite similar for the three popularity measures in most regressions. While the popularity measure based on all initiatives and referenda (IR) performs worst in most cases (it is never significant), the measure with the initiatives dropped (AR) performs best. However, dropping the initiatives from the IR measure or the 25 'noneconomic' referenda from the AR popularity measure (see appendix to this chapter) obviously does not make a big difference.

The AR and ER popularity measures are both significant in the yearly reaction function for the monetary base. The measure with the initiatives dropped (AR) is

---

67 Alesina/Roubini 1992 employ a one-quarter lag. They also experiment with alternative lag structures. See also Grier 1991 213.

also significant at the ten percent level in the quarterly reaction function for the monetary base. Experiments with zero- and one-quarter lags (not reported) show that the two-quarter lag performs best.

Table 4.3: Estimation Results for Popularity Measures in Reaction Functions

	Dependent variables			
	$\Delta \ln(MB)$	$\Delta_4 \ln(MB)$	$\Delta \ln(M1)$	$\Delta_4 \ln(M1)$
Popularity measure	Coefficient (t value)	Coefficient (p value)	Coefficient (p value)	Coefficient (p value)
IR_{t-2}	0.040 (1.468)	0.064 (0.1090)	0.020 (0.3013)	0.033 (0.1924)
AR_{t-2}	0.035* (1.712)	0.080** (0.0130)	0.018 (0.2510)	0.029 (0.1401)
ER_{t-2}	0.026 (1.176)	0.059* (0.0787)	0.015 (0.3431)	0.028 (0.1716)

The following equations are used: For $\Delta \ln(MB)$ as dependent variable equation 1.3 from table 1.9; for $\Delta \ln(M1)$ equation 1.6 from table 1.12; for $\Delta_4 \ln(MB)$ equation 1.9 from table 1.15; for $\Delta_4 \ln(M1)$ equation 1.12 from table 1.19. Numbers in parentheses are associated t statistics or p values; t statistics are calculated on the basis of HCSEs; * significant at 10 percent level; ** significant at 5 percent level.

There exists some association between the AR and ER measure and the growth rate of the monetary base. The positive sign implies that low popularity is associated with a more restrictive monetary policy. This might suggest that an unpopular executive retreats from interference with monetary policy, so that the central bank authorities can concentrate on price stability. But the conclusion that the Federal Council does influence SNB policy is not warranted for the following reasons. First, (and most importantly), there is no causality implied. Results might be driven by some third factor that influences both voting behavior and monetary policy. Second, significant coefficients can only be obtained from reaction functions, but not from autoregressions. Third, the number of missing observations that has to be linearly interpolated is rather high (26 observations in the IR, 34 in the AR, and 37 in the ER measure). This limits the informational content of these data.

Table 4.4: Estimation Results for Popularity Measures in Autoregressive Models

	Dependent variables	
	$\Delta_4\ln(MB)$	$\Delta_4\ln(M1)$
Popularity measure	Coefficient (t value)	Coefficient (p value)
IR_{t-2}	0.035 (0.873)	0.021 (0.4899)
AR_{t-2}	0.035 (1.158)	0.009 (0.6977)
ER_{t-2}	0.020 (0.600)	0.010 (0.6771)

The equation for $\Delta_4\ln(MB)$ is an AR(9). The equation for $\Delta_4\ln(M1)$ includes lags 1, 2, 4, 5 and 8 of the dependent variable as additional regressors. Numbers in parentheses are associated t statistics or p values. t statistics are calculated on the basis of HCSEs.

4.5.5 Estimation Results for Party Affiliation of Finance Ministers

Does monetary policy depend on which party is in control of the finance ministry? To test for effects of the finance minister's party affiliation on monetary policy dummy variables indicating a bourgeois or socialist finance minister are added to the regression equations. The dummy variable 'Socialist' is equal to one if a social democrat heads the finance department and zero otherwise (i.e. when a bourgeois party controls this department). The dummy variable 'Bourgeois' is defined analogously.

Tables 4.5 and 4.6 contain test results for the hypothesis that the change from radical to social democratic finance ministers affected the conduct of monetary policy. The coefficients on the variable 'Socialist' measure the difference in mean money growth rates with respect to the omitted category, the bourgeois finance ministers. (These are represented in the intercept.) Associated t or p values indicate whether this difference is significantly different from zero. Since all coefficients in the reaction function approach (table 4.5) fail to be significant, it must be concluded that the categorization into radical and social democratic finance ministers does not matter. But this categorization matters in the autoregression for the monetary base (table 4.6).

The estimation of the reaction functions (table 4.5) is confronted with the problem that the change in party affiliation of the finance minister coincides with the structural break detected earlier. (See section 1.5.1c.) Could this instability of the reaction function be due to omitted political variables? And asked more specifically: Could this structural break be caused, and, hence, be explained by the change in finance minister? There are at least two reasons why this explanation is unlikely to be correct.

First, regression analysis does not imply causality. There are other, more convincing explanations for the occurrence of the 1980 break. The most convincing argument is the creation of the European Monetary System in late 1979. It could also be argued that the 1980 break is caused by the revision of the National Bank Law in August 1979. But this explanation, too, is not convincing, because the revised legislation only established what had already been practice before. Still another argument could be the change in monetary theories that guided monetary policy, e.g. the breakthrough of monetarist thinking. But then several questions arise. Why could monetarist thinking break through? Was it because of turnover? And what caused this turnover?

Second, the SNB returned to monetary targeting in December 1979, *before* the change in finance ministry effectively occurred.

In addition to the problem of interpretation, the coincidence of the structural break for 1980 with the change of party in the finance ministry has technical implications, too. Technically, the reaction functions can only be estimated if the variable indicating the party affiliation of the finance minister enters with a lag. As is argued above, a lag of two quarters is reasonable. But the two-quarter lag does only allow for a transition from perfect to very strong multicollinearity.[68] This may not only explain the insignificant coefficients in table 4.5. It might even affect the signs of these coefficients.

Estimation results in the framework of autoregressive models (table 4.6) are likely to be more reliable, since there is no structural break for 1980 included. But these results do not support the predictions of partisan theory either. The coefficient is significant in the monetary base regression, but it shows the wrong sign. Partisan theory predicts that under a left-wing finance minister, money growth will be higher relative to a right-wing finance minister. Signs are just the opposite: Mean money growth rates are much lower under left-wing finance ministers (as is also illustrated by the results in table 4.7).[69]

Overall, there is no evidence that the change from bourgeois to socialist finance ministers affected monetary policy. And there is little reason to argue that the break in 1980 can be explained with the partisan change in the finance ministry.

---

68 The Pearson correlation coefficient between the dummy variables representing a bourgeois or social democratic finance minister and the two intercept dummies used to model the structural break is 0.95 (-0.95).

69 A parametrization with all categories included is not estimated for the reaction functions, since the equations already include dummy variables to model the structural break for 1980. In addition, the quarterly models also contain three seasonal dummies.

Table 4.5: Estimation Results for Party Affiliation of Finance Ministers in Reaction Functions

	Dependent variables			
	$\Delta \ln(MB)$	$\Delta_4 \ln(MB)$	$\Delta \ln(M1)$	$\Delta_4 \ln(M1)$
Dummy for party of finance minister	Coefficient (t value)	Coefficient (p value)	Coefficient (p value)	Coefficient (p value)
$Socialist_{t-2}$	-0.019 (-1.582)	-0.040 (0.2402)	0.006 (0.1685)	-0.004 (0.8344)

See notes on table 4.3. Coefficients measure the difference in mean money growth rates with respect to the omitted category, the bourgeois finance ministers. Associated t or p values indicate whether this difference is significantly different from zero.

Table 4.6: Estimation Results for Party Affiliation of Finance Ministers in Autoregressive Models

	Dependent variables	
	$\Delta_4 \ln(MB)$	$\Delta_4 \ln(M1)$
Dummy for party of finance minister	Coefficient (t value)	Coefficient (p value)
$Socialist_{t-2}$	-0.026** (-2.431)	-0.009 (0.1759)

See notes on table 4.4. Coefficients measure the difference in mean money growth rates with respect to the omitted category, the bourgeois finance ministers. Associated t or p values indicate whether this difference is significantly different from zero.
** significant at 5 percent level.

Table 4.7: Estimation Results for Party Affiliation of Finance Ministers in Autoregressive Models (Parametrization Without Intercept)

	Dependent variables	
	$\Delta_4 \ln(MB)$	$\Delta_4 \ln(M1)$
Dummy for party of finance minister	Coefficient (t value)	Coefficient (p value)
$Bourgeois_{t-2}$	0.026** (2.414)	0.019*** (0.0070)
$Socialist_{t-2}$	0.0002 (0.062)	0.010** (0.0101)
Joint F test	2.993* (0.0559)	5.404*** (0.0062)

See notes on table 4.4. Since all categories are included in the model, the intercept is dropped and coefficients measure mean money growth rates for each category. The joint F test indicates whether at least one of the two mean growth rates is significantly different from zero. * significant at 10 percent level; ** significant at 5 percent level; *** significant at 1 percent level.

4.5.6 Estimation Results for Individual Finance Ministers

Does monetary policy depend on who is finance minister? To answer this question a series of dummy variables indicating specific finance ministers is added to the regression equations. Test results are presented in tables 4.8 and 4.9. Displayed coefficients measure the difference in money growth rates with respect to the omitted category. (Here, the first finance minister is accounted for in the intercept.) Associated t or p values show whether this difference is significantly different from zero. A joint F test indicates whether at least one of these differences is significantly different from zero. Thus, it informs about whether this categorization matters. If the idiosyncratic argument is correct, changes of finance ministers should be associated with an intercept shift. Estimation results in the framework of the autoregressive models, but also for the yearly reaction function models suggest that a distinction among individual finance ministers does not matter. But it does matter in the quarterly reaction function models, especially with the monetary base as dependent variable.[70]

Do these results imply that monetary policies are unique to individual finance ministers? The fact that significant coefficients can only be obtained in quarterly models may suggest that results are related to the method of measuring changes in the data. Moreover, especially the seventies were characterized by economic and monetary turmoil, and money growth rates fluctuated considerably. The results

---

70 A model which allows also slope coefficients to vary across individual finance ministers would be preferable. See e.g. Chappell et al. 1993 186. Since there remain only few degrees of freedom, this approach is not pursued here.

found for the individual finance ministers could be generated by these events. Another possible explanation is that radical central bank chairmen tend to cooperate with radical finance ministers, but boycott social democratic finance ministers. (This would rather support the hypothesis that executive influence is ineffective.) Again, the methods of research applied here do not allow for the conclusion that individual finance ministers do in fact *cause* shifts in monetary policy.

If party affiliation were the appropriate independent political variable, there should be no intercept shift when Chevallaz and Stich became finance ministers. There should only be such a shift after Ritschard took over the finance department. These predictions of partisan theory are not confirmed by the pattern of results. The same information is provided by table 4.10, which contains estimation results for autoregressive models excluding the intercept. All coefficients measure mean money growth rates for each individual finance minister. Results again show that money grew much faster in periods with radical finance ministers in office.

Table 4.8: Estimation Results for Individual Finance Ministers in Reaction Functions

	Dependent variables			
	$\Delta\ln(MB)$	$\Delta_4\ln(MB)$	$\Delta\ln(M1)$	$\Delta_4\ln(M1)$
Dummy for individual finance minister	Coefficient (t value)	Coefficient (p value)	Coefficient (p value)	Coefficient (p value)
$Chevallaz_{t-2}$	-0.042*** (-2.262)	-0.004 (0.9228)	-0.021** (0.0439)	0.029 (0.2273)
$Ritschard_{t-2}$	-0.056*** (-2.617)	-0.039 (0.5004)	-0.008 (0.4227)	0.027 (0.4224)
$Stich_{t-2}$	-0.060*** (-2.926)	-0.047 (0.4368)	-0.012 (0.2230)	0.027 (0.4177)
Joint F test	3.843** (0.0130)	0.614 (0.6085)	2.147 (0.1014)	0.509 (0.6772)

See notes on table 4.3. Coefficients measure the difference in mean money growth rates with respect to the omitted category, i.e. Celio as finance minister. Associated t or p values indicate whether this difference is significantly different from zero. The joint F test indicates whether at least one of these differences is significantly different from zero. ** significant at 5 percent level; *** significant at 1 percent level.

Table 4.9: Estimation Results for Individual Finance Ministers in Autoregressive Models

	Dependent variables	
	$\Delta_4 \ln(MB)$	$\Delta_4 \ln(M1)$
Dummy for individual finance minister	Coefficient (t value)	Coefficient (p value)
$Chevallaz_{t-2}$	0.008 (0.298)	-0.006 (0.6601)
$Ritschard_{t-2}$	-0.016 (-0.582)	-0.018 (0.2683)
$Stich_{t-2}$	-0.019 (-0.712)	-0.014 (0.3352)
Joint F test	1.716 (0.1709)	0.759 (0.5204)

See notes on table 4.4. Coefficients measure the difference in mean money growth rates with respect to the omitted category, i.e. Celio as finance minister. Associated t or p values indicate whether this difference is significantly different from zero. The joint F test indicates whether at least one of these differences is significantly different from zero.

Table 4.10: Estimation Results for Individual Finance Ministers in Autoregressive Models (Parametrization Without Intercept)

	Dependent variables	
	$\Delta_4 \ln(MB)$	$\Delta_4 \ln(M1)$
Dummy for individual finance minister	Coefficient (t value)	Coefficient (p value)
$Celio_{t-2}$	0.019 (0.688)	0.026* (0.0972)
$Chevallaz_{t-2}$	0.027** (2.373)	0.020*** (0.0077)
$Ritschard_{t-2}$	0.003 (0.293)	0.008 (0.2559)
$Stich_{t-2}$	-0.001 (0.276)	0.012** (0.0151)
Joint F test	1.518 (0.2055)	2.763** (0.0331)

See notes on table 4.4. Since all categories are included in the model, the intercept is dropped and coefficients measure mean money growth rates for each category. The joint F test indicates whether at least one of the mean growth rates is significantly different from zero. * significant at 10 percent level; ** significant at 5 percent level; *** significant at 1 percent level.

4.6 Conclusions

Does the Swiss executive branch of government (the Federal Council) influence Swiss monetary policy? This question cannot be settled by a priori argument. An analysis of the de jure independence of the SNB shows that some executive influence could be expected. But this does not necessarily lead to a higher variability and level of inflation. The structure of the executive, commission government, tends to lower the variability of inflation. And the properties of the Swiss political market for monetary policy, especially the strong influence of the financial sector, help to explain the low level of inflation. The legitimacy that the central bank enjoys with influential interest groups also operates as a constraint on executive influence. Empirical tests of executive influence are confronted with great difficulties in the Swiss case. Commission government per se affects the ability to test for executive influence. Moreover, the lack of variation in the party composition of the commission government since 1959 requires alternative measures and tests. Two approaches are pursued. A first approach assumes that the Federal Council decides as a body. Hence, changes in preferences of all federal councillors must enter the variable measuring political influence. Since there exist no popularity polls for the Swiss executive, popularity measures based on national referenda are constructed. It is found that money growth rates are positively associated with some of these popularity measures.

A second approach assumes that each department head effectively decides. Two tests can be carried out then. First, it is tested whether monetary policy is affected by the party affiliation of the finance minister. This test is additionally complicated by the fact that the partisan change in the finance ministry coincides with a structural break detected earlier. But the argument that this break is caused by the partisan change is unconvincing. And results do not support the hypothesis that the change from bourgeois to social democratic finance ministers affected monetary policy. Second, it is tested whether monetary policy depends on individual finance ministers. Significant results can only be found for quarterly regression models.

Overall, there is no clear evidence for executive influence. Since regression analysis does not imply causality, significant results can only be interpreted as being consistent with executive influence. Results might be caused by some other factors. No convincing arguments can be put forward that changes in executive preferences are the most plausible cause for changes in money growth rates. Based on theoretical considerations and empirical analysis, the conclusion that the Swiss executive does in fact influence Swiss monetary policy is not warranted. According to Burdekin/Langdana (1992 105) the SNB enjoys perhaps the greatest level of autonomy of any of the world's central banks. The results of this study do not contradict this statement.

In the seventies and eighties Swiss monetary policy was confronted mainly with the trade-off between inflation and exchange rates. Two new developments challenge Swiss monetary policy in the nineties. First, uncertainties related to the creation of the European Monetary Union may accentuate this trade-off between inflation and exchange rates. Second, another trade-off, between inflation and unemployment, is gaining importance. While these developments may not suffice to upset the equilibrium in the political market for monetary policy, they will certainly increase political pressure on the SNB. A more serious test for SNB independence is still to come.

Appendix to Chapter 4

Table 4.11: 'Noneconomic' Referenda Dropped in the ER ('Economic' Referenda Only) Popularity Measure

Date	Subject of Referendum
20. 5. 1973	Jesuiten- und Klosterartikel
2. 12. 1973	Tierschutzartikel
25. 9. 1977	Erhöhung der Unterschriftenzahl für das Referendum
25. 9. 1977	Erhöhung der Unterschriftenzahl für die Verfassungsinitiative
4. 12. 1977	Politische Rechte. Bundesgesetz
4. 12. 1977	Einführung eines zivilen Ersatzdienstes
28. 5. 1978	Schutz der Schwangerschaft und Strafbarkeit des Schwangerschaftsabbruchs. Indikationenmodell
3. 12. 1978	Sicherheitspolizeiliche Aufgaben des Bundes
18. 2. 1979	Stimm- und Wahlrecht für 18jährige
18. 2. 1979	Fuss- und Wanderwege (Gegenvorschlag)
30. 11. 1980	Strassenverkehrsgesetz, Änderung (Gurtenobligatorium)
6. 2. 1982	Änderung des Strafgesetzbuches
2. 12. 1984	Hilfe für Opfer von Gewaltverbrechen (Gegenvorschlag)
22. 9. 1985	Koordination des Schuljahresbeginns (Gegenvorschlag)
5. 4. 1987	Abstimmungsverfahren bei Volksinitiativen mit Gegenentwurf
1. 4. 1990	Organisation Bundesrechtspflege
3. 3. 1991	Stimm- und Wahlrechtsalter 18
2. 6. 1991	Militärstrafgesetz
17. 5. 1992	Zivildienst
17. 5. 1992	Sexualstrafrecht
27. 9. 1992	Revision Parlamentsbetrieb (Geschäftsverkehrsgesetz)
26. 9. 1993	Bundesbeschluss gegen Waffenmissbrauch
26. 9. 1993	Bundesbeschluss Anschluss Laufental an Kanton Basel-Landschaft
25. 9. 1994	Verbot der Rassendiskriminierung
4. 12. 1994	Zwangsmassnahmen im Ausländerrecht

CHAPTER 5

Legislative Influence on Monetary Policy? The Case of Switzerland

5.1 Introduction

While executive influence on central banks is widely recognized, the legislature is usually not considered to be important in monetary policy, despite the fact that the central bank is a creation of the legislature and ultimately is accountable to it. The conventional wisdom is that legislators lack incentives to monitor and influence monetary policy. The view that government agencies operate independently of the legislature has been challenged by the theory of legislative control developed by Weingast. (Weingast/Moran 1983) Building on principal-agent models the theory of legislative control argues that principals are able to control their agents effectively. More recently, this theory has also been applied to the Federal Reserve. Grier (1991) and Havrilesky (1992) both report evidence for legislative influence by specialized legislative committees of the US legislature (the US Senate Banking Committee) on US monetary policy. But Beck (1990), who reworks an earlier version of Grier's analysis, finds that data that cover a slightly different time period reject Grier's results. The question of congressional influence on US monetary policy remains the subject of continuing debate.

So far, the theory of legislative control has only been applied to the US Congress. Evidence for legislative influence has been provided for several government agencies - such as the Antitrust Division of the Department of Justice, the Federal Trade Commission FTC, the International Trade Commission ITC, the Interstate Commerce Commission ICC, the National Labor Relations Board NLRB, the Securities and Exchange Commission SEC - and the Federal Reserve System. This chapter applies the theory of legislative control to the Swiss legislature. The question analyzed is whether the Swiss legislature or specialized legislative committees thereof have any influence on Swiss monetary policy. This provides at the same time an empirical test of the theory of legislative control - which is also referred to as the 'new' theory of bureaucracy here - under a different institutional setting than the existing work does.

An analysis of the institutional setting suggests that neither the Swiss legislature as a whole nor specialized committees thereof exert any influence on Swiss monetary policy. And in empirical tests no systematic legislative influence can be detected that is consistent with the predictions of the theory of legislative control. However, this does not allow for the general conclusion that this theory does only apply to the special features of the US Congress. After all, the Swiss central bank represents a formally independent agency. It may well be the case that there exists legislative influence on other Swiss government agencies that do not enjoy this degree of formal independence.

The chapter proceeds as follows. Section 5.2 presents the theory of legislative influence. For this purpose, the 'old' and 'new' theory of bureaucracy are reviewed. Section 5.3 discusses the application of the theory of legislative control to the Federal Reserve Board. Section 5.4 is an attempt to apply this theory to a different institutional environment, the SNB. Section 5.5 offers some concluding remarks.

5.2 The Theory of Legislative Influence (or the 'New' Theory of Bureaucracy)

In spite of its 'independent' status, a central bank is a government agency. (Alt 1991 42) Agencies might be either operationally *independent* and use their autonomy to maximize social welfare or bureaucratic utility. Or they might be operationally *dependent* and systematically be influenced by some other political actors. The question whether government agencies are independent of or controlled by their principals is the subject of the controversy between 'old' and 'new' theory of bureaucracy (the 'new' theory of bureaucracy being a theory of legislative control of government agencies). This section provides a brief summary of the debate between 'old' and 'new' theory of bureaucracy.

5.2.1 'Old' Theory of Bureaucracy: Bureaucratic Discretion

The bureaucratic discretion model (in its extreme version) argues that agencies are independent of the legislature. The two central issues are: Why are agencies autonomous? And how is this autonomy exercised in the making of agency policy? (Moe 1985 1094)

The *basic argument* is that bureaucrats enjoy discretion because of the lack of effective external and internal control. Therefore, agency behavior can only be predicted by explaining the behavior of senior bureaucrats.

External control of bureaucrats is ineffective mainly for two reasons, the existence of multiple principals, and the attenuation of property rights.

In the case of US federal agencies for instance, *multiplicity of principals*, which is required by the separation of powers, can arise from at least four sources. (Rowley 1992 122-123) First, within each legislative chamber the jurisdiction of oversight committees and subcommittees may overlap. Second, bicameralism involves separate oversight by committees of the House and the Senate. Third, jurisdictional conflict between the oversight and the appropriations committee arises in the congressional budgetary process. Finally, the 'independent' Presidency and Congress have competing jurisdictions.

As to the second reason for ineffective external control, the *property rights* of members of Congress are *attenuated* because offices are non-transferable and intergenerational linkages are absent. (Rowley 1992 198) In sum, oversight rights are seriously attenuated and relatively widely dispersed across several principals. This diffuse and attenuated ownership leads to shirking with the monitors and thus opens up opportunities for agency discretion.

Internal control of bureaucrats is ineffective because the outside labor market will exercise only minimal internal impact upon an agency, and because the internal incentives to efficient bureau monitoring are relatively low. (Rowley 1992 126, 198)

Because of this lack of effective external and internal control, bureaucrats enjoy *discretion.* Even without the problems implied by multiplicity of principals and attenuation of property rights, the principal may be unable to monitor the agent effectively because the agent controls the information from his policy area (especially the bureau's production function), because access to clientele allows the agent to foster agency-clientele alliances that help to protect it from nominal overseers, or because high costs of passing new legislation to redirect agency policy limits congressional action. (Weingast/Moran 1983 767)

The usual observations in numerous *case studies* about the relationship between the legislature and regulatory agencies seem to provide evidence for these assertions (see e.g. Wilson 1980): the lack of oversight hearings, the infrequency of congressional investigations and policy resolutions, the perfunctory nature of confirmation hearings of agency heads, the lack of ostensible congressional attention to or knowledge about the ongoing operation and policy consequences of agency choice, and the superficiality of annual appropriations hearings. (Weingast/Moran 1983 767) Because little monitoring activity can be observed, considerable shirking must occur, „so much that it is best to ignore the influence of the principal on agent decisions.“ (Weingast/Moran 1983 767 Fn. 2)

Since in the extreme version it is assumed that the legislature does not influence agency decisions, agency behavior can only be predicted by explaining the behavior of senior bureaucrats. What is needed is a *model of bureaucratic choice.* Attention shifts towards the motivations and incentive structures of senior bureaucrats to predict how they will respond to specific reward-cost structures.

Instead of relying exclusively on the narrow goal of expected wealth maximization, it is assumed that bureaucrats have multiple goals. Possible *motives* are power, money income, security, perquisites of office, easy life, patronage, desire to serve the public interest as individually perceived, and commitment to a specific program of action. (Rowley 1992 98-99) All these goals are purely selfish. Downs (1967) distinguishes five types of bureaucrats, depending on which of these goals are components of the utility function. While climbers consider power, income and prestige as the most important goals, conservers consider security, perquisites of office, the easy life, and patronage as most valuable. Zealots, advocates and statesmen are called mixed motive bureaucrats, because they combine the desire to serve the public interest and commitment to a specific program of action with some of the other goals. „Zealots are loyal to relatively narrow policies or concepts. They seek power both for its own sake and to effect the policies to which they are loyal ... Advocates are loyal to a broader set of functions or to a broader organization than are zealots ... Statesmen are loyal to society as a whole and seek power in order to influence significantly national policies and actions." (Rowley 1992 99) The desire to serve the public interest as individually perceived and the commitment to a specific program of action can be considered as ideological goals. The type of mixed motive bureaucrat thus indicates to what degree he will use his discretion to pursue ideological goals. Different combinations of motives will influence the behavior in predictable ways. Put another way, different types of bureaucrats will behave differently.

To predict the behavior of bureaucrats we also need to know their *reward-cost structure*. Bureaucrats are constrained by legislation (authoritative mandate), oversight by the various principals, and the size and composition of their budget. Surpluses of revenues over costs usually cannot be appropriated as direct personal income. Remuneration is based on time allocated without any bonus for good performance and without any penalty for deviance. Promotions are based more on seniority than on merit. (Rowley 1992 98, 105, 198)

If bureaucrats pursue narrowly selfish goals such as power, money income, security, perquisites of office and patronage, they will strive for a large and rapidly growing *budget*, because all these motives are positive monotonic functions of budget size. Easy life is a positive monotonic function of the budget's rate of growth, too. Depending upon the distribution of underlying preferences and the specific reward-cost structure, they will pursue a different balance between budget size and budget discretion. Bureaucrats will have this choice in the case of the demand-constrained bureau. In the case of the budget-constrained bureau, this choice is not available. (Rowley 1992 101-103)[1]

If ideological goals such as the desire to serve the public interest or the commitment to a specific program of action become important, a different budgetary policy will result. A strong preference for output of the bureau may lead bureaucrats to seek a maximum budget. The preference for non-output-related outlays makes budgetary discretion more important. And if ideological motives require a reduction in the bureau's activities, bureaucrats may even pursue policies of budgetary reduction.

The behavior of each type of bureaucrat in a specific environment can be predicted. These predictions can be compared with the evidence. *Empirical tests* usually compare budgets, productivity or costs of public bureaucracies with their private alternatives.

Most *criticisms* of the 'bureaucratic discretion' model follow implicitly from the 'congressional control' model. (See e.g. Wintrobe 1997; Moe 1997.) Niskanen's (1971, 1975) single-bureau model is a bilateral bargaining approach of bureau dominance. His monopoly bureau contrasts with the fact that in the budge-

---

[1] If the bureau is faced with a low-demand condition, its equilibrium output will be budget-constrained. Under a high-demand condition, its equilibrium output will be demand-constrained. See Niskanen 1971 chap. 5.

tary process many bureaus compete with each other. In the US for instance, up to two thousand federal agencies face only 13 subcommittees of the Appropriations Committee. (Weingast/Moran 1983 769 Fn. 5) The bureaucratic discretion model certainly underestimates the ability of the legislature to control agencies. The principal-agent problem implicit in the model is in fact eroded. (Rowley 1992 97)

5.2.2 'New' Theory of Bureaucracy: Legislative Control

The *congressional dominance approach* argues that agencies are effectively controlled by the legislature. (Weingast/Moran 1983 767) There is no disagreement about the observations from case studies cited above. However, the apparent absence of legislative monitoring is not accepted as evidence against legislative control. Instead it is argued that these observations are also consistent with the legislative control model. The reason is that agencies are controlled by much more subtle mechanisms. If these mechanisms work well, they provide appropriate ex ante incentives. Agencies will pursue legislative goals (i.e. serve legislative clientele) even if they receive little direct guidance from their overseers. (Weingast/Moran 1983 768) Therefore, we will observe rather few actual punishment. The overseer may even appear ignorant of agency proceedings because he gauges the success of programs through his constituents' reactions rather than through detailed study. (Weingast/Moran 1983 768) Since public hearings and investigations are resource-intensive activities, they will not be used for agency policies that operate smoothly. Instead, hearings and investigations are used to police areas that function poorly. This implies that „the more effective the incentive system, the less often we should observe sanctions in the form of congressional attention through hearings and investigations. Put another way, direct and continuous monitoring of inputs rather than of results is an inefficient mechanism by which a principal constrains the action of his agent.“ (Weingast/Moran 1983 769; see also McCubbins/Schwartz 1984.)

In this approach, the legislature-agency relationship is a straightforward application of the *principal-agent problem*. (Weingast 1984) The argument is analogous to the issues present in the debate over separation of ownership and control in large corporations. Shareholders need not actively monitor the day-to-day performance of managers because market institutions allow shareholders to remain ignorant. (Weingast/Moran 1983 792) The question is whether we can identify a similar strong set of incentive mechanisms in the legislative-bureaucratic relationship which obviates the need for direct legislative monitoring. It is these mechanisms of control available to legislators that the congressional control model focuses on. (Moe 1985 1094)

A set of factors enables the legislature to control government agencies effectively:

1. *Competition* among agencies in the budgetary process: Agencies are not really monopolies, since they have to compete in the budgetary process with many other agencies. The legislators pursuing their own electoral goals will favor

those agencies that provide the best clientele service. (Weingast/Moran 1983 169; Rowley 1992 120)

2. *Oversight* with ex post sanctioning: Oversight plays an important role in sanctioning errant agencies. Ex post sanctions include new legislation, specific prohibitions on activities, and other means that serve to embarrass agency heads, hurt future career opportunities, and foil pet projects. (Weingast/Moran 1983 769)
3. *Appointment* process: The legislature controls who gets appointed and reappointed. Therefore, it controls which experts gain influence and control of agency management. Veto power over appointments implies that the only changes in agency management we observe are those preferred by the legislature. (Weingast/Moran 1983 769 Fn. 6; Shughart et al. 1986 963; Rowley 1992 120)
4. Monitoring of agency behavior by *special interest groups:* Interest groups have 'individual' stakes in particular issues. They monitor agency behavior and provide 'their' legislators with the information gathered. (McCubbins/ Schwartz 1985; Weingast 1984)
5. *Agency design* by the principal: The legislature controls agency structure and design. (Macey 1992; McCubbins et al. 1989) Bureaucratic organizations can be designed differently. With alternative organizational designs having different implications for the control of these agencies legislators will prefer agency structures that alleviate the control problem. Shughart et al. (1986) develop a model of legislative control of bureaucratic policymaking that focuses on the differences between two alternative organizational structures, independent commissions and bureaus administered by a single department head. Their analysis suggests that, other things being equal, the output generated by the former will have a smaller variance. This reduction in variance facilitates congressional oversight. (Shughart/Tollison/ Goff 1986 962) This argument turns out to be important in the application to the Swiss executive. (See section 4.3.3.)
6. *Legislative committee system:* Congressional institutions, especially the committee system, allow legislators to economize on monitoring costs and to specialize in other activities more profitable for their own private objectives. According to Weingast/Moran (1983) a system of committees and subcommittees in the US Congress is the main reason why federal agencies are controlled effectively by the legislature.

Since the congressional control model assumes that agencies are controlled by the legislature, regulatory policymaking can only be understood by considering legislative politics. Therefore, a *model of legislative choice* which parallels the economic theory of markets is developed. (Weingast/Moran 1983 770-775; Weingast/Marshall 1988) The model builds on the assumption that each legislator 'votes his district'. This means that legislators supply benefits (money or favorable legislation) in exchange for votes and money to the politically responsive interests located within their district. Since interests are not uniformly distributed across districts, the potential for gains from trade within the legislature emerges. Contractual problems due to noncontemporaneous benefit flows and nonsimultaneous exchange (not all bills come up for a vote simultaneously) lead to failure of classical contracting. Repeated interaction is not always sufficient to prevent a failure of the legislative market. The anticipation of contractual problems leads to the emergence of particular legislative institutions that substitute for market exchange. Thus, legislative institutions are an endogenous response to ex post contractual problems.

The prominent institution that evolved in the US Congress is a system of *committees and subcommittees*. It is defined by the following three conditions: (Weingast/Marshall 1988 143)

1. Committees have near monopoly jurisdiction over a small set of policy issues. This affords committee members an extraordinary influence over a subset of policies.
2. A property rights system over committee seats called the 'seniority system' is established.
3. Vacant committee seats are assigned to legislators by bidding mechanisms. Committee members are assigned on the basis of self-selection. (Shepsle 1978)

Condition 1 defines the source of committee power and value, condition 2 defines the property rights system associated with committee positions, and condition 3 establishes an exchange mechanism over the rights established under conditions 1 and 2. (Weingast/Marshall 1988 143) Therefore, the committee system enforces the following trade among legislators: „(E)ach legislator gives up some influence over many areas of policy in return for a much greater influence over the one that, for him, counts the most." (Weingast/Moran 1983 771)

Among the effects of the legislative committee system (see Weingast/Marshall 1988 144-148), the *control of agencies* is the most relevant in the present context. A legislator's fortunes depend on his obtaining benefits for his constituents. Since constituent interests differ, legislators seek assignment to those committees that have the greatest marginal impact upon their electoral fortunes. (Weingast/Marshall 1988 145-146) Hence, committees are composed of members to whom policies established by the agencies they oversee are important electorially. (Shughart et al. 1986 963) Each legislator specializes in overseeing agencies most closely associated with his constituency, in return for sacrificing any interest in other agencies. (Rowley 1992 121)

A first *testable prediction* therefore is that committees are not representative of the entire legislature but are composed of 'preference outliers'. (Weingast/Marshall 1988 150-152) In general, committees will be composed of legislators with above-average support for policies within their jurisdiction. A second testable prediction which follows from the first one is that committee members receive a disproportionate share of the benefits from programs within their jurisdiction. A third testable comparative statics prediction is that as committee preferences change, so too will agency policy.[2] Predictions two and three reflect the general assertion that congressional committees effectively control agency behavior.

The congressional control model has been *criticized* on several grounds. The model critically depends on the assumption of near monopoly jurisdiction of the oversight committees. The assumed one-to-one nature of the principal-agent relationship contrasts with the multiplicity of principals faced in reality. (Rowley 1992 121, 126; Vachris 1996 225-227) The model is in fact entirely Congress-centered and pays almost no attention to the agencies themselves and to other principals such as the President. (Ferejohn/Shipan 1990) For this reason Moe (1987 and 1985) holds the model presently for unsuited to explain bureaucratic behavior and political control. (However, see the extensions in Calvert et al. 1989, Ferejohn/Shipan 1990, Steunenberg 1994, and Morris/Munger 1998. See also the review of the literature by Moe 1997.) The hypothesis of efficient control of agencies by the legislature seems to be overly optimistic.

Discretionary behavior or effective control of agencies? A final answer to this question can only be provided by *quantitative evidence*. The qualitative observations from case studies are compatible with the bureaucratic discretion and the legislative control model. Therefore, this qualitative evidence, though valuable, cannot be used to support either view. More appropriate quantitative tests must be developed to determine the superiority of one of the models. Since the two models are inconsistent with each other, the empirical test of one of them will also inform about the validity of the other. Here the focus is on empirical tests of the legislative control model.[3]

---

2 Hammond/Knott (1996 142) argue that this must not always hold. There are also conditions „under which agency policy will not change at all, despite substantial changes in the preferences of virtually *all* the elected officials."

3 Recent research, however, tries to synthesize the two competing models:
Vachris (1996) e.g. extends the 'new' theory of bureaucracy, which is termed the traditional principal-agent model, by modeling political markets as many agents (legislature, executive, and the bureau itself) competing for control over a common pool of resources. The problem then is to determine the relative influence of these agents on policy (outcomes). The application of the extended principal-agent model to the Antitrust Division of the Justice Department supports the hypothesis that the Congress, the President, and the bureaus themselves influence antitrust enforcement. Hence, „while congressional oversight does play a role in the determination of bureaucratic behavior, the Congress does not, in effect, dominate the bureaucracy." (Vachris 1996 236)
Hammond/Knott (1996) present a formal model of multi-institutional policy-making including congressional bodies, the executive, the courts, and the agency itself. „In our view, control of the bureaucracy is a function of the *interactions* of the president and Congress (and, in a broader perspective, the courts). For some agencies, these interactions lead to great autonomy; for other agencies these interactions lead to little autonomy." (Hammond/Knott 1996 163)
Another model which builds on multiplicity of principals and asymmetric information flows is developed by Hopenhayn/Lohmann 1996.

5.3 Application of the 'New' Theory of Bureaucracy to Central Banks: Legislative Influence on the Federal Reserve

The theory of legislative influence has been applied to several US government agencies, such as the Interstate Commerce Commission (Barke/Riker 1982), the Federal Trade Commission (Weingast/Moran 1983), the Securities and Exchange Commission (Weingast 1984), the National Labor Relations Board (Moe 1985), the International Trade Commission (Rowley/Thorbecke 1993; Butler 1995), and the Antitrust Division of the Department of Justice (Vachris 1996). Another area of application are central banks, especially the Federal Reserve System. (Grier 1991; Havrilesky 1992) Hence, the old question of central bank independence is addressed in the light of the more recent controversy in the theory of bureaucracy.

Central banks are perceived as government agencies. If they are operationally *independent*, they may use their discretion to pursue the public interest and maximize social welfare. In this perspective, monetary policy becomes a straightforward exercise in applied welfare economics. (Kane 1980 199) The more adequate the models of how monetary policy works, the easier for central banks to maximize social welfare. However, private interests may interfere! An independent central bank, enjoying discretion, may pursue its own (private) goals and maximize bureaucratic utility (budget, staff, prestige etc.).

A *dependent* central bank will effectively be controlled by its principals, and it will pursue their (public or private) interests. The set of potential principals includes the executive, the legislature (or specialized legislative committees), and special interest groups. Sections 5.3 and 5.4 explore legislative influence on central bank behavior.

An application of the theory of legislative control to central banks is appealing for the following general reasons. First, monetary policy „provides an ideal arena for quantitative analysis, since quantitative indicators of the variables are so readily available.“ (Beck 1984 787) Second, some central banks are considered as politically independent government agencies. Finding evidence for systematic political influence on these formally independent actors represents strong empirical support for the control hypothesis. Third, a central bank is an actor which takes very important decisions. It is evident that such decisions will not take place in a political vacuum. Instead, it can be assumed that political actors have an incentive to influence the monetary authority, given the additional fact that monetary policy instruments are much easier to manipulate than fiscal policy instruments.

This section discusses the application of the theory of legislative control to the US central bank, the Federal Reserve System. The legal and institutional background is presented in order to identify the control mechanisms available to the legislature. This serves to demonstrate that the potential for legislative influence exists. However, the mere existence of control mechanisms does not imply legislative control. To establish effective legislative control, two additional conditions must be satisfied. First, legislators must actually try to influence monetary policy. This addresses the incentive problem. And, second, the central bank must yield to that legislative pressure. It is especially the first condition that is questioned, as the discussion of the conventional wisdom on legislative oversight of monetary policy shows. The Weingast-Grier perspective on the Congress-Fed relationship, which basically argues that these two conditions are satisfied, is then set out. Finally, the evidence on congressional influence on US monetary policy is briefly summarized.

5.3.1 The Institutional Background

The US legislature has the capability to affect the monetary policy of the Federal Reserve System over three mechanisms:

1. Since the Fed is a creation of the legislature, it can change the legal status of the central bank.
2. It has the general oversight. To this end, Federal Reserve officials regularly appear to oversight hearings before the Senate and House Banking Committees.
3. Confirmation hearings: The Senate (Banking Committee) has to confirm the President's designations of governors of the Federal Reserve Board to serve as chairman and vice chairman of the board. Hence, it can influence who is in charge of monetary policy.

ad 1) The threat of *changing the legal status* of the central bank: Legislative influence arises from the ability (or power) of the legislative branch to amend the legal status of the central bank. This includes changes of the regulatory domain, budgetary, and monetary policy autonomy. (See Woolley 1984 139.) As a bureaucracy (agency) the central bank prizes its high level of independence. Therefore, it tries not to strongly alienate other governmental institutions like the legislature (and the executive branch) that can infringe on its independence. This makes it receptive to legislative (and executive) pressure. (Cukierman 1992 453) Ironically, monetary authorities bow to political pressure in order to maintain their 'independent' status. (Willett 1990 17; see e.g. Eizenga 1983 7.)

However, as Havrilesky (1992 19) argues, legislative attacks on central bank prerogatives may not necessarily lead the central bank to become more responsive to legislative preferences. Legislative threats may actually induce the central bank to closer cooperation with the executive, in order to have a political ally in the fight versus the legislature.[4]

Of course, the threat of changing the legal status of the central bank is more credible if central bank independence is not guaranteed by the constitution, so that only a change in legislation by simple majority rule is required.

---

[4] The public can be another valuable political ally for the central bank. Especially the German Bundesbank and the SNB regularly address the public to defend their monetary policy, also by trying to shift attention towards problems of fiscal policy.

ad 2) *Oversight hearings:* While the threat of change in the legal status may be the (ultimate and) most important weapon the legislature has to discipline a central bank, oversight hearings are the control device most extensively discussed in the literature, probably because of the controversy about their effectiveness. Based on House Concurrent Resolution 133 from March 1975, and Public Law 95-188 from November 1977, quarterly oversight hearings on the conduct of monetary policy are held alternately by the House and Senate Banking Committees of the US Congress.[5] These hearings are supposed to assure „that at least four times a year Congress is going to focus on what is happening to money supply, what is planned for the year ahead, and what the associated developments in production, employment and prices are likely to be." (Weintraub 1978 360)

As to the *effectiveness* of oversight hearings, most observers agree that they have little impact on monetary policy (at least after initial optimism has disappeared). (See e.g. Pierce 1978, Roberts 1978, Weintraub 1978, Havrilesky 1992 112.) „Congress has salved its conscience by passing a resolution and then a law but it has showed little interest in providing meaningful oversight of monetary policy." (Pierce 1978 364) While legislators are more interested in defining goals and basic guidelines for their achievement, the Fed's strategy is to direct attention away from policy objectives and toward technical questions about what the best monetary aggregate is and other technical areas. (Pierce 1978 364) For Roberts (1978 544) the oversight process is „more of a continuing dialogue and educational process rather than an exercise threatening the Fed's independence."

ad 3) *Senate confirmation:* House Concurrent Resolution 133 and Public Law 95-188 also require Senate confirmation of the President's designations of governors of the Federal Reserve to serve as chairman and vice chairman of the board. In empirical work on congressional influence only members of the Senate Banking Committee are found to have an impact on monetary policy. (See section 5.3.4.) This suggests that Senate confirmation of appointments - which represents an implicit veto power over presidential appointments - is the decisive mechanism of legislative influence.

To avoid a change in the legal status of the central bank, and to have reappointment by the Senate confirmed, central bank officials may well bow to legislative pressure (for lower interest rates, for example).

5.3.2 The Conventional Wisdom: Limits of Legislative Influence

Despite these potential control devices available to the legislature, *conventional wisdom* is that the legislature has little (if any) influence on monetary policy. Different arguments are put forward to support this view.

Following Woolley (1984) effective legislative oversight requires persistency and consistency. He argues that legislators do not have these capabilities, basically

---

5 For the exact wording of the legislation that requires oversight hearings see e.g. Weintraub 1978 345.

because they lack incentives to monitor monetary policy. (See also Pierce 1978; Weintraub 1978.)

On the one side, the expected vote-producing *benefits* from an involvement in monetary policy are rather limited for several reasons. First, monetary policy entails some difficult zero-sum tradeoffs. This creates complex pressures from interest groups. Some voters are usually harmed and rally for defense of their interests. Risk-avoiding legislators prefer other arenas to score electoral points and shift responsibility for monetary policy. Second, monetary policy does not redistribute resources as overtly as fiscal policy (and especially porkbarreling) does. Third, it is frequently argued that the distributive aspects of monetary policy do not translate neatly into the geography of legislative districts. (See e.g. Alt 1991 42.) This offers limited opportunities for porkbarreling. More generally, agency oversight, particularly central bank monitoring, has collective good character.[6]

On the other side, the *costs* of involvement into monetary policy to individual legislators are rather high for a number of reasons: Monetary policy issues are often technical. Direct communication with central bank authorities is relatively infrequent and difficult. (Havrilesky 1988 87) Moreover, agencies can engage in (positive) activities to discourage legislative oversight. (See Woolley 1984 137-138.)

Since benefits are limited and costs are high, legislators *lack the incentive* to systematically control monetary policy. Therefore, assignments to the committees specialized in monetary policy oversight are less attractive than other committee seats. This can also be observed on the relatively high rates of turnover at these committees. (See Woolley 1984 134 on this.) Attendance to oversight hearings is fairly low. And committee floor success is rather limited. (Woolley 1984 136)

Pierce (1978) lists two additional explanations for the absence of congressional influence. The first reason is the lack of public interest. The general public and many members of Congress simply know little about monetary policy. The second reason is the mystical quality of American central banking. „The Fed was able to imbue its activities with a mystical quality, arguing in effect that secrecy was required for effective central banking.“ (Pierce 1978 363)

Finally, monetary policy is not central to contemporary partisan conflict in the US. (See Woolley 1984 134.) Legislators, independent of their party affiliation, usually tend to prefer low interest-rates.

Usually, Congress shows interest in controlling monetary policy only in extreme cases. This is why it is observed that congressional oversight operates according to the 'fire-alarm' principle. (McCubbins/Schwartz 1984) And this is unlikely to establish a systematic impact on monetary policy.

---

6 For Swiss legislators, the vote-producing effect might be overestimated, especially if reelection is not endangered, or if the legislator does not run for reelection. His primary interest might be the future income, for instance by being appointed to the board of a major company. Because of competition for these positions the individual legislator may well have a private interest for engagement in monetary policy affairs.

Nevertheless, there regularly are legislative attempts to influence monetary policy. (For a discussion of these legislative attacks on the Federal Reserve see Havrilesky 1992 chap. 3; Woolley 1984 chap. 7.) It is well known from agency theory that there exist more effective ways to control an agency, the most effective control device being the budget. This raises a paradox: Why doesn't the legislature control the central bank's budget? Why did it decide to create a formally independent agency first and tries to influence it afterwards? In the literature, different explanations are offered for what Cukierman terms the legislative schizophrenia of Congress.[7]

A first reason why Congress gave the monetary authority broad powers to conduct monetary policy without providing meaningful guidelines for its use is to preserve the *effectiveness* of monetary policy. (Cukierman 1992 213) The conduct of monetary policy requires expertise. Therefore, it is reasonable to confer authority to specialists. (Goodman 1992 7)[8]

A second explanation is that the central bank's ultimate political purpose as an institution is to serve as the legislature's *whipping boy* or scapegoat. Incumbent politicians want to be able to blame the central bank for unpopular policies. In exchange the monetary authority can enjoy the privilege of independence. This hypothesis has been proposed by Kane (1980). The shift-of-responsibility argument put forward by Fiorina (1982) is similar to Kane's hypothesis.

According to a third hypothesis suggested by Havrilesky (1990) the main reason for central bank independence is to *mask* some of the *redistribution* of income effected by fiscal policy.

A fourth explanation is offered by Moser (1995 chap. 10). Independent central banks are created to mitigate the *time-inconsistency* problem in monetary policy. He argues that only those countries with a legislative system that comprises at least two veto players (parliamentary chambers, executive, or the people if a referendum exists) with different preferences with respect to monetary policy can credibly supply a partially independent central bank.

Finally, it has been argued that despite central bank independence, legislators get what they want from monetary policy, because Congress holds the key card. This is the basic proposition of the Weingast-Grier principal-agent model of the Congress-Fed relationship discussed subsequently.

7 „The collective schizophrenia in which Congress confers a large degree of legal independence on the Fed only to continually attempt to influence its policy by threatening to revoke this independence seems very much a US phenomenon.“ Cukierman 1992 466 Fn. 1.

8 Moreover, the theory of rational expectations teaches that monetary policy only works if it creates monetary surprises. The problem with the rational expectations argument is that it was developed *after* that independent central banks were established.

5.3.3 The Challenge: Legislative Influence on Monetary Policy

The hypothesis of benign congressional neglect of monetary policy has been challenged by Grier (1991). His principal-agent model of the Congress-Fed relationship builds on the paradigm of legislative control of bureaucratic policies introduced by Stigler (1971) and Peltzman (1976), and on its extensions to oversight committee control of bureaus by Weingast/Moran (1983), Weingast (1984), and Weingast/Marshall (1988).

In the *Weingast-Grier perspective* on the Congress-Fed relationship - this is the terminology adopted from Beck (1990) - Congress holds the key card, the congressional grant of independence to the Fed. It is the threat of removal of Fed independence - 'the big club behind the door' (Beck 1990 137) - that ultimately disciplines the Fed and induces it to comply with congressional preferences.

Because of the structure of the legislature congressmen do not have equal influence. Authority to recommend or withhold legislation, hold hearings, and oversee bureaus is allocated across a set of committees. *Committee membership* affords legislators disproportionate influence in affecting policies under their jurisdictions. (Denzau/Mackay 1983; Shepsle/Weingast 1987) The key congressmen influencing policies under their jurisdictions are committee and subcommittee leaders (chairmen). The possibility of disproportionate influence and the electoral motivation induce legislators to join committees that control legislation which is vital to their constituents. Therefore, committees are populated with 'high demand' preference outliers.[9]

Legislators serving constituents who demand specific monetary outcomes will try to obtain a seat in the committee that controls monetary policy, the *Congressional Banking Committee.* „When the Congressional Banking Committees are dominated by one type of legislator, say those with a pro-inflation constituency, there will be a policy equilibrium through time with high money growth. If, through electoral losses or retirements, the committees become dominated by low inflation legislators, there will be a corresponding change to a new equilibrium of lower money growth.“ (Grier 1991 204)

The major *refutable hypothesis* of Grier's model of congressional influence is the following comparative statics prediction: changes in the preferences of the Fed's sponsoring committees as a result of turnover in committee membership and especially committee leadership, ceteris paribus, will induce a corresponding change in Fed policy. (Grier 1991 204)

It is important to note that effective legislative control does not require continuing monitoring and detailed work rules (hearings and legislation). The absence of overt monitoring activity can be consistent with legislative control. It does not imply zero influence. (Weingast 1984; Grier 1991 206; Beck 1990 132)

---

9 See e.g. Benson 1981 on this common claim. However, Krehbiel 1990 finds no convincing evidence of preference outliers for members of the 96th to 99th Congress.

The Weingast-Grier perspective on the Congress-Fed relationship has been *criticized* by Beck (1988 and 1990 137). Usually, budgetary control is considered as the key power of a principal. Why did Congress give up this relatively low-cost means of controlling its agent, the Fed? Why does it rely on the threat of removal of Fed independence instead of moving towards budgetary control of the Fed? Because of this puzzle posed by the Weingast-Grier perspective Beck considers the argument as unreasonable.

5.3.4 Evidence on Congressional Influence

So far, evidence on legislative influence on central bank behavior is only available for the Fed.

Qualitative evidence is provided by Weintraub (1978), Pierce (1978) and Woolley (1984 chap. 7). Weintraub for instance reviews the history of congressional oversight of monetary policy and concludes that this oversight is ineffective. „Congress plays only a 'watchdog' role." (Weintraub 1978 349) A similar conclusion is reached by Pierce. Also skeptical about the effectiveness of legislative oversight is Woolley.[10]

The difficulty with qualitative evidence is that - because of observational equivalence - it cannot discriminate between ineffectiveness of legislative oversight and legislative control. Quantitative evidence is needed.

Quantitative evidence on legislative influence was first presented by Havrilesky (1988). His model builds on the assumption that the Fed responds to statements in the financial press on a weekly basis. Statements of congressmen reported in the Wall Street Journal are coded as +1 if they express interest for easier policy. They are coded as -1 if they express a desire for tighter policy. The sum of pluses and minuses for each week constitutes the 'signaling' index. Since these congressional 'signals' are of no value in predicting monetary policy (as measured by the growth rates of the money supply M1 and the monetary base), he concludes that „Congress exerts no effective, regular influence on monetary policy." (Havrilesky 1988 91)

The main problem with these results is that they are based on a very limited time period (from 1979 to 1984). Moreover, the disproportionate influence of committee members and especially committee leaders is not accounted for. (Grier 1991 210)

An interesting hypothesis is put forward by Havrilesky (1992 chap. 5): Congressional threats to Fed bureaucratic privileges condition the central bank's responsiveness to executive branch pressures. So there is legislative influence. But this influence operates not in the sense that Congress always gets the monetary policy it desires. Just the opposite may occur: Legislative pressure induces the Fed to cooperate with the Administration to rally support against the legislature.

---

10 Authors that stress the importance of Congress in monetary policymaking without presenting evidence are Kane 1980, Wagner 1986, and Hetzel 1990.

To test this hypothesis Havrilesky constructs a measure of legislative threat based on the number of legislative bills introduced that are aimed at the Fed's budgetary authority, regulatory domain or monetary policy autonomy during the 1964-1990 period. The first difference of the federal funds rate is then regressed not only on a variable measuring signals from the Administration to the Fed[11] (the pure-signaling model), but also on an interaction term constructed with the signaling index and the threat variable (the threat-augmented model). Empirical results appear to corroborate Havrilesky's conjecture that Fed responsiveness to Administration signaling is conditioned by congressional threat. (Havrilesky 1992 178)

Evidence supporting the hypothesis that Congress is able to influence the direction of Fed policy - as is postulated by the *legislative control model* - is provided by Grier (1991) and Havrilesky (1992 chap. 7).

The difficulty with an empirical test of the *Weingast-Grier perspective* is „that congressional dominance and congressional impotence are observationally equivalent with respect to congressional activity. Thus, the argument must turn on the indirect evidence of the relationship between some observable change in Congress and an observable change in agency output." (Beck 1990 136) The technical problem is to measure changes in agency policy and changes in preferences of the oversight committee, and to show that changes in agency behavior are systematically related to the changes in preferences of the overseers.

Changes in *preferences* of the oversight committee are a necessary condition for the comparative statics test to be applicable. One of the most obvious reasons for changes in preferences is turnover. Legislative turnover will bring in new legislators which may have different preferences or which represent different electoral districts and thus different interests. However, legislative turnover can neither be a necessary, nor a sufficient condition for changing committee preferences. In addition to turnover committee preferences may change as a result of changes in an incumbent's constituency. And committee preferences may remain unchanged if the old and new members represent the same (or similar) constituent interests. (Grier 1991 208)

Changes in preferences in the legislative oversight committees can be *measured* in at least two ways: party affiliation (if party membership is decisive), or some ratings based on legislators' voting records. In the case of the US, where party affiliation is not a reliable measure of political preferences, legislators' preferences are commonly measured by some ratings based on their voting records. The most frequently used rating is from ADA, the Americans for Democratic Action. This is also the measure used by Grier (1991). „ADA scores are not a perfect measure of senators' induced preferences over monetary policy. They do, however, allow for intra-party differences between legislators and there is a strong

[11] This variable is constructed analogously to the congressional 'signaling' index just described. See Havrilesky 1988 and 1992 for details.

connection between ADA scores and sources of electoral support." (Grier 1991 212)

Changes in *agency policy* are assessed by looking at key policy instruments and their application. The choice of the dependent variable depends on the specific agency under investigation.[12] For central banks the best choice appears to be the growth rate of the monetary base or the money supply M1. (See section 1.3.2a.)

Grier (1991) shows that changes in the leadership of the Senate Banking Committee - where changes are measured using ADA scores - are significantly correlated with monetary base growth. This suggests the existence of a systematic political influence on Fed behavior and is interpreted as evidence supporting the legislative control model.

Havrilesky (1992 chap. 7) also finds that US monetary policy is responsive to preferences of members of the Senate Banking Committee (the chairman). The remarkable thing is that he gets similar results although he measures legislative preferences differently. Havrilesky constructs a variable based on the number of times that legislators mention certain state-of-the-economy variables during the oversight hearings. This variable has a significant effect on the federal funds rate in the month after the hearing.

The fact that both authors find influence only for the Senate, but not for the House Banking Committee suggests that the Senate Banking Committee's confirmation authority seems to play a decisive role.

The empirical results of an earlier version of Grier's study have been contested by Beck (1990). While he reports a similar finding for the sample period analyzed by Grier (from 1961 to 1980), his replication of Grier's work for a longer sample period (from 1962 to 1987) yields results that are inconsistent with the Weingast-Grier hypothesis. He concludes that the Grier finding is artifactual. He is especially disturbed about the fact that the hypothesis is not supported for the House Banking Committee, because he is not convinced that confirmation power is the strongest tool for congressional sanction.

Since legislators tend to be more sensitive to high interest rates, and because the Fed directly controls the federal funds rate, the legislative control model should also predict a strong congressional impact on the federal funds rate. Beck finds no evidence that either House or Senate committee liberalism - as measured by ADA ratings - leads to lower interest rates.

The debate on the congressional influence on US monetary policy is continued in an issue of the Journal of Monetary Economics in 1996. Chopin et al. (1996a) extend Grier's analysis by considering a longer sample period and by considering the preferences of House oversight committee leaders, in addition to Senators. They conclude that Grier's evidence is not robust to these extensions. In his reply, Grier argues that Chopin, Cole and Ellis's claims are unfounded. „Properly meas-

---

12 For the Federal Trade Commission, for example, the case-bringing activity (number of cases and their distribution) can be chosen.

ured, both House and Senate leadership have a significant positive effect on base growth over Grier's (1991) original sample." (Grier 1996)

Although Grier's revised version of 1991 (with a sample period from 1958 to 1984) and Havrilesky's findings do support the legislative control model for the Fed, the quantitative evidence must be considered as being inconclusive. (See also Alt 1991 72.) For this reason, it is also of interest to test the legislative control model in a different institutional environment. This is attempted in the next section.

5.4 Legislative Influence on SNB Behavior?

In addition to the three general arguments listed in section 5.3, an application of the theory of legislative control to the SNB is interesting for the following two reasons.

First, it represents an application to a different institutional setting. In the controversy in the economic theory of bureaucracy institutions play a prominent role. The control hypothesis builds on special institutional arrangements. Are there institutional features in the Swiss political market that help to confirm the control hypothesis?

A second reason is the alleged independence of the SNB. It is considered as one of the most independent central banks in the world. An empirical test of the control hypothesis furthers the knowledge about the degree of its de facto independence.

As in section 5.3, the application to the SNB starts with a discussion of the institutional background. Then follows a brief review of legislative activities towards the Swiss central bank to illustrate legislative attention. Finally, an empirical test of the control hypothesis is performed.

5.4.1 The Institutional Background

The focus of the control hypothesis is on legislative influence on agency behavior. In this approach, the legislature is modeled as the principal and the central bank is interpreted as its agent. In the literature on legislative control a set of factors is put forward that enables the legislature to control its agencies effectively. (See section 5.2.2.) Here, a systematic analysis of these control mechanisms for the case of Switzerland is attempted. It shows that several of these control mechanisms are not available to the Swiss legislature in its relationship to the central bank, weakening the case for the control hypothesis.

The SNB is a federal agency, and as such, it is accountable to the Confederacy. (See e.g. Schmid 1980 47.) Article 39 (2) of the Federal Constitution FC stipulates that the central bank is managed with the collaboration and under the supervision of the Confederation. Article 63 of the National Bank Law NBL shows that the *legal oversight* of the Confederacy over the central bank is basically exercised by the executive, the Federal Council. (See sections 4.2.2 and 4.2.3.) The legislature, however, has very little oversight authority. Article 63 (1) of the NBL states that the Federal Assembly (i.e. National Council and Council of States) exercises oversight by approving an increase in equity capital. The Federal Assembly also determines on how the new capital is raised. (Article 6 (1) of NBL) The SNB's privilege of issuing money has to be renewed every 20 years. This renewal has to be accorded by the Federal Assembly. (Article 66 (1) of NBL) And decisions about SNB profits and losses as a result of changes in the mint par of exchange of the SFr have to be taken by the Federal Assembly. (Article 3 of 'Bundesgesetz über das Münzwesen')[13] Though these legal provisions could be used by the legislature to pressure the central bank, they are very unlikely to be relevant in practice.

The important thing is that the SNB is *not directly* accountable to the Federal Assembly. Therefore, it has not to report to the legislature. Article 63 (2 lit.k) of the NBL stipulates that the executive informs the Federal Assembly about the SNB's monetary policy. In practice, the executive informs legislative committees about current economic policies while representatives of the SNB are present.

Hence, there exists a *double-layer* principal agent relationship between legislature and central bank. The Federal Assembly can only influence SNB policy indirectly over the executive. The structure of the existing principal-agent relationships is crucial for the question whether one can expect any systematic legislative influence on SNB policy. This is why the two principal-agent relationships involved need to be discussed in more detail.

The executive (Federal Council) is elected by the legislature (the Federal Assembly). (Article 96 of FC) This constitutes a principal-agent relationship between the legislature and the executive. The analysis of the *legislature-executive relationship* is therefore a straightforward application of principal-agent theory.

The legislature has the general oversight over the executive. Article 85 of the FC enumerates the *mechanisms of legislative control* over the executive:

1. The legislature decides on the laws of organization and the mode of election of the federal authorities.
2. It determines salaries and allowances of the members of the federal authorities.
3. It elects the Federal Council.
4. It draws up of the annual budget and approves of the State's accounts as well as decrees on the floating of loans.
5. It has the general supervision of the federal administration.
6. It decides on conflicts of competence between federal authorities.

Despite these constitutional provisions (which include such important instruments as elections and budgets), the *conventional wisdom* is that the executive (the agent), together with the federal bureaucracy, actually dominates the legislature

13 The last time this stipulation was relevant was in December 1971 when the legislature had to decide on a SNB loss of 1243 millions of SFr. See e.g. AB 1971 1481-1490.

(the principal). (See e.g. Aubert 1987 218-220; Mastronardi 1991; Tschäni 1990 197.) The dominance of the executive is explained with several factors that constrain legislative influence.

A first set of arguments concerns the position of parliament in the political market in general. Institutional peculiarities such as federalism, the highly fragmented party system, and direct democracy lead to a *high diffusion* of political power in Switzerland. (See e.g. Kriesi 1990.)[14] With respect to its primary activity, legislation, parliament is not the exclusive site of policy-making. Cantonal legislatures enjoy considerable authority. The executive who prepares legislative bills and issues federal decrees is active in legislating, too. The initiative allows voters themselves to legislate directly. And with the referendum voters can intervene and control (to some extent) legislative activity of parliament. (Aubert 1987 232) It is especially the referendum that weakens the position of parliament as legislative authority.[15]

A second group of arguments concerns the *position* of legislators *vis-à-vis the executive.* The executive is a full-time authority, while legislators only work part-time. This tends to weaken their position vis-à-vis the executive. The executive has direct access to the know-how of the federal bureaucracy, which means that it has much more resources available. And the Federal Assembly has no possibility to withdraw confidence from the political executive during interelection periods.[16]

However, several arguments can be listed *against the hypothesis of executive dominance*. First, it is inconsistent with the fact that the Federal Council generally appears to comply with parliamentary decisions. Second, the argument with the diffusion of political power holds for the Federal Council, too. „With many important decisions being taken in the preparliamentary consultation process, in the Federal Assembly itself, and in the referenda, federal councillors have relatively little authority. Under these conditions it may not seem quite so crucial to many politicians who sits in the Federal Council." (Steiner 1982 332) And third, the effectiveness of legislative control over the executive also depends on two factors that are neglected in the political science literature (but do play an important role in the theory of legislative control), the organization of the executive, and the structure of the legislature. These two control mechanisms deserve further elaboration.

The executive is organized as a *commission government*. Why did the legislature - who controls agency structure and design - choose this particular form of

---

14 As an additional institutional peculiarity Kriesi (1990 35) lists the self-regulating society.

15 „Compared to representative democracies, parliament is not very important since most political battles are fought out through the referendum process. Consequently, there is little competition between the political parties and little difference in their ideologies, and the election and partisan competition of parliament have only minor consequences for political activity." (Schneider et al. 1981 232)

16 As an additional argument, Aubert (1987 218-220) lists simply the number of members in the two bodies.

government? One explanation is that the organizational design of agencies is a major control device for legislatures in their role as principals. (Macey 1992; McCubbins et al. 1989) Commission government facilitates legislative oversight. (See section 4.3.3 for details.)

The central element of the structure of the legislature is the *committee system*. Similarly to the US legislature, the two chambers of Swiss parliament have established a system of committees. This committee system evolved not just to increase legislative output. It is explicitly acknowledged that the standing committees play a prominent role in the supervision of the federal administration. (Tschäni 1990 195) In fact, their emergence is mainly seen as a response to oversight problems.

The committee system of the Swiss legislature is virtually untouched by scientific research. Here, only those aspects of the committee system are addressed that are supposed to be most relevant in the present context. Further research in this area is needed.[17]

Both chambers of the Swiss legislature specialized their legislative and oversight activities in a number of standing committees. (Besides, they also set up ad hoc committees if needed.) The committee system evolved over time. The last major reform in 1991 (Federal Law of October 4, 1991) mainly aimed at a higher degree of specialization in the committee system. As a result of this reform, all standing committees in both councils were completely renewed.

Standing committees can establish their own rules of procedure. The rules must be approved by their chamber, however.

In the National Council the bureau[18] determines the number of seats in standing committees. *Committee size* basically depends on the importance of the issues. The more important the issue, the larger the committee will be. Since 1991 committee size is determined according to the volume of legislative activity. Standing committees in the Council of States are smaller and have a fixed number of seats.

In the National Council the number of committee *seats per legislator* is restricted to two. There exists no such upper limit in the Council of States.

Committee seats and chairmanship are *assigned* according to the strengths of the fractions[19] in the respective chambers. If possible, the different official languages and the geographic regions are also considered as criteria for committee assignments. In the National Council the bureau appoints committee chairmen and

---

17 A description of the committee system in the Swiss legislature is provided by Nuspliger 1991.

18 Until 1991, the bureau in the National Council consisted of the president, the vice-president, and 8 more legislators (Stimmenzähler). Since 1992 the bureau includes the president, the vice-president, 4 more legislators (Stimmenzähler), and the presidents of the fractions.
The bureau in the Council of States is composed of the president, the vice-president, and 3 more legislators (2 Stimmenzähler and 1 Ersatzstimmenzähler).

19 Fractions include all members of the same party from both chambers. To form a fraction, at least five legislators have to join in one of the two chambers. Only members of fractions can get appointments to committees.

committee members after consultation with the fractions. Here, the presidents of the fractions seem to play a key role. In the assignment process the bureau is supposed to take care of the 'public interest' and to avoid a one-sided representation of special interests. In the Council of States all standing committees were appointed by the Council itself on the basis of a proposed list before 1991. After the reorganization of 1991 presidents, vice-presidents, and all members are appointed by the bureau.

Membership in a standing committee is *limited* to six years. Exceptions are allowed for important reasons only. If a member leaves a committee (because it reached the 6 year limit) it can only be appointed to that committee again after a break of two years. While the Council of States still has these term limits, the National Council decided to abandon them for standing committee members in 1991. Since then, terms are 4 years, with the possibility of reappointment.

The *chairmanship* of a standing committee changes every two years. (These term limits were not changed in the reform of 1991.) This implies a significant amount of turnover in committee leadership.

In both councils committee *jurisdictions* are determined by the bureau. Committees report to their chambers about the issues they were assigned to. And they present propositions about whether a bill should be approved or rejected. If a majority in the committee recommends to reject the bill, the minority may still propose to approve it. Within their jurisdictions, committees have the right to start parliamentary initiatives and to use all the other parliamentary instruments available to each individual legislator.

Committee meetings are confidential. The information released includes the decisions with the number of votes for and against, the essential petitions made, and the main positions taken in the discussions.

Each Council has a standing committee which is specialized in the *general oversight* of the administration (Geschäftsprüfungskommission). These committees control annual reports, monitor and investigate activities of the executive, the bureaucracy, and the federal courts, and make special inspections.[20]

The finance committees (Finanzkommissionen) are the second type of committee with general oversight authority. They are specialized in the *financial* aspects of the *oversight*. The budget becomes an effective control mechanism through the activity of these committees. Each chamber has its own finance committee. From among the members of both committees, a joint subcommittee, the finance delegation ('Finanzdelegation') consisting of 6 members is appointed.[21]

---

20 Since the reform of 1991 there exists also a joint subcommittee composed of 3 members of each oversight committee, called the 'Geschäftsprüfungsdelegation'. This subcommittee oversees secret service activities.

21 The activity of the finance committees and the finance delegation is based on Article 85 (10 and 11) of the FC. Details are regulated in Article 48-50 of the 'Geschäftsverkehrsgesetz' (Federal Law of the Legislature) and in a special regulation. (Systematic Collection SR 171.126)

The finance committees (and their subcommittees) can at any time request any relevant information from the Federal Council, from single department heads, from subordinate agencies, and from federal courts. They can engage the 'federal finance control' (a specialized control agency), and they can make inspections.

The finance delegation has unrestricted authority for inspection of all documents related to the budget and for getting access to relevant information from all agencies. For this purpose its members receive a special identity card.

Other standing committees have special oversight authority in their jurisdictions.

This brief description of the committee structure in the Swiss legislature reveals the following features that are relevant in the present context:

- Proposals that do not command a majority of votes in the committee can still become public policy, since the minority in the committee can make its own proposals to the legislature.[22]
- The closed-rule assumption does not apply. This means that committee proposals can be (and often are) amended in parliament. Under an open-rule setting the legislative committee will rationally anticipate the other legislators' responses to its proposals in parliament. It will not be able to make the sorts of proposals that are suggested by the model of legislative choice. (Ferejohn/Shipan 1990 4)[23]
- These two features imply that the committee has not complete agenda control in his jurisdiction.
- Term limits for committee membership and committee leadership prevent individual legislators from building up too powerful positions. To some extent, they also prevent legislators from a high degree of specialization into legislative areas. The property rights system over committee seats called the 'seniority system' (Weingast/Marshall 1988 143) is severely attenuated. Term limits for committee membership have been dropped in the National Council in the 1991 reform, improving (ceteris paribus) the preconditions for effective legislative oversight.
- There is a process of self-selection operating, especially in the Council of States. In the National Council, the presidents of the fractions appear to function as 'filters'.[24] As a result, committees are likely to be 'preference outliers'.[25] This tends to favor the argument of specialization and effective oversight.

Except for the process of self-selection, the special features of the committee system in the Swiss legislature attenuate the preconditions of the legislative control model. In an application to the Swiss setting, these qualifications must be

22 Individual members of the finance committees can also present their own proposals (that deviate from the majority) in the legislature.

23 See Ferejohn/Shipan 1990 7 on the importance of this assumption.

24 See Crain 1990 for a filtering theory of legislative committees.

25 However, there exists no empirical evidence on this for the Swiss legislature.

added to the general criticisms of the legislative control model listed in section 5.2.

To sum up this discussion on the legislature-executive relationship: There is no doubt that the legislature and its specialized committees have the *legal* authority to oversee the executive. But the question of *de facto* legislative control of the executive cannot be settled by a priori argument. There exists no evidence on this, and it is not intended to provide direct evidence on this question here.[26] The discussion illustrates that legislative control of the executive cannot be excluded. And it suggests that legislative influence - if it exists at all - will be weaker than in the US, because of the double-layer principal-agent relationship and because the committee system is less developed.

As to the second principal-agent relationship between the executive and the central bank, an analysis of the legal status of the SNB reveals that there is substantial possibility for executive influence. (See sections 4.2.2 and 4.2.3.) In empirical tests, no systematic influence from the executive on the central bank can be detected. However, this, too, does not rule out the existence of such influence.

The fact that the Swiss legislature possesses only *indirect oversight authority* over the central bank represents an important difference to the US institutional setting. The Federal Reserve is directly accountable to Congress. (Roberts 1978 543; MacLaury 1994 84) Congress (the Senate Banking Committee) can exercise its oversight authority by confirmations of appointments to the board and by hearings. The Swiss legislature possesses no similar control instruments. Parliamentary influence on central bank policy has to be exercised indirectly over the executive. This institutional setting tends to isolate the central bank from short-run developments and special (legislative) interests. This, of course, is an important reason why legislative preferences are not expected to influence the conduct of SNB policy.

A parliament basically has two functions, general oversight (over the activities of the executive) and legislation. Even if oversight may be ineffective, *legislative authority* may be relevant. The degree of legal independence conferred on the central bank ultimately depends on the decisions of political authorities as expressed through the legislative process. (Cukierman 1992 445) But there is no guarantee of that autonomy. (Hetzel 1990 112) Hence, the legislature has the possibility to change the degree of legal independence. (See Schmid 1980 116.) It is this threat of change in central bank status that may ultimately discipline the central bank.[27] This hypothesis is supported by the fact that it is generally agreed that oversight hearings are ineffective, and - given the long term of board members - confirmation hearings may not be that important either. (Beck 1990 138)

---

[26] The finding that the legislature does in fact influence monetary policy would at the same time provide indirect evidence for legislative control of the executive.

[27] This need not be a change of the NBL. Central bank independence may also be affected by changes of other legislation, e.g. legislation concerning policies towards the business cycle. See e.g. 'Motion' Jelmini, AB 1991 808.

Whether this threat of change in central bank status is effective depends on its credibility. The high costs of passing new legislation affect the credibility of this threat. The high diffusion of power (especially because of bicameralism and referenda) also limits the Federal Assembly's legislative authority. The more veto players, the more stable the system. (Moser 1996) This implies that the threat of legislative change is less credible!

Even with the absence of mechanisms of legislative influence on central bank behavior, the existence of such influence cannot be precluded. As Grier (1991 202 Fn. 3) notes, partisan modellers, for instance, „do not search for the mechanisms of influence, but test their theory on monetary outcomes.“ This could also be the empirical approach followed here.

The legislative control model mainly focuses on legislative committees as the decisive institutional arrangement that allows for effective agency oversight. (See section 5.2.2.) Although the legislature as a whole is not expected to have any impact, special committees are supposed to influence agency behavior. A testable hypothesis can be derived from this argument: Changes in political preferences of the special oversight committees should lead to changes in agency behavior.

Which committees can be expected to have a disproportionate (if any) influence on Swiss monetary policy? This question cannot easily be answered, since neither the legislature nor specialized committees have direct oversight authority over the central bank. The list of committee jurisdictions established by the bureaus of the two Councils (Zuteilung der Arbeitsbereiche 1991) assigns issues concerning banks, money, credits and currency to the *economics committee* (Wirtschaftskommission). Hence, one would expect that legislative questions concerning central banking fall into the jurisdiction of this committee.[28]

However, this must not necessarily be the case. The existing committee jurisdictions were determined only in November 1991. The economics committee did not exist before Fall 1979. And the assignment of issues also depends on the volume of legislative activities. Here, the finance committee, and a subcommittee thereof - the finance delegation - are also picked out for the following reasons:

1. In addition to financial oversight, the finance committees can also be assigned other issues by their councils. Legislative activity in the past shows that issues concerning the SNB were often assigned to the finance committee. (See e.g. AB 1995 1595, 1992 2136, 1976 1612.)
2. Not all standing committees are of the same importance. Proxy measures for the importance of committees are committee size, length of its existence, frequency of meetings, existence of written rules of procedures, and size and precision of these regulations. Using these proxy measures the finance committees can probably be considered as the most important among all committees.

[28] This was also confirmed to the author by Mrs. G. Puca Kunz of the Parliamentary Services who actually makes the assignments on the basis of the list mentioned.

And the subcommittee of the finance committees, the finance delegation, is of even greater importance.[29]

3. The finance committee has a long tradition, while other committees that might be relevant (such as the economics committee) were only created more recently. Empirical tests for the finance committees can be performed for longer time periods, yielding more reliable estimates.

Therefore, the hypothesis that special legislative committees influence Swiss monetary policy is tested not only for the economics committee, but also for the finance committee and the finance delegation. But before, a brief review of legislative activity towards the SNB during the era of flexible exchange rates is presented.

5.4.2 Legislative Activity towards the SNB

This section presents a brief summary of legislative activity towards the SNB in the National Council (House of Representatives). The discussion is restricted to the National Council for the following reasons: First, it is not intended to provide a complete account of the activity of the Swiss legislature towards the SNB and its policy, but to illustrate that legislators do care about central banking and monetary policy. Second, as a comparison for the years from 1983 to 1996 reveals, legislative activity in the Council of States (Senate) is quite similar to the one in the National Council, though it is less numerous.[30] Third, in the empirical tests employed in the next section, data on the National Council only can be employed.

Identifying legislative activity towards the SNB is not an easy task, not just because of its overall quantity. Very often, the SNB is indirectly involved, as is the case for instance in the numerous debates on interest rates (especially mortgage rates). To simplify the discussion, only the most obvious legislative activity towards monetary policy is considered here. Also, the focus is on legislative activities initiated by members of the National Council, but not on legislative activities initiated by the executive branch of government, nor on routinely held debates on regular reports. Hence, not included in this list are

- annual reports and debates on the federal decree to save the currency (Schutz der Währung) from 1971 to 1979

---

[29] Article 50 (7) of the Federal Law of the Legislature stipulates that all decisions made by the Federal Council which affect the oversight of credits and the budget in general have to be submitted to the finance delegation on a regular basis. (See also Article 15 of the regulation of the finance committees and the finance delegation.) Since many monetary decisions affect the budget, the assumption that the finance delegation will be informed about them in an early stage may not be unreasonable.

[30] This can be explained with the fact that the Council of States consists of a smaller number of legislators, and with the difference in party composition of the two chambers. Legislative attacks on the SNB frequently (but not only) come from legislators situated on the left and the extremes of the political spectrum. These groups are more sizable in the National Council than they are in the Council of States.

- the extended deliberations about the so-called 'Konjunkturartikel' held in Spring 1974. In these debates, monetary policy plays a very important role.
- report on 'Konjunkturdämpfung' (AB 1974 1849). Widespread criticism of a too restrictive monetary policy is addressed at the executive and the SNB.
- statements made in the debate on the revision of the NBL in 1978
- attacks on SNB policy in debates on the situation on the labor market. For instance, in an extended debate on unemployment, business cycles and monetary policy on October 8, 1992, (AB 1992 2100) many legislators belonging to different parties attack the SNB for its too restrictive monetary policy.[31]
- statements made by individual legislators in discussions about questions related to the SNB and its policy. These statements are often much more critical than the formal documents handed in.

The remaining selection of legislative activity in the National Council from 1970 to 1996 is listed in table 5.6 in the appendix to this chapter. This list provides an interesting account of the problems in the monetary domain that preoccupied Swiss legislators.

The table lists the date that each legislative activity is brought in along with its number in parentheses, the type of legislative activity, name and party membership of the legislator(s) initiating the activity as well as the number of sponsors, the original title, a brief description, a classification into standard topics, and the source.

Swiss legislators can choose among several legislative 'instruments' to advance their policies:[32]

- Parliamentary initiative (PI): Article 93 of the FC grants each legislator the right of initiative. A parliamentary initiative orders the legislature to work out a law.

The other legislative 'instruments' are defined in the regulations of the two councils:

- 'Motion' (MO): A 'Motion' orders the executive to work out a federal law or a federal decree, or to take some measures. The executive has to declare whether it accepts the 'Motion'.
- 'Postulat' (PO): With a 'Postulat' the executive is ordered to examine whether a federal law or a federal decree, or some measures should be taken. The executive has to declare whether it accepts the 'Postulat'.
- 'Interpellation' (IN): An 'Interpellation' serves to ask information from the executive about important developments and problems. A discussion in the legislature only takes place if the council approves.

---

31 Frey Walter for instance concludes: „Ich meine, es ist nun die Aufgabe des Parlaments ... sich auf politischer Ebene für einen Kurswechsel der Nationalbank einzusetzen." AB 1992 2138.

32 In general, a legislative majority is more difficult to obtain if an 'instrument' representing a more serious attack is chosen. The individual legislator, having a preference for being successful in the chamber (i.e. approval by a majority) will account for the trade off between importance of the 'instrument' and probability of success.

- Simple question (Einfache Anfrage EA): Simple questions serve to get information from the executive on matters concerning the confederacy.

Legislators also have the opportunity to ask questions (Fragestunde FS) concerning actual problems.

The abbreviations in the column headed with 'type' inform about the legislative instrument being used. The instrument chosen is an indicator of how serious the legislative attack is supposed to be.[33]

The column with the names and party membership of the legislators who initiate the activity also helps to determine the weight of a legislative attack. The importance of legislative activity depends on the party membership, or more generally on the position of the corresponding legislator in the political spectrum. Legislative attacks can also be attributed more weight if they are sponsored by fractions or signed by several other legislators. Therefore, the number in brackets indicates how many other legislators also signed. Moreover, - combined with the other columns - this column serves to identify a crude relationship between parties and political preferences. It also helps to answer the question whether members of various political parties differ in their activity towards the SNB. (Who is most active?)

Legislative statements frequently address several issues. In the column headed with 'description', only the most important issue(s) related to monetary policy and the central bank is (are) assessed. It is also indicated whether there is a discussion. If applicable, voting results are added, too.

Most legislative activities towards the SNB can be classified into the following main categories:

1. Inflation rates are too high: Executive and SNB are urged to fight inflation. (I)
2. The SFr is either too strong or too weak: Executive and SNB are pressured to stabilize exchange rates. (X) They are asked to 'bring down' exchange rates - defined as units of SFr per 1 (or 100) unit(s) of foreign currency - to improve the competitiveness of Swiss industries. (XH) This is the more frequent case. Or a stronger SFr is demanded to fight the problem of imported inflation. (XL)
3. Increase the amount of central bank profits to be handed over to fiscal authorities: Legislators suggest to sell gold coins, adjust the value of gold reserves, change policy concerning holdings of currency reserves, or openly demand for handing over more profits to fiscal authorities. (P) Usually, a corresponding change in the FC or in the NBL is proposed. The question of central bank profits regularly comes up whenever SNB profits rise due to an appreciation of gold and/or currency reserves, while the fiscal authorities are running large deficits.
4. Monetary policy is too restrictive: legislators ask for a less restrictive monetary policy to avoid negative effects on growth and employment. (M)

---

33 'Interpellationen' and simple questions (einfache Anfragen) can be declared urgent (dringlich). This is another indicator for the importance of legislative activities.

5. Legislators want the executive to work out reports (e.g. whether or not to join the European Monetary System). This is usually the mildest form to signal preferences. (Q)

To simplify access to the table, the column headed with 'topic' contains the abbreviations that indicate the category of each legislative activity (if applicable).

Legislative activity in the National Council from 1970 to 1996 can be briefly summarized as follows:

In the early seventies - before the transition to flexible exchange rates - legislators are primarily worried about inflation. Most of them address the executive to fight inflation by administrative measures (e.g. price stops and wage controls). In Fall 1972 several legislators point at the importance of a control of the money supply in the fight against inflation and explicitly ask to stop interventions in the exchange rate market. On January 23 1973 the SNB changes to the regime of flexible exchange rates!

In 1974, many legislators agree that monetary policy meanwhile is too restrictive, as the extended debate on the report on 'Konjunkturdämpfung' reveals. Fischer's 'Interpellation' is a quite pronounced criticism of the too restrictive monetary policy. Executive and central bank are criticized for not perceiving the danger of an artificially created recession. The fact that 98 more legislators sign this 'Interpellation' also illustrates the widespread agreement in the National Council.

In 1975 (and afterwards) legislators are primarily preoccupied with the stability of exchange rates. In late 1977 and in 1978 - after two years of relative calm (1976 and 1977) - the weakness of the US$ and the DM induces legislators to ask for interventions in the exchange rate market. In 'Interpellationen' of September 18 and 19 1978 the social democrats, the radicals, and the members of the Swiss people's party, all point at the suffering Swiss industries faced with a strong SFr and ask for measures. Especially the social democrats criticize the SNB's monetarist approach and ask for more activism in monetary policy. According to them, Switzerland should join the 'snake' or peg its exchange rate to the DM. Just before these 'Interpellationen' are debated in the National Council on October 2, the SNB announces an exchange rate target! (It is hard to avoid the impression that the SNB ceded to these political pressures in order to avoid harsh criticisms from the legislature.) Schwarzenbach and Fischer (Bremgarten) soon point at the danger of rising inflation rates as a result of the monetary expansion. Especially Schwarzenbach's question of November 27 1979 again illustrates that legislators are well aware of the relationship between money supply and inflation.

Legislative activity in the early eighties is preoccupied with rising inflation rates, rising mortgage rates, and a weakening SFr as the source of imported inflation. In June 1980 for instance the rise in mortgage rates triggers several (6) legislative actions towards lower mortgage rates. The executive is pressured to intervene directly, or indirectly over the SNB and the Banking Commission. The rest of the eighties is dominated by the problem of exchange rate stability.

After mid 1989 interest rates gain center stage. The rise in mortgage rates triggers harsh criticism by the social democrats. In their 'Interpellation' of June 1989 they call the SNB's interest rate policy irresponsible.

During 1990 and early 1991 several legislators - including members of the radical party - demand a less restrictive monetary policy. The 'Motion' Feigenwinter intends to increase the transparency of monetary policy by forcing the SNB to publish its goals and plans and to defend its policy in parliamentary hearings twice a year. According to the 'Motion' Jelmini (Council of States) the executive shall prepare legislation that allows for improved coordination of fiscal and monetary authorities in order to increase the effectiveness of economic policy. David raises the question of responsibility for the failure in the fight against inflation. And Tschopp addresses the alleged disagreement between members of the executive and the SNB's president. In Fall 1992 'Interpellationen' of the social democratic party, the Swiss people's party, and the green party attack SNB policy and ask the executive to use all its weight to change the too restrictive monetary policy. This criticism is again repeated by Strahm and the social democratic party in November 1994. The social democrats also want the SNB to be explicitly accountable to the legislature (justify its policy annually before parliament). Since the attacks are led by influential members of all major parties, legislative majorities in the National Council become viable.[34] This inevitably increases the pressure on the SNB for a more expansionary monetary policy.

In 1994 and 1995 legislators from almost all parties focus on exchange rate stability. Especially the social democrats make the central bank responsible for job losses.

Legislative activity towards *central bank profits* deserves special attention. Activities in this area clearly intensify over the period under investigation. In 1973 Fischer is preoccupied with the losses due to the weakness of the US$. In 1975 Albrecht proposes to sell gold coins and to use the return to cover fiscal deficits. The 'Motion' Schmid points into the opposite direction. Schmid proposes several legislative changes that would strengthen the independence of the SNB. He clearly sees a conflict of interest between the requirement to earn profits and the goal of price stability. For this reason he proposes to liberate the SNB from the pressure to earn profits. In April 1978 two legislative attacks are directed towards more transparency in the SNB's annual accounts.

In 1980 the price increase of gold induces several legislators to propose that at least part of the gold reserves should be sold to earn profits (though these profits need not be handed over to fiscal authorities). In November and December 1982, three 'Motionen' ask for an increase in the amount of central bank profits to be handed over to the fiscal authorities and require a change in central bank legislation. All three 'Motionen' are accepted as 'Postulate'. Between 1984 and 1988

---

[34] An interesting question is whether these developments are due to worsening economic conditions or whether a change in legislative preferences - as a result of turnover due to the election in Fall 1991 - also plays a role.

Meier signals his preoccupation with central bank profits. In June 1984 he proposes a diversification of currency holdings. In February 1985 he suggests a change in the distribution of central bank profits (increase the share of the Confederacy and reduce the share of the cantons). In December 1985 he addresses the loss of the central bank as a result of the changes in the US$ exchange rate. And in September 1988 he proposes to sell US$ to avoid losses as a result of the $ devaluation.

Legislative attacks on SNB profits intensify in the nineties. In a parliamentary initiative, Hafner proposes to sell the gold reserves to cover fiscal budget deficits. The legislative committee which deliberates this proposition comes up with an 'attenuated' proposal that is accepted as a 'Postulat'. And in October 1990 the 'Motion' Theubet also aims at an increase in the amount of SNB profits to be transferred to fiscal authorities. It appears as if these legislative attacks are successful: In February 1992 - a few days before the 'Motion' Theubet is debated in the National Council (March 9) - executive and SNB agree that the amount of central bank profits delivered to fiscal authorities is increased (from 5.093 millions) to 600 millions annually, beginning with 1991. (See e.g. AB 1995 1595.)

But given the dramatic rise in fiscal deficits, not all legislators seem to be satisfied with this agreement. The 'Motion' Spielmann, which asks for a valuation of assets in annual accounts at market prices, or the 'Postulat' of members of the independent party, which proposes to invest half of the gold reserves in interest rate earning bonds, or the 'Interpellation' Weyeneth, which questions the functions of the local SNB branches, ultimately all evidence legislative interest in SNB profits. The 'Motion' of the finance committee from January 1995 - accepted as 'Postulat' in March 1996 - appears to be the most serious attack on central bank profits so far. And as the 'Interpellation' Tschopp shows, it will not be the last one. Meanwhile, two studies by Ungern-Sternberg that criticize the SNB's management of its assets (1996a) and the modest transfers of central bank profits to fiscal authorities (1996b) have come to the support of these legislative attacks, still increasing the pressure on the SNB. Not surprisingly, M. Lusser, the leaving chairman of the SNB, stated in an interview in April 1996 that one of the biggest challenges facing his successors will be the question of central bank profits! (Brenner/Hofmann 1996 31) Already in the beginning of June 1996 the Federal Council appoints a commission consisting of members of the SNB and the finance department that shall investigate the SNB's management of its assets and its policy towards transfers of central bank profits to fiscal authorities. (See Brenner 1996 25.) In 1997 the National Bank Law is partially revised in order to allow for a more profitable management of the central bank's assets. In Spring 1998 the SNB and the Federal Council agree that the SNB shall deliver 1.5 billions of SFr annually from 1999 to 2003.

This brief discussion of legislative activity towards monetary policy in general and the SNB in particular reveals several points:

- Legislators are aware of the importance of monetary policy and they do care about it. They understand the relationship between monetary policy (money

supply) on the one side and interest rates, exchange rates, inflation, employment and growth on the other side.
- They are informed about what is going on in monetary policy. Several legislative questions evidence that legislators watch central bank behavior. Also, they address the SNB directly in order to get information they want. (See e.g. AB 1995 563.)
- They do not hesitate to propose changes in central bank legislation to achieve a change in monetary policy. More recent legislative activity shows that the threat of change in legislation (e.g. direct accountability to the legislature, hearings) is also used to exert pressure on the SNB. Legislators are clearly aware of the usefulness of this instrument.
- The type of instrument chosen, the party affiliation of legislators initiating legislative activity, and the number of legislators sponsoring these activities suggest that the weight of legislative actions increased in the nineties.
- Who is most active? Clearly, members of political parties situated on the left of the political spectrum and members of small parties not represented in the executive act more frequently on monetary policy affairs.
- In the early seventies under the regime of fixed exchange rates the central bank enjoys only very little discretion. All legislative criticisms and complaints are directed at the executive. This changes under the regime of flexible exchange rates. Now the SNB has the discretion to determine the money supply. All legislative attacks are still addressed at the executive (as a body), because the legislature has no direct access to the central bank. It can only exert influence over the executive. Therefore, the executive is pressured to intervene with the central bank, for instance for lower interest rates etc. This illustrates the existence of a double-layer principal agent relationship.
- Most legislative attempts address policy directives rather than SNB independence. This appears to be another difference to the Congress-Fed relationship. (See Grier 1991 206.)

Analyzing legislative activity towards the central bank is one way to address the question whether there exists any legislative influence on monetary policy. However, this does not provide clear-cut evidence for the following reasons. If there is control, then such legislative activity need not develop at all. And if such activity exists, it does not imply that the SNB considers this as a credible threat. This depends on who initiates this legislative activity and how many legislators are likely to support it. (Or stated differently: It depends on which allies the central bank can rely on to defend its formally independent position). To overcome these limitations, more formal tests are required.

5.4.3 Evidence on Legislative Influence: An Empirical Test

The SNB is formally independent from the legislature. But as Cukierman (1992 333) notes, political authorities find subtle ways to influence the course of monetary policy.[35] Therefore, an empirical test of the hypothesis of legislative influence on Swiss monetary policy is performed. This provides at the same time a test of the 'new' theory of bureaucracy in a different institutional environment.

The major refutable comparative statics prediction of the legislative control model is that as preferences of the relevant oversight committee(s) change, agency behavior will change, too.[36] The main difficulty with an empirical test of this hypothesis is the measurement of political preferences and changes thereof.

A standard measure for political preferences is *party affiliation*. But three major problems are involved with this measure.

First, party affiliation is not always a reliable indicator of political preferences of Swiss legislators, because party loyalty is rather low.[37] (Aubert 1987 229; Lehner 1985 119; Steiner 1982 321) Evidence on intraparty differences is provided by Lüthi et al. (1991) and Hohl (1996).[38]

Second, party affiliation shows rather little variation in the Swiss legislature, and, (presumably) also in the committees. If, for instance, all parties of the National Council are grouped into a block of left and right wing parties (following the classification in Fuchs 1990 18), the ratio of the left wing parties to the whole legislative body shows only little variation: it is 0.335 in 1971, 0.365 in 1975, 0.34 in 1979, 0.325 in 1983, 0.33 in 1987 and 1991. Party composition of the committees is also very stable. (See below for two examples.) Since this affects the comparative statics condition, it becomes difficult to measure any influence from these variables.

Third, the existence of several political parties raises the problem of locating them in the policy space. (See Steiner 1982 323.)

One alternative[39] to get more reliable and more sensitive measures of (changes in) legislator's preferences is to use some *ratings* based on roll call votes of the individual legislators. In the US various lobby groups publish such ratings on a regular basis. The intention is „to provide an idea of a legislator's general ideol-

---

35 And he adds: „Many papers in Mayer (1990) reach a similar conclusion". Cukierman 1992 Fn. 1 469.

36 In section 5.2 three testable predictions are stated. Here, only the third is tested empirically, because there is not enough evidence available on the committee system.

37 The lack of party loyalty (or the fact that political parties are rather weak) may explain the existence of an elaborated committee system. As Weingast/Marshall (1988 158) note, the committee system is an institutional alternative to political parties to enforce legislative trades.

38 Both studies calculate the Rice-Index for the parties represented in the National Council. The Rice-Index is the difference between the percentage of the majority and the percentage of the minority of a party in a vote. Values are in the closed interval between 0 and 100. A value of 0 indicates that a party is equally divided in a vote. A value of 100 results if all party members vote the same position.
Hohl (1996) also compares the votes of individual legislators with the recommendations of party conventions ('Abstimmungsparolen') for ten initiatives.

39 The two alternatives employed by Havrilesky are not viable. There are no oversight hearings that yield information on legislative preferences. And signaling by legislative activity is too sporadic to serve as a useful variable.

ogy and the degree to which the legislator represents different groups' interests." (Barone/Ujifusa 1989 xiv) Probably the best known rating is from Americans for Democratic Action, a liberal lobby group founded in 1947. ADA ratings have been extensively used in scientific research (see e.g. Grier 1991 211), mainly because this lobby group uses a broad spectrum of issues for its vote analysis, and because the ratings are available since 1948 on an annual basis.

Since such ratings do not exist for Swiss legislators, they have to be constructed first. The precondition is the availability of a sufficient number of *roll call votes* (Abstimmungen unter Namensaufruf). In the National Council (Council of States) a roll call vote will only take place if 30 (10) members request so. In the Council of States, this virtually never happens, making a construction of ratings for senators not viable. In the National Council roll call votes do not occur very often either, and also quite irregularly for the period before 1984. Their number increases after 1984, and it explodes after 1993 with the introduction of an electronic voting system. A rating (similarly to the one provided by ADA) can be constructed for the National Council for the period after 1975. Because of the few roll call votes during the 1975 to 1983 period, ratings have to be constructed for four-year legislative periods (from 1975 to 1979 and from 1979 to 1983). Beginning with 1984 all ratings are established on an annual basis.

The ratings are *constructed* as follows (see also Jeitziner/Hohl 1997 and Hohl/Jeitziner 1997): First, ten roll call votes are selected for each legislative period (1975 to 1979 and 1979 to 1983) or each year (after 1983).[40] Criteria are low abstentions, low absences, broad spectrum of issues, national rather than regional questions, left versus right rather than extremes versus the political middle. Second, for each vote it is determined how a typical member of the political left and the right should have voted. Third, all votes are converted into ratings. For each individual legislator, the voting record is analyzed and points are distributed. If the legislator votes the left position, he gets a -1. If he votes the right position, he gets a +1. If he is absent, or if he abstains, he gets a 0.[41] All pluses and minuses are then summed. Hence, all votes are weighted equally. A legislator can get a minimum of -10 points and a maximum of +10 points. A value of -10 implies that a legislator always voted the left position and that he was never absent and/or abstained. He is a perfect 'liberal' (in the American terminology). A value of +10 means that a legislator always voted the right position and that he was never absent and/or abstained. This value indicates the most 'conservative' position.

These ratings are then used as *measures of legislators' preferences.* For preferences of the whole council, committees, and subcommittees the arithmetic mean

---

40 It would be preferable to choose a larger number of roll call votes, e.g. twenty (as ADA does). But there are simply not enough roll call votes available. The number of ten is a minimum and corresponds with the number of roll call votes in the 1975 to 1979 period. For later periods, this number allows for some choice among roll call votes.

41 This system, which deviates from the practice of ADA, was chosen to account for the numerous absences and also the quite frequent abstentions in the Swiss legislature. Especially the treatment of absences remains a controversial issue.

of the members' ratings are employed. Three different versions are tried out. The first version uses the current (annual) rating for each committee member. This variable exhibits the highest amount of variation. But it is most vulnerable to the selection of roll call votes. To reduce this dependence on the choice of roll call votes, a second version is constructed on the basis of the lifetime ratings of each individual legislator. While the minimum number of roll call votes included remains ten, the lifetime rating can be based on a maximum of 140 roll call votes for legislators sitting in the National Council for the five legislative periods from 1975 to 1995.[42] The problem with this variable is that it neglects the possibility that a legislator changes its preferences over time, especially across (re)election periods. This problem is accounted for in the third version of preference measures which uses ratings for (four-year) legislative periods. Except for the two legislative periods from 1975 to 1983, where each legislative rating is based on just 10 votes, all subsequent legislative ratings are based on 40 roll call votes each. This appears to be the most plausible preference measure for individual legislators.

Preference measures for the following *legislative bodies* of the National Council are constructed:

- the National Council as a whole (period after 1975.4)
- the economics committee (period after 1979.4)
- leadership of the economics committee (period after 1979.4)
- finance committee (period after 1975.4)
- leadership of the finance committee (period after 1975.4)
- finance delegation (period after 1975.4)

The *economics committee* consisting of 23 members was established in December 1979. After the reorganization in December 1991 the committee was enlarged to 25 members and renamed 'Kommission für Wirtschaft und Abgaben'. A look at the party composition shows that the right wing parties (christian democrats, radicals, Swiss people's party, liberals, freedom party) always occupy 16 of the 23 (25) seats. In 1991, the social democrats and the green party each win one additional committee seat. If political preferences of this committee are measured with party affiliation, the only change that can be measured occurs in 1991, when the ratio of the right wing parties falls from 0.70 to 0.64.

The *finance committee* has a much longer tradition. Its size increased over time, apparently to allow for a proportional representation of smaller fractions. After the 1975 elections the committee was enlarged from 19 to 23 seats. And in the reorganization of 1991 the committee size was fixed at 25 seats. The share of the right wing majority fluctuated only very slightly: Before the elections of 1975 it was 0.63. After the elections from 1975 this share was 0.65. Committee seats were won by the right wing parties in the 1979 election, raising their proportion to 0.74. The 1983 election resulted in some losses (0.70). And the reorganization af-

[42] While only 4 national councillors (Hubacher, Jaeger, Nebiker, Oehler) achieve this record, 22 legislators reach 4 legislative periods. Their lifetime rating is based on a maximum number of 130 roll call votes.

ter the 1991 elections changed this proportion only slightly (0.68). Hence, if party affiliation or party composition is employed as preference measure for the finance committee, only little variation can be observed, making it very difficult to detect any relationship with monetary policy.

Party affiliation of the three national councillors sitting in the *finance delegation* shows no variation at all. The three seats of this subcommittee (neglecting the other three seats taken by senators) are always occupied by one member of the radical, christian democratic, and social democratic party.

If the ratings are employed instead, considerably more variation can be measured. Table 5.1 lists summary statistics for all legislative variables. Figure 5.1 plots the three versions of the preference measure employed for the economics committee. And Figure 5.2 displays the two measures constructed for the finance committee and the finance delegation.[43]

Table 5.1: Summary Statistics for Legislative Variables[a]

Variable	N	Mean	Std. Dev.	Minimum	Maximum
ECLE	63	0.7032	0.9934	-0.6630	1.9020
ECLI	63	0.9303	0.5411	-0.0200	1.5430
ECRA	63	0.7111	1.1633	-0.9600	3.1300
FCLE	79	1.1846	0.9007	-0.1680	2.1520
FCLI	79	1.0015	0.6893	0.0670	1.9090
FDLE	79	1.3140	1.1308	0.0330	4.0000
FDLI	79	0.9461	0.7342	0.0330	2.4000
PECLE	63	0.6758	6.4334	-8.2500	9.0000
PECLI	63	0.5548	6.0128	-8.2000	7.6000
PECRA	63	0.5161	6.9371	-10.000	10.000
PFCLE	79	1.0949	6.3436	-9.5000	8.5000
PFCLI	79	0.5103	6.0482	-9.4000	7.4000

[a] For variable definitions see table 5.2. Statistics on ECLE, ECLI, ECRA, PECLE, PECLI and PECRA are for 1979.4 to 1995.2. Statistics on the other variables are for 1975.4 to 1995.2.

Figure 5.1 shows that most of the time the average score for the economics committee is positive, indicating a 'conservative' position. The measure based on current ratings ECRA exhibits the highest amount of variation, and the measure based on lifetime ratings ECLI shows the least variation. The Pearson correlation coefficient between the current rating ECRA and the rating for legislative periods ECLE is 0.87. The other correlation coefficients are 0.63 for ECLE and ECLI, and 0.57 for ECLI and ECRA. Also visible are the effects of elections with subsequent

43 The measure constructed for the finance delegation is the average score of the three national councillors. The three senators also sitting in this subcommittee are not included.

renewal of the committee. After the 1983 election 9 of 23 committee members are replaced. Based on the current and legislative ratings ECRA and ECLE, this results in a shift in legislative preferences towards more conservatism. The lifetime rating ECLI, however, rather suggests an opposite move towards 'liberalism'. Since the current and legislative ratings ECRA and ECLE are based on only 10 roll call votes for the first legislative period, the lifetime rating ECLI is a more reliable preference measure for this period. The 1987 election brings no dramatic shifts in preferences, although 18 of 23 committee members are replaced. The peak for the measure based on current ratings ECRA in 1989 is probably due to the selection of roll call votes, since no turnover can be observed. For the period between 1983 and 1988 current and legislative ratings ECRA and ECLE exhibit a trend towards more conservatism. The lifetime rating ECLI rather indicates stability in committee preferences. After the 1991 election and the reorganization of the committee system, 21 new members are appointed to the economics committee which is now counting 25 seats. This turnover results in a quite dramatic shift of committee preferences towards 'liberalism'. Average scores for all three preference measures now indicate a position left to the political middle.

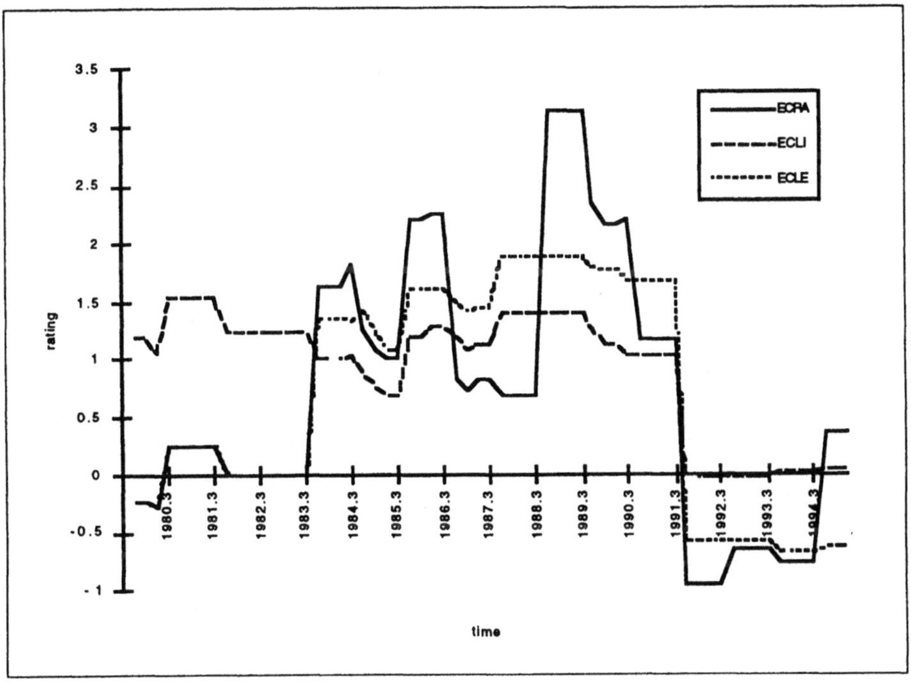

Figure 5.1: Ratings for Economics Committee (Average Scores)
For definitions and sources of legislative preference measures see table 5.2.

Figure 5.2 shows a similar basic pattern for the finance committee and the finance delegation. Except for the legislative rating for the finance committee FCLE after the 1991 election, the average scores always indicate a conservative position. The measures based on legislative ratings again exhibit more variation than those based on lifetime ratings. The Pearson correlation coefficient between the two measures for the finance committee is 0.95. It is 0.93 for the two measures of the finance delegation.

After the 1979, 1983 and 1987 elections, 8, 12, and 9 members of a total of 23 are replaced in the finance committee. The largest turnover in this committee occurs after the 1991 election, with 17 newly appointed members out of a total of 25. The shift towards conservatism after the 1979 election is probably due to the selection of roll call votes. From 1980 to 1991 the measure based on lifetime ratings FCLI suggests a trend towards 'liberalism', while the legislative rating FCLE remains stable except for a blip between 1984 and 1986. As with the economics committee, the 1991 election results in a dramatic shift towards 'liberalism'.

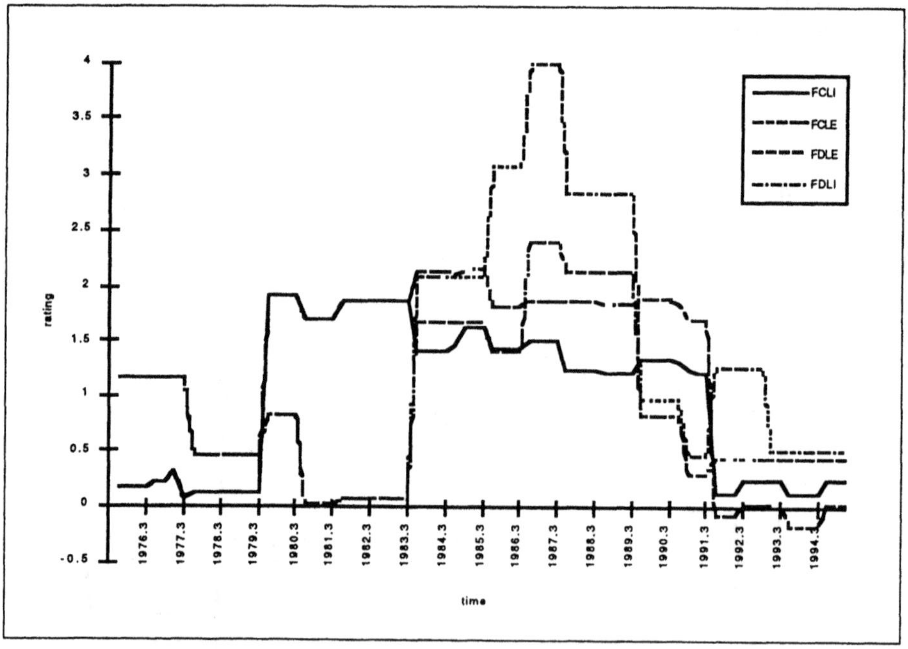

Figure 5.2: Ratings for Finance Committee and Finance Delegation (Average Scores)
For definitions and sources of legislative preference measures see table 5.2.

The two measures for the finance delegation (FDLE and FDLI) follow a somewhat different pattern. Here, the shift towards conservatism begins after the 1983 election and peaks in 1987. Changes towards 'liberalism' take place in December 1987 and 1989, before the 1991 elections. Average scores for the finance delegation need to be interpreted with caution, however. Since they are composed of only three individual ratings, they are much more sensitive to turnover. Moreover, the preferences of the three senators also sitting in this subcommittee are not assessed.

The ratings are then used to test the hypothesis of legislative control in the framework of reaction functions and in autoregressive model specifications.

The *reaction function* developed in chapter 1 assumes that the central bank systematically responds to those key economic variables that are usually regarded as the most important determinants of monetary policy (i.e. inflation, exchange, growth, and interest rates). Here, the central bank is also assumed to systematically respond to shifts in legislative preferences. Hence, a variable LEGISLATURE representing the different measures of legislative preferences is added to the reaction function. The regression equation for the monetary base as dependent variable with all economic variables expressed as nonseasonal differences is

$$\Delta\ln(MB)_t = \beta_0 + \beta_1\Delta\ln(MB)_{t-1} + \beta_2\Delta\ln(CPI)_{t-1} + \beta_3\Delta\ln(DMN)_{t-1}$$
$$+\beta_4\Delta\ln(GDP)_{t-1} + \beta_5\Delta DR_{t-1} + \beta_6 SD1_t + \beta_7 SD2_t + \beta_8 SD3_t$$
$$+\beta_9 LEGISLATURE_{t-2} + \varepsilon_t$$

(See tables 1.2 and 5.2 for variable definitions and data sources.)

Reaction functions with both quarterly and yearly rates of change are estimated for the monetary base and the money supply M1 as dependent variables. (For a detailed outlining of the estimation procedure see section 1.5.1.) Since most series are not seasonally adjusted regressions with quarterly rates include three seasonal dummies (SD1, SD2, SD3). In the annual models seasonality is removed by the definition of the yearly rates of change.

In the *autoregressive model specifications* money growth rates are regressed on lagged dependent variables, a constant, and the legislative variable. The autoregressive terms are included to control for changes in the economy, similar to the economic regressor variables in the reaction function approach. The autoregressive model is first estimated excluding the variables representing legislative preferences. (See section 3.5.2 for a description of how the 'best' autoregressive model is chosen.) The model selected is then tested for structural breaks. The inefficiency of OLS in the presence of heteroskedasticity is corrected by using HCSEs. Finally, the variables measuring legislative preferences are added to these autoregressive models.

All legislative variables enter the regression equations with a *lag* of two quarters. This accounts for a reasonable interval between change in legislative preference and change in monetary policy. Nevertheless, experiments with alternative lag structures (one-, three- and four-quarter lags) are also carried out.

Table 5.2: Definitions of Legislative Preference Measures[a]

Variable	Definition
ECLE	average score of economics committee based on ratings for legislative periods of individual legislators
ECLI	average score of economics committee based on lifetime ratings of individual legislators
ECRA	average score of economics committee based on current (annual) ratings of individual legislators
FCLE	average score of finance committee based on ratings for legislative periods of individual legislators
FCLI	average score of finance committee based on lifetime ratings of individual legislators
FDLE	average score of finance delegation based on ratings for legislative periods of individual legislators
FDLI	average score of finance delegation based on lifetime ratings of individual legislators
PECLE	presidency of the economics committee: chairman's rating for legislative periods
PECLI	presidency of the economics committee: chairman's lifetime rating
PECRA	presidency of the economics committee: chairman's current (annual) rating
PFCLE	presidency of the finance committee: chairman's rating for legislative periods
PFCLI	presidency of the finance committee: chairman's lifetime rating

[a] Source: roll call votes from 'Amtliches Bulletin' (analogue to the Congressional Record); ratings compiled by Hohl (1996) and listed in Hohl/Jeitziner 1997.

To predict signs for the legislative variables in the present application, an important additional *assumption* is required: Members with low ratings (<0) indicating a left position tend to prefer a more expansionary monetary policy, because they value employment (and growth) most. Members with high ratings (>0) indicating a right position tend to prefer a more restrictive monetary policy, because they are especially averse to inflation. Changes in the monetary aggregates should therefore be negatively associated with variables measuring legislative preferences. Hence, significant negative coefficients on the political variables are consistent with the hypothesis of legislative influence.

While this assumption about the relationship between ratings and preference for monetary policy is probably correct for legislators situated on the left of the political spectrum, it is *problematic* for the political right. Members of the right-wing parties affiliated with export industries and tourism pressure for a less restrictive monetary policy whenever their constituency suffers from a strong SFr. Hence, these legislators - having a conservative rating - will often vote the left position in questions related to monetary policy. This could be observed for instance in Fall 1978 and in Fall 1992. (See the discussion of the legislative activity towards the SNB in section 5.4.2.) This possible lack of correlation between positive values of the rating and preference for restrictive monetary policy is the basic weakness of the present empirical approach. It would also be a plausible explanation for insignificant coefficients on the political variables in the regressions that follow.

The question about the relationship between the position on the political spectrum (operationalized with ratings) and the preference for monetary policy has already been raised for the US - though it may be less of a problem for US than for Swiss legislators. As Woolley (1984 134) notes, legislators, independent of their party affiliation, generally prefer a more expansionary monetary policy (because they all value low interest rates). Similarly, Beck (1990 Fn. 10 and 12) criticizes that general liberalism, as measured by the ADA ratings, might not correctly reflect preferences for easy money, or for low interest rates. Monetary policy issues may often lie outside the basic partisan cleavage.

Grier (1991), being well aware of this difficulty, demonstrates that ADA scores do strongly affect the source of senators' campaign funds. Hence, there must be economic content in the ADA ratings. He interprets this as indirect evidence on the relationship between ratings and legislators' induced preferences over monetary policy.

This indirect evidence cannot be provided for Swiss legislators, since no figures on campaign financing are available. But even if this information were available, the problem would only be shifted to the level of the interest groups. Interest groups situated on the right of the political spectrum supporting 'conservative' legislators might still prefer a more expansionary monetary policy under certain circumstances. To solve this problem, it would be necessary to determine which interest groups favor what type of monetary policy, depending on the economic situation. Then, legislators' induced preferences over monetary policy could be inferred with the help of their interest group affiliation. Unfortunately, an (annually updated) list of interest group affiliation of Swiss legislators (Register der Interessenbindungen) exists only since 1985.

More direct evidence on the relationship between ratings and induced preference for monetary policy could be gained from an analysis of roll call votes on monetary policy issues. Because of the lack of such votes, this is not viable either.

Influence of the Economics Committee?

Observations on the economics committee are only available since 1979.4 (if contemporaneous values are employed). Hence, regressions are for the period from 1979.4 to 1995.2 - not accounting for lost observations due to lag structures.

In the *reaction function* approach, no structural breaks can be identified for this period. Correction for heteroskedasticity is needed for the regressions on the monetary base. Estimation results for two-quarter lags are reported in table 5.3.

Each entry is based on a separate regression including the control variables listed in the text and lags of the dependent variable to whiten the errors. Estimates for the control variables are not reported in order to preserve space. The only significant coefficient is found in the annual monetary base equation: The preference of the economics committee based on the version with current ratings ECRA is positively associated with monetary base growth. However, the coefficient shows an unexpected positive sign. Hence, the hypothesis of the legislative control model is not supported.

Table 5.3: Estimation Results for Economics Committee in Reaction Functions (1980.3 to 1995.2)

	Dependent variables			
	$\Delta\ln(MB)$	$\Delta_4\ln(MB)$	$\Delta\ln(M1)$	$\Delta_4\ln(M1)$
Preference measure	Coefficient (t value)	Coefficient (t value)	Coefficient (p value)	Coefficient (p value)
$ECRA_{t-2}$	-0.0002 (-0.107)	0.007*** (3.012)	-0.0002 (0.9095)	-0.0002 (0.9447)
$ECLE_{t-2}$	-0.002 (-0.986)	0.004 (1.399)	-0.0003 (0.9242)	0.001 (0.7551)
$ECLI_{t-2}$	-0.0002 (-0.048)	0.005 (1.087)	0.0003 (0.9521)	0.003 (0.7043)
$PECRA_{t-2}$	-0.0005 (-1.393)	-0.0005 (-1.043)	0.0002 (0.6485)	0.0004 (0.4186)
$PECLE_{t-2}$	-0.0005 (-1.441)	-0.0005 (-1.099)	0.0002 (0.6580)	0.0004 (0.4476)
$PECLI_{t-2}$	-0.0004 (-1.140)	-0.0003 (-0.775)	0.00001 (0.9843)	0.00001 (0.8729)

All equations include the variables listed in the text as additional regressors. Both nonseasonal models ($\Delta\ln(MB)$ and $\Delta\ln(M1)$) include three seasonal dummies, but no lagged dependent variables. In the equation for $\Delta_4\ln(MB)$ 8 lags of the dependent variable are added. In the equation for $\Delta_4\ln(M1)$ lags 1, 2, 4, 5 and 8 of the dependent variable serve also as regressors. Numbers in parentheses are associated t statistics or p values; t statistics are calculated on the basis of HCSEs; *** significant at 1 percent level.

The same legislative variables are also tested in yearly *autoregressive* model specifications. For the monetary base as dependent variable, an AR(8) model is chosen. For the annual M1 model an AR(11) excluding lags 3, 6, 7 and 9 is selected. The legislative variables are then added to both autoregressive models one at a time. None of them turns out to be significant. Therefore, results are not reported here.

Does the economics committee or its leadership exert any systematic influence on Swiss monetary policy? Empirical results do not support this hypothesis.

Influence of the Finance Committee?

Since ratings can only be established for the period after 1975.4, observations on the finance committee are also only available for the period from 1975.4 to 1995.2 (neglecting lost observations due to lag structures).

In the *reaction function* approach, tests for structural stability identify a 'regime' shift for 1980. (See section 1.5.2.) However, because of the small number of observations that remains for the period before 1980, the structural break is not incorporated. Table 5.4 lists the estimated coefficients for the legislative variables with a two-quarter lag. Significant coefficients are only found in the annual money supply equation for the variables measuring the preferences of the finance delegation. But they exhibit an unexpected positive sign.

The variables measuring the preferences of the finance committee and the finance delegation are also estimated in *autoregressive* model specifications. With the monetary base as dependent variable, an AR(5) model is chosen for the period from 1976.3 to 1995.2.[44] For the same period the 'best' model with the money supply M1 as dependent variable is again an AR(11) excluding lags 3, 6, 7 and 9. No structural breaks are imposed. In the monetary base model correction for heteroskedasticity is needed. Since none of the coefficients turns out to be significant, results are not reported here.

Hence, also for the finance committee, results do not support the legislative control model.

Influence of the National Council?

A variable measuring the preferences of the National Council as a whole is also tested for the period from 1975.4 to 1995.2. This variable is the average score of the National Council based on the current (annual) ratings of individual legislators. It is never significant. The legislative control model predicts that the legislature as a whole does not exert any influence on monetary policy. Results do not contradict this hypothesis.

For a number of reasons the empirical results have to be interpreted with *caution*.

A first and basic weakness of the present approach follows from the assumption about the relationship between ratings and preferred monetary policy that needs to be introduced. Whether the negative relationship that is assumed between legislative ratings and preferred money growth rates really exists is an empirical question. Legislators from right-wing parties affiliated with export industries and tourism can often be observed to pressure for less restrictive monetary policy.

---

44 The 'best' autoregressive model specification changes with the time period being covered.

Table 5.4: Estimation Results for Finance Committee and Finance Delegation in Reaction Functions (1976.3 to 1995.2)

	Dependent variables			
	$\Delta\ln(MB)$	$\Delta_4\ln(MB)$	$\Delta\ln(M1)$	$\Delta_4\ln(M1)$
Preference measure	Coefficient (t value)	Coefficient (t value)	Coefficient (p value)	Coefficient (p value)
$FCLE_{t-2}$	-0.002 (-0.323)	0.004 (0.732)	0.00001 (0.9978)	0.004 (0.3523)
$FCLI_{t-2}$	-0.002 (-0.284)	0.004 (0.543)	0.0001 (0.9774)	0.004 (0.4118)
$PFCLE_{t-2}$	-0.0001 (-0.208)	0.0007 (1.343)	0.0001 (0.7570)	0.0008 (0.1285)
$PFCLI_{t-2}$	-0.00001 (-0.115)	0.0007 (1.306)	0.0001 (0.7634)	0.0008 (0.1418)
$FDLE_{t-2}$	-0.004 (-1.221)	-0.002 (-0.497)	0.003 (0.1743)	0.008** (0.0233)
$FDLI_{t-2}$	-0.005 (-1.031)	-0.002 (-0.233)	0.004 (0.2709)	0.011** (0.0360)

All equations include the variables listed in the text as additional regressors. Both nonseasonal models ($\Delta\ln(MB)$ and $\Delta\ln(M1)$) include three seasonal dummies. In the equation for $\Delta\ln(M1)$ the lagged dependent variable is dropped. In the equation for $\Delta\ln(MB)$ lags 2 and 3, in the equation for $\Delta_4\ln(MB)$ lags 1 to 5, and in the equation for $\Delta_4\ln(M1)$ lags 1 to 9 of the dependent variable enter also as regressors. Numbers in parentheses are associated t statistics or p values; t statistics are calculated on the basis of HCSEs; ** significant at 5 percent level.

Hence, the assumption of a negative relationship between ratings and preferred money growth rates is problematic. Insignificant coefficients on the legislative variables might be caused by this difficulty. Unfortunately, hard evidence on this relationship is not viable because of lack of data (no roll call votes on monetary policy issues available).

A second problem is that we can only look at (committees of) the National Council, but not at the Council of States, because no ratings for senators can be constructed. This might not be a big problem, however, since both chambers have equal rights. Moreover, the analysis of legislative activity suggests that with the National Council the more active chamber is considered.

A third difficulty is abstention from and representation in committee work. As in the Council as a whole, it is rather common that not all committee members are actually present. Moreover, each committee member can be represented by some other member. To address this problem, all documents on committee meetings would have to be screened. The present approach abstracts from these difficulties. It is assumed that committee members will be present if decisive votes have to be taken. And it is further assumed that abstaining members will be (if at all) represented by legislators with similar preferences.[45]

Finally, empirical results critically depend on the quality of the ratings. The quality of the ratings itself depends on the availability (especially number) of roll call votes. The introduction of the electronic voting system in 1993 promises significant improvements for future work with this variable.

5.5 Conclusions

The theory of legislative control predicts that specialized legislative committees effectively control agency behavior. This hypothesis has been analyzed for several US government agencies, including the Federal Reserve Board. This chapter applies the theory of legislative control to a different institutional setting. It is questioned whether the Swiss legislature, or specialized committees thereof, exert any influence on Swiss monetary policy. The underlying institutional setting is investigated and some empirical tests are performed. Theoretical and empirical results do not support the hypothesis of legislative influence for the case of Switzerland. So far, it appears as if legislative influence on monetary policy - if it exists at all - may well be a feature that is unique to the US political market.

---

45 A look at replacements in committees indicates that this second assumption may not be unrealistic. Very often, the new committee member has a very similar rating as his predecessor had.

Appendix to Chapter 5

Table 5.5: Legislative Activity Towards the SNB in the National Council

Date Number	*Type* *	*Name (Party**, Canton) {Sponsor}*	*Title (Original)*	*Description*	*Cate-gory* ***	*Source* ****
1.3.71 10 842	IN	Stich (S, SO) {40}	Teuerungsbe-kämpfung	measures to fight inflation	I	71: 781 812 818
17.3.71 10 894	MO	Wartmann (V, TG) {22}	Inflationsbe-kämpfung	measures to fight inflation	I	71: 778 812
17.3.71 10 902	IN	Gasser (C, OW) {35}	Bekämpfung der Teuerung	measures to fight inflation	I	71: 779 812
16.6.71 10 965	MO	(Wyss)-Stich (S, SO) {37}	Notenbank-Instrumentarium	more effective instruments for SNB; accepted		72: 669
20.9.71 11 027	IN	Eibel (R, ZH)	Wirtschaftliche und währungspo-litische Lage	economic and monetary situation	Q	71: 1082
16.12.71 11 140	IN	Blatti (R, BE) {15}	Währungslage	developments in international monetary policy	Q	72: 689 702
17.12.71 11 142	IN	Eisenring (C, ZH) {18}	Währungs- und handelspolitische Lage	developments in international monetary policy	Q	72: 691 702
16.3.72 105	KA	Oehen (P, BE)	Inflationsbe-kämpfung	measures to fight inflation (imported inflation and growth of population)	I XL	72: 1362
24.4.72 120	KA	Jaeger (U, SG)	Faktische Abwertung des SFr	depreciation of the SFr (vis-à-vis DM and Schilling)	XL	72: 1366
25.4.72 123	KA	Keller (R, TG)	Teuerungsabwehr	measures to fight inflation	I	72: 1367
25.4.72 125	KA	Fischer (R, BE)	Frankenauf-wertung	explain appreciation and depreciation of SFr	XL	72: 1368
22.6.72 168	KA	Schalcher (L, ZH)	Preis- und Lohnstopp	price stops and wage controls	I	72: 1866
27.6.72 11 354	IN	Franzoni (C, TI) {13}	Währungslage	monetary situation	X	72: 1279

29.6.72 177	KA	Lehner (C, VS)	Währungs- politische Massnahmen	measures against influx of foreign capital and negative effects on less developed regions	I	72: 1885
5.10.72 222	KA	Tschumi (V, BE)	Geldentwertung	measures against index mechanisms	I	72: 2468
6.10.72 228	KA	Bächtold (U, BE)	Teuerungs- bekämpfung	consider measures suggested by Kellenberger	I	72: 2469
27.11.72 233	KA	Breiten- moser (C, BS)	Mangelnde Inflationsbe- kämpfung	asks for price stops and wage controls	I	72: 2476
27.11.72 234	KA	Biel (U, ZH)	Internationaler Währungsfonds	Switzerland and IMF: executive shall clarify its position	Q	72: 2469
27.11.72 11 461	IN	Stich (S, SO) {31}	Teuerungsbe- kämpfung	measures to fight inflation: importance of monetary policy	I	72: 1910 2279
27.11.72 11 462	MO	Biel (U, ZH)	Teuerungsbe- kämpfung	measures to fight inflation: minimum reserves and stop interventions in exchange rate market	I	72: 1901 2279
27.11.72 11 464	PO	Reich (P, ZH)	Teuerungsbe- kämpfung	stop interventions in exchange rate market; for credit controls	I	72: 2311
27.11.72 11 467	IN	Schmid (S, SG) {54}	Internationaler Währungsfonds	investigate whether to join the IMF	Q	73: 279
27.11.72 11 470	MO	Hürlimann (C) {14}	Teuerungsbe- kämpfung	control of money sup-ply (as one measure to fight inflation)	I	72: 1905 2279
28.11.72 243	KA	Bräm (P, ZH)	Inflationsbe- kämpfung: Konferenz	asks for reduction of money supply and transition to flexible exchange rates	I	72: 2477
4.12.72 11 486	PO	Müller- Zürich (P, ZH)	Konjunktur- steuerung	stop interventions in exchange rate market	I	72: 2289
11.12.72 11 501	PO	Oehen (P, BE)	Inflationsbe- kämpfung	use exchange rate po-licy to fight inflation	I	72: 2284
5.3.73 11 575	IN	Muheim (S, LU) {29}	Kreditrestrik- tionen	executive shall intervene with SNB that application of 'Kreditbeschluss' takes into account regional differences	M	73: 284
5.3.73 311	KA	Breiten- moser (C, BS)	Abwertungs- spekulationen	administrative and legislative measures by SNB to prevent speculation	X	73: 410

7.3.73 11 599	IN	Baum-berger (R, AR) {32}	Währungs-situation	measures to stabilize exchange rates; join IMF	XH	73: 288 301 322
7.3.73 318	KA	Villard (S, BE)	Exportindustrie: Währungskrise	Confederacy shall help industries hurt by exchange rate fluctuations	XH	73: 410
8.3.73 327	KA	Leuten-egger (V, ZH)	Inflationsbe-kämpfung: Arbeitsgruppe	appoint a committee to work out measures to fight inflation	I	73: 411
12.3.73 333	KA	Jaeger (U, SG)	Schweizerische Währungspolitik	executive shall present a clear concept concerning exchange rate policy	X	73: 412
6.6.73 391	KA	Meier Josi (C, LU)	Konjunkturmass-nahmen: Emissionskon-trolle	criticism of executive and SNB in applying the 'Emissions-kontrolle'	M	73: 1009
20.6.73 11 704	IN	Nauer (S, ZH) {21}	Finanzinfor-mation	criticism of SNB for not making public financial information (thus collaborating with private banks)		73: 1833
20.6.73 414	KA	Riesen (S, FR)	Kreditbeschluss	harsh criticism of SNB for not taking into account special circumstances in application of 'Kreditbeschluss'	M	73: 1012
25.6.73 431	KA	Schmid (S, SG)	Inflationsbe-kämpfung	intensify fight against inflation (in addition to policy measures taken by monetary authorities)	I	73: 1411
26.6.73 437	KA	Fischer (R, BE)	Aufwertungsver-lust der SNB	SNB losses due to weakness of the $	P	73: 1402
18.9.73 452	EA	Blatti (R, BE)	Kreditbeschrän-kung: Sonderfälle	criticism of applica-tion of 'Kreditbe-schluss' by SNB; shall account for regional differences	M	73: 1846
18.9.73 11 764	IN	Fischer (R, BE) {38}	Währungsverluste der Nationalbank	responsibility for losses due to changes in exchange rates	P	73: 1540
25.9.73 11 775	PO	Salzmann (U, BE) {6}	Währungsschutz-anleihen	issue bonds to steri-lize money with cen-tral banks; accepted	I	73: 1582
28.1.74 567	EA	Diethelm (S, SZ)	Nationalbank: Zinssätze	interest rates too high; feeds into inflation	I	74: 198

29.1.74 578	EA	Bräm (P, ZH)	Nationalbank: Wahlkriterien	Does qualification or party affiliation determine appointments do SNB board of directors?	Q	74: 1089
4.3.74 11 943	PO	Eisenring (C, ZH) {20}	Kreditbeschluss: Anwendung	less restrictive monetary policy, because economic situation changed; accepted	M	74: 1478
14.3.74 620	EA	Rothen (S, SO)	Zinspolitik	SNB raised discount and lombard rate; rising interest rates and inflation	I	74: 1108
21.3.74 647	EA	Groli-mund (R, SO)	Kreditbegrenzung: Baukredite	no minimum reserves and no limits on credits (construction suffers from high interest rates)	M	74: 1101
20.6.74 673	EA	Jelmini (C, TI)	Nationalbank. Goldreserve	adjust mint par of exchange	P	74: 1111
25.6.74 12 043	IN	Fischer (R, BE) {98}	Kreditpolitik der Nationalbank	monetary policy is too restrictive (deflationary) danger of artificially created recession	M	74: 1478
27.6.74 12 057	PO	Eibel (R, ZH)	Stabilitätspolitik	ineffectiveness of restrictive monetary policy to fight inflation; less restrictive monetary policy; use fiscal policy to fight inflation, too; accepted	M	74: 1262
17.9.74 12 090	MO	Franzoni (C, TI) {18}	Teuerungsbekämpfung	for implementation of money growth rule; accepted	I	74: 1813
24.9.74 12 107	IN	Oehler (C, SG)	Devisen-operationen	measures to stabilize exchange rates	X	75: 356
26.9.74 722	EA	Butty (C, FR)	Bankenliquidität	increase liquidity with banks	M	74: 1949
3.10.74 12 129	MO	Baumann (V, AG) {52}	Geldpolitik der Nationalbank	lower interest rates; accepted	M	74: 1756
3.10.74 12 134	MO	Biel (U, ZH)	Teuerungsbekämpfung	control money supply; vote; not accepted as PO with 15:56	I	75: 158
11.12.74	PO	Kommission des NR	Inflationsbekämpfung	continue to fight inflation, but less restrictive; widespread agreement in debate; accepted	M	74: 1884

27.1.75 75.606	EA	Albrecht (C, NW)	Goldmünzen-verkauf	sell gold coins; use return to cover fiscal deficits	P	75: 598
27.1.75 75.610	EA	Egli (C, LU)	SFr: Wechselkurs	measures to stabilize exchange rates (join the 'snake')	XH	75: 431
28.1.75 75.612	EA	Butty (C, FR)	Negativzinsen auf Auslandsgeldern	amount and use of negative interest rates 'earned'	Q	75: 582
28.1.75 75.613	EA	Chavanne (S, GE)	Abwehr von Auslandsgeldern	use of charges earned with fight against in-flux of foreign capital	Q	75: 582
28.1.75 75.615	EA	Rothen (S, SO)	Exportindustrie/ Uhrenindustrie	measures to stabilize exchange rates	XH	75: 432
5.3.75 75.638	EA	Künzi (R, ZH)	Konjunkturmass-nahmen	financial help of SNB to cantons		75: 432
6.3.75 75.339	IN	Sozialde-mokrati-sche Fraktion	Wirtschaftslage	for a weaker SFr and lower interest rates	M XH	75: 426
11.3.75 75.646	EA	Letsch (R, AG)	Kurs des SFr	stabilize exchange rates; SFr too expensive	XH	75: 599
12.3.75 75.345	IN	Landes-ring der Unab-hängigen	Konjunkturpolitik	stabilize exchange rates, but without inflation; join the 'snake'	X	75: 428
18.3.75 75.658	EA	Bräm (P, ZH)	Wechselkurs-spaltung	against 'splitting' of exchange rates	X	75: 1038
18.3.75 75.659	EA	Bräm (P, ZH)	Alternative zur Wechselkurs-spaltung	cooperation among countries to stabilize exchange rates	X	75: 1038
23.9.75 75.450	IN	Cantieni (C, GR) {34}	Zinspolitik	lower interest rates	Q	75: 1606
23.9.75 75.779	EA	Eisenring (C, ZH)	Währungsschlan-ge: Beitritt	Should Switzerland join the 'snake'?	Q	75: 1526
25.9.75 75.460	MO	Sozial-demo-kratische Fraktion	Bekämpfung der Rezession	change of NBL (which allows for a more activist mone-tary policy); discus-sion and vote: accepted with 52:20		76: 508
2.10.75 75.796	EA	Staehelin (U, AG)	Goldbestand der Nationalbank	sell gold to avoid further losses	P	75: 1908
3.12.75 75.818	EA	Oehen (P, BE)	Neue 100-Franken Note	criticism of new 100 SFr bank-note		75: 1919
10.12.75 75.825	EA	Chavanne (S, GE)	Negativzinsen	negative interest rates not effective enough; other measures to re-duce influx of money	XH	78: 405

16.12.75 75.832	EA	Baechtold (S, VD)	Währungsmass-nahmen	measures against too expensive SFr	XH	76: 406
18.12.75 75.502	IN	Carobbio (T, TI)	Hypothekarzinsen	executive shall inter-vene with SNB to bring down mortgage rates	M	76: 219
18.3.76 76.659	EA	Butty (C, FR)	Währungs-schlange	join the 'snake' (after France left)	X	76: 852
10.6.76 76.693	EA	Meizoz (S, VD)	SFr: Währungs-spekulation	gentlemen agreement: why did SNB not take these measures against exchange rate speculations before?	XH	76: 1275
1.12.76 76.816	EA	Schwar-zenbach (-, ZH)	Neue Banknoten: Kosten	costs of replacing all bank-notes		77: 436
24.3.77 77.332	PO	Schmid (S, SG) {1}	Schweizerische Nationalbank	proposes several legislative changes that would strengthen independence of SNB; accepted		78: 866
8.12.77 77.814	EA	Dafflon (T, GE)	Dollarkurs	amount of $ bought since 1970? Losses thereby? Effects of weakness of $ on Swiss economy	XH Q	78: 419
15.12.77 77.513	PO	Eisenring (C, ZH)	Lage der schweizerischen Wirtschaft	crisis of the $ and economic situation: measures; accepted	XH	78: 235
15.12.77 77.842	EA	Cantieni (C, GR)	Devisenmarkt	weakness of $ (and DM): intervene	XH	78: 169
19.1.78 78.315	IN	Cantieni (C, GR) {6}	Fremdenverkehr: Währungsverluste	weakness of $ and losses of tourism industry	XH	78: 984
6.3.78 78.631	EA	Schatz (R, SG)	Schutz der Wäh-rung: Grund-stückerwerb durch Ausländer	foreigners should not be allowed to buy real estate in Switzerland	XH	78: 1015
19.3.78 78.471	IN	Fraktion schweize-rische Volks-partei	Währungs-situation	protect domestic industries from cheaper imports: tariffs in the amount of decline in price	XH	78: 1296
17.4.78 78.659	EA	Jaeger (U, SG)	Nationalbank: Rechnungsablage	asks for more trans-parency in the annual accounts	P	78: 1454
19.4.78 78.672	EA	Condrau (C, ZH)	Europäische Währungs-schlange	since measures so far not effective: join the 'snake'	Q	78: 1455
19.4.78 78.674	EA	Schmid (S, SG)	SNB: Jahres-rechung 1977	asks for more trans-parency in the annual accounts	P	78: 1454

18.9.78 78.453	IN	Sozialdemokratische Fraktion	Beschäftigungslage	criticism of monetarism and for more activism in monetary policy; discussion	M	78: 1274
18.9.78 78.454	IN	Freisinnig-demokratische Fraktion	Wirtschaftslage: Massnahmen	strength of SFr and competitiveness of Swiss industries: measures; discussion	XH	78: 1286
25.10.78 78.536	IN	Richter (R, NE)	Währungsmassnahmen	join the EMS to avoid exchange rate fluctuations	XH	79: 91
27.11.78 78.824	EA	Schwarzenbach (-, ZH)	Nationalbank: Stützungskäufe	interventions on exchange rate markets; monetary expansion and risk for rising inflation rates	I	78: 1960
7.12.78 78.854	EA	Grobet (S, GE)	Nationalbank: Indiskretionen	insider: reputation of SNB endangered		79: 443
8.3.79 79.624	EA	Schmid (S, SG)	Europäische Währungskooperation	exchange rate stability endangered as result of EMS	X	79: 908
19.3.79 79.643	EA	Bussey (S, VD)	SFr: Wechselkurs	SFr too expensive; problems for export industry	XH	79: 908
22.3.79 79.667	EA	Villard (S, BE)	Nationalbank und Uhrenindustrie	SFr too expensive; problems for export industry (watches)	XH	79: 908
7.6.79 79.692	EA	Fischer-Bremgarten (-, AG)	Neuer Inflationsschub	rising inflation rates as result of excessive money supply	I	79: 1358
13.6.79 79.706	EA	Meizoz (S, VD)	Hypothekarzins	measures to lower mortgage rates		79: 1374
5.10.79 79.537	IN	(Baumgartner)-Soldini (-, GE)	Schweiz-IDA: Erklärung des Nationalbankpräsidenten	criticism of statement made by SNB director Leutwiler		80: 14
3.12.79	FS	Riesen (S, FR)	Beziehungen mit Liechtenstein (Währung, Gesellschaftsrecht)	statements made by SNB director Leutwiler on the relationship Switzerland-Liechtenstein	Q	79: 1494
10.12.79	FS	Reichling (V, ZH)	Währung	exchange rate too high	XH	79: 1566
3.3.80 80.606	EA	Schüle (R, SH)	Nationalbank: Goldmünzen	sell gold coins to earn profits	P	80: 824
10.3.80	FS	Biderbost (C, VS)	Nationalbank: Goldpreisgewinne	central bank profits: use part of it	P	80: 133
10.3.80	FS	Meier Fritz (-, ZH)	Schweizerfranken	intervene in exchange rate market	XL	80: 133

10.3.80	FS	Schüle (R, SH)	Schweizerfranken	SFr too weak; imported inflation	XL	80: 133
17.3.80 80.370	PO	Soldini (-, GE)	Nationalbank: Goldreserve	use SNB reserves to buy coal		81: 807
4.6.80 80.426	PO	Hubacher (S, BS)	Hypothekarzins-satz	measures to bring down mortgage rates		80: 1325
5.6.80 80.427	IN	Unabhängige und evangel. Fraktion	Hypothekarzins	measures to bring down mortgage rates		80: 1325
9.6.80 80.434	IN	Grobet (S, GE)	Hypothekarzins	executive shall intervene directly or over the SNB against rise in mortgage rates		80: 1325
4.3.81 81.322	IN	Herczog (T, ZH)	Wirtschaftslage	stronger SFr to fight imported inflation, but without hurting exports; discussion	XL	81: 1767 82: 675
9.3.81	FS	Meizoz (S, VD)	Hypothekarzins	measures against rising mortgage rates		81: 244
9.3.81	FS	Neukomm (S, BE)	Teuerungsbe-kämpfung	measures to fight inflation	I	81: 121
9.6.81	FS	Müller (S, BE)	Währungs-situation	rising $ and imported inflation	XL	81: 583
21.9.81 81.448	PO	Uchten-hagen (S, ZH)	Zinspolitik und Inflationsbe-kämpfung	for a restrictive monetary policy, but additional (administrative) measures to bring down interest rates and inflation		81: 1751 82: 537
21.9.81 81.455	IN	Christlich-demokratische Fraktion	Teuerungsbe-kämpfung	criticism of SNB policy: inflation has not been fought effectively enough	I	81: 1261
22.9.81 81.466	IN	Hubacher (S, BS)	Massnahmen gegen die Teuerung	too restrictive monetary policy and high interest rates that feed into inflation	M	81: 1262
22.9.81 81.467	IN	Unabhängige und evangel. Fraktion	Teuerung und Inflation	for steady money growth rates and political independence of the SNB; against exchange rate policy		81: 1262
23.9.81 81.472	IN	Carobbio (T, TI)	Geldpolitik und Inflationsbe-kämpfung	criticizes restrictive monetary policy as measure against inflation: leads to increased unemployment	M	81: 1765

1.10.81 81.725	EA	Carobbio (T, TI)	Internationaler Währungsfond	criticizes statements made by Leutwiler (SNB director) at IMF meeting		81: 1794
7.12.81	FS	Schüle (R, SH)	Nationalbank: Diskont- und Lombardsatz	lower interest rates	M	81: 1514
10.12.81 81.766	EA	Blocher (V, ZH)	Nationalbank: Beteiligung an Orell Füssli	SNB as shareholder of private corporation: legitimization?	Q	82: 586
8.3.82 82.343	PO	Günter (U, BE)	Goldparität: Änderung	adjust mint par of exchange; not accepted		82: 1433
21.6.82	FS	Butty (C, FR)	Währungs-anpassungen	realignment in EMS: impacts on Switzerland?	XH	82: 811
24.6.82 82.681	EA	Rothen (S, SO)	Währungspolitik	monetary policy in the future? exchange rate?	Q	82: 1490
21.9.82 82.492	IN	Christlich-demokratische Fraktion	Wirtschaftslage	continue to fight inflation	I	82: 1163
21.9.82 82.494	IN	Schweizerische Volkspartei	Wirtschaftslage	stabilize exchange rates	X	82: 1165
21.9.82 82.495	IN	Unabhängige und evangel. Fraktion	Wirtschaftslage	ensure price stability and stability of real exchange rates	I X	82: 1166
21.9.82 82.497	IN	Fraktion der PdA/PSA/POCH	Wirtschaftslage	take measures with respect to exchange rates and interest rates	X	82: 1167
8.10.82	FS	Hofmann (V, BE)	Währungsfonds: Beitritt	questions concerning a participation in the IMF (worried about costs)	Q	82: 1277
8.10.82 82.729	EA	Eisenring (C, ZH)	Verhältnis SFr/Deutsche Mark	stabilize DM exchange rate; join EMS?	X	82: 1843
30.11.82 82.901	MO	Unabhängige und evangel. Fraktion	Ertragsüberschüsse der Nationalbank: Ablieferung	increase amount of central bank profits to be delivered to fiscal authorities; accepted as PO	P	83: 988
15.12.82 82.934	MO	Schmid (S, SG)	Nationalbank: Ermittlung und Verwendung des Gewinns	increase amount of central bank profits to be delivered to fiscal authorities; accepted as PO	P	83: 988

16.12.82 82.935	MO	Feigen-winter (C, BL)	Nationalbank: Gewinne und Exportrisiko-garantie	increase amount of central bank profits to be delivered to fiscal authorities; accepted as PO	P	83: 989
28.1.83 83.628	EA	Ganz (S, SH)	SFr: Überbewertung	SFr too strong	XH	83: 1075
2.2.83 83.321	MO	Carobbio (T, TI)	Hypothekarzins: Stabilisierung	stabilize mortgage rates (executive and SNB shall collaborate on this); accepted as PO		83: 986
18.6.84	FS	Meier (N, ZH)	SNB-Devisen: Diversifikation der Anlagen	SNB should diversify its currency holdings	P	84: 807
1.10.84	FS	Meier (N, ZH)	Dollarkurs: Intervention der Nationalbank	intervene in exchange rate market; $ too expensive; risk of imported inflation	XL	84: 1284
5.3.84 84.318	MO	Meier (N, ZH)	Nationalbankge-setz: Revision	distribution of central bank profits: increase share of Confederacy and reduce share of cantons; accepted	P	85: 724
18.3.85	FS	Meier (N, ZH)	SNB: Fernbleiben von Zentralbank-interventionen	SFr too weak	XL	85: 537
16.12.85	FS	Meier (N, ZH)	Nationalbank: Milliardenver-luste?	loss in central bank profits as a result of change in US$ exchange rate	P	85: 2077
10.10.86 86.956	MO	Leuenber-ger Moritz (S, ZH)	Bankengesetz: Priorität für Teilrevision	changes in SNB sta-tistics as measure against capital flight from developing countries; accepted as PO		87: 510
11.3.87 87.333	IN	Ogi (V, BE) {22}	Eindämmung der Währungs-fluktuationen	exchange rate stabili-ty: What can be done? What has been done?	X	87: 1026
1.12.87 87.931	IN	Fraktion der SVP	Währungsstabili-tät und Beschäfti-gungssituation	exchange rate stabi-lity (How can it be secured?)	X	87: 1776
1.12.87 87.932	IN	Sozialde-mokrati-sche Fraktion	Wirtschafts- und Beschäftigungs-lage	provide enough liquidity to prevent recession	M	87: 1777

10.12.87 87.951	IN	Christlich-demokratische Fraktion	Kurssturz an der Börse: Auswirkungen auf die Schweizer Wirtschaft	stabilize exchange rates	X	88: 931
29.2.88 88.309	PO	Christlich-demokratische Fraktion	Beitritt der Schweiz zum Europäischen Währungssystem EWS	investigate whether Switzerland should join the EMS	X	88: 1480
20.6.88 88.658	EA	Meier (N, ZH)	Währungspolitik der Nationalbank	sell US $ to avoid losses as a result of $ devaluation	P	88: 1537
6.10.88 88.764	PO	Schüle (R, SH)	Liberalisierung der Schweizer Finanzmärkte	role of Swiss monetary policy in European integration (worried about competitiveness of financial sector); accepted	Q	88: 1937
17.3.89 89.430	IN	Schüle (R, SH)	Aussenwert des SFr und Inflationsgefahr	SFr too weak; danger of imported inflation	XL	90: 930
6.6.89 89.454	IN	Sozial-demokratische Fraktion	Entwicklungen auf dem Hypothekarzinsmarkt	interest rates are too high; discussion	M	89: 1795 1884
8.2.90 90.345	IN	Freisinnig-demokratische Fraktion	Anstieg des schweizerischen Zinsniveaus	lower interest rates and inflation rates		90: 1847
18.6.90	FS	Hafner Rudolf (G, BE)	Einlösungspflicht für Banknoten	SNB shall no longer be obliged to redeem bank-notes		90: 1054
21.6.90 90.244	PI	Hafner Rudolf (G, BE)	Goldvorrat der Nationalbank	sell gold reserves to cover fiscal budget deficits; vote against with 40:18	P	91: 1910
19.11.90 ad 90.244	PO	Kommission des NR	Golddeckung der Banknoten	context Hafner: several changes in FC and NBL concerning gold reserves; accepted		1915
1.10.90	FS	Béguelin (S, VD)	Entwicklung der Hypothekarzinsen	more expansionary monetary policy	M	90: 1695
1.10.90	FS	Hafner Rudolf (G, BE)	Beeinflussungsversuche durch die Nationalbank	SNB influences legislators in opposition to executive		90: 1693
5.10.90 90.860	IN	Bonny (R, BE)	Geldpolitik der Nationalbank	critical questions concerning the too restrictive monetary policy; discussion	M	90: 2485 92: 374

5.10.90 90.873	MO	Theubet (C, JU)	Verteilung des Gewinns der SNB zwischen Bund und Kantonen	increase amount of profits to be transferred to fiscal authorities	P	92: 376
10.12.90 90.925	PO	Freisinnig-demokratische Fraktion	Schweiz und Europäisches Währungssystem (EWS)	executive shall investigate whether to join the EMS; accepted	Q	91: 769 92: 435
14.12.90 90.980	PO	Weder Hansjürg (U, BS)	Goldvorrat der Nationalbank: Transfer in die Schweiz	executive shall investigate whether the SNB's gold reserves should be transferred to Switzerland; accepted	Q	91: 770
18.3.91	FS	Portmann (C, GR)	Geldmengenpolitik	less restrictive monetary policy	M	91: 534
21.3.91 91.3093	MO	Feigenwinter (C, BL) {9}	Veröffentlichung der Ziele und Pläne der Nationalbank	change NBL to increase transparency of monetary policy, (SNB shall publish goals and plans; hearings in parliament twice a year)		-
30.9.91 91.3237	MO SR	Jelmini (C, TI)	Konjunkturpolitik: Gesetz zum Vollzug von Artikel 31 quinquies BV	executive shall prepare legislation that allows for improved coordination of fiscal and monetary authorities in order to increase effectiveness of economic policy; vote against with 50:75		92: 582
28.11.91 91.1107	EA	Maeder (U, AR)	Nationalbank als Totengräberin des ältesten Schweizer Verlags	criticism of SNB's policy as shareholder of Orell Füssli Verlag		92: 670
2.12.91	FS	David (C, SG)	Teuerungsbekämpfung	Why is SNB not successful in its fight against inflation? Is this due to the instruments used, the methods employed, or are there persons responsible for this?	I	91: 2189
9.12.91	FS	Tschopp (R, GE)	Beziehungen Bundesrat-Nationalbank	addresses alleged disagreement between members of the executive and the SNB's president	Q	91: 2285

29.1.92 92.3014	IN	Sozialde-mokra-tische Fraktion	Verschlechterung der Wirtschafts-lage und zuneh-mende Arbeits-losigkeit	lower interest rates; discussion	M	92: 584 599
9.6.92	FS	Zisyadis (-, VD)	Aussagen eines Nationalbank-direktors zur Arbeitslosigkeit	criticism of state-ments made by SNB director Zwahlen	Q	92: 853
17.6.92 92.1057	EA	Daepp (V, BE)	Volkswirtschaft-liche Auswirkun-gen bei einer Festsetzung der Hypothekarzinse bei 7 Prozent	measure to prevent mortgage rates from climbing above 7 percent: subsidies from SNB		92: 2240
21.9.92 92.3370	IN	Sozialde-mokra-tische Fraktion	Geld- und Konjunkturpolitik	lower interest rates and exchange rates	M	92: 2112 2140
22.9.92 92.3380	IN	Fraktion Schweize-rische Volks-partei	Geldpolitik der Nationalbank	monetary policy too restrictive, interest rates and exchange rates too high; measures	M	92: 2116 2140
22.9.92 92.3383	IN	Grüne Fraktion	Geld- und Konjunkturpolitik	lower interest rates; measures to stabilize exchange rates	M	92: 2115 2140
16.12.93 93.3636	MO	Spielmann (-/S, GE)	Neubewertung der National-bankbestände	valuation of assets in annual accounts at market prices; vote against with 19:77	P	94: 564
17.6.94 94.3279	PO	LDU/EVP Fraktion	Umwandlung der Goldreserven der Nationalbank	invest about half of gold reserves in bonds and use interest rate returns to cover fiscal spending; vote against with 23:82	P	95: 561
30.11.94 94.1141	EA	Strahm Rudolf (S, BE)	Hypothekarzins-erhöhung und Politik der Nationalbank	lower interest rates; more expansionary monetary policy; very critical on SNB policy and on board (too dogmatic)	M	94: 2567

29.11.94 94.3495	IN	Sozialdemokratische Fraktion	Schweizerfranken und Kapitalmarktzinsen	exchange rates and interest rates too high; effects on employment and distribution; want SNB to be explicitly accountable to the legislature (justify its policy annually before parliament); discussion	M	95: 992 96: 228
29.11.94 94.3497	IN	Oehler (C, SG)	Währungspolitik und Schweizer Wirtschaft	stabilize exchange rates; lower interest rates; critical questions, also on executive-SNB relationship	XH M	95: 972
16.12.94 94.3568	IN	Weyeneth (V, BE) {11}	Aufgaben der Agenturen und Zweigstellen der Nationalbank	functions of local SNB branches? Does executive pressure SNB to reduce their number or to eliminate all of them? (efficiency of SNB operations)	P	95: 971
16.12.94 94.3569	IN	Weyeneth (V, BE) {5}	Vorgehen bei übermässigem Kursanstieg	measures to stabilize exchange rates if SFr rises excessively	XH	95: 974
18.1.95 95.3001 (94.073)	MO	Finanzkommission des NR	Reingewinnausschüttung der Schweizerischen Nationalbank	increase amount of profits handed over to fiscal authorities (Confederacy and cantons); accepted as PO with 70:48 votes	P	95: 1595 96: 448
13.3.95 95.5024	FS	Hubacher (S, BS)	Hoher Frankenkurs. Werkplatz Schweiz	strong SFr and SNB policy also responsible for job losses; measures?	XH M	95: 517
13.3.95 95.5036	FS	Tschopp (R, GE)	Nationalbank: Pool starker Währungen	form a pool including all 'hard' currencies in order to stabilize exchange rates	XH	95: 536
13.3.95 95.5037	FS	Duvoisin	Starker SFr und Exporte	strong SFr: measures to preserve competitiveness of export industries	XH	95: 517
18.9.95 95.3354	IN	Tschopp (R, GE)	Massnahmen gegen eine erneute Rezession	measures against too strong SFr; vote for discussion with 107:41	XH	96: 624

21.9.95 95.3382	PO	Kühne (C, SG) {12}	Währungspolitik der Nationalbank	executive shall pressure the SNB to give more weight to the goal of exchange rate stability; accepted in vote by 62:36	M XH	96: 450
5.12.95 95.1138	IN	Sozialdemokratische Fraktion	Frankenkurs und Wirtschaftslage	bring exchange rate down (above 85 SFr per 100 DM)	XH	96: 643
4.3.96 96.3016	IN	Tschopp (R, GE)	Währungsreserven: Änderung der Politik	change policy concerning holdings of currency reserves and gold	P	

* *type of legislative activity:*
EA einfache Anfrage (simple question)
FS Fragestunde (questions)
IN Interpellation
KA kleine Anfrage
MO Motion
PI Parlamentarische Initiative (parliamentary initiative)
PO Postulat

** *political parties:*
C Christlich-demokratische Partei (christian democratic party)
F Freiheits-Partei (freedom party)
G Grüne Partei (green party)
L Liberale Partei (liberal party)
N Nationale Aktion (national action party)
P Frei-republikanische und nationale Partei (republican movement party)
R Freisinnig-demokratische Partei (radical or free democratic party)
T Partei der Arbeit und autonome sozialistische Partei (labor party; communists)
S Sozialdemokratische Partei (social democratic party)
U Landesring der Unabhängigen/evangelische Volkspartei (independents party/evangelical party)
V Schweizerische Volkspartei (Swiss people's party)
\- ohne Parteizugehörigkeit (no party membership)

*** *main concern of legislative activity:*
I inflation
M for a less restrictive monetary policy
P central bank profits
Q work out reports and answer questions
X stabilize exchange rates
XH for a weaker SFr
XL for a stronger SFr

**** *Source:*
indicates volume and page in 'Amtliches Bulletin' (analog to Congressional Record)

NR Nationalrat (National Council or House of Representatives)
SR Ständerat (Council of States or Senate)

List of Abbreviations

AB	Amtliches Bulletin
ADA	Americans for Democratic Action
ARCH	autoregressive conditional heteroskedasticity
BAK	Konjunkturforschung Basel AG
Créa	Centre de recherches économiques appliquées
DM	Deutschmark
EA	einfache Anfrage
ETH	Eidgenössische Technische Hochschule in Zürich
FC	Federal Constitution (Bundesverfassung)
FS	Fragestunde
FTC	Federal Trade Commission
GARCH	generalized autoregressive conditional heteroskedasticity
ICC	Interstate Commerce Commission
IFS	International Financial Statistics
IN	Interpellation
ITC	International Trade Commission
KOF	Konjunkturforschungsstelle der Eidgenössischen Technischen Hochschule Zürich
ML	Maximum Likelihood
MO	Motion
NBL	National Bank Law (Nationalbankgesetz)
NLRB	National Labor Relations Board
OECD	organization for economic cooperation and development
OLS	ordinary least squares
PDL	polynomial distributed lag
PI	parliamentary initiative (Parlamentarische Initiative)
PO	Postulat
SFr	Swiss franc
SGZZ	St.Galler Zentrum für Zukunftsforschung
SIC	Swiss Interbank Clearing System
SNB	Swiss National Bank
SR	Systematische Rechtssammlung
WLS	weighted least squares

List of Tables and Figures

Tables

Figures

References

Abrams, Richard K., Richard Froyen, and Roger N. Waud (1980), „Monetary Policy Reaction Functions, Consistent Expectations, and the Burns Era“, Journal of Money, Credit, and Banking 12, No. 1, 30-42.

Alesina, Alberto (1987), „Macroeconomic Policy in a Two-Party System as a Repeated Game“, Quarterly Journal of Economics 102, 651-678.

Alesina, Alberto (1988), „Macroeconomics and Politics“, in NBER Macroeconomics Annual, Cambridge MA, 13-52.

Alesina, Alberto (1989), „Politics and Business Cycles in Industrial Democracies“, Economic Policy 8, 55-98.

Alesina, Alberto, Gerald D. Cohen, and Nouriel Roubini (1992), „Macroeconomic policy and Elections in OECD Democracies“, Economics and Politics 4, 1-30.

Alesina, Alberto, Gerald D. Cohen, and Nouriel Roubini (1993), „Electoral Business Cycle in Industrial Democracies“, European Journal of Political Economy 9, 1-23.

Alesina, Alberto, and Nouriel Roubini (1992), „Political Cycles in OECD Economies“, Review of Economic Studies 59, 663-688.

Alesina, Alberto, and Jeffrey Sachs (1988), „Political Parties and the Business Cycle in the United States, 1948-1984“, Journal of Money, Credit, and Banking 20, No. 1, 63-82.

Alesina, Alberto, and Lawrence H. Summers (1993), „Central Bank Independence and Macroeconomic Performance: Some Comparative Evidence“, Journal of Money, Credit, and Banking 25, No. 2, 151-162.

Allen, Stuart D. (1986), „The Federal Reserve and the Electoral Cycle“, Journal of Money, Credit, and Banking 18, No. 1, 88-94.

Alt, James E., and A. Chrystal (1983), Political Economy. Berkeley.

Alt, James E. (1991), „Leaning into the Wind or Ducking out of the Storm? U.S. Monetary Policy in the 1980s“, in Alberto Alesina, and Geoffrey Carliner (eds.), Politics and Economics in the Eighties. Chicago and London, 41-77.

Alt, James E, and John T. Woolley (1982), „Reaction Functions, Optimization, and Politics: Modelling the Political Economy of Macroeconomic Policy“, American Journal of Political Science 26, No. 4, 709-740.

Ammann, Yves (1995), „Le budget de plein emploi - un réexamen“, Office fédéral des questions conjoncturelles. Etude numéro 20, Berne.

Amtliches Bulletin der Bundesversammlung (AB). Nationalrat. Vol. 1970-1996.

Andrews, Donald W. K. (1993), „Tests for Parameter Instability and Structural Change with Unknown Change Point“, Econometrica 61, No. 4, 821-856.

Aubert, Jean-Francois (1987), So funktioniert die Schweiz. 5. überarb. Aufl., Bern.

Bach, G. L., and James Stephenson (1974), „Inflation and the Redistribution of Wealth“, Review of Economics and Statistics 56, 1-13.

Bade, Robin, and Michael Parkin (1985), „Central Bank Laws and Monetary Policy“, Working Paper, Department of Economics, University of Western Ontario.

Banaian, King, Richard C. K. Burdekin, and Thomas D. Willett (1995), „On the Political Economy of Central Bank Independence“, in Kevin D. Hoover and Steven M. Sheffrin (eds.), Monetarism and the Methodology of Economics. Essays in Honour of Thomas Mayer. Aldershot, 178-197.

Banaian, King, Leroy O. Laney, and Thomas D. Willett (1986), „Central Bank Independence: An International Comparison“, in E. F. Toma and Mark Toma (eds.), Central Bankers, Bureaucratic Incentives, and Monetary Policy. Dordrecht, 199-217.

Baltensperger, Ernst (1985), „Disinflation - The Swiss Experience 1973-1983“, Zeitschrift für Wirtschafts- und Sozialwissenschaften 105, 271-293.

Baltensperger, Ernst, und Peter Böhm (1984), „Geldmengenpolitik und Inflationskontrolle. Möglichkeiten, Kosten, flankierende Massnahmen", Beilage zur 'Volkswirtschaft'.

Barke, Richard P., and William H. Riker (1982), „A Political Theory of Regulation with Some Observations on Railway Abandonments", Public Choice 39, 73-90.

Barone, Michael, and Grant Ujifusa (1989), The Almanac of American Politics 1990. Washington.

Barro, Robert J. (1974), „Are Government Bonds Net Wealth?", Journal of Political Economy 82, 1095-1117.

Barro, Robert J. (1977), „Unanticipated Money Growth and Unemployment in the United States", American Economic Review 67, No. 2, 101-115.

Barro, Robert, and David Gordon (1983), „Rules, Discretion, and Reputation in a Model of Monetary Policy", Journal of Monetary Economics 12, 101-122.

Barsky, R. B., and J. A. Miron (1989), „The Seasonal Cycle and the Business Cycle", Journal of Political Economy 97, 503-534.

Barth, James, Robin Sickles, and Philip Wiest (1982), „Assessing the Impact of Varying Economic Conditions on Federal Reserve Behavior", Journal of Macroeconomics 4, No. 1, 47-70.

Beaulieu, Joseph J., and Jeffrey A. Miron (1992), „A Cross Country Comparison of Seasonal Cycles and Business Cycles", Economic Journal 102, 772-788.

Beaulieu, Joseph J., and Jeffrey A. Miron (1993), „Seasonal Unit Roots in Aggregate U.S. Data", Journal of Econometrics 55, 305-328.

Beck, Nathaniel (1982), „Presidential Influence on the Federal Reserve in the 1970s", American Journal of Political Science 26, No. 3, 415-445.

Beck, Nathaniel (1984), „Domestic Political Sources of American Monetary Policy: 1955-82", The Journal of Politics 46, 786-817.

Beck, Nathaniel (1987), „Elections and the Fed: Is there a Political Monetary Cycle?", American Journal of Political Science 31, No. 1, 194-216.

Beck, Nathaniel (1988), „Politics and Monetary Policy", in Thomas D. Willet (ed.), Political Business Cycles: The Political Economy of Money, Inflation, and Unemployment. Durham, N. C., 366-395.

Beck, Nathaniel (1990), „Congress and the Fed: Why the Dog does not Bark in the Night", in Thomas Mayer (ed.), The Political Economy of American Monetary Policy. Cambridge, 131-150.

Belke, Ansgar (1993), „Theorien des Politischen Konjunkturzyklus", WISU, H. 11, 919-922.

Belke, Ansgar (1996), Politische Konjunkturzyklen in Theorie und Empirie. Eine kritische Analyse der Zeitreihendynamik in Partisan-Ansätzen. Tübingen.

Bell, William R., and Steven C. Hillmer (1992), „Issues Involved with the Seasonal Adjustment of Economic Time Series", in Svend Hylleberg (ed.), Modelling Seasonality, 83-138.

Benson, Bruce L. (1981), „Why are Congressional Committees Dominated by 'High-Demand' Legislators? - A Comment on Niskanen's View of Bureaucrats and Politicians", Southern Economic Journal 47, No. 1, 68-77.

Berger, Helge (1996), „The Bundesbank's Path to Independence. Evidence from the 1950s", Münchener Wirtschaftswissenschaftliche Beiträge, Nr. 96-09.

Berger, Helge, and Ulrich Woitek (1995), „Are there Political Business Cycles in Germany?", Münchener Wirtschaftswissenschaftliche Beiträge, Nr. 95-06.

Bernholz, Peter (1987), „Auf der Suche nach stabilem Geld. Radikale Vorschläge für eine Privatisierung der Währungsordnung", Neue Zürcher Zeitung 285, Dienstag, 8. Dezember, S. 41.

Berthold, Norbert, und Rainer Fehn (1994), „Verursachen Wahlen einen Politischen Konjunkturzyklus?", WiSt, H. 4, 166-175.

Blancpain, Jean-Pierre (1987), „Geldpolitik im Dilemma“, Neue Zürcher Zeitung, Nr. 295, 19./20. Dezember, 33.

Bohley, Peter und Armin Jans (Hrsg.) (1990), Einführung in die Wirtschafts- und Sozialstatistik der Schweiz, Haupt.

Borins, Sanford F. (1972), „The Political Economy of 'the Fed'“, Public Policy 20, 174-198.

Botschaft über die Revision des Nationalbankgesetzes vom 27. Februar 1978. Bundesblatt, 130. Jg, Bd. 1, 769-848.

Bowles, Paul, and Gordon White (1994), „Central Bank Independence: A Political Economy Approach“, Journal of Development Studies 31, No. 2, 235-264.

Box, G. E. P., and D. A. Pierce (1970), „Distribution of Residual Autocorrelations in Autoregressive-Integrated Moving Average Time Series Models“, Journal of the American Statistical Association 65, 1509-1526.

Brenner, Beat (1993), „Paradoxes an der Schweizer Geldpolitik“, Neue Zürcher Zeitung, 11./12. Dezember, Nr. 289, 31.

Brenner, Beat (1994), „Wenn weniger Macht Stärke bedeutet. Weise Trennung von Bankenaufsicht und Geldpolitik. Ein Referat von Markus Lusser“, Neue Zürcher Zeitung, 6. Juli, Nr. 155, 20.

Brenner, Beat (1995), „Unterstützung für den Kurs der Nationalbank. Robert Studer gegen Abweichungen vom geldpolitischen Zielpfad“, Neue Zürcher Zeitung, 17. Februar, Nr. 40, 27.

Brenner, Beat (1996), „Überprüfung der SNB-Anlagepolitik. Schaffung einer gemischten Arbeitsgruppe“, Neue Zürcher Zeitung, 4. Juni, Nr. 127, 25.

Brenner, Beat, und Daniel Hofmann (1996), „Notenbanken müssen unabhängig und glaubwürdig sein. Ein Gespräch mit dem scheidenden Nationalbankpräsidenten Markus Lusser“, Neue Zürcher Zeitung, 27./28. April, Nr. 98, 31.

Brüggemann, Imke, and Jürgen Wolters (1997), „Money and Prices in Germany. Empirical Evidence for 1962 to 1996“, Diskussionsbeiträge des Fachbereichs Wirtschaftswissenschaft der Freien Universität Berlin, Nr. 19.

Buchanan, James M. (1976), „Barro on the Ricardian Equivalence Theorem“, Journal of Political Economy, 84, 337-342.

Bundesgesetz über den Geschäftsverkehr der Bundesversammlung sowie über die Form, die Bekanntmachung und das Inkrafttreten ihrer Erlasse (Geschäftsverkehrsgesetz) (Federal Law of the Legislature) vom 23. März 1962. Stand am 1. Januar 1995.

Buomberger, Peter, und Beat Schwab (1993), „Sind die schweizerischen Staatsdefizite eine Belastung für unsere Zukunft?“, Schweizer Monatshefte für Politik, Wirtschaft, Kultur, 1-16.

Burdekin, Richard C. K. (1987), „Swiss Monetary Policy: Central Bank Independence and Stabilization Goals“, Kredit und Kapital 20, 454-466.

Burdekin, Richard C. K. (1994), „Inflation, Output and Wages in Europe, 1971-1989: Did Membership in the European Monetary System Matter?“, Rivista Internationale di Scienze Economiche e Commerciali 41, No. 10-11, 827-852.

Burdekin, Richard C. K., and Farrokh K. Langdana (1992), Budget Deficits and Economic Performance. London and New York.

Burdekin, Richard C. K. and Mark E. Wohar (1990), „Monetary Institutions, Budget Deficits and Inflation: Empirical Results for Eight Countries“, European Journal of Political Economy 6, 531-551.

Butler, David Alan (1995), Does 'Independent' Mean 'Free from Influence'? Escape Clause Decision-Making at the United States International Trade Commission. New York and London.

Caesar, R. (1980), „Die Unabhängigkeit der Notenbank im demokratischen Staat. Argumente und Gegenargumente“, Zeitschrift für Politik 4, 347 ff.

Caesar, R. (1981), Der Handlungsspielraum von Notenbanken. Theoretische Analyse und internationaler Vergleich. Baden-Baden.

Cagan, Phillip (1985), „Financing the Deficit, Interest Rates, and Monetary Policy", in Phillip Cagan, (ed.), The Economy in Deficit. Essays in Contemporary Economic Problems. Washington and London, 195-221.

Calvert, Randall L., Matthew D. McCubbins, and Barry R. Weingast (1989), „A Theory of Political Control and Agency Discretion", American Journal of Political Science 33, No. 3, 588-611.

Camen, Ulrich, Hans Genberg, and Michael Salemi (1990), „Optimal Monetary Policy and the Revealed Preference Function of the Swiss National Bank", in P. Artus and Y. Barroux (eds.), Monetary Policy: A Theoretical and Econometric Approach. Dordrecht, 3-14.

Cameron, D. (1984), „Social Democracy, Corporatism, Labor Quiescence and the Representation of Economic Interest in Advanced Capitalist Society", in J. Goldthorpe (ed.), Order and Conflict in Contemporary Capitalism. New York.

Capitelli, René, und Peter Buomberger (1990), „Zur Geldpolitik der achtziger Jahre: Einige grundsätzliche Überlegungen", Schweizerische Zeitschrift für Volkswirtschaft und Statistik 126, 535-550.

Cargill, Thomas F. (1995), „The Statistical Association between Central Bank Independence and Inflation", Banca Nazionale del Lavoro Quarterly Review 193, 159-172.

Carvalho, Fernando J. Cardim de (1995/1996), „The Independence of Central Banks: A Critical Assessment of the Arguments", Journal of Post Keynesian Economics 18, No. 2, 159-175.

Caspar, Luzian (1994), „Kontroverse um Fed-Vize Blinder: 'Inflations-Softie' ante portas?", Basler Zeitung, 10. September, Nr. 211.

Cecco, Marcello (1983), „Discussion", in Donald R. Hodgman (ed.), The Political Economy of Monetary Policy: National and International Aspects, 204-205.

Chappell, Henry W., Thomas M. Havrilesky, and Rob Roy McGregor (1993), „Partisan Monetary Policies: Presidential Influence Through the Power of Appointment", Quarterly Journal of Economics 108, No. 1, 185-218.

Charemza, Wojciech W., and Derek F. Deadman (1997), New Directions in Econometric Practice. 2nd ed., Cheltenham.

Chopin, Marc C., C. Steven Cole, and Michael A. Ellis (1996), „Congressional Influence on US Monetary Policy: A Reconsideration of the Evidence", Journal of Monetary Economics 38, 561-570.

Clausen, Volker, und Manfred Willms (1993), „Unabhängigkeit der Zentralbank", WiSt, H. 12, 605-610.

Crain, Mark W. (1990), „Legislative Committees: A Filtering Theory", in W. Mark Crain and Robert D. Tollison (eds.), Predicting Politics. Ann Arbor, 149-166.

Cukierman, Alex (1992), Central Bank Strategy, Credibility, and Independence. Theory and Evidence. Cambridge, MA.

Cukierman, A., and A. Meltzer (1986), „A Positive Theory of Discretionary Policy, the Cost of a Democratic Government and the Benefits of a Constitution", Economic Inquiry 24, 367-388.

De Haan, J., and D. Zelhorst (1990), „The Impact of Government Deficits on Money Growth in Developing Countries", Journal of International Money and Finance 9, 455-469.

Demopoulos, G.D, G. M. Katsimbris, and S. M. Miller (1987), „ Monetary Policy and Central-Bank Financing of Government Budget Deficits", European Economic Review 31, 1023-1050.

Denzau, Arthur T., and Robert J. Mackay (1983), „Gatekeeping and Monopoly Power of Committees: An Analysis of Sincere and Sophisticated Behavior“, American Journal of Political Science 27, 740-761.

Denzau, Arthur T., and Michael C. Munger (1986), „Legislators and Interest Groups: How Unorganized Interests Get Represented“, American Political Science Review 80, No. 1, 89-106.

Dickey, David A. (1993), „Seasonal Unit Roots in Aggregate U.S. Data“, Journal of Econometrics 55, 329-331.

Dickey, David A., and Wayne A. Fuller (1979), „Distribution of the Estimators for Autoregressive Time Series with a Unit Root“, Journal of the American Statistical Association 74, 427-431.

Dickey, David A., and Wayne A. Fuller (1981), „Likelihood Ratio Statistics for Autoregressive Time Series with a Unit Root“, Econometrica 49, 1057-1072.

Downs, Anthony (1967), Inside Bureaucracy. Boston.

Dueker, Michael, and Andreas M. Fischer (1996), „Inflation Targeting in a Small Open Economy: Empirical Results for Switzerland“, Journal of Monetary Economics 37, 89-103.

Dwyer, Gerald P. (1982), „Inflation and Government Deficits“, Economic Inquiry 20, 315-329.

Dwyer, Gerald P. (1985), „Federal Deficits, Interest Rates, and Monetary Policy“, Journal of Money, Credit and Banking 17, 655-681.

Eijffinger, Sylvester (ed.) (1997), Independent Central Banks and Economic Performance. Cheltenham.

Eijffinger, Sylvester, and Eric Schaling (1993), „Central Bank Independence in Twelve Industrial Countries“, Banca Nazionale del Lavoro Quarterly Review 184, 49-89.

Eijffinger, Sylvester, and Eric Schaling (1995), „Central Bank Independence: Criteria and Indices“, in Hans-Hermann Francke und Eberhart Ketzel (Hrsg.), Konzepte und Erfahrungen der Geldpolitik. Berlin, 185-218.

Eijffinger, Sylvester, Eric Schaling, and Marco Hoeberichts (1998), „Central Bank Independence: A Sensitivity Analysis“, European Journal of Political Economy 44, 73-88.

Eiker, F. (1967), „Limit Theorems for Regressions with Unequal and Dependent Errors“, Proceedings of the Fifth Berkeley Symposium on Mathematical Statistics and Probability, Vol. 1, Berkeley, 59-62.

Eizenga, Weitze (1983), „The Independence of the Federal Reserve System and of the Netherlands Bank“, SUERF Series, Tilburg.

Engle, R. F. (1982), „Autoregressive Conditional Heteroscedasticity, with Estimates of the Variance of United Kingdom Inflations“, Econometrica 50, 987-1007.

Engle, R. F., C. W. J. Granger, S. Hylleberg, and H. S. Lee (1993), „Seasonal Cointegration. The Japanese Consumption Function“, Journal of Econometrics 55, 275-298.

Federal Constitution of the Swiss Confederation, unofficial translation, March 1980.

Fenno, Richard Jr. (1978), Home Style: House Members in their Districts. Boston, MA.

Ferejohn, John, and Charles Shipan (1990), „Congressional Influence on Bureaucracy“, Journal of Law, Economics and Organization 6, 1-20.

Fiorina, Morris (1974), Representatives, Roll Calls, and Constituencies. Lexington, MA.

Fiorina, Morris (1982), „Legislative Choice of Regulatory Process: Legal Process or Administrative Process“, Public Choice 39, 33-66.

Fischer, Andreas M. and Michel Peytrignet (1990), „Are Larger Monetary Aggregates Interesting? Some Exploratory Evidence for Switzerland Using Feedback Models“, Schweizerische Zeitschrift für Volkswirtschaft und Statistik 126, No. 4, 505-519.

Fischer, Andreas M. und Mathias Zurlinden (1994), „Geldpolitik mit formellen Inflationszielen: eine Übersicht", Geld, Währung und Konjunktur, Quartalsheft der Schweizerischen Nationalbank, No. 1, 65-76.
Fischer, Stanley (1994), „Modern Central Banking", in Forrest Capie, Stanley Fischer, Charles Goodhart, and Norbert Schnadt (eds.), The Future of Central Banking. Cambridge, 262-308.
Fischer, Stanley (1995), „Central Bank Independence Revisited", American Economic Association: Papers and Proceedings 85, No. 2, 201-206.
Forder, James (1998), „The Case for an Independent European Central Bank: A Reassessment of Evidence and Sources", European Journal of Political Economy 44, 53-71.
Frey, Bruno S. (ed.) (1997), Political Business Cycles. Cheltenham.
Frey, Bruno S., and Friedrich Schneider (1981), „Central Bank Behavior. A Positive Empirical Analysis", Journal of Monetary Economics 7, 291-315.
Friedman, B. M., and K. N. Kuttner (1989), „Money Income and Prices After the 1980s", NBER Working Paper No. 2852.
Friedman, Milton (1982), „Monetary Policy: Theory and Practice", Journal of Money, Credit and Banking 14, 98-118.
Froyen, Richard T. (1974), „A Test of the Endogeneity of Monetary Policy", Journal of Econometrics 2, 175-188.
Fuchs, Jakob (1990), Staatskunde. 4. Aufl., Rothenburg.
Fürstenberg, Reinhard (1980), „Monetary Policy in Switzerland. The Performance During the Seventies", Arbeitspapier Nr. 106, Institut für Weltwirtschaft Kiel.
Gärtner, Manfred (1994a), „Democracy, Elections, and Macroeconomic Policy: Two Decades of Progress", European Journal of Political Economy 10, 85-109.
Gärtner, Manfred (1994b), „The Quest for Political Cycles in OECD Economies", European Journal of Political Economy 10, 427-440.
Gärtner, Manfred (1995), „Die Nationalbank und die Inflation. Notenbankunabhängigkeit als Fetisch oder Stein der Weisen?", in Andreas Brandenberg (Hrsg.), Standpunkte zwischen Theorie und Praxis. Handlungsorientierte Problemlösungen in Wirtschaft und Gesellschaft. Festschrift für Hans Schmid. Bern, Stuttgart und Wien, 421-437.
Geschäftsreglement des Nationalrates vom 22. Juni 1990 (Stand am 1. Juli 1995).
Geschäftsreglement des Ständerates vom 24. September 1986 (Stand am 1. Januar 1995).
Giannaros, Demetrios S., and Bharat R. Kolluri (1985), „Deficit Spending, Money, and Inflation: Some International Empirical Evidence", Journal of Macroeconomics 7, No. 3, 401-417.
Godfrey, L. G. (1978), „Testing for Higher Order Serial Correlation in Regression Equations when the Regressors Include Lagged Dependent Variables", Econometrica 46, 1303-1313.
Goodhart, Charles A. E. (1994), „Game Theory for Central Bankers: A Report to the Governor of the Bank of England", Journal of Economic Literature 32, 101-114.
Goodhart, Charles A. E., and Dirk Schoenmaker (1995), „Should the Functions of Monetary Policy and Banking Supervision be Separated?", Oxford Economic Papers 47, 539-560.
Goodman, John B. (1992), Monetary Sovereignty. The Politics of Central Banking in Western Europe. Ithaca and London.
Granger, C. W. J., and Paul Newbold (1974), „Spurious Regressions in Econometrics", Journal of Econometrics 2, 111-120.
Greene, William H. (1990), Econometric Analysis. New York and London.
Grier, Kevin B. (1987), „Presidential Elections and Federal Reserve Policy: An Empirical Test", Southern Economic Journal 54, No. 2, 475-486.

Grier, Kevin B. (1989), „On the Existence of a Political Monetary Cycle", American Journal of Political Science 33, No. 2, 376-389.

Grier, Kevin B. (1991), „Congressional Influence on U.S. Monetary Policy", Journal of Monetary Economics 28, 201-220.

Grier, Kevin B. (1996), „Congressional Oversight Committee Influence on US Monetary Policy Revisited", Journal of Monetary Economics 38, 571-579.

Grier, Kevin B., and Michael C. Munger (1991), „Committee Assignements, Constituent Preferences, and Campaign Contributions", Economic Inquiry 29, 24-43.

Grier, Kevin B., and Howard E. Neiman (1985), „Deficits, Politics, and Money Growth", Economic Inquiry 25, 201-214.

Grilli, Vittorio, Donato Masciandaro, and Guido Tabellini (1991), „Political and Monetary Institutions and Public Financial Policies in the Industrial Countries", Economic Policy 13, 342-392.

Gruner, Erich, and Kenneth J. Pitterle (1983), „Switzerland's Political Parties", in Howard R. Penniman (ed.), Switzerland at the Polls. The National Elections of 1979. Washington and London, 30-59.

Gujarati, D. (1970), „Use of Dummy Variables in Testing for Equality between Sets of Coefficients in Linear Regressions: A Generalization", The American Statistician 24, No. 5, 18-21.

Hamburger, Michael J., and Burton Zwick (1981), „Deficits, Money and Inflation", Journal of Monetary Economics 7, 141-150.

Hamilton, James D. (1994), Time Series Analysis. Princeton.

Hammond, Thomas H., and Jack H. Knott (1996), „Who Controls the Bureaucracy?: Presidential Power, Congressional Dominance, Legal Constraints, and Bureaucratic Autonomy in a Model of Multi-Institutional Policy-Making", Journal of Law, Economics, and Organization 12, No. 1, 119-166.

Hartwig, Karl-Hans (1983-84), „Bundesbankautonomie und Inflationsbekämpfung: Politische Ökonomie des Notenbankverhaltens", List-Forum 12, 307-322.

Hartwig, Karl-Hans (1995), „Bundesbankverhalten und Geldmengensteuerung", in Jürgen Siebke und H. Jörg Thieme (Hrsg.), Geldpolitik. Zwanzig Jahre Geldmengensteuerung in Deutschland. Baden-Baden, 69-92.

Harvey, Andrew C. (1990), An Econometric Analysis of Time Series. 2nd ed., New York et al.. (1st ed. 1981).

Hatanaka, M. (1974), „An Efficient Two-step Estimator for the Dynamic Adjustment Model with Autoregressive Errors", Journal of Econometrics 2, 199-220.

Havrilesky, Thomas (1987), „A Partisanship Theory of Fiscal and Monetary Regimes", Journal of Money, Credit, and Banking 19, No. 3, 308-325.

Havrilesky, Thomas (1988), „Monetary Policy Signaling from the Administration to the Federal Reserve", Journal of Money, Credit, and Banking 20, No. 1, 83-101.

Havrilesky, Thomas (1990), „Distributive Conflict and Monetary Policy", Contemporary Policy Issues 8, 50-61.

Havrilesky, Thomas (1992), The Pressures on American Monetary Policy. Dordrecht.

Havrilesky, Thomas, and John Gildea (1991), „The Policy Preferences of FOMC Members as Revealed by Dissenting Votes", Journal of Money, Credit, and Banking 23, 130-138.

Havrilesky, Thomas, and John Gildea (1995), „The Biases of Federal Reserve Bank Presidents", Economic Inquiry 33, 274-284.

Havrilesky, Thomas, and James Granato (1993), „Determinants of Inflationary Performance: Corporatist Structures vs. Central Bank Autonomy", Public Choice 76, 249-261.

Havrilesky, Thomas, Robert Sapp, and Robert Schweitzer (1975), „Tests of the Federal Reserve's Reaction to the State of the Economy: 1964-1974", Social Science Quarterly 55, No. 4, 835-852.

Hayek, Nicolas G. (1995), „Geldpolitik im Gesamtinteresse?", Neue Zürcher Zeitung, Samstag/Sonntag, 11./12. März, Nr. 59, 27.
Haynes, Stephen E., and Joe A. Stone (1989), „An Integrated Test for Electoral Cycles in the U.S. Economy", Review of Economics and Statistics 71, 426-434.
Hendry, David F. (1989), PC-GIVE: An Interactive Econometric Modelling System. Version 6.0/6.01. Institute of Economics and Statistics and Nuffield College, University of Oxford, Oxford.
Hendry, David F. (1995), Dynamic Econometrics.
Hendry, David F., and Jurgen A. Doornik (1996), Empirical Econometric Modelling Using PcGive for Windows. London et al.
Hendry, David F., and Neil R. Ericsson (1991), „Modeling the Demand for Narrow Money in the United Kingdom and the United States", European Economic Review 35, 833-886.
Hetzel, Robert L. (1990), „The Political Economy of Monetary Policy", in Thomas Mayer (ed.), The Political Economy of American Monetary Policy. Cambridge, 99-114.
Hibbs, Douglas A. (1977), „Political Parties and Macroeconomic Policy", The American Political Science Review 71, 1467-1487.
Hibbs, Douglas A. (1987), The American Political Economy. Cambridge, MA.
Higgins, Richard S., William F. Shughart II, and Robert D. Tollison (1987), „Dual Enforcement of the Antitrust Laws", in R. J. Mackay, J. C. Miller III and B. Yandle (eds.), Public Choice and Regulation. Stanford, 154-180.
Hodgman, Donald R., and Robert W. Resek (1983), „Determinants of Monetary Policy in France, The Federal Republic of Germany, Italy and the United Kingdom: A Comparative Analysis", in Donald R. Hodgman (ed.), The Political Economy of Monetary Policy: National and International Aspects, 147-170.
Hoffmann, Stefan (1990), „Die Durchführung der Geldpolitik in der Schweiz", Geld, Währung und Konjunktur, Quartalsheft der Schweizerischen Nationalbank, No.1, 73-78.
Hohl, Tobias (1996), Messung von Politikerpräferenzen. Lizentiatsarbeit, Universität Freiburg.
Hohl, Tobias, and Bruno Jeitziner (1997), „Parlamentarierratings 1975 - 1995", Working Paper, Seminar für Wirtschafts- und Sozialpolitik der Universität Freiburg.
Hopenhayn, Hugo, and Susanne Lohmann (1996), „Fire-Alarm Signals and the Political Oversight of Regulatory Agencies", Journal of Law, Economics, and Organization 12, No. 1, 196-213.
Hotz-Hart, Beat, Stefan Mäder, und Patrick Vock (1995), Volkswirtschaft der Schweiz. Zürich.
Hylleberg, Svend (1992), „General Introduction", in Svend Hylleberg (ed.), Modelling Seasonality, 3-14.
Hylleberg, Svend, R. F. Engle, C. W. J. Granger, and B. S. Yoo (1992), „Seasonal Integration and Cointegration", Journal of Econometrics 44, 1990, 215-238; reprinted in Svend Hylleberg (ed.), Modelling Seasonality, 425-448.
Issing, Otmar (1983), „Geldpolitik", Gablers Wirtschaftslexikon, 11. Aufl.
Jarque, C. M., and A. K. Bera (1980), „Efficient Tests for Normality, Homoscedasticity and Serial Independence of Regression Residuals", Economics Letters 6 (3), 255-259.
Jeitziner, Bruno (1995), „A Reaction Function Study for the Swiss National Bank", Working Paper, Seminar für Wirtschafts- und Sozialpolitik der Universität Freiburg/Schweiz, Freiburg.
Jeitziner, Bruno, and Tobias Hohl (1997), „Measuring Political Preferences: Ratings for Members of the Swiss National Council", Swiss Political Science Review 3 (4), 1-27.

Joines, Douglas H. (1990), „Seasonality and the Monetization of Federal Budget Deficits", Economic Inquiry 28, 413-441.

Jordan, Thomas J. (1993), Seigniorage, Defizite, Verschuldung und Europäische Währungsunion. Bern u. a.

Jordan, Thomas J. (1994), „Der Stand der schweizerischen Fiskalpolitik. Eine Analyse anhand neuer Fiskalindikatoren", Schweizerische Zeitschrift für Volkswirtschaft und Statistik 130, No. 2, 193-206.

Judge, George G., R. Carter Hill, William E. Griffiths, Helmut Lütkepohl, and Tsoung-Chao Lee (1988), Introduction to the Theory and Practice of Econometrics. 2nd ed., New York et al.

Kane, Edward J. (1980), „Politics and Fed Policymaking. The More Things Change the More they Remain the Same", Journal of Monetary Economics 6, 199-211.

Karras, Georgios (1994), „Macroeconomic Effects of Budget Deficits: Further International Evidence", Journal of International Money and Finance 13, No. 2, 190-210.

Kästli, René (1995), „Auf der Suche nach Indikatoren für die schweizerische Geldpolitik", in Andreas Brandenberg (Hrsg.), Standpunkte zwischen Theorie und Praxis. Handlungsorientierte Problemlösungen in Wirtschaft und Gesellschaft. Festschrift für Hans Schmid. Bern, Stuttgart und Wien, 449-463.

Kath, Dietmar (1995), „Bundesbankautonomie und politische Entscheidungsprozesse", in Jürgen Siebke und H. Jörg Thieme (Hrsg.), Geldpolitik. Zwanzig Jahre Geldmengensteuerung in Deutschland. Baden-Baden, 53-68.

Keller, Karl (1994), „Rückblick auf 20 Jahre verfehlter Währungs- und Geldpolitik", Neue Zürcher Zeitung, 8./9. Januar, Nr. 6, 17.

Kennedy, Peter (1992), A Guide to Econometrics. 3rd. ed., Cambridge, Mass.

Kirchgässner, Gebhard, and Marcel Savioz (1997), „Monetary Policy Forecasts for Real GDP Growth: An Empirical Investigation for the Federal Republic of Germany", Mimeo, University of St.Gallen.

Klein, Martin, and Manfred J. M. Neumann (1990), „Seigniorage: What Is It and Who Gets It?", Weltwirtschaftliches Archiv 126, No. 2, 205-221.

Kleinewefers, Anne (1996), „Die Geldpolitik in Deutschland, Holland, Österreich und der Schweiz", mimeographed, Universität Bern.

Kmenta, Jan (1986), Elements of Econometrics. 2nd ed., New York and London.

Koutsoyiannis, A. (1977), Theory of Econometrics. An Introductory Exposition of Econometric Methods. 2nd ed., New York.

Krehbiel, Keith (1990), „Are Congressional Committees Composed of Preference Outliers?", American Political Science Review 84, No. 1, 149-163.

Kriesi, Hanspeter (1990), „Political Power and Decision Making in Switzerland", in Janet Eve Hilowitz (ed.), Switzerland in Perspective. Westport, 35-50.

Kydland, Finn E., and Edward C. Prescott (1977), „Rules Rather Than Discretion: The Inconsistency of Optimal Plans", Journal of Political Economy 85, 473-491.

Landes, W. M., and R. A. Posner (1975), „The Independent Judiciary in an Interest-Group Perspective", Journal of Law and Economics 18, 875-901.

Landmann, Oliver, und Jürgen Jerger (1997), „20 Jahre Geldmengensteuerung in der Schweiz: Erfahrungen und Alternativen", mimeo, Universität Freiburg im Breisgau.

Landon, Stuart, and Bradford G. Reid (1990), „Government Deficits and Money Growth", Review of Economics and Statistics 72, 382-389.

Laney, Leroy O (1985)., „An International Comparison of Experiences with Monetary Targeting: A Reaction Function Approach", Contemporary Policy Issues 3, 99-112.

Laney, Leroy O., and Thomas D. Willett (1983), „Presidential Politics, Budget Deficits, and Monetary Policy in the United States, 1960-76", Public Choice 40, No.. 1, 53-69.

Lang, Günter, und Peter Welzel (1992), „Budgetdefizite, Wahlzyklen und Geldpolitik: Empirische Ergebnisse für die Bundesrepublik Deutschland 1962-1989", Jahrbücher für Nationalökonomie und Statistik 210, No. 1-2, 72-85.

Lange, Carsten (1995), Seigniorage. Eine theoretische und empirische Analyse des staatlichen Geldschöpfungsgewinnes. Berlin.

Lardaro, Leonard (1992), Applied Econometrics. New York.

Leamer, E. (1978), Specification Searches: Ad hoc Inference with Nonexperimental Data. New York.

Lehner, Franz (1985), „Das Schweizerische Konkordanzmodell als Alternative zum Parlamentarismus", Jahrbuch für Neue Politische Ökonomie 4, 108-136.

Levy, Mickey D (1981)., „Factors Affecting Monetary Policy in an Era of Inflation", Journal of Monetary Economics 8, 351-373.

Lim, Quek Peck (1983), „Why Swiss Monetarism Works", Euromoney, 211-214.

Lindbeck, A. (1976), „Stabilization Policies in Open Economies with Endogenous Politicians", American Economic Review (Papers and Proceedings) 66, 1-19.

Lindsey, David E., and Henry C. Wallich (1987), „Monetary Policy", The New Palgrave, 508-515.

Lombra, R., and M. Moran (1980), „Policy Advice and Policymaking at the Federal Reserve", in K. Brunner and A. Meltzer (eds.), Monetary Institutions and the Policy Process. Supplement to the Journal of Monetary Economics.

Lothian, J. R. (1976), „The Demand for High-Powered Money", American Economic Review 66, 56-68.

Lusser, Markus (1984), „Die Grenzen der Geldpolitik in einer offenen Volkswirtschaft", Geld, Währung und Konjunktur, Quartalsheft der Schweizerischen Nationalbank, No. 4, 59-63.

Lusser, Markus (1992), „Die volkswirtschaftliche Bedeutung der Schweizerischen Nationalbank", Geld, Währung und Konjunktur, Quartalsheft der Schweizerischen Nationalbank, No. 1, 63-72.

Lüthi, Ruth, Luzius Meyer, und Hans Hirter (1991), „Fraktionsdisziplin und die Vertretung von Partikulärinteressen im Nationalrat", in Parlamentsdienste (Hrsg.), Das Parlament - oberste Gewalt des Bundes. Bern, 53-72.

Macey, Jonathan R. (1992), „Organizational Design and Political Control of Administrative Agencies", Journal of Law, Economics, and Organization 8, No. 1, 93-110.

MacLaury, Bruce K. (1994), „The Fed: Reconciling Autonomy and Democracy", in David C. Colander and Dewey Daane (eds.), The Art of Monetary Policy. New York, 75-84.

Maddala, G. S. (1992), Introduction to Econometrics. 2nd. ed, New York et al.

Maennig, Wolfgang, und Adrian Hunger (1996), „Seignorageverluste - Hemmnis für die Europäische Währungsunion?", WiSt, Heft 5, 227-232.

Marti, Urs (1994), „Besorgte Schweizer Exporteure. Währungspolitische Demarche beim Bundesrat", Neue Zürcher Zeitung, 4. November, Nr. 258, 21.

Mastronardi, Philippe (1991), „Zur Wirksamkeit der parlamentarischen Verwaltungskontrolle im Bund", in Parlamentsdienste (Hrsg.), Das Parlament - oberste Gewalt des Bundes. Bern, 351-368.

Mayer, Thomas (ed.) (1990), The Political Economy of American Monetary Policy. Cambridge.

Mayhew, David R. (1974), Congress: The Electoral Connection. New Haven.

McCallum, Bennett T. (1978), „The Political Business Cycle: an Empirical Test", Southern Economic Journal 44, 504-515.

McCallum, Bennett T. (1989), Monetary Economics. Theory and Policy. New York and London.

McCubbins, Matthew D., Roger G. Noll, and Barry R. Weingast (1989), „Structure and Process, Politics and Policy: Administrative Arrangements and the Political Control of Agencies", Virginia Law Review 75, No. 2, 431-482.

McCubbins, Matthew D., and Thomas Schwartz (1984), „Congressional Oversight Overlooked: Police Patrols versus Fire Alarms", American Journal of Political Science 28, No. 1, 165-179.

McMillin, W. Douglas (1986), „Federal Deficits, Macrostabilization Goals, and Federal Reserve Behavior", Economic Inquiry 24, 257-269.

Meyer, Hans (1986), „The Role of the Swiss National Bank in the Payment System", Journal of Bank Research, 190-193.

Mills, Terence C. (1992), Time Series Techniques for Economists. Cambridge.

Miron, J. A. (1994), „The Economics of Seasonal Cycles", in C. A. Sims (ed.), Advances in Econometrics. 6th World Congress, Cambridge.

Miron, J. A., and S. P. Zeldes (1988), „Seasonality, Cost Shocks, and the Production Smoothing Model of Inventories", Econometrica 55, 877-908.

Missong, Martin, und Philippe Herrault (1990), „Geldpolitik, Staatsverschuldung und europäische Währungskooperation. Eine kritische Analyse internationaler Vergleiche von Zentralbankreaktionsfunktionen am Beispiel Deutschland - Frankreich", Schweizerische Zeitschrift für Volkswirtschaft und Statistik 126, No. 4, 567-580.

Mizon, Grayham E. (1995), „A Simple Message for Autocorrelation Correctors: Don't", Journal of Econometrics 69, 267-288.

Moe, Terry M. (1985), „Control and Feedback in Economic Regulation: The Case of the NLRB", American Political Science Review 79, No. 4, 1094-1116.

Moe, Terry M. (1987), „An Assessment of the Positive Theory of 'Congressional Dominance'", Legislative Studies Quarterly 12, No. 4, 475-520.

Moe, Terry M. (1997), „The Positive Theory of Public Bureaucracy", in Dennis C. Mueller (ed.), Perspectives on Public Choice. A Handbook. Cambridge, 455-480.

Morris, Irwin, and Michael Munger (1998), „First Branch, or Root? The Congress, the President, and the Federal Reserve", Public Choice 96, 363-380.

Moser, Peter (1995), Checks and Balances in Democracies. A Survey of the Positive Theory of Political Institutions with Applications to Decision-Making in Switzerland, the European Union, and to Central Bank Independence. St. Gallen.

Moser, Peter (1996), „Why is Swiss Politics so Stable?", Swiss Journal of Economics and Statistics 132, No. 1, 31-61.

Mueller, Dennis C. (1989), Public Choice II. A Revised Edition of Public Choice. Cambridge, MA.

Münster, Petra (1994), „Niederländisches Plädoyer für eine harte Interpretation der Maastricht-Kriterien. Mit Blick auf die WWU vernachlässigte Staatsschuldenquote", Neue Zürcher Zeitung, 9. Dezember, Nr. 258, 29.

Nationalbankgesetz (National Bank Law) vom 1. 10. 1979.

Nautz, Dieter (1997), „Wie brauchbar sind Multiplikatorprognosen für die Geldmengensteuerung der Bundesbank?", Discussion Paper No. 40, Humboldt-Universität zu Berlin.

Nedwed, Harald (1992), Notenbankenfreiheit. Theoretische Analyse und historische Erfahrungen aus der Schweiz im 19. Jahrhundert. Basel.

Nelson, Charles R., and Heejoon, Kang (1984), „Pitfalls in the Use of Time as an Explanatory Variable in Regression", Journal of Business and Economic Statistics 2, 73-82.

Neumann, Manfred J. M. (1991), „Central Bank Independence as a Prerequisite of Price Stability", in Commission of the European Communities (ed.), The Economics of EMU. Background Studies for European Economy. No. 44: „One market, One Money" (European Economy, Special ed. No. 1), 79 ff.

Newey, Whitney K., and Kenneth D. West (1987), „A Simple Positive Semi-Definite, Heteroskedasticity and Autocorrelation Consistent Covariance Matrix", Econometrica 55, 703-708.
Nicholls, D. F., and A. R. Pagan (1983), „Heteroscedasticity in Models with Lagged Dependent Variables", Econometrica 51 (4), 1233-1242.
Nickell, Stephen (1985), „Error Correction, Partial Adjustment and all that: An Expository Note", Oxford Bulletin of Economics and Statistics 47, No. 2, 119-129.
Nilles, Délia (1994), „Le monétarisme helvétique est-il mort en 1988?", cahiers de recherches économiques, Université de Lausanne, no. 9415.
Niskanen, William A. (1971), Bureaucracy and Representative Government. Chicago.
Niskanen, William A. (1975), „Bureaucrats and Politicians", Journal of Law and Economics 28, 617-643.
Niskanen, William A. (1978), „Deficits, Government Spending, and Inflation", Journal of Monetary Economics 4, 591-602.
Nordhaus, William D. (1975), „The Political Business Cycle", Review of Economic Studies 42, 169-190.
Nuspliger, Kurt (1991), „Die Stärkung der parlamentarischen Kommissionen", in Parlamentsdienste (Hrsg.), Das Parlament - oberste Gewalt des Bundes. Bern, 223-241.
Osborn, Denise R. (1990), „A Survey of Seasonality in UK Macroeconomic Variables", International Journal of Forecasting 6, 327-336.
Osborn, Denise R. (1993), „Seasonal Cointegration", Journal of Econometrics 55, 299-303.
Parkin, Michael (1987), „Domestic Monetary Institutions and Deficits", in James M. Buchanan, Charles K. Rowley, and Robert D. Tollison (eds.), Deficits. New York, 310-337.
Parkin, Michael, and Robin Bade (1978), „Central Bank Laws and Monetary Policies: A Preliminary Investigation", in Michael G. Porter and Michael E. Burns (eds.), The Australian Monetary System in the 1970s. Melbourne, 24-39.
Peltzman, Sam (1976), „Toward a More General Theory of Regulation", Journal of Law and Economics 19, 211-240.
Perron, P. (1989), „The Great Crash, the Oil Price Shock and the Unit Root Hypothesis", Econometrica 57, 1361-1401.
Perry, George L. (1987), „Deficit Financing", The New Palgrave, 762-764.
Persson, Torsten, and Guido Tabellini (1990), Macroeconomic Policy, Credibility and Politics. London.
Persson, Torsten, and Guido Tabellini (1993), „Designing Institutions for Monetary Stability", Carnegie-Rochester Conference Series on Public Policy 39, 53-84.
Pierce, James L. (1978), „The Myth of Congressional Supervision of Monetary Policy", Journal of Monetary Economics 4, 363-370.
Pierce, James L. (1979), „The Political Economy of Arthur Burns", Journal of Finance 34, 485-496.
Posen, Adam (1993), „Central Bank Independence Does Not Cause Low Inflation: The Politics Behind the Institutional Fix", mimeo, Harvard University.
Posen, Adam (1995), „Declarations are not Enough: Financial Sector Sources of Central Bank Independence", in Ben S. Bernanke, and Julio J. Rotemberg (eds.), NBER Macroeconomics Annual, 253-274.
Prast, Henriette M. (1996), „Commitment Rather than Independence: An Institutional Design for Reducing the Inflationary Bias of Monetary Policy", Kyklos 49, No. 3, 377-405.
Protopapadakis, A. A., and J. J. Siegel (1987), „Are Money Growth and Inflation Related to Government Deficits? Evidence from Ten Industrialized Economies", Journal of International Money and Finance 6, 31-48.

Ramsey, J. B. (1969), „Tests for Specification Errors in Classical Linear Least Squares Regression Analysis", Journal of the Royal Statistical Society B 31, 350-371.

Reglement für die Finanzkommissionen und die Finanzdelegation der eidgenössischen Räte vom 8. November 1985.

Reuber, G. L. (1964), „The Objectives of Canadian Monetary Policy, 1949-1961: Empirical Trade-offs and the Reaction Function of the Authorities", Journal of Political Economy 72, , 09-132.

Rich, Georg (1985), „Die Inflationsbekämpfung als Aufgabe der schweizerischen Geldpolitik", Geld, Währung und Konjunktur, Quartalsheft der Schweizerischen Nationalbank, No. 1, 60-69.

Rich, Georg (1989), „Geldmengenziele und schweizerische Geldpolitik: eine Standortbestimmung", Geld, Währung und Konjunktur, Quartalsheft der Schweizerischen Nationalbank, No. 4, 345-360.

Rich, Georg (1990), „Capitelli und Buomberger zur schweizerischen Geldpolitik: Der Wechselkurs als Deus ex machina?", Schweizerische Zeitschrift für Volkswirtschaft und Statistik 126, 553-564.

Rich, Georg (1992), „Die schweizerische Teuerung: Lehren für die Nationalbank", Geld, Währung und Konjunktur, Quartalsheft der Schweizerischen Nationalbank, No. 1, 73-88.

Rich, Georg (1995), „Monetary Targets as a Policy Rule: Lessons from Swiss Experience", Paper presented at Bank of Canada, June 23.

Rich, Georg, and J. P. Béguelin (1985), „Swiss Monetary Policy in the 1970s and 1980s", in Monetary Policy and Monetary Regimes. A Symposium dedicated to Robert E. Weintraub. Rochester, 76-111.

Roberts, Steven M. (1978), „Congressional Oversight of Monetary Policy", Journal of Monetary Economics 4, 543-556.

Rogoff, Kenneth (1985), „The Optimal Degree of Commitment to an Intermediate Monetary Target", Quarterly Journal of Economics 100, No. 4, 1169-1190.

Rogoff, Kenneth (1990), „Equilibrium Political Budget Cycles", American Economic Review 80, 21-36.

Rogoff, Kenneth, and Anne Sibert (1988), „Elections and Macroeconomic Policy Cycles", Review of Economic Studies 55, 1-16.

Rowley, Charles K. (1992), The Right to Justice. The Political Economy of Legal Services in the United States. Aldershot.

Rowley, Charles K., and Willem Thorbecke (1993), „The Role of the Congress and the Executive in U.S. Trade Policy Determination: A Public Choice Analysis", in Meinhard Hilf and Ernst-Ulrich Petersman (eds.), National Constitutions and International Law. Dordrecht, 347-370.

Schiemann, Jürgen, und Stefan Alshuth (1994), „Der Grad der Zentralbankautonomie und sein Einfluss im gesamtwirtschaftlichen Prozess. Eine international vergleichende Rangkorrelationsanalyse", Aussenwirtschaft 49, H. 4, 579-600.

Schiltknecht, Kurt (1977), „Die Geldpolitik der Schweiz unter dem System flexibler Wechselkurse", Schweizerische Zeitschrift für Volkswirtschaft und Statistik 113, No. 1, 1-26.

Schiltknecht, Kurt (1983), „Switzerland - The Pursuit of Monetary Objectives", in P. Meek (ed.), Central Bank Views on Monetary Targeting, New York, 72-79.

Schmid, Beat (1979), Die Unabhängigkeit der Schweizerischen Nationalbank und ihre rechtliche Stellung. Bern.

Schneeweiss, Hans (1990), Ökonometrie. 4. überarbeitete Aufl., Heidelberg.

Schneider, Friedrich (1979), „Ein polit-ökonomisches Modell des Zentralbankverhaltens bei endogenem Staat", in C. Chr. v. Weizsäcker (Hrsg.), Staat und Wirtschaft. Berlin, 473-502.

Schneider, Friedrich (1985), Der Einfluss von Interessengruppen auf die Wirtschaftspolitik. Eine empirische Untersuchung für die Schweiz. Bern und Stuttgart.

Schneider, Friedrich, Werner W. Pommerehne, and Bruno S. Frey (1981), „Politico-Economic Interdependence in a Direct Democracy: The Case of Switzerland", in Douglas A. Hibbs, and Heino Fassbender (eds.), Contemporary Political Economy. Studies on the Interdependence of Politics and Economics. Amsterdam, 231-248.

Schultes, Dieter (1994), Bestimmungsfaktoren der Geldpolitik der Deutschen Bundesbank. Berlin.

Schürmann, Leo (1980), Nationalbankgesetz und Ausführungserlasse. Bern.

Schwab, Beat (1993), „Zyklische und strukturelle Komponenten der schweizerischen Staatsdefizite", SBG-Arbeitspapier.

Schwab, Beat (1994a), „Ausmass und Folgen der Staatsdefizite und Staatsverschuldung in der Schweiz", Dokumentation Wirtschaftskunde der Gesellschaft zur Förderung der schweizerischen Wirtschaft, 4/5.

Schwab, Beat (1994b), „Definitions- und Messprobleme von Budgetdefiziten und Staatsverschuldung", Schweizerische Zeitschrift für Volkswirtschaft und Statistik 130, No. 3, 403-419.

Sheehan, Richard G. (1992), „U.S. Influences on Foreign Monetary Policy", Journal of Money, Credit, and Banking 24, No. 4, 447-464.

Shepsle, Kenneth A. (1978), The Giant Jigsaw Puzzle. Democratic Committee Assignments in the Modern House. Chicago and London.

Shepsle, Kenneth A. (1992), „Bureaucratic Drift, Coalitional Drift, and Time Consistency: A Comment on Macey", Journal of Law, Economics and Organization 8, No. 1, 111-118.

Shepsle, Kenneth A., and Barry R. Weingast (1987), „The Institutional Foundations of Committee Power", American Political Science Review 81, No. 1, 85-104.

Shughart II, William, Robert D. Tollison, and Brian L. Goff (1986), „Bureaucratic Structure and Congressional Control", Southern Economic Journal 52, No. 4, 962-972.

SNB (1975), „Revision der Geldmengenstatistik", Beilage zum Monatsbericht der Schweizerischen Nationalbank, No. 8, 1-6.

SNB (1982a), „Zur Revision der monetären Statisktik: Die neuen Daten für die schweizerische Notenbankgeldmenge", Beilage zum Monatsbericht der Schweizerischen Nationalbank, Heft Nr. 2, 3-13.

SNB (1982b), 75 Jahre Schweizerische Nationalbank. Zürich.

SNB (1985), „Revision der Geldmengenstatistik", Geld, Währung und Konjunktur, Quartalsheft der Schweizerischen Nationalbank, No. 1, 51-56.

SNB (1988), „Monetary Policy in 1989", Geld, Währung und Konjunktur, Quartalsheft der Schweizerischen Nationalbank, No. 6, 271-272.

SNB (1995a), „Revision der Geldmengenstatistik", Geld, Währung und Konjunktur, Quartalsheft der Schweizerischen Nationalbank, No. 1, 61-69.

SNB (1995b), Functions, Instruments, Organisation. 9th, revised ed., Zürich.

Soh, Byung Hee (1986), „Political Business Cycles in Industrialized Democratic Countries", Kyklos 39, No. 1, 31-46.

Spahn, Heinz-Peter, und Georg Ziemes (1992), „Abhängigkeit versus Autonomie der Notenbank. Ein spieltheoretisches Modell monopolistischer Koordination in der Wirtschaftspolitik", Jahrbücher für Nationalökonomie und Statistik 210, H. 3-4, 219-232.

Spörndli, Erich (1994), „Aktuelle Fragen der schweizerischen Geldpolitik", in Dieter Duwendag (Hrsg.), Geld- und Währungspolitik in kleinen, offenen Volkswirtschaften. Berlin, 43-54.

Stein, H. (1985), Presidential Economics. New York.

Steiner, Jürg (1982), „Switzerland: 'Magic Formula' Coalitions", in Eric C. Browne and John Dreijmanis (eds.), Government Coalitions in Western Democracies. New York, 315-334.

Steunenberg, Bernard (1994), „Regulatory Policymaking in a Parliamentary Setting", Jahrbuch für Neue Politische Ökonomie 13, 36-57.

Stigler, George (1971), „A Theory of Regulation", Bell Journal of Economics and Management Science 2, 3-21.

Taylor, Mark P. (1995), „The Economics of Exchange Rates", Journal of Economic Literature 33, No. 1, 13-47.

Theil, Henri (1971), Principles of Econometrics. New York.

Thieme, H. Jörg (1993), „Geldtheorie", WiSt, H. 4, 171-180.

Tietmeyer, Hans (1993), „Staatsschulden und Geldwertstabilität im grenzüberschreitenden Vergleich", in Hugo J. Hahn (Hrsg.), Geldwertstabilität und Staatsschulden. Baden-Baden, 69-87.

Tschäni, Hans (1990), Profil der Schweiz. Zürich.

Turnovsky, Stephen J., and M. E. Wohar (1987), „Alternative Modes of Deficit Financing and Endogeneous Monetary and Fiscal Policy in the U.S.A. 1923-1982", Journal of Applied Econometrics 2, 1-25.

Tzermias, Nikos (1994), „Die Notenbank als Hüterin der Vollbeschäftigung? Vorstoss von Fed-Gouverneur Blinder", Neue Zürcher Zeitung, 30. August, Nr. 201, 21.

Uhlig, Andreas (1994), „Höhere Realzinsen als Folge der Staatsdefizite", Neue Zürcher Zeitung, 3. Oktober, Nr. 230, 11.

Ungern-Sternberg, Thomas von (1996a), „The Swiss National Bank and Seignorage", cahiers de recherches économiques, Université de Lausanne, no. 9601.

Ungern-Sternberg, Thomas von (1996b), „Die Gewinnausschüttung der Schweizerischen Nationalbank", cahiers de recherches économiques, Université de Lausanne, no. 9610.

Vachris, Albert M. (1996), „Federal Antitrust Enforcement: A Principal-Agent Perspective", Public Choice 88, 223-238.

Vaubel, Roland (1993), „Eine Public-Choice-Analyse der Deutschen Bundesbank und ihre Implikationen für eine Europäische Währungsunion", in Dieter Duwendag und Jürgen Siebke, Europa vor dem Eintritt in die Wirtschafts- und Währungsunion. Berlin, 23-79.

Wagner, Richard E. (1986), „Central Banking and the Fed: A Public Choice Perspective", Cato Journal 6, No. 2, 519-538.

Wallis, K. F. (1967), „Lagged Dependent Variables and Serial Correlated Errors: A Reappraisal of Three-Pass Least Squares", Review of Economics and Statistics, 555-567.

Walsh, Carl (1995), „Optimal Contracts for Central Bankers", American Economic Review 85, No. 1, 150-167.

Wasserfallen, Walter, and Guido Kürsteiner (1994), „Interest Rates and Exchange Rates under Money Supply Targets", Journal of Monetary Economics 33, 201-230.

Weingast, Barry R. (1984), „The Congressional-Bureaucratic System: A Principal-Agent Perspective (with Applications to the SEC)", Public Choice 44, 147-191.

Weingast, Barry R., and William J. Marshall (1988), „The Industrial Organization of Congress; or, Why Legislatures, Like Firms, Are Not Organized as Markets", Journal of Political Economy 96, No. 1, 132-163.

Weingast, Barry R., and Mark J. Moran (1983), „Bureaucratic Discretion or Congressional Control? Regulatory Policymaking by the Federal Trade Commission", Journal of Political Economy 91, No. 5, 765-800.

Weintraub, Robert E. (1978), „Congressional Supervision of Monetary Policy", Journal of Monetary Economics 4, 341-362.

White, H. (1980), „A Heteroskedastic-Consistent Covariance Matrix Estimator and a Direct Test for Heteroskedasticity", Econometrica 48, 817-838.

Wild, Carl (1992), „Die Nationalbank hat eine Scharte auszuwetzen", Basler Zeitung, 12. Dezember, Nr. 292.

Willet, Thomas D., with Edward Keen (1990), „Studying the Fed: Toward a Broader Public-Choice Perspective", in Thomas Mayer (ed.), The Political Economy of American Monetary Policy. Cambridge, 13-25.

Willms, Manfred (1990), „Grundprobleme eines europäischen Zentralbankstatuts", Wirtschaftsdienst 70, 521-556.

Willms, Manfred (1992), Internationale Währungspolitik. München.

Wilson, James (1980), The Politics of Regulation. New York.

Wintrobe, Ronald (1997), „Modern Bureaucratic Theory", in Dennis C. Mueller (ed.), Perspectives on Public Choice. A Handbook. Cambridge, 429-454.

Woll, Artur (1988), „Die Unabhängigkeit der Deutschen Bundesbank muss gesichert werden!", Wirtschaftsdienst 3, 122-124.

Wolters, Jürgen (1996), „Neuere Verfahren der Saisonbereinigung. Eine Einführung", IFO Studien 42(3), 279-286.

Wood, John H. (1967), „A Model of Federal Reserve Behavior", in George Horwich (ed.), Monetary Process and Policy: a Symposium. Richard D. Irwin, Inc.: Homewood, 135-166.

Woolley, John T. (1983), „Political Factors in Monetary Policy", in Donald R. Hodgman (ed.), The Political Economy of Monetary Policy: National and International Aspects, 177-203.

Woolley, John T. (1984), Monetary Politics. The Federal Reserve and the Politics of Monetary Policy. Cambridge University Press.

Zurlinden, Mathias (1996), „Devisenmarktinterventionen der Schweizerischen Nationalbank 1986-1994", Geld, Währung und Konjunktur, Quartalsheft der Schweizerischen Nationalbank, No. 2, 163-187.

Zuteilung der Arbeitsbereiche an die ständigen Kommissionen. Beschlüsse der Büros vom 8. November 1991.

Contributions to Economics

Hagen Bobzin
Indivisibilities
1998. ISBN 3-7908-1123-8

Helmut Wagner (Ed.)
Current Issues in Monetary Economics
1998. ISBN 3-7908-1127-0

Peter Michaelis/Frank Stähler (Eds.)
Recent Policy Issues in Environmental and Resource Economics
1998. ISBN 3-7908-1137-8

Jessica de Wolff
The Political Economy of Fiscal Decisions
1998. ISBN 3-7908-1130-0

Georg Bol/Gholamreza Nakhaeizadeh/Karl-Heinz Vollmer (Eds.)
Risk Measurements, Econometrics and Neural Networks
1998. ISBN 3-7908-1152-1

Joachim Winter
Investment and Exit Decisions at the Plant Level
1998. ISBN 3-7908-1154-8

Bernd Meyer
Intertemporal Asset Pricing
1999. ISBN 3-7908-1159-9

Uwe Walz
Dynamics of Regional Integration
1999. ISBN 3-7908-1185-8

Michael Carlberg
European Monetary Union
1999. ISBN 3-7908-1191-2

Giovanni Galizzi/Luciano Venturini (Eds.)
Vertical Relationships and Coordination in the Food System
1999. ISBN 3-7908-1192-0

Gustav A. Horn/Wolfgang Scheremet/Rudolf Zwiener
Wages and the Euro
1999. ISBN 3-7908-1199-8

Dirk Willer
The Development of Equity Capital Markets in Transition Economies
1999. ISBN 3-7908-1198-X

Karl Matthias Weber
Innovation Diffusion and Political Control of Energy Technologies
1999. ISBN 3-7908-1205-6

Heike Link et al.
The Costs of Road Infrastructure and Congestion in Europe
1999. ISBN 3-7908-1201-3

Simon Duindam
Military Conscription
1999. ISBN 3-7908-1203-X